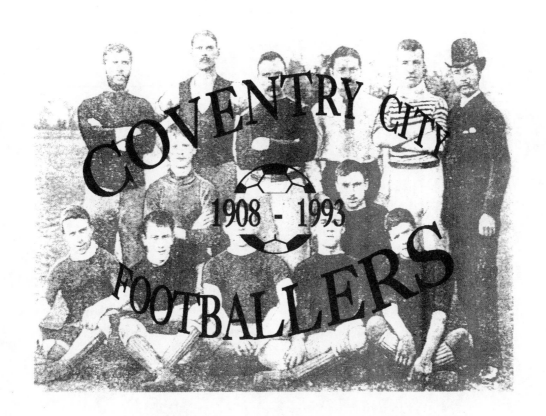

The Complete
Who's Who

Martin and Paul O'Connor

Published by:
Yore Publications
12 The Furrows, Harefield,
Middx. UB9 6AT.

British Library Cataloguing–in–Publication Data.
A catalogue record for this book
is available from the British Library.

ISBN 1 874427 45 3

YORE PUBLICATIONS specialise in football books,
generally of an historic theme,
relating to both League and non–League football.
Please see page 222, or send a S.A.E. to
the above address for full details of these
and other books (plus relevant football videos).

Free Newsletters are circulated three times per year

Printed by The Bath Press

ACKNOWLEDGEMENTS

This book is the fruit of many years research by the authors who have received tremendous aid, information, and encouragement to continue and complete the project from many people.

The most important of these are our respective wives, Margaret and Marina, who have tolerated our moods of extreme ecstasy, or deepest depression as the team's result dictates. Also Liz, our daughter/sister, who has accompanied us to games since 1977.

Ray Spiller, and his creation the Association of Football Statisticians, who have provided an inspiration and a deep well of information and knowledge which has not only been of benefit to the authors, but also to other compilers.

Amongst members who have proved very helpful we must include the late Morley Farrow and Alex Wilson, together with Garth Dykes, Les Triggs, Steve Phillips, Robert Jex, Brian Pead, Ray Goble, Michael Braham, Terry Frost, Richard Lindsay, Robert McElroy, Keith Farnsworth, Barry Hugman, Paul Taylor, Doug Lamming, Jack Rollin, Barry Hugman, Wade Martin, Paul Joannu, Eugene MacBride and George Sheridan. We apologise for omitting any other member who has given un-stinting of their time and has not been mentioned.

The staff at the British Newspaper Library at Colindale are given special thanks for their unfailing help and cheerfulness, even under the most trying circumstances, especially the Library Assistants under the late George Evans, and now, Terry Dillingham.

Also to be thanked are the staff of the Local Studies Department of the Coventry City Library, and the Coventry Evening Telegraph for the provision of photographs.

Thanks also to Dean Miller and Kevin Monks, Coventry City fans in the original meaning of the word – fanatics. People who support the team through thick and thin and are the backbone of the support; the Mobbs Family, George "Jock" Hudson, Maurice "Taff" Lloyd and Chris Sutcliffe, who have shared our emotions at every home game during the last decade.

Finally special thanks to Rod Dean, David Brassington, who also provided photographs, Don Chalk and Jim Brown who complied *"Coventry City – A Complete Record 1883 – 1991"*, a work which we used extensively. These people provided a source which was knowledgable, enthusiastic and encouraging.

Martin & Paul O'Connor
August 1993

CONTENTS

		Page
Key to Players' Pages	....	9
The Story So Far....	....	10
Birmingham League	....	16
Southern League	....	18
The Great War	....	40
World War 2	....	41
Football League Players:	....	43
Adams to Bytheway	....	44
Caine to Gynn	....	69
Hackett to Knox	....	105
Lager to Nutt	....	131
Oakey to Ryan	....	158
St John to Van Gool	....	182
Waldock to Young	....	208
Addendum	....	221
Yore Publications	....	222

Key to Players pages

Most abbreviations are self explanatory,
the list below is an explanation of the less obvious:

Name:

Where a name is shown in brackets, this is
the player's more popular name or nickname.

Career (where known):

Date of transfer to that specific club is shown
F/T = Free Transfer
c/s = Close season
pro = Date signed as a professional
WW1 = First World War
WW2 = Second World war
Appearances and goals. The first (or only) figure represents the number of
appearances in that competition. When followed by a plus sign and a suffixed
's', this shows the additional number of substitute appearances made. A dash
followed by a number indicates the number of goals scored. A dash ('–') and
no other figure indicates a playing staff member who made no appearances in
that competition that season.
Example:
23+3s–10 = 23 full appearances, 3 substitute appearances, 10 goals.
12 – 3 = 12 full appearances, 3 goals scored.

Debut:

(a) = 'away' game. (h) = 'home game.
letters in brackets at end of line show the position played in that match,
e.g. (OL) = Outside left, (CH) = Centre half, etc.

General:

Players who commenced their Coventry City career in the Southern
League are also indicated under the Football League players' section.

1883 – 1993: The Story So Far .....

1891

Since the formation of Coventry City in October 1883 as Singers Football Club, it has been a history of struggle allied to continual progress, from a works-based team to its position as proud members of the Football Association Premier League.

This progression has taken the club through the Birmingham and Southern Leagues, before the First World War, and then through all the Divisions of the Football League up to membership of the Premier League. Coventry City were the first club to have played in every Division of the Football League, including Division Three North in 1925-26 and Division Four in 1959-60; and along the way the club won the F.A. Cup in May 1987.

Singers F.C. were founded by workmen at the Singer Cycle Works in Alma St, Hillfields. The credit for founding the club goes to William Stanley who – along with players "Cock" Heath, Harry Banks and Joe Collins – had belonged to an earlier local football club, Coventry Association, which had at that time just folded.

Coventry Association were powerful enough to have had fixtures with Aston Villa as early as 1876, however it had been unable to establish itself because Rugby Union was by far the most popular game in Coventry at the time.

Singers F.C. grew, and its local derbies with Rudge F.C. – a competitor on the football field and as a cycle manufacturer – helped to establish a strong side which, by 1891, had won the Birmingham Junior Cup in two successive seasons. Two members of this side, Frank Mobley and Will Dorrell went on to have long and successful careers in first class football.

In 1894 the club joined the Birmingham League but players were still employees of the works. This system meant that Singers were unable to play or sign professional players from outside the cycle industry in order to improve the quality of the side, and thus their League positions were always lowly.

May 1898 saw the club change its name to Coventry City F.C., but to no avail on the field as the team continued to flounder. A move to the Highfield Road ground in 1899 signalled an even more dismal time with record defeats, including 0-14 against Aston Villa Reserves, and last place in the League in 1902. During 1901-02, the club sent a side of reserves and local players to Worcester to play Berwick Rangers in the F.A. Cup. The subsequent 2-11 drubbing is still their heaviest defeat in this competition.

In the close season of 1902 some significant players were obtained in Craythorne and Tarplin, amongst others, and a gradual improvement took place. In the years that followed other quality players joined so that by the 1907-08 season

Coventry City F.C. had a powerful side which beat Brierley Hill Alliance on September 21st 1907 in the F.A. Cup First Qualifying Round, 6-2 away, and subsequently won another six ties to reach the First Round Proper.

A thrilling game at home to Crystal Palace was lost 2-4 but the Cup run stirred local people and the club's potential could be seen. At the end of the season the club applied to join the Southern League and was duly elected and so begins the story of Coventry City as a full professional club.

A theme running through the history of the club is the one of a large step forward, followed by a desperate struggle, but progress being finally achieved with the odd disaster thrown in. So it was with the membership of the Southern League. The initial season of 1908-09 commenced with a home draw and then the next five games were all lost. The first victory was a 3-1 win away at Bristol Rovers, and the first home win was two weeks later, 3-2 against Watford. A final position of 20th, one off the bottom, was a disappointment to all.

For the following season player-manager Harry Buckle made some important signings in Bob Evans, Frank Sarl, Eli Bradley, Patsy Hendren and the return of Billy Smith which greatly improved the strength of the team. A final position of 8th could have been improved upon but for the attentions of the F.A. Cup run that year, which saw victories over Wrexham and Kettering Town in the Preliminary Rounds and defeats for Preston North End, Portsmouth and Nottingham Forest in the competition proper. This produced a Quarter-Final tie with mighty Everton which was lost 0–2 at Highfield Road before 19,095 spectators.

In 1910–11 another useful F.A. Cup run saw both Sheffield Wednesday and Brighton & Hove Albion eliminated before City, without Bob Evans in goal, were thumped 0–5 by Burnley at Turf Moor.

The club was unable to hold on to its better players and a gradual decline resulted in the calamity of relegation to the Southern League Division Two in April 1914, and yet another period of trauma for the club.

The privations of war, travelling distances of the clubs in this section were in South Wales, small crowds and player unavailability due to enlistment or essential war work, resulted in the club losing large amounts of money.

By May 1915 the club was broke with no paid officials and few players. The Football Association in conjunction with the Football League and Southern League decided to abandon all first class football for the duration of the war.

A few odd games were played in the period 1915–18 but nothing of an organised nature and losses were still being incurred. At this point director David Cooke came to the rescue by settling all the club's debts and appointing William Clayton as manager.

City applied for, and obtained, membership of the Football League, Midland Section and competed in this competition using players already on the clubs books from before the war, players employed locally in engineering and munitions industries, servicemen on leave or stationed locally, and in some cases, players borrowed from opponents, when City failed to raise a full eleven.

The results were encouraging enough for the club to apply for Football League membership. This was gained in March 1919 and with David Cooke as Chairman and William Clayton as manager the club set about signing players for this momentous season.

The first game in Football League, Division Two was at home to Tottenham Hotspur. After the horrors of a war which decimated a generation of young men there was great excitement and expectation as City set off on their new adventure.

Once again the theme surfaced, Tottenham won the first game 5–0 at a canter, City went eleven games without scoring a goal, players came and went, managers were changed and still the team lost.

On Christmas morning 1919, the Coventry City record in Division Two was:–
Played: 19, Won: 0, Drawn: 5, Lost: 14
Goals for: 4. Goals against: 39
Points: 5. Position: 22

Even with this appalling record, 19,000 spectators turned up for the first Christmas game after the war and how they were rewarded – a 3–2 win against Stoke. The following day in the return fixture at Stoke, City lost 1–6, the scorer was Quinn ·· Peter Quinn.

From then until the season's close a further eight wins were recorded together with six draws and a bit of skulduggery, the club finished twentieth, and avoided relegation. Some years later both Bury and Coventry City officials were banned from football for life by the Football Association after being found guilty of fixing a game at Bury.

The following seasons became a habitual battle to preserve Division Two status and were known as *"The Stormy Period"* but the inevitable relegation came in May 1925 when the club finished bottom of League Division Two.

A season in Division Three North followed, before Coventry City settled for another period of mediocrity in Division Three South, until the arrival on the 8th April 1931, of Harry Storer, and so started the most successful and exciting period for City to that date. With the acquisition of Clarrie Bourton in the 1931 close season the Bantams now had a goal scoring centre forward who was the idol of the fans – there were many male children christened Clarence at this time as a salute by happy fathers to their hero.

Wins accumulated and goals scored soared, and the League positions improved from 12th – 1931–32 – followed in successive seasons by 6th, 2nd, 3rd and eventually in May 1936 the club finished first and obtained promotion. Here tradition was changed, as City started well, and in the years up to the outbreak of war they were a leading side in Division Two, and on the fringe of promotion to Division One.

1931

This fine side containing, George Mason, Harry Barratt, Les Warner and Ted Roberts, was not able to realise its potential. The Second World War deprived these and other excellent players of the prime of their careers.

The Club played intermittently during the early War years before joining the Football League North Division in August 1942 until May 1945, and then the Football League South in 1945–46.

When League football restarted in August 1946, the City were confident of promotion, but 7th was their best position and the club was eventually relegated in April 1952.

Another dark period ensued, with even a season in Division Four in 1958–59. Then in November 1961 the Nadir of modern times was reached, when King's Lynn inflicted a 1–2 defeat in the Second Round of the F.A. Cup. It was not just the result which was so lamentable, but the performance itself was devoid of pride, competence or wit.

Within a week Chairman Derrick Robbins had appointed Jimmy Hill as the new Manager. Hill arrived with a large new broom and changes followed thick and fast – a new playing strip – all sky blue – training regime, coaching staff, club song and bingo on supporters' trains.

There were many in football who thought Hill was brash and a showman, but he knew how to market the product which was his responsibility – Coventry City – and attendances boomed as fans flocked to watch a product they wanted – a winning team.

What people tended to overlook was the fact that Jimmy Hill had a technical acumen, was a superb judge of a player – both his ability and character – as well as a motivator of men. The importance of Jimmy Hill to the club cannot be underestimated.

His legacy is still with us – we are the Sky Blues, we sing the club song – words by J.H., and we play in the top echelon of English football, and it was J.H. who achieved that promotion.

Recently, on the radio Tom Watt, actor and football fan, said that if you asked a football supporter to name his six most memorable moments he would name at least three which applied to his own club. Well, when J.H. was at Highfield Road it seemed we had a memorable moment every week, such was the excitement that was generated.

And then of the eve of that first season in Division One in August 1967, supporters were stunned – this word used in its original sense not the tabloid cliché – by the news of Hill's resignation.

The season that followed produced memorable moments galore as, at last, Coventry City played the leading clubs in the land and in 1970-71 they played Bayern Munich in the European Fairs Cup.

On September 30th 1972 a 1-3 home defeat to Chelsea, was maybe not so historic to most people, except it was the last game of Jeff Blockley for the club – he scored an own goal – but it was the first game viewed by 5 year old Paul O'Connor and it was love at first sight. A love which has withstood moments of high drama – Bristol City 2-2 – when defeat would have meant relegation, and the Sky Blues had lost a 2-0 lead. They were desperate for the final whistle, when news of Sunderland's defeat came through, and the rest of the game was played out in the most friendly of manners.

On January 27th 1981, a 35,468 crowd packed in for the first leg of the Football League Cup Semi-Final with West Ham United, and witnessed a pulsating game. West Ham took a two goal lead after Garry Thompson – who ran a million miles that night – scored an own goal as he chased a West Ham player into the City penalty area. Then Thompson upped a gear to score two goals with an all action display, full of stamina, aggression and no little skill, so that City took a 3-2 lead to Upton Park for the second leg. Unfortunately an injury time goal did for them.

Who could ever forget the Terry Gibson hat-trick against all-conquering Liverpool on December 1983? Or the final run in to season 1984-85 when nothing less then three wins in the last three games would ensure First Division survival. A Stuart Pearce penalty at Stoke City, with future City striker Ian Painter missing from the spot in turn, gave a slender hope. Then a miss-hit shot from Brian Kilcline gave the Sky Blues a nervous and

fortuitous win over Luton Town. The final game was set for Sunday, the 26th of May 1985, against the newly crowned champions Everton, who came to Coventry to entertain their fans with an exhibition display.

The morning was bright, sunny and warm. The excitement intense, and the result a 4-1 win to Coventry amidst ecstatic relief from the fans. Steve Ogrizovic in his first season at the club, viewed the scenes of jubilation and said: " *If this is how our supporters react to avoiding relegation, what will it be like when we win something?* " Well, in the Spring of 1987, Steve discovered that support for the club could reach heights and produce feelings that reduced hardened and normally tacit men to tears, as City's run in the F.A. Cup culminated in triumph at Wembley in the Final. I'm sure all fans will have their special memories of that time, for me it was at Hillsborough, F.A.Cup Sixth Round against Sheffield Wednesday, first half, Score 0-0. The ball is loose in mid-field, and Lloyd McGrath wins a 40-60 challenge with his opposite number.

Then as the ball runs loose again, he wins it back with another numbing tackle, a short pass to Dave Bennett, and a quick through ball to Cyrille Regis and bang! 1-0.

What scenes at Hillsborough a few week later in the Semi-Final against Leeds United, when City win 3-2 in extra time against a tough uncompromising side, in a competitive but entertaining game.

And then the finale at Wembley when City came from behind twice to lift the Cup. The Cup Winning Side had some exceptionally good players but was essentially a team who played and strived for one another. It was a case of the whole being greater than the sum of its parts.

Since then we have endured shock defeats at Sutton United and Northampton Town, where the fans were soaked by torrential rain which fell all afternoon, as well as depressed by an unsatisfactory display by the team.

To follow Coventry City is not for those who seek perpetual glory, but is for a more average supporter who knows disappointment, but when the team do achieve, they can savour the moment all the more for its rarity.

This book is for those supporters young and old. Whether their hero was Clarrie Bourton, George Lowrie, George Hudson, Ferguson or Wallace, Cyrille Regis or Mick Quinn. Or again, Leslie Jones, Peter Hill, Ian Gibson or Dave Bennett. Or the players that the Coventry fan really loves, George Mason, George Curtis, Lloyd McGrath – men who had heart, courage and a great love of their club.

We hope the reader enjoys reading about the men who have played for Coventry City and gets as much pleasure as we have in researching this book.

1986/87

BIRMINGHAM LEAGUE DAYS, AND BEFORE

During the club's early days in the Birmingham League, and before, most of the players were juniors, but some blossomed to become Football League players. Amongst these were:–

Arthur Arrowsmith, played for Stoke at outside right after playing for Coventry in season 1905–06.

Sam Bayley, who came from Leamington, spent the 1899–1900 season with Small Heath.

Arthur Beadworth, had a long career after joining Leicester Fosse from Hinckley Town in 1900. He played in turn for Coventry City, Preston North End, Manchester United, Swindon Town, Blackburn Rovers, New Brompton and finally spent the 1906–07 season with Burton United in Division Two.

W. Layton

Archie Bostock, played in 1880's for Singers F.C. as a young man, went on to play for Shrewsbury Town, West Bromwich Albion and Burton Swifts. He was capped for Wales.

W. Buckingham, joined Coventry City in the summer of 1901 from Tottenham Hotspur. He played in the infamous F.A. Cup tie against Berwick Rangers which was lost 2–11.

Reuben Craythorne. After starring at Coventry City for three seasons, Reuben – who came from Kidderminster Harriers – went to Notts Co. where he was a first team regular in Division One for 10 years. Later joined Darlington.

H. Davis. A Scot who joined Walsall Town Swifts in Division Two from Cambuslang Hibs., and onto Coventry City in the 1900 close season.

J. Davis. After a season with Burton United in Division Two, joined Coventry City in the summer of 1906, but was unable to break into the first team on a regular basis.

Will Dorrell. Will played for Singers F.C. in the Birmingham Junior Cup Final of 1891, was immediately taken by Leicester Fosse, and from 1894–96 he played in Division One with Aston Villa. He then returned to Leicester Fosse, moved to Burslem Port Vale, and finally Belper Town. Two of his sons played League football, and one – Arthur – played for England in the twenties.

Harry Edwards. Another of the Birmingham Junior Cup Winners team. Joined Small Heath in 1892, and then went on to Leicester Fosse, Derby County, and Wolverton Town – when they played in the Southern League.

William Edwards. Left Singers F.C. in 1896 and spent the following season with Small Heath.

Arthur Flavell. Arthur was the regular goalkeeper for Singers in their first season in the Birmingham League in 1894–95. Later he joined West Bromwich and Millwall. He was a reserve team player at both clubs.

Caesar Jenkyns. A heavyweight Welsh International centre–half, known for his robustness, who joined Coventry City late in his career (1902–03 season), after playing for Small Heath, Woolwich Arsenal, Newton Heath and Walsall in the Football League. He gained eight Welsh caps.

John Kearns. John joined Coventry City from Hartshill United in 1903. He then went in turn to Birmingham, Aston Villa and Bristol City. He played in Division One for 10 years.

John Kifford. A Scot who came from Abercorn F.C. to Derby County, and then moved to Bristol Rovers, Portsmouth, West Bromwich Albion, Millwall, Carlisle United and Coventry City. Was club trainer for a while when he retired in 1908.

W. Layton. Spent two seasons in Wolverhampton Wanderers first team before joining Coventry City in the summer of 1906.

Albert Lewis. Many fans in the early days believed Albert to be the finest player City had up to the Great War. He joined West Bromwich Albion for the first time in 1904 from Stafford Rangers. He joined Coventry City in 1906, had two sparkling seasons before joining Northampton Town, and then in 1913 he returned to West Bromwich Albion.

Jim McIntyre. Started with Walsall Swifts before joining, in turn; Notts Co., Northampton Town, Reading and Coventry City. Returned in 1928 to become the club manager.

Frank Mobley. The darling of the Singers F.C. supporters. A strong goal scoring centre–forward who led the Birmingham Junior Cup winning team. He left for Small Heath in 1892, and after spending season 1896/97 with Bury, and then Gravesend in the Southern League, before returning to Coventry City for a short period in 1900.

Albert Lewis

E. Peers. Came to Coventry City in 1904 after a League career which started at Walsall Swifts and took in Nottingham Forest, Burton United and Swindon Town.

L. Pember. An Aston Villa Reserve who joined Walsall and then Doncaster Rovers – during a brief stay in Division Two – before coming to Coventry City for season 1904–05.

Dick Ray. Dick became a well known Football League manager. His football playing career started with Burslem Port Vale in 1894, before going on to play for Crewe Alexandra, Manchester City, Coventry City (Feb to May 1903), Stockport Co., Chesterfield, Leeds City and finally Huddersfield Town.

W. Tarplin. Came to City from Small Heath Albion in 1901, and joined Notts County in 1903 – where he spent 5 seasons – and after a season at Reading he left the first class football scene.

Oliver Taylor. A goalkeeper who joined City from West Bromwich Albion where he spent two seasons. Joined Coventry in 1903, where he stayed for another two seasons.

J. Tooth. Joined Aston Villa from the Army, where he served in the 11th Hussars. Unable to break into the first team he joined Burton United for season 1905–06 and joined Coventry a year later for two fine seasons.

The Southern League

ALDEN, W.F.
Winger
Born: Bristol
Career: Rogers' FC, Mardy c/s 1909, Merthyr Town c/s 1910, Coventry City c/s 1911, Llanelly c/s 1912, Aberdare c/s 1913.

Coventry City	Southern League	F.A.Cup
1911–12	8	–

Debut: 16/9/1911 v Stoke (h) 3–2 (OL)

Alden had a lot of success in South Wales football in the Southern League Division 2, but he was not able to displace Albert Holmes in City's first team.

ALDERSON, Robert Gordon (Bob)
Outside Right
Born: Newcastle–Upon–Tyne
Career: Wellbourne F.C., Coventry City May 1914

Coventry City	Southern League	F.A.Cup
1914–15	16 – 2	–

Debut: 5/9/14 v Brentford (a) 1–3 (OR)

Bob was a regular during the dark season of 1914–15, when City were in Southern League Division 2. A native of the North East, he was one of many junior players signed from that area. As a Sergeant, he served in the Tyne Electrical Engineers during The Great War.

ALLAN, John
Centre Forward
Born: Carlisle
Career: Benwell St. James, Bentwick Mission, Newcastle North End, Bedlington United, Everton c/s 1909, Leeds City July 1912, Rochdale c/s 1913, Coventry City c/s 1914, Walsall c/s 1920

Coventry City	S.League	F.League	F.A.Cup
1914–15	24 – 22	–	1
1919–20	–	5	–
Total	24 – 22	5	1

Debut: 5/9/14 v Brentford (a) 1–3 (CF)

Jack was brought up in the North East, eventually joining Everton, where he was a more than useful reserve. He was signed by Scott–Walford for Coventry, having already played for him at Leeds City. During the 1914–15 season, Jack was a prolific scorer. He scored in 5 successive games – it would have been six, but the game against Mardy was expunged. He also contributed 3 hat–tricks, a fourth against Abertillery was discounted when their record was expunged.

ARCHER, Arthur (Sol)
Goalkeeper
Born: Atherstone c. 1883
Died: Stafford May 1931
Career: Atherstone Athletic, Hartshill Utd, Atherstone Town, Polesworth Athletic, Kidderminster Harriers, Coventry City c/s 1908, Atherstone Town c/s 1909 until 1921

Coventry City	Southern League	F.A.Cup
1908–09	14	3

Debut: 3/10/08 v Plymouth Argyle (h) 1–2 (Goal)

A good shot stopper, but he was less than sure on crosses. At 5 feet 9 inches tall and weighing 13 stone, he was solid and able to withstand the physical approach of forwards which was prevalent at the time. Sol had a good run in the first team following the loss of form of Joe Moult, but he lost his place after a 6–1 defeat at Luton Town.

ARNOLD, Thomas (Tommy)
Forward
Born: Coventry
Career: Foleshill Great Heath, Coventry City c/s 1904, Woolwich Arsenal c/s 1905, Coventry City c/s 1906, Retired 1911

Coventry City	Southern League	F.A.Cup
1904–05	–	3 – 1
1908–09	23 – 9	3
1909–10	22 – 5	2 – 3
1910–11	4 – 1	–
Total	49 – 15	8 – 4

Debut: 8/10/04 v Halesowen (Birm. Lge.) (a) 3–2 (OL)

Tommy was a product of Foleshill football–which was very strong at the time, and after a season with City, he was signed by Arsenal, for whom he made

2 appearances before he returned. A hard player to dispossess, Tom was a valuable regular during City's first 2 seasons in the Southern League and especially during the FA Cup runs. Tom became the club trainer in 1912.

BARNACLE, Richard (Dick)
Full Back
Born: Coventry
Career: Foleshill St. Georges, Coventry City c/s 1908, Newport Co. c/s 1919

Coventry City	Southern League	F.A.Cup
1908–09	13	2
1909–10	2	–
1910–11	15 – 1	3
1911–12	30	2
1912–13	23	2
1913–14	30	–
1914–15	15	1
Total	128 – 1	10

Debut: 3/10/08 v Plymouth Argyle (h) 1–2 (RB)

Foleshill provided City with a regular supply of footballers who were robust, durable and redoubtable and Dick was the epitome of this breed. Tall, tough and quick, a good reader of the game and possessed of great coolness, he was signed as a reserve, but forced his way into the first team by sheer ability, whilst working as a full time miner. Harry Parkes signed him for Newport County, to establish them after The Great War, but injury ended his career after only 1 game.

BENNETT, F.
Right Half
Born: Coventry
Career: Lord Street Juniors, Coventry City April 1914.

Coventry City	Southern League	F.A.Cup
1914–15	4*	–

* Bennett may have played five games – no accurate line-up record v Swansea on Easter Monday.

Debut: 27/3/15 v Llanelly (h) 1–0 (OR)

A local player who was in reserve during that awful season of 1914–15.

BIVINS, Arthur
Full Back
Born: Aldermans Green, Coventry 1885.
Career: Clifton Victoria, Coventry City 1907, Worcester City c/s 1909, Longford F.C.

Coventry City	Southern League	F.A.Cup
1908–09	4	

Debut: 1/9/08 v Crystal Palace (h) 1–1 (LB)

A member of a well known local sporting family, Arthur joined the club in 1907 as a reserve. In August 1908, he played so well in the pre-season trials, that he was included in the first 4 Southern League games, all of which were lost. He returned to the reserves after losing form and in the following season he joined Worcester City. At 5 feet 9½ inches tall and 13 stone 7 pounds, he was described as hefty and powerful.

BLAKE, Sid
Goalkeeper
Born: Whitley Bay
Career: Willington Athletic, Whitley Athletic October 1904, Newcastle United January 1905, Queens Park Rangers 1906/07, Whitley Bay 1907/08, North Shields Athletic 1908/09, Newcastle Utd May 1909 (£30), Coventry City May 1914, Retired 1917.

Coventry City	Southern League	F.A.Cup
1914–15	19	1

Debut: 5/9/14 v Brentford (a) 1–3 (Goal)

Sid joined Newcastle United and made his Football League debut as an outside left, before finding his best position in goal. It was in the latter position

19

that he was signed by manager Scott-Walford for The City. A competent and reliable goalkeeper, Sid provided a firm base for the side and when he retired in 1918, he became the club trainer.

BOSTON, Ernest (Ernie)
Centre Forward
Born: Coventry 11th January 1888
Died: Coventry 14th January 1941
Career: Victoria Swifts, Lord Street Juniors, Clifton Victoria, Coventry City c/s 1907, Retired 1914.

Coventry City	Southern League	F.A.Cup
1908–09	10	–
1909–10	5	–
1910–11	9	–
1911–12	11	–
1912–13	5 – 2	–
1913–14	14 – 1	–
Total	54 – 3	–

Debut: 26/9/08 v Southend Utd. (h) 2–5 (CH)
Honours: Captained England Juniors v Scotland, March 1912

Ernie was an excellent reserve team player who could never achieve a regular first team place, but always gave his all when called upon. At 5 feet 9 inches and 11 stone, he was a little lightweight for top class football, but was speedy. He did manage a fairly lengthy run in the Southern League during the dreadful 1913–14 relegation season, but left in the close season.

BOURNE, G.
Right Half
Born: Foleshill
Career: Foleshill Great Heath, Coventry City Sept 1909.

Coventry City	Southern League	F.A.Cup
1909–10	1	–

Debut: 18/10/09 v Queens Park Rangers (a) 0–4 (RH)

Yet another player from the Foleshill area, who was described as a natural footballer, being a smart tackler and accurate passer of the ball. His sole appearance in the first team was in the 0–4 defeat at Queens Park Rangers and he left shortly afterwards.

BRADLEY, Eli John
Centre Half
Born: Dudley December 1882
Died: May 1952

Career: Bilston United, Dudley Town, West Bromwich Albion July 1905, Luton Town July 1908, Coventry City c/s 1909, Hearts of Midlothian October 1912, Dudley Town November 1913, Retired 1919.

Coventry City	Southern League	F.A.Cup
1909–10	37 – 4	6 – 1
1910–11	33 – 10	4
1911–12	27 – 4	2
1912–13	7 – 1	–
Total	104 – 19	12 – 1

Debut: 1/9/09 v Swindon Town (a) 1–2 (CH)
Honours: England Junior International v Scotland 1899
3 Southern League appearances (with City)

Eli was the backbone of the City team, being influential in the Southern League and the FA Cup. He was a hard tackling, whole hearted half back, who was never beaten at a time when football was a real hard man's game. His worth was recognised by the Southern League, who selected him for all 3 inter-league matches during 1911–12. After only a few games in the 1912–13 season, he left for Hearts and was a sensation in Scotland, until he sustained a serious knee injury which ended his first class career.

BROWN, Ivor
Inside Right
Born: Derby 1st April 1888
Died: 1966
Career: Ripley Athletic, Tottenham Hotspur 1909, Coventry City c/s 1911, Reading c/s 1913, Swansea Town c/s 1914, Porth c/s 1920.

Coventry City	Southern League	F.A.Cup
1911–12	22 – 8	–
1912–13	33 – 11	–
Total	55 – 19	–

Debut: 2/9/11 v Northampton T. (h) 1–2 (IR)

As the club consolidated it's place in the Southern League, Ivor Brown had 2 very useful seasons at City, after spending some time at Tottenham in the reserves. He was clever on the ball, but a little slow and it was this lack of pace which prevented him reaching the very top.

BUCKLE, Harry Redmond
Outside Left
Born: Belfast 1882
Career: Cliftonville Casuals, Cliftonville Olympic, Cliftonville

May 1901, Sunderland October 1902, Portsmouth May 1906, Bristol Rovers c/s 1907, Coventry City c/s 1908 player/manager, Belfast Celtic c/s 1911, Glenavon c/s 1914, Belfast Utd September 1917 (player/manager/sec.), Fordsons September 1922

Coventry City	Southern League	F.A.Cup
1908–09	39 – 16	3
1909–10	38 – 17	6 – 1
1910–11	36 – 9	4 – 1
Total	113 – 42	13 – 2

Debut: 1/9/08 v Crystal Palace (h) 1–1 (OL)
Honours: 2 Irish International Caps
      3 Irish League appearances
      1 Southern League appearance
      Irish League Cup Runners–up Medal 1924
      Irish League Cup Winners Medal 1926

During the club's first season in the Southern League, Harry Buckle provided the only glimpses of class. He arrived at City in his prime, as an Irish international, and showed exceptional ability with a "piledriver" of a shot. During those first 2 seasons in the League, Buckle was the top scorer for the club and included the first 2 hat–tricks recorded at top class level. Harry was tall for a winger at 6 feet, but this helped him to withstand the sturdy challenges at first class level. At the end of his first season, Harry was appointed as the first team manager, as well as still playing. He was very successful in establishing the club's position in the League, as well as leading them to 2 super FA Cup campaigns. He left during the summer of 1913, to join Belfast Celtic and embarked on a very successful career in Irish football, both as a player and administrator. He won an Irish Cup Winners medal at the age of 45 with Fordsons in 1926, when he combined playing with managerial and secretarial duties! For a while, he worked in the Belfast Shipyards. In September 1912, he was badly injured in the face by an iron bolt which was fired at him and on another occasion, he was set upon by his work mates as he left the premises, and thrown in the river.

BUNN, Thomas (Tommy)
Inside Left

Born: South Bank, Middlesbrough
Career: South Bank, Wolverhampton Wanderers 1912, Coventry City November 1913.

Coventry City	Southern League	F.A.Cup
1913–14	1	–

Debut: 22/11/13 v Reading (a) 0–1 (IL)

Came in November 1913 for a month's trial and after playing in the reserves, he was given a League chance, but was "hardly a success" as Nemo reported in the Midland Daily Telegraph. He left when his trial period expired.

CAMWELL, C.
Centre Forward

Born: Coventry
Career: Clifton Victoria, Coventry City c/s 1908, Rugby Town 1909

Coventry City	Southern League	F.A.Cup
1908–09	1	1

Debut: 28/11/08 v Brighton & H.A. (h) 2–1 (CF)

Camwell was one of the local players in the reserves during the first season in the Southern League. After playing in the Coventry and North Warwickshire League, he was given his chance in November 1908 following injury to Ike Turner. Camwell failed to score in either of the games he played, where his inexperience, lack of pace and stamina were exposed. He left for Rugby Town where he had a happier time.

CASEY, Thomas J.
Outside Left

Born: Oswestry
Career: Oswestry Town, Coventry City c/s 1914

Coventry City	Southern League	F.A.Cup
1914–15	1*	–

* Casey may have played two games – no accurate line–up record v Swansea on Easter Monday.

Debut: 3/4/15 v Newport Co. (a) 1–0 (OL)

A young reserve in that last season before the postponement of League football during The Great War.

CHAPLIN, Alfred (Freddy)
Wing Half

Born: Foleshill 1879
Career: Bablake School, Foleshill St. Pauls, Foleshill Great Heath, Coventry City 1902, Small Heath May 1903, Woolwich Arsenal c/s 1905, Coventry City c/s 1907, Retired 1912 then Longford F.C.

Coventry City	Southern League	F.A.Cup
1907–08	–	8
1908–09	35	3
1909–10	37	5 – 1
1910–11	24	4
1911–12	31 – 1	2
Total	127 – 1	22 – 1

Debut: 1/9/08 v Crystal Palace (h) 1–1 (CH)
Honours: England Junior International v Scotland 1903

Freddie was one of the products of Foleshill football and after playing for City in the Birmingham League during 1902–03, he went to Football League clubs before returning to Coventry. He became a dependable and valuable member of the team, although at 5 feet 9 inches tall and 11 stone, he was considered slight for a half back of the time. Despite this, he always played with great heart and was a general utility player on occasion with credit. Although Freddie scored only 2 goals in senior football, they were both noteworthy. The first was the only goal of the game at Portsmouth in the FA Cup 2nd round during the epic cup run of 1909–10. His second goal was in his final game for the club in April 1912.

CRAIG, Robert
Outside Left/Left Half

Born: Newcastle–Upon–Tyne
Career: North Shields Athletic, Coventry City May 1913, Nuneaton Town c/s 1919, Hinckley United c/s 1920, Retired c.1925.

Coventry City	Southern League	F.A.Cup
1913–14	14 – 1	–
1914–15	11	–
Total	25 – 1	–

Debut: 3/9/13 v Gillingham (a) 2–0 (OL) 1 goal

A Tynesider who came straight into the first team and scored on his debut, but this was the only goal he scored. He left the club at the end of the Great War and had some local success.

CRUTCHLEY, J.C.
Right Half

Career: Coventry City 1914, Halesowen 1915, Portsmouth 1919, Hednesford Town c/s 1920.

Coventry City	Southern League	F.A.Cup
1914–15	11	–

Debut: 2/1/15 v Brentford (h) 3–2 (RH)

A raw junior who came into the first team during the 1914–15 season when more experienced players were unavailable.

DAVIES, Claude
Outside Left

Born: Bangor, North Wales
Career: Bangor University, Coventry City c/s 1910, Rugby Town c/s 1911 until 1915.

Coventry City	Southern League	F.A.Cup
1910–11	2	–

Debut: 8/10/10 v Brighton & H.A. (h) 0–2 (OL)

A teacher who played as an amateur, mainly for City reserves and Rugby Town. His two appearances were as a replacement for Harry Buckle who was injured, a hard act to follow.

DAVISON, George
Centre Forward

Born: Newcastle–Upon–Tyne
Career: Blyth Spartans, Coventry City c/s 1913, Bristol Rovers c/s 1914, West Stanley c/s 1920.

Coventry City	Southern League	F.A.Cup
1913–14	38 – 18	1 – 1

Debut: 3/9/13 v Gillingham (a) 2–0 (CF)

A prolific goalscorer at Blyth Spartans, George was the top scorer during the poor season of 1913–14, with 19 goals, when no other player scored more than 6, hence the club's relegation to Southern League Division 2. In the penultimate league game, he scored a hat–trick against Watford at home and netted again in the last game. At the end of the season, he was eagerly signed by Bristol Rovers.

DEXTER, George
Right Back

Born: Hucknall, Notts
Career: Bestwood Colliery, Coventry City c/s 1912, Preston North End c/s 1914, Hucknall Byron 1919, Norwich City 1919–20.

Coventry City	Southern League	F.A.Cup
1912–13	–	–
1913–14	11	–
Total	11	–

Debit: 7/2/14 v Cardiff City (a) 1–2 (RB)

In the Southern League days, City obtained their players from 3 main sources, Foleshill, the North-east and Nottinghamshire areas. All being mining areas which bred a determined, unyielding type of player. George came from the Nottinghamshire mining area and spent a season and a half in the reserves before forcing his way into the first team during the difficult season of 1913–14, to fill one of the full back positions which had been such a problem. Nemo described him as "a good hard back and a good tackler and kicker". At the end of that season, he was signed by Preston North End in the Football League.

DOBSON, Harold (Harry)

Inside Right

Born: Newcastle–Upon–Tyne
Career: North Shields Athletic, Coventry City May 1913, Newport County c/s 1919, Southend United February 1922

Coventry City	Southern League	F.A.Cup
1913–14	15 – 2	1
1914–15	18 – 14	1
Total	33 – 16	2

Debut: 3/9/13 v Gillingham (a) 2–0 (IR) 1 goal

A young Tynesider who scored on his debut in September 1913, but had to overcome two injuries before the end of that most disappointing of seasons, which restricted his appearances. He became a regular during 1914–15, scoring 14 goals in only 18 games, which did not include a hat–trick against Mardy in a 6–0 win which was expunged when Mardy resigned from the League. After the war, Harry had a successful career with Newport County and Southend United.

DODD, Samuel

Centre Half

Born: Birkenhead
Career: Birkenhead FC, Sheffield Wednesday May 1904, Stockport County c/s 1905, Coventry City c/s 1908.

Coventry City	Southern League	F.A.Cup
1908–09	11	3

Debut: 19/9/08 v Millwall (a) 0–3 (RH)

Sam was one of the experienced Football League players signed to help establish City in the initial Southern League season. In the event, he was unable to maintain a regular first team place in a struggling side, even though Nemo in the Midlands Daily Telegraph described his play as "skilful and determined".

DORAN, John Francis D.C.M., M.M. (Jack)

Inside/Centre Forward

Born: Dublin
Career: Newcastle Empire FC, Coventry City May 1914, Norwich City c/s 1919, Brighton & Hove Albion 1919/20, Manchester City August 1922, Crewe Alexandra January 1924, Mid–Rhondda c/s 1924, Shelbourne 1924/25, Fordsons c/s 1925, Boston United.

Coventry City	Southern League	F.A.Cup
1914–15	1 – 2	–

Debut: 20/3/15 v Ebbw Vale (a) 3–1 (IR) 2 goals
Honours: 3 Ireland Full Caps

Although born in Dublin, Jack was brought up in Newcastle upon Tyne, where City found him in junior football. He joined the Army in September 1914, which restricted him to only 1 first team appearance when he scored twice. Whilst on service with R.A.O.C, he was awarded both the D.C.M and M.M. After the war, he joined Norwich City and Brighton, where he scored with typical regularity and it was during this time that he won his 3 caps.

DOUGHERTY, James

Half Back

Born: New Brighton 1880
Career: Wallasey Rovers, Liscard, Y.M.F.S.A., Chorley, New Brighton Tower c/s 1900, Small Heath 1901, Coventry City c/s 1908, Stirchley United c/s 1909.

Coventry City	Southern League	F.A.Cup
1908–09	13	3

Debut: 19/9/05 v Millwall (a) 0–3 (LH)

Jim was one of the experienced players City signed for their Southern League debut season, but he struggled to hold down a regular place. His lack of pace exposed him, although his judgement was sound and his passing accurate.

DRENNAN, Thomas Alexander (Tom)

Left Back

Born: Long Eaton September 1885
Career: Long Eaton St. Helens FC, Aston Villa 1904 North-ampton Town c/s 1905, Coventry City c/s 1908.

Coventry City	Southern League	F.A.Cup
1908–09	16 – 1	3

Debut: 26/9/08 v Southend Utd (h) 2–5 (LB)

Made a good partner to Juggins during his time at City, but lost his place after a 4–1 defeat at Northampton Town in January 1909. Quick and a good tackler, Tom had 3 very successful seasons at Northampton Town prior to joining City.

ENRIGHT, Joe
Inside Left

Born: Athlone
Career: Shelbourne, Leeds City c/s 1910, Newport County October 1913, Coventry City c/s 1914, Athlone Town during 1914–18 War when on leave

Coventry City	Southern League	F.A.Cup
1914–15	21 – 7	1 – 1

Debut: 19/9/14 v Pontypridd (a) 3–2 (IL)
Honours: 1 Ireland Full Cap
1 Irish League appearance

Signed by Scott–Walford for the second time in the summer of 1914, Joe had a useful season for City, scoring on average once every three games, including 4 goals against Newport in November 1914 in a 10–1 win. During the Great War, he served with the Army in the R.A.O.C. until 1919, when he returned to Ireland.

EVANS, Robert Owen (Bob)
Goalkeeper

Born: Wrexham 1881
Died: Coventry 8th March 1962
Career: Stansty Villa, Wrexham c/s 1898, Blackburn Rovers June 1903 (£150), Croydon Common c/s 1908, Coventry City May 1909, Birmingham c/s 1913 (£50), Nuneaton Town c/s 1914, Retired 1915.

Coventry City	Southern League	F.A.Cup
1909–10	34	6
1910–11	37	3
1911–12	34	2
1912–13	21	2
Total	126	13

Debut: 1/9/09 v Swindon Town (a) 1–2 (Goal)
Honours: 10 Wales Full Caps (5 with City)

Along with Bradley and Saul, Bob Evans made up a defence that lifted City up the league and provided the basis of 2 FA Cup runs. In Evans, the club had

a first class goalkeeper who had already won 5 caps for Wales. He went on to appear another 5 times for Wales whilst with City, the club's first international. He gave many brave, agile and skilful displays and was considered to be amongst the elite of goalkeepers of his day. When he retired, he became a referee in local football, as well as secretary of his local branch of the National Federation of Discharged and Demobilised Sailors and Soldiers, and the Coventry and District Football Benevolent Society – immersing himself in local causes.

FARRANT, Samuel George
Inside Forward

Born: Bristol 27th May 1885
Career: Bristol St. Georges FC, Grays Utd c/s 1903, Bristol City 1904, Stockport Co. 1905, Workington 1906, Luton Town May 1907, Coventry City c/s 1908, Aberdare c/s 1909.

Coventry City	Southern League	F.A.Cup
1908–09	14 – 3	–

Debut: 1/9/08 v Crystal Palace (h) 1–1 (IR)

Sam was a high goalscorer in the local football leagues, but was never able to reproduce this form subsequently, and he was unable to hold down a regular place at the highest levels. He achieved more success in Southern League Division 2 circles with Aberdare. In the language of the time, he was described as "cool and pretty". He played in City's first Southern League match, but after a knee injury in November, he was never able to regain his place and left the following summer, and in 1910 emigrated to South Africa.

FEEBURY, Albert
Half Back

Born: Hucknall, Notts. 1891
Career: Hucknall, Nottingham Forest, Coventry City c/s 1911, Crystal Palace July 1914, Folkestone c/s 1924.

Coventry City	Southern League	F.A.Cup
1911–12	7	–
1912–13	33 – 2	2
1913–14	25 – 3	1
Total	65 – 5	3

Debut: 2/9/11 v Northampton T. (h) 1–2 (LH)

Albert was a miner who was heavily built, but he had great stamina and was a trier whose first season with City was disrupted by injury. He took over the centre half position when Bradley left. Being 5 feet 10½ inches tall and 13 stone, he had the physique to do the job. He made some appearances for the club during the Great War whilst a Crystal Palace player. When with Palace, he helped them to the Football League Division 3 Championship in 1921.

FISHER, Frederick (Fred)
Left Back

Born: Wednesbury
Career: Wednesbury Old Athletic, Coventry City c/s 1910, Wednesbury Old Athletic c/s 1911.

Coventry City	Southern League	F.A.Cup
1910–11	1	–

Debut: 8/4/11 v Plymouth Argyle (a) 0–6 (LB)

After spending a season in the club's reserve side, Fred got his first team chance at Plymouth, who promptly won 6–0! This turned out to be his only appearance and he left at the end of the season.

FISHER, W. Albert (Albert)
Inside Left

Born: Birmingham
Career: Ashbury Richmond 1900, Soho Caledonians 1902, Aston Villa 1902, Bristol City c/s 1903, Brighton & Hove Albion c/s 1905, Manchester City June 1906, Bradford c/s 1907, Coventry City c/s 1908, Merthyr Town c/s 1909 (player-manager).

Coventry City	Southern League	F.A.Cup
1908–09	6	3 – 1

Debut: 1/9/08 v Crystal Palace (h) 1–1 (IL)

After making a single appearance for Aston Villa in the First Division, Albert became a regular with Bristol City in Division 2, scoring 22 goals in 50 League starts. He then played for a succession of teams without achieving the same success. City signed him for their initial season in the Southern League and after playing the first game, he could not hold on to his place. Although he had good ball control, his shooting was inaccurate, and he spent most of the season in the reserves. In the close season of 1909, he was appointed player manager at Merthyr Town and later managed Notts County.

FULLJAMES, William (Bill)
Right Half

Born: Cleethorpes 1889
Died: 27th August 1959
Career: Grimsby Rovers, Grimsby Town 1911, Scunthorpe & Lindsey United c/s 1912, Coventry City c/s 1914, Nuneaton Town c/s 1919, Caerphilly Town c/s 1922.

Coventry City	Southern League	F.A.Cup
1914–15	9	–

Debut: 5/9/14 v Brentford (a) 1–3 (RH)

Scott–Walford, the new City manager, had seen Bill playing for Scunthorpe United in non–League football and signed him as the regular right half for the 1914–15 season. After joining the Forces in December 1914, he ceased playing for City, and later joined the coaching staff.

GILBERT, Herbert
Centre Half

Born: Coventry 1885
Career: Foleshill St. Pauls, Herberts Athletic, Coventry City 1905, Foleshill Great Heath

Coventry City	Southern League	F.A.Cup
1907–08	–	8 – 2
1908–09	12	–
Total	12	8 – 2

Debut: 3/10/08 v Plymouth Argyle (h) 1–2 (CH)

Bert had 2½ seasons in the Birmingham League as the regular City centre half, and missed only 6 games. Then, just before the first Southern League match, he contracted peritonitis in August, and missed the start. He played one game in October, but was not able to regain his place until the end of February, and played well in a period when the results improved. Despite this, he was released at the end of the season.

GORDON, John (Jack)
Left Back

Born: Arbroath
Career: Parkhead FC (Arbroath), Arbroath December 1904, Hibernian September 1906, Brentford 1908, Leith Athletic c/s 1909, Coventry City c/s 1910, Leith Athletic c/s 1911.

Coventry City	Southern League	F.A.Cup
1910–11	11	–

Debut: 3/9/10 v Queens Park Rangers (a) 0–5 (LB)

For his second taste of English football, Jack signed for City and started the season as first choice left back, but his first game was a 0–5 defeat at QPR. After a few games, he was replaced by Dick Barndale. He briefly regained his place in December, but both games he played in were lost with 7 goals being conceded. He never made the first team again.

GRETTON, H.
Outside Right

Born: Basford, Notts
Career: Bulwell White Star, Coventry City c/s 1912, Grantham Town December 1914.

Coventry City	Southern League	F.A.Cup
1912–13	–	–
1913–14	19	–
1914–15	–	–
Total	19	–

Debut: 11/10/13 v Swindon Town (a) 1–6 (OR)

Gretton was signed in the summer of 1912 as a raw youth who had made a grand reputation in local football. After a season and a half learning his trade in the reserves, he was promoted to the first team to claim the outside right position on a regular basis, and held his place until the end of the season. He was young, light and fast, and being a whole-hearted trier he was the type of player that Coventry crowds have taken to their hearts. Unfortunately, he got his chance when the team were labouring and his form faded, which prompted his release.

HALL, Francis (Frank)
Outside Right

Born: Coventry
Career: Foleshill Albions, Coventry City c/s 1913.

Coventry City	Southern League	F.A.Cup
1913–14	1	–

Debut: 25/4/14 v Norwich City (a) 1–1 (OR)

Frank spent a season at Highfield Road in the reserves and his one and only first team game was at Norwich in a 1–1 draw. He did not impress and left the club within a week.

HANSON, William
Left Back

Born: Rushall c. 1888
Career: Rushall Red Cross FC, Aston Villa, Coventry City January 1909, Bradford (PA) July 1910.

Coventry City	Southern League	F.A.Cup
1908–09	19	–
1909–10	27	5
Total	46	5

Debut: 9/1/09 v New Brighton (a) 1–0 (LB)

Billy joined City to replace Drennan at left back and stiffen the defence after a poor run. The effect was immediate, when 4 of the next 5 games were won. With his speed and hard tackling, he had good distribution and seldom made mistakes. His defensive role was one of the keys to the splendid FA Cup run in his second season, when City reached the quarter finals for the first time. At the end of the season, it came as no surprise to find him snapped up by Bradford to play Division 2 League Football.

HARKINS, John
Wing Half

Born: Musselburgh
Died: Killed in World War 1
Career: Black Watch Regiment, Middlesbrough September 1906, Broxburn Athletic c/s 1908, Bathgate c/s 1909, Leeds City August 1910, Darlington c/s 1912, Coventry City c/s 1914

Coventry City	Southern League	F.A.Cup
1914–15	16* – 1	1

* Harkins may have played seventeen games – no accurate line–up record v Swansea on Easter Monday.

Debut: 5/9/14 v Brentford (a) 1–3 (LH)

Middlesbrough bought John out of the Army where he had impressed playing for his regiment against Celtic in a Scottish Cup tie the previous season. A regular at all of his clubs, he joined City during May 1914, when he lined up again with manager Scott–Walford, for whom he had played at Leeds City. A strong, hard working and clever Scot who lost his life during the Great War, after returning to military service.

HARRIS, George Abner
Left Back/Left Half

Born: Halesowen January 1878
Died: June 1923
Career: Haden Hill Rose FC, Halesowen, Coombs Wood, Halesowen, Aston Villa June 1901, West Bromwich Albion 1909, Wellington Town c/s 1910, Coventry City c/s 1912, Retired 1915.

Coventry City	Southern League	F.A.Cup
1912–13	30	2
1913–14	25	–
1914–15	4 – 1	–
Total	59 – 1	2

Debut: 5/9/12 v Swindon Town (h) 2–1 (LB)
Honours: England Junior International 1906

An experienced player, his best season for City was 1912–13, but the difficulties of the following season, when City were relegated, took their toll on George's form. A heavy player who used his weight to good effect, but he had lost a lot of his pace during his time at City, although made up for this with his excellent passing. On retirement, he became a licensee and later worked in heavy industry. His death was caused by an industrial accident.

HENDREN, Elias (Patsy)
Family name (O'Hanrahan)
Forward

Born: Chiswick 5th February 1889
Died: London 4th October 1962
Career: St. Nicholas FC 1903, Sanderson's FC 1905, Queens Park Rangers c/s 1906, Brentford November 1907, Manchester City March 1908, Coventry City October 1909, Brentford c/s 1911, Retired 1927.

Coventry City	Southern League	F.A.Cup
1909–10	23 – 10	6 – 3
1910–11	4 – 1	–
Total	27 – 11	6 – 3

Debut: 30/10/09 v Watford (a) 3–0 (IL) 2 goals
Honours (Football): England Victory International 1920
Southern League v Football League 1913–14
(Cricket): 51 tests for England

Patsy, who changed his name from O'Hanrahan to the Anglicised version of Hendren, had two parallel sporting careers. As well as being better than the average footballer, he was also one of the best batsman in the World, playing over 50 times for England; His highest score was 205 not out, and during his career he made 57610 runs at an average of 50.80. He may also have been the first player to wear protective head gear against West Indian fast bowlers at Lord's in 1933, after he had been struck on the head by their fast bowlers 2 years earlier. Patsy, who also had a cheerful nature and was a great dressing room asset, joined City and made an immediate impact, scoring 2 goals from inside left. The following season, he was plagued by a series of injuries and eventually moved on to Brentford where he played for another 17 years with some success, gaining an England Victory cap in 1920. At Brentford, he became a left winger, which proved to be his best position and from which his career blossomed.

HICKLETON, William R.
Right Half

Born: Newcastle–Upon–Tyne c. 1884
Career: Wallsend Park Villa, Portsmouth c/s 1905, Northampton Town c/s 1907, Coventry City c/s 1909, Brentford c/s 1911.

Coventry City	Southern League	F.A.Cup
1909–10	34	6
1910–11	20	3
Total	54	9

Debut: 1/9/09 v Swindon Town (a) 1–2 (RH)

A Tynesider who had not established himself at either Portsmouth or Northampton Town, he started the season 1909–10 in the City first team and had a storming campaign in both the Southern League and FA Cup. During his second season, he was injured a couple of times, and this affected his form towards the end, hence reducing his appearances. He then had two seasons for Brentford.

HICKMAN, J.
Centre Forward

Career: General Electric Works FC, Coventry City December 1908.

Coventry City	Southern League	F.A.Cup
1908–09	3 – 2	–

Debut: 12/12/08 v Brentford (h) 1–2 (CF)

A free scoring centre forward from the Birmingham Works League. He joined City the week after appearing in a representative game, and within hours, made his debut as the 8th centre forward of the season. He was 22 years old and at 5 feet 10 inches tall and 12 stone, he had an excellent physique, worked hard and was not timid, but he was slow, with poor ball control.

HILL, Walter
Forward

Born: Birmingham
Career: Birmingham Small Arms Co. FC, Coventry City c/s 1910.

Coventry City	Southern League	F.A.Cup
1910–11	3	–

Debut: 3/9/10 v QPR (a) 0–5 (IR)

Walter was signed from Birmingham Works League football, where he played for BSA and he went straight into the City first team and rapidly out again after a 0–5 defeat. Nemo in the Midland Daily Telegraph, reported "Hill did not make a big impression". Hill's second appearance was in a 0–6 defeat at Plymouth, but in his final appearance, City drew 1–1 at home to Millwall.

HODGE, W.F. (Chips)
Wing Half/Inside Forward

Career: Barnes FC, Croydon Common c/s 1907, Coventry City c/s 1908, Hastings & St. Leonards United c/s 1909.

Coventry City	Southern League	F.A.Cup
1908–09	2	–

Debut: 12/9/08 v New Brompton (h) 3–4 (LH)

Chips was a regular at Croydon Common, but was very much a reserve at Coventry with only 2 first team games in the initial Southern League season. His first game was at left half and a week later, he played centre forward in an emergency. He did have ability, which he showed in the reserves, but he was not able to reproduce this in the first team.

HOLMES, Albert (Bert)
Outside Left

Born: Mansfield
Career: Mansfield Mechanics, Coventry City c/s 1911, Heart of Midlothian February 1914, Coventry City March 1914, Portsmouth c/s 1915.

Coventry City	Southern League	F.A.Cup
1911–12	30 – 3	2
1912–13	38 – 8	2
1913–14	26 – 6	1
1914–15	8	1
Total	102 – 17	6

Debut: 2/9/11 v Northampton T. (h) 1–2 (OL)

A strong, dangerous winger from the Nottinghamshire coalfield. Bert was a first- teamer from the start and only missed out through injury that first season. An ever-present in his second, as he would have been in 1913–14, but was suspended for "training irregularities" in early February 1914. His only hat-trick for City was from outside left in the Southern League game at Highfield Road against Northampton Town on March 29th 1913. In this game, City led 4–0 at half time, but had to hold on for a 4–4 draw in the end. He signed for Hearts in the Scottish League, for whom he made 3 appearances, but soon returned to City.

HOPKINS, J.
Forward

Career: Willenhall Pickwick, Wolverhampton Wanderers January 1904, New Brompton c/s 1907, Coventry City c/s 1908

Coventry City	Southern League	F.A.Cup
1908–09	2	–

Debut: 14/11/08 v Leyton (h) 2–1 (IL)

Hopkins came as an experienced player for the initial Southern League season, but he was unable to establish a first team place. He did not distinguish himself in either game. No trace of his subsequent career has been found.

JACKSON, Steve
Full Back

Born: Smethwick
Died: Killed in action during World War I
Career: Hay Mills FC, Coventry City c/s 1911.

Coventry City	Southern League	F.A.Cup
1911–12	1	–
1912–13	5	–
1913–14	6	–
Total	12	–

Debut: 14/10/11 v Crystal Palace (a) 0–3 (LB)

A young eager reserve who did well when called into first team action, but whose limitations were exposed in Southern League football. Joined the Army early in World War 1 and was subsequently killed in action.

JACQUES, William
Goalkeeper

Born: Northfleet 8th December 1888
Died: 6th June 1925
Career: Northfleet, Coventry City c.s 1911, Tottenham Hotspur c/s 1914, Retired 1923 due to illness.

Coventry City	Southern League	F.A.Cup
1911–12	4	–
1912–13	17	–
1913–14	36	1
Total	57	1

Debut: 11/11/11 v Watford (a) 2–6 (Goal)

Bill was one of the few players who enhanced his reputation during the 1913–14 season. An excellent shot stopper, with a powerful physique, which he translated into achieving great length with both his kicking and his punching. He went straight into the Tottenham first team where he remained until illness struck in 1922, which led to his retirement, and his early death aged 36. Bill had the great misfortune to miss out on a Cup Final medal in 1921 when he was injured during the build up.

JARVIS, John Walter
Centre Forward

Born: Kenilworth 1888
Career: Longford St. Thomas', Hawkesbury FC, Kenilworth Town, Coventry City September 1912, Kenilworth Town c/s 1913, Nuneaton Town December 1913.

Coventry City	Southern League	F.A.Cup
1912–13	1	–

Debut: 12/10/12 v Crystal Palace (a) 0–3 (CF)

At 5 feet 10 inches tall and 12 stone, Jack was tall with a good physique, who scored a lot of goals in local junior football, but his elevation to the first team exposed his lack of ability and real speed for the highest class.

JOHNSON, Samuel
Left Half

Born: Colne c.1885
Career: Newton Heath Albion, Colne 1904, Blackpool c/s 1905, Colne FC c/s 1907, Exeter City c/s 1908, Coventry City c/s 1909, Leeds City June 1911.

Coventry City	Southern League	F.A.Cup
1909–10	12	1
1910–11	36	4
Total	48	5

Debut: 4/12/09 v Kettering (a) 5–0 (LH) FA Cup

Sam arrived at City after a spell in the Football League with Blackpool and another with Exeter City in the Southern League. Once he had established himself in the first team, he became a regular. As a wing half, he was described as energetic and a hard worker, giving good support from left half. He left in June 1911, being signed by Scott–Walford at Leeds City.

JONES, Fred
Inside Forward

Born: Newstead, Notts 25th December 1888
Career: Sutton Junction, Notts County c/s 1907, Coventry City c/s 1911, Notts County c/s 1912, Coventry City c/s 1913, Southampton c/s 1914, Coventry City c/s 1919, Pembroke Dock 1920/21, Wrexham 1921/22, Ebbw Vale 1922/24.

Coventry City	S.League	F.League	F.A.Cup
1911–12	37 – 22	–	2 – 1
1913–14	19 – 4	–	–
1919–20	–	1	2 – 1
Total	56–26	1	4 – 2

Debut: 9/9/11 v Brighton & HA (a) 1–3 (IL)

Fred had 3 different spells at Highfield Road, the first season being the best when he was the club's highest scorer. He scored one hat–trick for City against Plymouth Argyle at Highfield Road on March 2nd 1912 in a League game. At the end of that season, he returned to Notts County, but soon came back to City, where he was frustrated by injury. He never recovered his earlier free scoring form, but he was still 3rd highest scorer – with only 4 goals. In his final spell, he managed only one Football League appearance.

JONES, Herbert (Harry)
Wing Half

Career: Dudley Town, Coventry City January 1904 to c/s/1909.

Coventry City	Southern League	F.A.Cup
1904–05	–	4
1907–08	–	8
1908–09	6	–
Total	6	12

Debut: 16/1/04 v Stoke Reserves (a) 1–3 (RH)

Harry served Coventry well for four and a half seasons in the Birmingham League and was the club's captain as they set off on their initial season in the Southern League. His play was described at the time as "tenacious, resourceful and hard working". He did not rely on "brawn and muscle". Harry found Southern League football very difficult and lost his place after 6 games. He played out the rest of the season, his last with City, in the reserves.

JUGGINS, Eleander (Eli)
Full Back

Born: Bilston
Career: Willenhall Swifts, Darlaston, Wolverhampton Wands. c/s 1904, Coventry City 1907, Retired 1914.

Coventry City	Southern League	F.A.Cup
1907–08	–	8 – 4
1908–09	28 – 2	1
1909–10	20	1
1910–11	16	1
1911–12	2	–
1913–14	2	1
Total	68 – 2	12 – 4

Debut: 21/9/07 v Brierley Hill (a) 6–2 (RB) 1 goal FA Cup

Variously described as "Herculean" and "a heavy-weight", Eli, with his powerful 5 feet 9 inch and 14 stone frame, was a tower of strength during the first Southern League season. His tackling was powerful and his anticipation made up for his distinct slowness in recovery. After 2 seasons in the first team, he became a regular reserve team player and captain. He joined the club training staff in 1911 and made only occasional appearances in emergencies after that.

KIMBERLEY, Walter
Wing Half/Centre Forward

Born: Birmingham
Died: Killed in action in World War I
Career: Aston Manor FC, Aston Villa c/s 1907, Coventry City c/s 1912, Walsall c/s 1914.

Coventry City	Southern League	F.A.Cup
1912–13	10 – 1	1
1913–14	11	1
Total	21 – 1	2

Debut: 21/9/12 v Stoke (h) 5–2 (CF) 1 goal

At Aston Villa, Walter was a reserve player, who made 7 First Division appearances, but did not get another chance in the following two seasons, which culminated in his signing for City. He was a half back in the reserves, but was drafted in as an emergency centre forward in September 1912 and scored on his debut. He was fairly tall and good in the air, but his lack of speed was quite pronounced and he returned to the reserves after 3 games. His further games were at centre or left half where his quick tackling and strong kicking were best utilised. During the war, he was posted as a prisoner of war in October 1914, and then reported as killed in action, although this has not been substantiated.

LAWRANCE, William
Full Back/Wing Half

Born: Bladon, Co. Durham
Career: Sunderland Royal Rovers, Coventry City c/s 1913, Sunderland Royal Rovers c/s 1914.

Coventry City	Southern League	F.A.Cup
1913–14	4	–

Debut: 3/9/13 v Gillingham (a) 2–0 (LB)

Lawrance was a young North–Easterner who was unable to retain his first team place, and he returned North after City's relegation from Southern League Division 1.

LEE, Thomas
Outside Left

Born: Bolton c.1885
Career: Erith FC, Arsenal c/s 1906, West Ham United c/s 1907, Coventry City c/s 1909, Colne FC c/s 1910.

Coventry City	Southern League	F.A.Cup
1909–10	6	–

Debut: 25/9/09 v Portsmouth (a) 0–0 (OL)

Tommy was a reserve at both Arsenal and West Ham United, and at City he was understudy to Harry Buckle, so his first team appearances were restricted. After a season in the City reserves, he went to Colne in his native Lancashire.

LEGGE, Samuel George Frederick (Sam)
Inside Left

Born: Willenhall
Died: Walsall August 1973
Career: Willenhall Swifts, West Bromwich Albion August 1906, Worcester City April 1907, West Bromwich Albion May 1908, Coventry City June 1909.

Coventry City	Southern League	F.A.Cup
1909–10	9 – 1	–

Debut: 18/9/09 v West Ham Utd (h) 2–2 (IL)

Sam spent his only season at Coventry in the reserves. He eventually made his first team debut when Tubby Warren was injured, but although he had a powerful shot, a lack of pace precluded him from the highest class.

McCULLOCH, Alexander
Centre Forward

Born: Edinburgh
Career: Bonnyrigg Rose Athletic, Leith Athletic April 1907, Middlesbrough September 1907, Newcastle United February 1908 (£200), Brentford c/s 1908, Bradford November 1908 (£100), Swindon Town c/s 1909, Reading 1910, Swindon Town c/s/1911, Coventry City October 1912, Raith Rovers c/s 1913, St. Bernards c/s 1915, Alloa Athletic October 1915, Broxburn United 1915–16, Dunfermline Athletic March 1917, Heart of Midlothian c/s 1918, Lincoln City c/s 1919, Aberaman, Merthyr Town 1920/21, Llanelly c/s 1921.

Coventry City	Southern League		F.A.Cup
1912–13	23 – 4		2

Debut: 26/10/12 Southampton (a) 0–0 (CF)

Alex had a long career, but did not stay too long with any one club. He came to City to solve the goalscoring problem, but his total left something to be desired. At 5 feet 10 inches and 12 stone, he was a hard worker who dribbled and passed well and was highly mobile. All he lacked, was a scoring touch.

MARR, Andrew (Andy)
Outside Right
Born: Newcastle–Upon–Tyne
Career: Ashington, Coventry City May 1912, Wolverhampton Wanderers c/s 1913, Gateshead May 1914.

Coventry City	Southern League		F.A.Cup
1912–13	1		–

Debut: 21/3/13 v Exeter City (h) 0–1 (OR)

Andy came from Ashington, the town which was to produce the famous Milburn and Charlton football families, in the Tyneside coalfield. He was fast and a good crosser of the ball, but he was young and inexperienced. Wolves took him at the end of his only season at City and he was used in their reserves before finally returning to the North.

MARVIN, W.T.
Centre Half
Career: Hinckley United, Derby Co. c/s 1907, Coventry City c/s 1908, Nuneaton Town c/s 1909, Rugby Town c/s 1911.

Coventry City	Southern League		F.A.Cup
1908–09	32 – 1		–

Debut: 5/9/08 v Crystal Palace (h) 1–1 (CH) 1 goal

A young centre–half who held a first team place down at centre half during the first season in the Southern League. Marvin scored his only goal on his debut and was credited with the City's first goal in the Southern League. Nemo referred to him in the following encouraging terms: "a good lad...Strenuous worker...never–say–die attitude.." But he was quite inexperienced and soon joined

Nuneaton Town in the Birmingham League during the 1909 close season, after just one hectic season at City.

MEUNIER, James (Jim)
Left Back
Born: Manchester c.1885
Career: Heaton Moor, Stockport Co. 1903, Manchester City c/s 1904, Southport Central c/s 1906, Everton c/s 1908, Lincoln City c/s 1912, Coventry City July 1914, Hyde United c/s 1919, Macclesfield December 1919

Coventry City	Southern League		F.A.Cup
1914–15	10		1

Debut: 5/9/14 v Brentford (a) 1–3 (LB)

Jim had been a reserve team player at each of his previous clubs, but his experience was utilised immediately by Coventry in their only season in the Southern League Division 2. He was the regular first choice until he joined the Army, and left in November 1914, although he made a couple more appearances when on leave. Like many footballers of the day, Jim was a good enough cricketer to be employed as a League Professional by New Brighton C.C.

MITCHELL, Joseph (Joe)
Forward
Born: Coventry
Career: Lord Street Juniors, Coventry City c/s 1912, Nuneaton Town c/s 1914, Retired during War.

Coventry City	Southern League		F.A.Cup
1912–13	18 – 3		2 – 1
1913–14	4		–
Total	22 – 3		2 – 1

Debut: 19/10/12 v Plymouth Argyle (h) 2–3 (IL)

Joe had a good run in the first team in 1912–13 where his all action style allied with his passing ability made him a popular player with the Coventry supporters. He scored the City goal at Old Trafford against Manchester United in the FA Cup 1st Round game on 11th January 1913 in the 1–1 draw. He was injury prone in his second season and went to Nuneaton Town in 1914, and after the War he was playing rugby for a local Coventry club.

MORRIS, Thomas Henry (Tom)
Centre Half

Born: Grimsby 1884
Died: Killed in action World War 1
Career: Haycroft Rovers, Grimsby Rovers, Grimsby Town February 1906, Brighton & Hove Albion May 1907, Leeds City February 1909, Scunthorpe & Lindsey Utd c/s 1913 (player-coach), Coventry City c/s 1914.

Coventry City	Southern League	F.A.Cup
1914–15	17 – 2	1

Debut: 5th September 1914, Brentford (a) 1–3 (CH)

As City started their 1914–15 season, Scott Walford the new manager, signed known quantities to stiffen the side. One of these new players was Tom, who had played at Leeds City when Scott–Walford was manager. Tom was an excellent centre–half who gave the team a tremendous solidity and direction. He joined the Army in March 1915 and was killed in action.

MOULT, Joe
Goalkeeper

Born: Birmingham
Career: Aston Holy Trinity, Arden Hill, Aston Villa, Coventry City January 1908, Crystal Palace c/s 1909, Walsall c/s 1910.

Coventry City	Southern League	F.A.Cup
1908–09	26	–

Debut: 1/9/08 v Crystal Palace (h) 1–1

Joe came to the City from Aston Villa reserves and had a good start being first choice goalkeeper. During those early games he won nothing but praise for his performances. However, none of these early games were won, and after a 2–5 defeat at home to Southend United, Joe was dropped. In the reserves he regained his confidence and natural talent. Being nearly 6 feet tall and very commanding, he reclaimed the first team spot until near the season's close. He then joined Crystal Palace as a reserve before spending four seasons at Walsall where he had an excellent reputation.

NEWBIGGING, Alexander (Sandy)
Goalkeeper

Born: Lanark 1880

Career: Lanark Athletic, Abercorn c/s 1897, Lanark United September 1900, Queens Park Rangers c/s 1901, Nottingham Forest October 1901, Reading c/s 1905, Rangers c/s 1906, Reading c/s 1908, Coventry City c/s 1909, Retired Summer 1910 (made 1 Scottish Cup appearance for Inverness Thistle February 1911).

Coventry City	Southern League	F.A.Cup
1909–10	8	–

Debut: 4/9/09 v Crystal Palace (h) 1–1

Sandy spent his final season in football at Coventry as understudy to Bob Evans, although Inverness Thistle persuaded him to turn out in a Scottish Cup tie for them, following the encouragement from his ex–team mate Walter Wilson who was then at that club. He had a long life and attended the Rangers Centenary celebrations when aged 99 years.

PARKES, Harold Arnold (Harry)
Outside Right

Born: Halesowen September 1888
Died: Basford March 1947
Career: Halesowen Grammar School, Coombs Wood FC, Halesowen, West Bromwich Albion February 1906, Coventry City May 1908, West Bromwich Albion May 1914, Newport Co. 1919 (manager).

Coventry City	Southern League	F.A.Cup
1908–09	11 – 2	–
1909–10	12 – 1	–
1910–11	33 – 11	4 – 1
1911–12	36 – 7	2 – 1
1912–13	38 – 12	2 – 1
1913–14	32 – 1	1
Total	162 – 34	9 – 3

Debut: 25/12/08 v Swindon Town (h) 1–1 (OR)

Harry had a long career in football starting at West Bromwich Albion as a player in 1906, and ending with the managership of Notts Co. He was a whole–hearted player with a will–to–win, who was skilful, quick and thrusting. His goal scoring record was average but he was top scorer 1910–11, and again in 1912–13. During this latter season he scored a hat–trick against West Ham United in a 4–1 win. At Newport Co. he played a Southern League game as goalkeeper in an emergency. He later managed Chesterfield, Lincoln Mansfield, and Notts County.

During the 1911–12 season Nottingham Forest had a serious problem at centre forward and heard of a local centre–forward – Henry Poole – who was scoring lots of goals for his club. Henry was subsequently signed and played in the Football League within days. Alas his youth and inexperience were obvious in what proved to be his only first team appearance for Forest. He joined Coventry during the following summer and spent the whole season in the reserves making his only first team appearance during an injury crisis. Nemo's description was "dashing and a clever header of the ball".

PARTON, J.
Full Back

Born: Oxford
Career: Dudley FC, Coventry City c/s 1911, Halifax Town c/s 1914.

Coventry City	Southern League	F.A.Cup
1911–12	12	–
1913–14	12	1
Total	24	1

Debut: 23/9/11 v Luton Town (a) 4–2 (RB)

Parton's play was described at the time as steady and reliable, but he was a mainly reserve player in his three years at the club, initially as cover for Jim Thomson and Dick Barnacle. He eventually had a first team run in the 1913–14 season, but was dropped and left for Halifax Town in the Midland League.

POOLE, Harold
Forward

Born: Hucknall, Notts
Career: Newstead Rangers, Nottingham Forest April 1912, Coventry City c/s 1912, Sutton Town c/s 1913.

Coventry City	Southern League	F.A.Cup
1912–13	1	–

POWELL, Herbert
Forward

Born: c.1887
Career: Treharris FC, Nottingham Forest c/s 1904, Gresley Rovers c/s 1905, Grantham Avenue February 1906, Chesterfield c/s 1906, Barnsley February 1907, Carlisle United c/s 1907, New Brompton c/s 1908, Coventry City c/s 1909, Rotherham Town c/s 1911, Portsmouth c/s 1913, Boscombe c/s 1914, Brentford c/s 1915, Worksop Town c/s 1919, Grantham FC March 1922, Retford Town 1922/23, Sutton Town c/s 1923.

Coventry City	Southern League	F.A.Cup
1909–10	20 – 11	1
1910–11	6 – 2	1
Total	26 – 13	2

Debut: 25/9/09 v Portsmouth (a) 0–0 (IL)

Bert had a long career in football and played for a host of sides, possibly more than those detailed above – in a career lasting 20 years. At Coventry he was the cover centre–forward to Billy Smith and finished second top scorer to Buckle with 11 goals in 20 games. After a disappointing second season he moved on again.

ROBINSON, Arthur Charles (Nat)
Goalkeeper

Born: Coventry 28th February 1878
Career: Allesley FC, Singers January 1895, Small Heath c/s 1899, Chelsea c/s 1908, Coventry City c/s 1910, Retired 1915.

Singers FC	Southern League	F.A.Cup
1895–96	–	–
1896–97	–	1
1897–98	–	1
1998–99		2
Coventry City		
1910–11	1	1
1911–12	–	–
1912–13	–	–
1913–14	–	–
1914–15	5	–
Total	6	5

Debut: 1/2/1896 v W.B.A. Reserves (a) 1–4
Honours: 2 Football League appearances

Joined Singers FC in January 1895 as a half back, but in an emergency – only six men turned up – he played in goal for the Reserves v Foleshill St. Lawrence, in April 1895 and found his true position. Within 12 months he was the first team goalkeeper. He joined Small Heath and was their first choice goalkeeper for 8 seasons, before a spell at Chelsea for 2 seasons in their reserve team. At Small Heath he performed so well that he was selected twice to represent the Football League. A truly fine goalkeeper who was a character. Upon his return to Coventry he acted as understudy to Bob Evans and only played when Bob was either injured or away on international duty. He retired in 1911 and kept the Red Horse. In 1914–15 season he was called up again, in an emergency, as cover for Sid Blake.

ROGERS, E.
Goalkeeper

Born: Wiltshire
Career: Sunbeam Motors FC, Coventry City c/s 1913.

Coventry City	Southern League	F.A.Cup
1913–14	2	–

Debut: 13/1/14 v Portsmouth (h) 2–2 (Goal)

Came as understudy to Bill Jacques and after a half season he got his chance when Bill was injured in the New Year 1914. The side had already gone 5 games without a win, so a 2–2 draw in his first game was acceptable, but his next game was a 1–4 defeat, and this proved to be his last.

SAUL, Percy
Full Back

Born: Rotherham c.1881
Career: Thornhill FC, Gainsborough Trinity c/s 1901, Plymouth Argyle c/s 1904, Liverpool c/s 1906, Coventry City c/s 1909, Rotherham Town c/s 1911, Rotherham Co. (player/manager) c/s 1919.

Coventry City	Southern League	F.A.Cup
1909–10	31	6
1910–11	29	2
Total	60	8

Debut: 1/9/09 v Swindon Town (a) 1–2 (LB)

Percy was an enormous influence on the City, particularly in the cup run of 1909–10. He was still one of the best left backs in the country when he joined the club from Liverpool, where he was first choice in each of his three seasons at Anfield. Another cup run in 1910–11 was brought to an abrupt end with a 0–5 defeat at Burnley when both Evans and Saul were absent through injury. It was generally agreed that the result would have been different if Saul's Yorkshire grit had been employed. Later Percy became the Rotherham County manager.

SHIELDS, Tommy (Tom)
Full Back

Born: Co. Durham
Career: Newbiggin Colliery, Choppington FC, Coventry City May 1914, Fulham, Hartlepools United c/s 1919.

Coventry City	Southern League	F.A.Cup
1914–15	4	–

Debut: 20/3/15 v Ebbw Vale (a) 3–1 (RB)

Tom was signed as reserve cover but was thrust into first team action as players joined the Armed Services. During the War, he played for Fulham whilst serving in the Army, and at the end of hostilities moved back North.

SMITH, John
Centre/Inside Forward

Born: Wednesfield 1882
Career: Cannock FC, Stafford Road FC, Wolverhampton Wanderers July 1902, Birmingham c/s 1906, Bristol Rovers c/s 1907, Norwich City c/s 1908, Luton Town c/s 1909, Millwall March 1911, Coventry City May 1912.

Coventry City	Southern League	F.A.Cup
1912–13	17 – 4	–

Debut: 5/9/12 v Swindon Town (h) 2–1 (IL) 2 goals

A short, powerful player, who arrived at Coventry as an experienced forward. He scored twice on his debut but then only netted two more goals all season. John had played first team football in the Football League at Wolves and Birmingham but certainly made his name in the Southern League.

SMITH, William (Billy)
Centre Forward

Born: West Bromwich 1882
Career: West Bromwich Baptists FC, Worcester City, West Bromwich Albion 1902, Coventry City 1907, Birmingham c/s 1908, Coventry City c/s 1909, Nuneaton Town c/s 1912, Coventry City September 1913, Retired summer 1914.

Coventry City	Southern League	F.A.Cup
1909–10	22 – 8	4 – 1
1910–11	23 – 7	4 – 1
1911–12	19 – 9	2
1913–14	15	–
Total	79 – 24	10 – 2

Debut: 7/9/07 v Halesowen (h) 4–2 (IR)

Billy had three different spells with the club. In his first season in the Birmingham League he scored 33 goals in 33 games which encouraged Birmingham to sign him. He returned to City for their most successful seasons in the Southern League and FA Cup. He was a terrific shot but was also good at spreading the play, being adept at bringing wingers into the game. His most famous goal was against Sheffield Wednesday in the FA Cup 1st round tie at Hillsborough. Billy's third spell at the club, after a season at Nuneaton Town, was very disappointing in a very dismal season which culminated in relegation.

SPARKES, W.
Left Back

Born: Coventry
Career: Royal Warwickshire Regiment, Coventry City c/s 1908, Royal Warwickshire Regiment.

Coventry City	Southern League	F.A.Cup
1908–09	1	–

Debut: 12/9/08 v New Brompton (h) 3–4 (LB)

Sparkes was a soldier stationed at Budbrooke Barracks, and signed as an amateur for City during the summer of 1908. After giving very impressive displays in the pre-season trials he was given his chance following an injury to Juggins. Unfortunately he did not fulfil his promise and returned shortly afterwards to his Regiment.

STYLES, Leonard (Len)
Half Back

Born: Coventry
Career: St. Michaels, Coventry City c/s 1909 until 1914.

Coventry City	Southern League	F.A.Cup
1909–10	–	–
1910–11	–	–
1911–12	–	–
1912–13	3	–
1913–14	–	–
Total	3	–

Debut: 5/4/13 v Queens Park Rangers (a) 0–4 (CH)

Len signed for City in the close season of 1909 and proved a steady useful reserve team player who got his chance during April 1913, but it was back to the reserves the following season.

TALBOT, William
Right Half

Born: Coventry
Career: Foleshill Great Heath, Coventry City 1908.

Coventry City	Southern League	F.A.Cup
1908–09	1	–

Debut: 12/9/08 v New Brompton (h) 3–4 (RH)

Bill was a well-known footballer from the Foleshill area and got his chance in only the third Southern League game as a replacement for the club captain. The result was a 3–4 home defeat and the local newspaper said that he "was not a success". He spent the rest of the season in the reserves, and then left the club.

THOMSON, James Hunter
Right Back

Born: Shetland 1884
Career: Edinburgh Myrtle F.C., Leith Athletic, Heart of Midlothian, Abercorn January 1903, Leith Athletic October 1903, Portsmouth c/s 1906, Coventry City June 1911, Bury c/s 1913, Nelson (player/manager) c/s 1919.

Coventry City	Southern League	F.A.Cup
1911–12	31	2
1912–13	38	–
Total	69	2

Debut: 2/9/11 v Northampton Town (h) 1–2 (RB)

Jim was a first team player with all the clubs for whom he played. Nemo described him as "a resourceful and controlled full back who was cool under pressure". He became club captain, following the departure of Eli Bradley, until the season's end when he was signed by Bury, where he spent two seasons in the Football League.

TICKLE, Charles H.
Outside Right

Born: Birmingham 1884
Career: Selly Oak St. Marys, Bournbrook, Small Heath c/s 1902, Coventry City July 1908, Retired 1911.

Coventry City	Southern League	F.A.Cup
1908–09	40 – 5	3 – 1
1909–10	36 – 4	6
1910–11	35 – 10	4 – 1
Total	111 – 19	13 – 2

Debut: 1/9/08 v Crystal Palace (h) 1–1 (OR)
Honours: England Junior International v Scotland
1 Football League appearance

A delightful winger who was good enough to play for the Football League the season before he joined the City. In the language of the day he was described as "a drawing room footballer" and "dainty and dexterous", as well an excellent crosser of the ball. He laid on many chances during his three seasons at Coventry when he was first choice outside right.

TOSSWILL, John Speare (Jack)
(Inside Right)

Born: Eastbourne 1890
Died: 28th September 1915 in action
Career: Eastbourne, Hastings & St. Leonards, Aberdare, Tunbridge Wells Rangers, Maidstone United, Queens Park Rangers c/s 1911, Liverpool June 1912, Southend United c/s 1913, Coventry City November 1913.

Coventry City	Southern League	F.A.Cup
1913–14	17	–

Debut: 8/11/13 v Plymouth Argyle (a) 3–0 (IR)

Manager Scott–Walford signed Jack as City were hit by injuries, and he did remarkably well right from the start as they won their first game in 11 matches. However, they only managed three more victories in the final 25 games. Jack had done enough to be offered new terms and he re-signed for the 1914–15 season. But when war was declared in August 1914, he joined the Army before reporting for pre-season training. He lost his life in action in September 1915.

TURNBULL, Frederick Stephen (Boxer)
Forward

Born: Wallsend 1888
Career: Carvelle FC, Wallsend Park Villa, Newcastle City, Ashington, Coventry City c/s 1911, Southampton October 1912, North Shields Athletic c/s 1913.

Coventry City	Southern League	F.A.Cup
1911–12	34 – 12	2
1912–13	4	–
Total	38 – 12	2 – 0

Debut: 16/9/11 v Stoke (h) 3–2 (IR) 1 goal

The Midland Daily Telegraph said "Boxer was bustling and effective.....a great crowd pleaser.....but a little small and light for the highest class". Boxer eventually returned to Tyneside football.

TURNER, Isiah Samuel (Ike)
Centre Forward
Born: Oldbury August 1882
Career: Oldbury Town, Darlaston c/s 1902, West Bromwich Albion September 1904, Brierley Hill Alliance c/s 1905, Bristol Rovers c/s 1906, Coventry City c/s 1908, Dudley Town c/s 1910, Retired 1913.

Coventry City	Southern League	F.A.Cup
1908–09	27 – 8	–
1909–10	5	–
Total	32 – 8	–

Debut: 1/9/08 v Crystal Palace (h) 1–1 (CF)
Honours: England Junior International

Ike was the regular centre–forward during City's first season in the Southern League. A good player with control and speed but perhaps he lacked some aggression. He was unable to keep his place the following season, and was replaced by the crowd pleasing Billy Smith.

TURNER, Robert Frewin (Leggy)
Outside Left
Born: Leicester 15th July 1885
Died: Darlington 15th February 1959
Career: Leicester Imperial, Leicester Fosse March 1905, Everton April 1909, Preston North End July 1911, Darlington c/s 1912, Coventry City c/s 1914, Retired 1919.

Coventry City	Southern League	F.A.Cup
1914–15	13 – 1	1

Debut: 5/9/14 v Brentford (a) 1–3 (OL)

Bob came from a sporting family, for his father was a county cricketer with Leicestershire – as he was himself – and his brother Richard played football for Leicester Fosse, Portsmouth and Leyton. A quick outside left who did well for the City in Southern League Division 2, creating many chances for other forwards but he did score in the 10–1 thrashing of Newport in November 1914. He joined the Army in January 1915 and severed his connection with the club. In their book "Fossils & Foxes" Smith and Taylor relate that most of his former team–mates at Leicester Fosse attended his wedding the day before an away League game at Nottingham Forest, which Fosse lost 0–12. Then three days later Bob played for Everton when they beat a more sober Leicester team 4–2!

WAKINSHAW, Robert (Bob)
Forward
Born: Cullarcoats
Career: Wallsend Slipway FC, Coventry City c/s 1912

Coventry City	Southern League	F.A.Cup
1912–13	2	–

Debut: 9/4/13 v Portsmouth (a) 1–2 (OL)

Bob was a young Tynesider who spent a season in Coventry City reserves, eventually playing in two games at the season's end, when there was an injury crisis at the club. Subsequent movements of this player have not been traced.

WARREN, George (Tubby)
Inside Left
Born: Hinckley
Died: In action World War 1
Career: Hinckley Town, Leicester Fosse December 1903, Gresley Town c/s 1904, Nuneaton Town c/s 1906, Coventry City c/s 1907, Willenhall Swifts c/s 1911, Stockport County October 1911, Nuneaton Town c/s 1912.

Coventry City	Southern League	F.A.Cup
1907–08	–	6 – 6
1908–09	31 – 15	2 – 1
1909–10	17 – 9	5 – 2
1910–11	26 – 7	–
Total	74 – 31	13 – 9

Debut: 21/9/07 v Brierley Hill Alliance (a) 6–2 (CF) 1 goal FA Cup

Tubby was small and light but scored regularly, having good stamina and excellent passing skills. He was one of the few successes of the club's initial season in the Southern League and had three excellent seasons with City. Later he lost his life when he was killed in action when serving in the Army.

WELCH, Harold
Forward
Born: Coventry
Career: Foleshill Great Heath, Coventry City c/s 1910, Retired during the War.

Coventry City	Southern League	F.A.Cup
1910–11	15 – 4	4
1911–12	4	–
1912–13	9 – 3	1
1913–14	9 – 2	1
1914–15	9*	–
Total	46 – 9	6

* Welch may have played only eight games – no accurate line-up record v Swansea on Easter Monday.

Harry came from the 'fertile' Foleshill area, and spent his time at City as a more than useful reserve team player. He was self-possessed and an accurate passer of the ball who always gave a good account of himself, and scored some fine goals.

WILSON, Walter
Left Back

Born: Scotland c.1886
Career: Dykehead 1901, Albion Rovers c/s 1903, Bathgate c/s 1904, Inverness Thistle c/s 1907, Aston Villa c/s 1908, Coventry City c/s 1909, Inverness Thistle c/s 1910, Dumbarton c/s 1912, Renton October 1913, joined King's Own Scottish Borderers March 1914.

Coventry City	Southern League	F.A.Cup
1909-10	4	-

Debut: 2/9/09 v Northampton Town (h) 1-0 (LB)

Walter had a long and relatively successful career in Scottish non-League football, but did not make the top in England. He did not appear in the Villa first team and played only four games for City. He came in when Percy Saul was injured and grew in confidence during his games, after a shaky start and became a good reserve back. Later, when serving with the King's Own Scottish Borderers in France during the Great War, he suffered severe injuries and was nominated for the Military Medal.

YATES, William (Billy)
Right Half

Born: Birmingham 1884
Career: Witton Shell Shop FC, Erdington FC, Aston Villa March 1903, Brighton and Hove Albion c/s 1905, Manchester United c/s 1906, Heart of Midlothian c/s 1907, Portsmouth c/s 1908, Coventry City June 1911, Retired 1914.

Coventry City	Southern League	F.A.Cup
1911-12	38	2
1912-13	38	2
1913-14	30	1
Total	106	5

Debut: 2/9/11 v Northampton T. (h) 1-2 (RH)
Honours: Scottish Cup Runners-up Medal 1908

Billy had an eventful career including a season at Heart of Midlothian when he appeared in the Scottish Cup Final. At Coventry he was a hard driving wing half who was the work horse of the side.

He became club captain, but was sorely troubled by injury during 1913-14 when the club were relegated, at a time when his qualities were most needed. At the end of that season Billy retired and became landlord of the Dyers Arms.

★ ★ ★ ★ ★ ★ ★ ★ ★ ★ ★ ★ ★ ★ ★

THE GREAT WAR – SEASON 1918–19

Coventry City during the 1918–19 season competed in the Football League Midland Section and were able to select some well-established players who were working locally. These included Jesse Pennington the England full-back, Sid Bowser, and on one occasion at Huddersfield – Fred Bullock – who was loaned by the home club when City arrived short.

We have been unable to identify all the players concerned as reports on football matches, and indeed football in general, during the Great War was sketchy but we have listed below, those we know:-

T. Aston	– Oldbury Town
Josiah Bennett	– Southampton, Birmingham, Pontipridd, Lincoln City and Bristol Rovers
J. Bell	– Birmingham
Ernie Best	– Birmingham, Brighton & Hove Albion
Alf Bishop	– Halesowen, Wolverhampton, Wanderers, Wrexham
Sid Bowser	– Willenhall, West Bromwich Albion, Distillery, Walsall
Chris Buckley	– Brighton & Hove Albion, Aston Villa, Arsenal
Fred Bullock	– Ilford, Huddersfield Town and England
Emmin Dunn	– Nuneaton Town, Wolverhampton Wanderers 1914–15, Nuneaton Town
Howard Gregory	– Birchfield Trinity, West Bromwich Albion
L. Hopkins	– Brierley Hill Alliance, Cardiff City
Harry Howell	– Burslem Swifts, Burslem P.V., Stoke, Wolverhampton W., Southampton, Northfleet, Accrington St., Mansfield T.
W.A. Littlewood	– Worcester City, Aston Villa, Wellington Town
Herbert Middlemiss	– Stalybridge Rovers, Stockport C., Tottenham H., Queen's Park Rangers
Jack Needham	– Mansfield Town, Birmingham, Wolverhampton Wanderers, Hull City
A. Newman	– Causeway Green Villa, Stockport County
F. Osborne	– Worcester City, Swindon Town, Brighton & Hove Albion, Weymouth
Jesse Pennington	– Dudley Town, West Bromwich Albion and England
J. Pugh	– Luton Town, Brighton & H. A., Abertillery, Manchester U., Wrexham
Sam Richardson	– Great Bridge Celtic, West Bromwich Alb., Newport County, Aldershot
George Savage	– West Bromwich Utd., Newport County, Willenhall, West Bromwich A.
Frank Waterhouse	– Wednesbury Old Athletic, West Bromwich Albion, Derby County
G.H. Wild	– Halifax Town, Bradford City, Halifax Town, Barnoldswick Town
Charles Wilson	– Atherstone Town, Tottenham Hotspur, Huddersfield Town, Stoke, Stafford R., Atherstone Town, Wrexham, Shrewsbury T., Alfreton T.

Three other groups also played. Those included in the main text who appeared were:-

Jack Allan, Sid Blake, George Chaplin, Bob Craig, Dalton, Billy Fulgames, Gallagher, Albert Lindon, Tommy Lowes, Percy Mackrill, Dick Roberts, Chris Sambrooke, Sheldon, Lance Sheldon, A. Smith and Charlie Smith.

A second group we have been unable to identify positively:-

Adkins	– A one game centre forward.
Brookes	– An outside right who played against Birmingham.
Davis	– An inside forward who scored twice in seven games.
Edwards	– Wing half tried in April 1919 in two games.
Hennessey	– A winger tried late in the season.
Johnstone	– A Birmingham junior who had a trial, brother played for Aston Villa.
Edward Pate	– A Birmingham junior who played once in an emergency.
Richards	– A left half played one game.
Tye	– Birmingham-born junior used when City unable to raise a full side.
White	– A one-game trialist.
Wootton	– From Birmingham. Played three games at outside left.

And finally several men played under pseudonyms; "Andrews" and "Wells", who were tried on a couple of occasions.

COVENTRY CITY IN WORLD WAR TWO

After closing down following the German blitz on the City, the football club re-opened for business in August 1942.

During this period established first-teamers were used – when available – juniors, guests and many locals. The following is a list – where we have been able to we have identified each player and named their club or clubs. The people listed in the main text for Football League appearances have been omitted.

L. Abrahams   – A local goalkeeper.

A. Bainbridge   – Served locally in the R.A.F.

E. Batchelor   – A local.

Jose Bilboa   – Wolves. A Basque refugee.

S.L. Bennett   – Local.

L.A. Bolan   – Lowestoft Town, Tottenham H, Southend Utd.

W.A. Bond   – Local

John C. Bowles   – Cheltenham Town, Newport Co, Accrington S., Stockport Co, Winsford Utd.

T. Brown   – Bedworth Utd.

Alf Calverley   – Huddersfield Town, Mansfield Town, Arsenal, Preston N.E., Doncaster Rovers.

W.J. Carey   – Sedgley Park, Aston Villa, Bury.

S.A. Chapman   – Morris–Motors FC (Coventry)

J. Cook   – Coventry Tile FC

F. Copson   – Morris–Motors FC

S.H. Cornwell   – Norwich City

C. Craven   – Boston Utd, Grimsby Town, Manchester Utd, Birmingham, Tamworth, Sutton Town.

A. Cryer   – Local

A. Currie   – Irish junior

Neil Dougall   – Burnley, Birmingham City, Plymouth Argyle and Scotland

Thomas Dougall   – Morris–Motors FC, Brentford, Sunderland and Yeovil Town.

F.L. Douglas   – Ansley St. Johns.

P. Doyle   – GEC FC.

George Edwards   – Narberth GS, Swansea Town, Birmingham City, Cardiff City and Wales.

Thomas Eggleston   – Derby County, Leicester C, Watford

J. Evans   – R.A.F.

J.T. Evans   – Trialist from the Birmingham Works League.

Ken Faulkner   – Smethwick Highfield, Birmingham City, Oldbury T.

J. Fitzpatrick   – GEC FC

R. Gardner   – Morris–Motors FC

Ron Garner   – Broadway Old Boys

Ray Goddard   – Red Rovers, Wolverhampton Wanderers, Chelsea, Plymouth Argyle, Exeter C.

K.L. Green   – Local junior.

N.R. Greenway   – Coventry Gauge FC.

K.H. Grubb   – Local junior.

H. Hale   – Imperial Sports FC (Leamington)

Arthur Harris   – Nuneaton Town, Southend Utd, Bedworth Utd

Fred Harris	– Osbourne Ath, Birmingham City.
Eric Houghton	– Aston Villa, Notts Co and England
C.W.H. Humphries	– Paget Rangers, Walsall.
J.H. Jarvis	– East Fife.
Owen Johnson	– Derby Co, Bradford City, Shrewsbury T.
Fred Keeble	– Morris–Motors FC, Albion Rovers, Grimsby T, Notts Co.
Don Kelly	– Torquay Utd.
Laurie Kelly	– Wolverhampton W., Huddersfield Town, Nuneaton Borough.
J.T. Kendall	– Riley FC.
D. Kerry	– Local.
J. King	– Birmingham FC.
D. Lapworth	– S.S. Cars FC.
J. Laurie	– Morris–Motors FC.
Jack Lee	– Blackburn Rovers.
Glyn Lewis	– Crystal Palace, Bristol City, Barry Town.
Joe Loughran	– Birmingham FC, Luton Town, Burnley, Southend Utd.
Colin Lyman	– Southend United, Northampton Town, Tottenham H, Port Vale, Nottingham Forest, Notts County.
A. McKeown	– A.W.A. Baginton.
Jim McKeown	– Morris–Motors FC.
Horace Matthews	– A.W.A. Baginton.
Gil Merrick	– Solihull Town, Birmingham City and England.
J.P. Miles	– Local.
Frank Mitchell	– Birmingham City, Chelsea, Watford, also Warwickshire Cricketer. Born in Australia.
A. Morton	– Morris–Motors FC.
Peter Murphy	– Dunlop FC, Birmingham City, Tottenham H, Rugby Town.
D. Murphy	– Local.
W.G. Nash	– Morris–Motors FC.
J. Newbold	– Coventry Gauge FC.
Les Owens	– Charlton Athletic, Doncaster Rovers, Southport.
R.G. Paul	– Nuneaton Borough.
Henry Quinney	– Morris–Motors FC, Northampton T, Wolverhampton Wanderers.
Walter Quinton	– Rotherham United, Birmingham City, Brentford, Southend Utd, Shrewsbury Town.
F.H. Robinson	– Daimler FC
A.S. Setchell	– Coventry Tile FC
Ray Shaw	– Darlaston, Birmingham C.
Chris Simmonds	– Rootes FC, Millwall, Barry Town, Leyton Orient, Workington.
Sam Small	– Bromsgrove Rovers, Birmingham C, West Ham United, Brighton & Hove Albion
Charles Smith	– Yeovil Town, Exeter City, Aberdeen, Torquay United.
F.W. Taylor	– Standard Aero FC
J. Thacker	– Lincoln City, Morris Motors FC.
Eddie Vinall	– Folkestone, Sunderland, Norwich City, Luton Town, Walsall.
J.L. Walker	– Humber FC.
R. Ward	– A.W.A. Baginton.
K.C. Watkins	– Humber FC.
T. Whitcroft	– Ansley St. Johns.
W.C. Wright	– Modern Machine Tools FC.

THE FOOTBALL LEAGUE

PLAYERS

A – Z

1919/20 to 1992/93

ADAMS, Michael Richard (Micky)
Left Back
Born: Sheffield 8th November 1961
Career: Apprentice Gillingham, pro November 1979, Coventry City July 1983, Leeds United January 1987 (£115,000), Southampton March 1989 (£250,000).

Coventry City	League	F.A.Cup	Lge.Cup
1983–84	16+1s–1	4	–
1984–85	30+1s–3	2	2
1985–86	29+2s–3	1	3
1986–87	10+1s–2	–	4 – 1
Total	85+5s–9	7	9 – 1

Debut: 29/8/83 v Tottenham H (a) 1–1 (OL)

Signed by Bobby Gould, Adams was bought as a left back, but early in his City career he found it difficult to adapt to facing Division 1 wingers. He was switched to outside left, a position which he made his own, even keeping the enigmatic Peter Barnes out of the side. He left City because he could not command a regular place once Nick Pickering had been signed. He moved onto Leeds and faced City in the epic semi-final clash at Hillsborough in April 1987. How he is now an established left back at Southampton.

ALDECOA, Emilo G.
Outside Left
Born: Spain 30th November 1922
Career: Wolverhampton Wanderers 1943, Coventry City 1945, Athletic Bilbao 1947.

Coventry City	League	F.A.Cup
1945–46	WWII	2
1946–47	29	–
Total	29	2

Debut: 31/8/46 v. Burnley (a) 1–1 (OL)

Aldecoa came to England in 1937 at the age of 14 as a refugee from the Basque region of Spain. He settled in Stafford where he married a local girl, played for Wolves during the War, and moved to City in 1945. He was a consistent outside left who impressed on his day. He took the opportunity to return to his home Basque region with Athletic Bilbao, where he played sufficiently well to earn international honours.

ALDERSON, Brian Roderick
Forward
Born: Dundee 5th May 1950
Career: Lochee Harp, Coventry City July 1970, Leicester City July 1975 (£150,000), New England Teamen March 1978, Atlanta Chiefs March 1980.

Coventry City	League	F.A.Cup	Lge.Cup
1970–71	12+3s–1	1	3+1s
1971–72	5+3s	–	–
1972–73	32+1s–13	4 – 3	1 – 1
1973–74	40 – 9	6	6 – 6
1974–75	27+4s–6	3 – 2	1
Total	116+11s–29	14 – 5	11+1s–7

Debut: 5/9/70 v. Huddersfield T. (h) 0–0 (sub)
Full Debut: 19/9/70 v. Chelsea (h) 0–1 (OL)
Honours: 1 Scotland U–23 cap

Alderson made an impressive start as a left winger, but it was not until Colin Stein was signed in October 1972 that Alderson had a regular striking partner. The partnership blossomed and Alderson scored 17 goals in 1972/3 and 15 goals the season after. With such impressive form he earned a call-up for the Scotland U–23 team. Without Stein, Alderson was not the same player and struggled to score. With the emergence of Mick Ferguson alongside David Cross, Alderson was sold to Leicester where the goals dried up and after a disappointing time, he moved to the USA.

ALDERTON, James H. (Jim)
Wing Half

Born: Wingate, 6th December 1924
Career: Wolverhampton Wanderers January 1935, Coventry City October 1947, Darlaston c/s 1953.

Coventry City	League	F.A.Cup
1947–48	16	–
1948–49	14	–
1949–50	3	1 – 1
1950–51	25	1
1951–52	4	–
1952–53	–	–
Total	62	2 – 1

Debut: 25/10/47 v. Doncaster R. (h) 1–0 (LH)

In the late forties, City had a strong midfield which was difficult to break into. Alderton found it hard to command a place and had to be satisfied with runs whenever Snape, Barratt or Simpson were injured. His own injuries did not help and he finally moved. During the war, he guested for Notts County and Chester.

ALLARDYCE, Samuel (Sam)
Centre Half

Born: Dudley 19th October 1954
Career: Apprentice Bolton Wanderers, pro November 1971, Sunderland July 1980 (£150,000), Millwall September 1981 (£35,000), Tampa Bay Rowdies c/s 1983, Coventry City September 1983, Huddersfield Town July 1984, Bolton Wanderers July 1985, Preston North End August 1986, West Bromwich Albion c/s 1989, Preston North End 1992–93.

Coventry City	League	F.A.Cup	Lge.Cup
1983–84	28 – 1	1	3

Debut: 24/9/83 v. Sunderland (a) 0–1 (CH)

Bobby Gould needed an experienced centre–half at the heart of his makeshift side in 1983, and he discovered that Allardyce was playing in the USA after being released by Third Division Millwall. He was short of pace but not commitment and played his part in helping the club escape relegation. He wasn't offered a new contract, and moved on, spending his later playing days around the North before taking a coaching job at WBA, where he was

forced to appear as a sub in an emergency. He then coached at Preston, and in an emergency played 3 times during the 1992–93 season.

ALLAN, John
(See 'Southern League' section)

ALLEN, Brynley W. (Bryn)
Inside Forward

Born: Gilfachgoch 28th March 1921
Career: Swansea Town 1938, Cardiff City 1945, Newport County October 1947, Cardiff City August 1948, Reading May 1949, Coventry City February 1950, Hereford United January 1953, Barry Town c/s 1953, Haverfordwest 1957.

Coventry City	League	F.A.Cup
1949–50	16 – 8	–
1950–51	40 – 14	1
1951–52	28 – 4	3 – 1
1952–53	4	–
Total	88 – 26	4 – 1

Debut: 4/2/50 v. Leeds United (h) 0–4 (IL)
Honours: 2 Wales Full Caps (both at City)
Welsh Cup Winners medal 1954–55
Welsh Cup Runners up medal 1939–40

After spending the war playing for Swansea and Cardiff, the blond and slight Allen made his mark in peacetime as a free–scoring forward with the Bluebirds. Surprisingly, he was allowed to move to Division 3(S) Newport County, where he stayed briefly before moving to Reading. City snapped Allen up in February 1950. He impressed greatly and earned two Welsh caps. He was replaced by Eddy Brown and moved into non–league football at Hereford.

ALLEN, Robert (Bob)
Outside Left

Born: Belfast 16th January 1939
Career: Denbigh Town, Wolverhampton Wanderers September 1957, Coventry City July 1959, Nuneaton Borough.

Coventry City	League	F.A.Cup	Lge.Cup
1959–60	–	–	
1960–61	3 – 1	–	–
1961–62	22 – 1	–	–
1962–63	–	–	–
Total	25 – 2	–	–

Debut: 30/8/60 v Bradford C. (a) 1–4 (IL)

Signed by Billy Frith, Allen could not establish a regular place in the team. The arrival of Jimmy Hill, saw the manager try a number of combinations. As Allen could play in a number of positions, he clocked up a number of games, but once Hill had decided on his squad, Allen was released.

ALLEN, Thomas (Tommy)
Goalkeeper
Born: Moxley 1st May 1897
Died: Castle Bromwich 10th May 1968
Career: Wednesbury Old Athletic, Bilston United, Hickmans Institute, Wolverhampton Wanderers, WWI, Sunderland May 1919, Southampton May 1920, Coventry City June 1928, Accrington Stanley July 1932, Northampton Town September 1933, Kidderminster Harriers August 1934, Retired 1936.

Coventry City	League	F.A.Cup
1928–29	42	1
1929–30	42	4
1930–31	37	3
1931–32	33	1
Total	154	9

Debut: 25/8/28 v Norwich C. (h) 3–0 (Goal)

Allen emerged at Sunderland and was seen as a good prospect for the future, but an oversight meant that he was not kept on the club's retained list. He was snapped up by Southampton, where he proved to be an excellent keeper for 8 years. He was signed by his former colleague at the Dell, James McIntyre, and helped City to it's best season since joining the Football League. His slight build often left him the prey of centre forwards, but his agility was outstanding. At the age of 35, he moved to Accrington. After retiring, Allen settled in Coventry.

ALLON, Thomas George (George)
Right Half
Born: Ashington 27th August 1899
Died: Spring 1983
Career: Usworth Colliery, Coventry City February 1921, Nuneaton Town August 1925, Peterborough & Fletton United c/s 1926, Northampton Town November 1926 (£1,000), Wigan Athletic c/s 1932.

Coventry City	League	F.A.Cup
1920–21	–	–
1921–22	36 – 1	3
1922–23	31	1
1923–24	4	–
1924–25	3 – 1	–
Total	74 – 2	4

Debut: 24/9/21 v Wolverhampton W. (h) 3–1 (RH)

George Allon had impressed in the reserves at the start of the 1921–22 season and was pushed into the first team following some poor results. He became a regular for two seasons, but was an enigmatic player. When City were under pressure he could be relied on, being a good defender who was at his best, "when it came to a scrimmage or packing the goal", but when the team were on top he was unable to help with the constructive play of the side. After losing his place, he spent 2 seasons in the reserves, playing only a further 7 games. His last match was the 0–5 thumping by Oldham in February 1925. He went on to make 185 League appearances for Northampton Town before joining Wigan Athletic for the club's inaugural season.

ALSOP, Gilbert Arthur (Gil)
Centre Forward
Born: Frampton Cotterill 10th September 1911
Died: Walsall 16th April 1992
Career: Coalpit Heath, Bath City 1927, Coventry City December 1929, Walsall October 1931, West Bromwich Albion November 1935 (£3,000), Ipswich Town May 1937, Walsall November 1938, Retired 1947.

Coventry City	League	F.A.Cup
1929–30	6	–
1930–31	10 – 4	–
1931–32	–	–
Total	16 – 4	–

Debut: 22/2/30 v Crystal Palace (h) 1–0 (IR)

The bustling Alsop was regarded as a prospect for the future by manager James McIntyre, but the latter's departure and replacement by Harry Storer, changed Alsop's career. Storer brought in the striking partners Clarrie Bourton and Jock Lauderdale and the 20 year old Alsop was sold to Walsall. He hit the headlines, scoring the first of the 2 goals for the Saddlers team that sensationally knocked Arsenal from the F.A. Cup in 1933. He was a prolific scorer, scoring 125 League goals in only 159 League games for the Fellows Park club. He moved to First Division WBA, but moved onto Southern League Ipswich Town after only 1 League game. He helped Ipswich achieve League status before returning to Walsall, where he finished his career. During the war he guested for Leicester City, Luton Town, Mansfield Town and North-ampton. In all football, he scored 297 goals in his 18 year career. Alsop has the distinction of having a stand named after him at the Bescot Stadium, the new home of Walsall.

ARCHER, John William (Jack)
Left Half

Born: Wednesbury
Career: Wednesbury, Walsall 1929/30, Everton c/s 1931 (£4,500), Coventry City June 1936, Plymouth Argyle November 1938, Retired 1946.

Coventry City	League	F.A.Cup
1936–37	32	3
1937–38	37	1
1938–39	7	–
Total	76	4

Debut: 29/8/36 v Doncaster Rovers (a) 1–1 (LH)

Jack Archer was a stylish left half from Everton, where he played only 15 first team games in 5 years. On his return to the Midlands he played in City's side that was close to gaining promotion to Division 1 for the first time. He established a fine partnership with left back Walter Metcalf, but lost his place to Harry Boileau and was sold to Plymouth. At the outbreak of the war, he joined the RAF, but broke his leg in a match against the Army. It took 18 months to heal and after a few guest appearances for Hull City, Luton Town and Tranmere Rovers, he retired from football and returned to work in Coventry.

ARMESON, Laurence R.
Left Half

Born: Rotherham
Career: Rotherham YMCA, Sheffield United, Rotherham United 1935/36, Coventry City April 1936–45.

Coventry City	League	F.A.Cup
1936–37	–	–
1937–38	–	–
1938–39	7	–
Total	7	–

Debut: 15/10/38 v Bury (h) 0–0 (LH)

After failing to make the grade at Sheffield United, Armeson appeared twice for his home town club Rotherham United, before being signed by Harry Storer in April 1936. With City having a strong squad, he only played when Harry Boileau was injured. During the war, he guested for Northampton Town, Chester, Barnsley, West Ham United, Hull City and Mansfield Town, and retired from football in 1945.

ASHALL, George H.
Outside Left

Born: Killamarsh 29th September 1911
Career: Broadsworth Main, Huddersfield Town, Upton Colliery, Frickley Colliery August 1935, Wolverhampton Wanderers December 1935, Coventry City c/s 1938.

Coventry City	League	F.A.Cup
1938–39	37 – 4	1
1945–46	WWII	–
1946–47	17 – 6	2 – 1
1947–48	8	–
Total	62 – 10	3 – 1

Debut: 27/8/38 v Burnley (h) 1–1 (OL)
Honours: 1 appearance for the Football League.

After being released by Huddersfield, Ashall was a late developer being taken on as a professional at the age of 24. He became a regular in the Wolves side, but was seen by Harry Storer as an important source of inspiration for City's push to Division 1. After a good first season, the war intervened and by the time League action recommenced he was 35 years old. He received an injury in September 1947 against WBA which ended his career. During the war, he guested for Northampton.

ASHCROFT, Charles Thomas (Charlie)
Goalkeeper

Born: Chorley 3rd July 1926
Career: Chorley, Liverpool May 1945, Ipswich Town June 1955, Coventry City June 1957, Chorley c/s 1958.

Coventry City	League	F.A.Cup
1957–58	19	–

Debut: 24/8/57 v. Reading (h) 1–0 (Goal)
Honours: 1 England 'B' cap

After selling Reg Matthews, City were without any experienced goalkeeper. Ashcroft was considered an appropriate short–term option. He had previously suffered a broken arm which had not healed properly. Consequently, City signed a goalkeeper who couldn't straighten his arm! He stayed at City for only one season before returning to his home town club.

ASKEW, H. Frederick J. (Fred)
Right Half

Born: Coventry
Career: Lord Street Juniors, Warwick Town c/s 1923, Coventry City October 1926, Morton c/s 1929, Atherstone c/s 1930, Hinckley, Leamington Town.

Coventry City	League	F.A.Cup
1926–27	2	–
1927–28	6	–
1928–29	–	–
Total	8	–

Debut: 18/4/27 v Aberdare (a) 7–0 (RH)

Signed from Warwick Town, Askew was seen as an excellent half back for the future and showed his potential with some sparkling performances in the reserves. He found the transition to the League side difficult and could not oust William Brown from the right half position. After being released, he played only once for Morton before returning to his native Warwickshire.

ASTLEY, John (Jack)
Right Back

Born: Warrington 1910
Career: Chadwicks Recreation, Warrington Bedouins, Chester, Southport 1930/31, Shelbourne, Brentford May 1933, Coventry City February 1936, Retired 1944.

Coventry City	League	F.A.Cup
1935–36	14	–
1936–37	42	3
1937–38	42	1
1938–39	42	1
Total	140	5

Debut: 22/2/36 v Cardiff C. (h) 5–1 (RB)

Astley spent his early career in the North-west, playing twice for Southport before spending a couple of seasons for Shelbourne in the Irish League. He was brought back by Harry Curtis of Brentford and impressed in their 2nd Division side. Unable to hold his place in the Bees' 1st Division side, Harry Storer swooped and signed Astley in February 1936 from under the nose of Newport County. Whilst at City, Astley never missed a game and set up a fine full back partnership with Walter Metcalf, proving to be a constructive full back who helped the club to the brink of Division 1. During the war, Astley became an officer in the Army and remained in the services rather than return to football once hostilities had ended. He eventually returned to Coventry to live. Off the field, Astley was as stylish as on it, often being seen in Plus Fours!

ATHERTON, Peter
Centre Half

Born: Orrell 6th April 1970
Career: YTS Wigan Athletic, pro February 1988, Coventry City August 1991 (£329,000).

Coventry City	League	F.A.Cup	Lge.Cup
1991–92	35	–	–
1992–93	39	1	2
Total	74	1	2

Debut: 24/8/91 v QPR (a) 1–1 (CH)
Honours: 1 England U–21 Cap (at City)

Atherton had impressed City manager Terry Butcher whilst playing for Wigan against City in the FA Cup in January 1991. Butcher tried to buy the blond haired centre half several times before finally securing his signature. He stepped straight into Trevor Peake's boots – who had been sold to Luton – and has never looked back. He has shown himself to be a strong, tough-tackling centre half who has adapted well to the Premier League and earned an England U–21 cap.

AUSTIN, John Frank (Frank)
Wing Half/Full Back

Born: Stoke 6th July 1933
Career: Toton, Coventry City July 1950, Torquay United February 1963.

Coventry City	League	F.A.Cup	Lge.Cup
1950–51	–	–	
1951–52	–	–	
1952–53	2	–	
1953–54	37 – 1	1	
1954–55	30	–	
1955–56	40	1	
1956–57	31	–	
1957–58	33 – 1	1	
1958–59	14	–	
1959–60	41	2	
1960–61	29	3	–
1961–62	37	2	1
1962–63	8	–	–
Total	302 – 2	10	1

Debut: 11/4/53 v Newport Co. (h) 0–1 (LH)

Signed by Harry Storer, Austin proved to be a splendid servant for City during a time of great upheaval. He was a player of great style who started as a wing half but was converted to full back and established his place for a number of seasons. His ability to slot into either full back or wing half position ensured that Austin joined the elite band of players that have played over 300 games for City. At the start of Jimmy Hill's rebuilding programme, Austin was released and moved on to Torquay United where he ended his League career.

AVRAMOVIC, Rodojko (Raddy)
Goalkeeper
Born: Rijeka, Yugoslavia 29th November 1949
Career: N.K. Rijeka, Notts County August 1979 (£200,000), Inter Montreal May 1983, Coventry City September 1983 (£40,000), Retired 1984.

Coventry City	League	F.A.Cup	Lge.Cup
1983–84	18	4	2

Debut: 17/9/83 v. Leicester City (h) 2–1 (Goal)
Honours: 3 full Yugoslavia caps

This highly intelligent goalkeeper arrived at Meadow Lane as part of the wave of Yugoslav imports in the late 1970's. He gave four years good service to County before being released in a cost cutting exercise. Picked up by City after a short spell in Canada, he fitted the bill. The only other City 'keeper was 17 year old Suckling, and in Bobby Gould's team of "misfits" he provided valuable experience at the back. His professional career was to end however, on a sour note due to two costly errors which turned his manager against him. In January 1984, under heavy pressure, Raddy

allowed a clearance from Watford 'keeper Steve Sherwood bounce over him into an empty net. A month later, in a poor team performance versus Stoke, the third goal in the 2–3 Coventry defeat came from a cross which Avramovic pushed into his own net; Gould was furious and publicly sacked him. Avramovic continued to train, waiting for his manager to eat humble pie. It never happened and Avramovic returned to his native Yugoslavia to become a lawyer.

BABB, Philip (Phil)
Defender
Born: Lambeth 30th November 1970
Career: YTS, Millwall, pro 1988, Bradford City August 1990 (F/T), Coventry City July 1992 (£500,000).

Coventry City	League	F.A.Cup	Lge.Cup
1992–93	27+7s	1	2

Debut: 15/8/92 v Middlesbrough (h) 2–1 (Sub)
Full Debut: 23/9/92 v Scarborough (h) 2–0 (Mid) League Cup
Honours: 1 Republic of Ireland Full Cap (at City)

After failing to make the grade at Millwall, Babb moved to Bradford City on a free transfer and showed himself to be a strong tackling left back who could play at centre forward when called upon. His £500,000 fee to City in July 1992 seemed to be excessive, but now he has established himself in the Premier League he has shown that his tackling and pace has made him equally capable at left back or centre half. He impressed Jack Charlton sufficiently to earn a call up to the Irish international side.

BACON, Arthur
Centre Forward
Born: Birdholme 1905
Died: Derby January 1941
Career: New Tupton Ivanhoe, Chesterfield September 1923, Derby County October 1923, Manchester City December 1928, Reading June 1929, Chesterfield June 1932, Coventry City June 1933, Burton Town, March 1937, Tamworth (Trial) 1937/8.

Coventry City	League	F.A.Cup
1933–34	14 – 16	–
1934–35	1	–
1935–36	1 – 1	–
1936–37	–	–
Total	16 – 17	–

Debut: 14/12/33 v Norwich C. (h) 0–0 (CF)

Bacon was a strong and robust forward, who was characterised by his short back and sides haircut and his venomous shooting. He was a reserve team player prior to his signing for Reading, and on the 3rd April 1931, he scored the club's record individual tally for a match – 6 against Stoke. A disappointing spell at Chesterfield was followed by him signing for City as cover for Clarrie Bourton. He got his chance through an injury to City's centre forward. His goals included five against Gillingham (City's equal highest individual total in a match), and four versus Crystal Palace – in consecutive matches. Unbelievably, after Bacon's tremendous displays, he was dropped to make way for Bourton. He suffered an eye injury with City and moved onto Burton Town. He died in 1941 after an air raid on Derby, when he was serving as a special constable.

BAKER, Clive Edward
Goalkeeper
Born: North Walsham 14th March 1959
Career: Apprentice Norwich City, pro July 1977, Barnsley c/s 1984, Coventry City August 1991 (F/T), Ipswich Town August 1992 (F/T).

Coventry City	League	F.A.Cup	Lge.Cup
1991–92	–	–	1

Debut: 8/10/91 v Rochdale (a) 0–1 (Goal) League Cup

After being a regular understudy at Norwich, Baker became a dependable keeper at Barnsley for seven years and hardly missed a match. City gave him the opportunity of returning to Division 1, but his only appearance in his 12 months at the club came at Rochdale in the League Cup. Ironically he had the opportunity to play in March 1992 following injury to Steve Ogrizovic, only for him to suffer from appendicitis. Whilst at City he obtained an Open University degree in mathematics. At Ipswich he has become a trusty keeper.

BAKER, Gerard Austin (Gerry)
Forward
Born: New York 11th April 1938
Career: Larkhill Thistle, Chelsea June 1955, Motherwell January 1957, St. Mirren c/s 1959, Manchester City November 1960, Hibernian November 1961, Ipswich Town December 1963, Coventry City November 1967 (£20,000), Brentford (loan) October 1969, Margate 1970, Nuneaton Borough c/s 1970, Bedworth United.

Coventry City	League	F.A.Cup	Lge.Cup
1967–68	18+1s–4	3 – 1	–
1968–69	8+3s–1	–	–
1969–70	1	–	–
Total	27+4s–5	3 – 1	–

Debut: 11/11/67 v. Fulham (h) 0–3 (IR)
Honours: 4 full USA caps (all at City)

Gerry Baker's most successful periods came at Hibs. and Ipswich, but wherever he went he was always in the shadows of his taller, more successful brother Joe, who played on the Continent and was an England international. Nevertheless, both players played for their country – Gerry for the USA – although both brothers were brought up in Scotland. It was for St. Mirren that Gerry bagged 10 goals in a Scottish Cup match in January 1960 against Glasgow University in a 15–0 victory, which still stands as the club's highest victory. Baker was signed by Noel Cantwell to help City avoid relegation but never really impressed. He left City to move into non–league football and continued to live in the Coventry area. The sporting family connections continue for his daughter is Lorraine Baker, the British Olympic middle–distance runner.

BAKER, James Edward (Jim)
Right Half
Born: Trethomas June 1904
Career: Lovell's Athletic, Wolverhampton Wanderers May 1926, Coventry City May 1929, Lovell's Athletic c/s 1932, Coventry City February 1933, Bristol City June 1935, Colchester United c/s 1937.

Coventry City	League	F.A.Cup
1929–30	27 – 3	–
1930–31	42 – 4	3
1931–32	39 – 1	2
1932–33	8 – 1	–
1933–34	39 – 2	2
1934–35	27	–
Total	182 – 11	7

Debut: 31/8/29 v Merthyr Town (h) 3–2 (RH)

Just 2 months after buying Ted Watson from Wolves, James McIntyre raided the reserve side of the Molineux club again to acquire the services of Jimmy Baker. After irregular League appearances at Wolves, he became a regular choice for City, starting as a wing half, but switching to centre half with great effect.

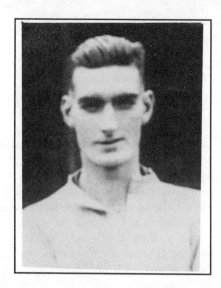

Despite making over 100 appearances in 3 seasons, he moved to his native Wales, playing for Lovell's Athletic – the works side for the well known confectionary company. Within 8 months, he returned to Highfield Road as the regular right half. He remained first team choice, but Harry Storer was anxious to see Billy Frith progress. Baker was sold to Bristol City, but only played 11 times in 2 seasons, before being attracted to the newly formed Colchester United. He finally hung up his boots during the war.

BALL, Christopher George (Chris)
Outside Right
Born: Leek 15th March 1907
Died: June 1991
Career: Leek St. Luke's, Coventry City 1926/7, Colwyn Bay July 1929, Bristol Rovers August 1930, Bristol City August 1931, Walsall February 1932, Cradley Heath, Brierley Hill Alliance.

Coventry City	League	F.A.Cup
1926–27	–	–
1927–28	8	–
1928–29	2	–
Total	10	–

Debut: 7/4/28 v Torquay U. (a) 3–2 (OR)

It took Ball almost 2 years as a professional before making his League debut, when he made eight consecutive appearances as a right winger, although his best position was inside right. Making no progress, he tried his luck with Colwyn Bay. After a season, he was signed by Bristol Rovers, making

17 appearances before moving across the city to Ashton Gate. He played only 3 games before transferring to Walsall, where he made 123 appearances and scored 23 goals in three and a half seasons. His play was typified by ferocious tackling and he has the distinction of being one of the four ex–City men to appear for the Saddlers in the remarkable 2–0 victory over Arsenal in the F.A. Cup in 1933.

BALL, John
Inside Right
Born: Hazel Grove, 29th September 1899
Career: Silverwood Colliery, Sheffield United 1919/20, Bristol Rovers 1921, Wath Athletic 1922, Bury 1923, West Ham United c/s 1929, Coventry City May 1930, Stourbridge c/s 1931, Hinckley United c/s 1932.

Coventry City	League	F.A.Cup
1930–31	23 – 4	3

Debut: 30/8/30 v Notts Co. (h) 1–2 (IR)
Honours: 1 England full cap

Ball's career hit its peak at Bury. In 202 League matches he scored 81 goals and earned an England cap against Ireland in October 1927, but he was almost lost to the game. He had played 6 Division One matches for Sheffield United and 25 games for Bristol Rovers, and it took Bury to revive his League career where he rewarded them by scoring 14 goals as they were promoted to Division 1. Despite scoring 9 goals in 15 matches at Upton Park, Ball signed for City in May 1930.

BAMBER, John David (David)
Centre Forward
Born: St. Helens 1st February 1959
Career: Manchester University 1977, Blackpool August 1979, Coventry City May 1983 (£50,000), Walsall March 1984, Portsmouth December 1984, Swindon Town November 1985, Watford June 1988, Stoke City December 1988 (£150,000), Hull City February 1990, Blackpool (loan December 1990) January 1991.

Coventry City	League	F.A.Cup	Lge.Cup
1983–84	18+1s–3	0+1s	2 – 1

Debut: 27/8/83 v Watford (a) 3–2 (CF)

After graduating in Economics from Manchester University, Bamber had impressed Bobby Gould whilst at Blackpool, and the player was Gould's first signing for City. He only scored four goals in an unhappy time when he suffered from illness. With promotion–seeking Portsmouth, he produced just 4 goals, but his career was revived at Swindon, where he scored 47 goals for the Robins before unsuccessful spells elsewhere. This curly haired big striker's career has flourished once more since his return to Bloomfield Road.

BANNISTER, Gary
Forward

Born: Warrington 22nd July 1960
Career: Apprentice Coventry City, pro May 1978, Detroit Express (loan) April 1980, Sheffield Wednesday August 1981 (£100,000), Queen's Park Rangers August 1984 (£200,000), Coventry City March 1988 (£300,000), West Bromwich Albion March 1990 (£250,000), Oxford United (loan) March 1992, Nottingham F. August 1992 (F/T), Stoke City May 1993 (F/T).

Coventry City	League	F.A.Cup	Lge.Cup
1978–79	3+1s – 1	–	1
1979–80	5+2s	–	–
1980–81	9+2s – 2	2	1
1987–88	7+1s – 1	–	–
1988–89	22+2s– 8	–	3 – 2
1989–90	10+1s– 2	–	2
Total	56+9s–14	2	7 – 2

Debut: 26/8/78 v Norwich C (h) 4–1 (Sub) Lge.Cup
Full Debut: 30/8/78 v Chester (a) 1–2 (OR)
Honours: 1 England U–21 cap

Bannister had two spells at City, but in neither did he achieve what was expected of him. He started as a right winger but was sold to 2nd Division Sheffield Wednesday once Peter Bodak had established a first team place. He was a revelation at Hillsborough, scoring 65 goals in only three seasons and earning his England U–21 cap after his transformation to a striker. After scoring 66 goals at Loftus Road in 3½ seasons, he signed for City. He battled with David Speedie for a striker's position and failed to score the goals expected of him. It seemed his career was declining after his release from WBA, but after a short trial he was given a contract by Nottingham Forest for whom he played frequently in 1992/93 season.

BARNES, David
Left Back

Born: Paddington 16th November 1961
Career: Apprentice Coventry City, pro May 1979, Ipswich Town May 1982 (F/T), Wolverhampton Wanderers October 1984 (£35,000), Aldershot August 1987, Sheffield United July 1989.

Coventry City	League	F.A.Cup	Lge.Cup
1979–80	3	–	–
1980–81	–	–	–
1981–82	6	4	–
Total	9	4	–

Debut: 15/4/80 v Bolton W. (a) 1–1 (LB)

When Barnes was at City he was understudy to Bobby McDonald and then Brian Roberts. He was given a free transfer in May 1982 because he had been involved in unsavoury off the field incidents. He appeared 17 times for Ipswich before signing for Wolves in October 1984, where he stayed as the club descended from Division 2 to Division 4. After two fruitful years at Aldershot he transferred to Sheffield United, and has been a useful squad player for the Blades.

BARNES, James (Jim)
Outside Left

Born: Atherstone 1905
Career: Atherstone, Coventry City 1927/8, Walsall June 1929, Watford c/s 1931, Exeter City June 1933, York City 1934, Atherstone c/s 1935.

Coventry City	League	F.A.Cup
1927–28	8	–
1928–29	–	–
Total	8	–

Debut: 13/2/28 v Crystal Palace (h) 2–2 (OL)

Following a 0–7 reverse at Walsall, the speedy Jim Barnes, was given a try after wholesale team changes were made. He showed his pace but his passing was erratic and he lost his place to "Cute" Herbert. Unable to impress new manager James McIntyre he was sold to Walsall, who were managed by his ex–City boss James Kerr. Showing good wing play, he scored 17 goals in 76 games. This encouraged Watford to invest in his services. Ironically, he kept Billy Pick out of the Hornets' side, the player that City boss McIntyre chose in preference to Barnes.

BARNES, Peter S.
Outside Left

Born: Manchester 10th June 1957
Career: Apprentice Manchester City, pro April 1974, West Bromwich Albion July 1979 (£748,000), Leeds United August 1981 (£900,000), Real Betis (Spain) August 1982 (£110,000), Leeds United August 1983, West Ham United (loan), August

1984, Manchester United (loan) September 1984, Coventry City October 1984 (£65,000), Manchester United June 1985 (£50,000), Manchester City January 1987 (£15,000) Bolton Wanderers (loan) October 1987, Port Vale (loan) December 1987, Hull City March 1988 (F/T), Sporting Farnese (Portugal) August 1988 (F/T), Bolton Wanderers October 1988, Sunderland February 1989, Stockport County March 1989 (player-coach), Hamrum Spartans (Malta)c/s 1989, Drogheda 1989–90, Northwich V.1990–91, USA Indoor League, Mossley 1991–92.

Coventry City	League	F.A.Cup	Lge.Cup
1984–85	18 – 2	–	1

Debut: 6/10/84 v. Watford (a) 1–0 (OL)
Honours: 22 England full caps
        1 England 'B' cap
        9 England U–21 caps
        1 Football League appearance
        League Cup Winners Medal 1975–76

Barnes was a winger of great skill and could enchant a crowd. The son of Manchester City favourite Ken Barnes, Peter's skinny frame and natural ball control earned him rave reviews and full caps. His move to WBA further enhanced his career, with a more than passing comparison with George Best. His move to Leeds, who were struggling against relegation, showed his limitations. His inconsistencies were a liability and he moved to the Continent, and lost his England place. His return to Leeds was unsuccessful, but Bobby Gould was prepared to sign him on. Despite some fantastic moments (his dribble to beat countless defenders against Southampton at a foggy Highfield Road was captured by television) Barnes' erratic form could not be accommodated in City's struggling side. He lost his place to Micky Adams. Signed by his former WBA boss Ron Atkinson for Manchester United, Barnes sparkled as the club went eleven games unbeaten at the start of 1985/6 but he then once again lost his place. Throughout his career, Barnes was a luxury item and it is sad that so few managers at either club or national level could harness his abounding talent.

BARR, Hugh
Inside Right
Born: Ballymena 17th May 1935
Career: Ballymena United, Linfield c/s 1961, Coventry City July 1962, Cambridge United January 1965.

Coventry City	League	F.A.Cup	Lge.Cup
1962–63	34 – 12	7 – 2	1
1963–64	13 – 3	2	–
1964–65	–	–	1
Total	47 – 15	9 – 2	2

Debut: 18/8/62 v. Notts County (h) 2–0 (IR)
Honours: 3 full Northern Ireland caps (2 at City)
        1 Northern Ireland 'B' cap
        Northern Ireland Amateur International
        5 appearances for Irish League
        Irish Cup Winners Medal 1961–62

Barr was a tall and heavy inside forward who had a successful career in Northern Ireland before being signed by Jimmy Hill at the age of 27. He made a great impression during his time at City, but preferred to be a part–time professional. Hill could not accept this arrangement and consequently Barr moved to non–league Cambridge United, where he combined playing with his job as a teacher.

BARRATT, Harold (Harry)
Wing Half
Born: Headington 25th December 1918
Died: Coventry 25th September 1989
Career: Herberts Athletic, Coventry City 1934, Retired April 1952.

Coventry City	League	F.A.Cup
1934–35	–	–
1935–36	–	–
1936–37	–	–
1937–38	1	–
1938–39	4 – 1	–
1945–46	WWII	2 – 1
1946–47	33 – 7	2
1947–48	38	2
1948–49	37	1
1949–50	26 – 2	–
1950–51	30 – 2	1
1951–52	1	–
Total	170 – 12	8 – 1

Debut: 9/4/38 v. Blackburn Rovers (h) 3–2 (IR)

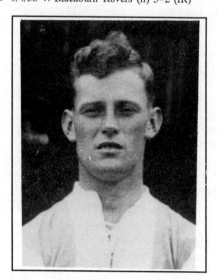

Signed by Harry Storer, Barratt was in awe of his manager and during Storer's two spells at City, showed great loyalty to the man who helped establish his career. The son of an ex–Southampton full back, he moved to Coventry during his early years. Barratt played only five games before the war, but was a cornerstone of the side during the war and the five years afterwards. His favourite position was in the half back line, but he could play inside forward if necessary. In total, he played in nine positions for City, including a spell in goal after Alf Wood was injured. He took great pride in being appointed City skipper, a position he held for five years until his retirement, which was caused by a knee injury at Notts County on the opening day of the 1951/2 season. After retiring, he managed Rugby Town and Snowdown Colliery and was responsible for grooming George Curtis. Until his death, he was National Coach for the British Crown Green Bowls Association.

BARRY, Roy A.
Centre Half
Born: Edinburgh 19th September 1942
Career: Musselburgh, Heart of Midlothian c/s 1960, Dunfermline Athletic late 1966, Coventry City October 1969, Crystal Palace September 1973 (£45,000), Hibernian February 1975, East Fife c/s 1976 (player–manager).

Coventry City	League	F.A.Cup	Lge.Cup
1969–70	14+1s	2	–
1970–71	1	–	–
1971–72	27 – 1	1	–
1972–73	40 – 1	4	2
1973–74	–	–	–
Total	82+1s–2	7	2

Debut: 1/11/69 v. Chelsea (a) 0–1 (sub)
Full Debut: 15/11/69 v. Burnley (a) 0–0 (CH)

Signed as the replacement for George Curtis, Barry had a big act to follow. Despite being only five feet nine, he was an impressive centre–half who had an uncompromising style. He came to City with a reputation for being a "hatchet man", but at City he was never in trouble. After some impressive performances, he broke his leg in March 1970 against Sheffield Wednesday. It took Barry 14 months to return and he played two more solid seasons for City before signing for Crystal Palace. He moved back to his home town with Hibs before a short spell as player–manager of East Fife. He was last heard of living in London.

BASSETT, George R.
Full Back
Born: Birmingham 12th May 1943
Career: Coventry City August 1961, Worcester City c/s 1963, Retired c/s 1973.

Coventry City	League	F.A.Cup	Lge.Cup
1961–62	1	–	–
1962–63	–	–	–
Total	1	–	–

Debut: 24/4/62 v. Bristol City (a) 2–3 (OL)

Bassett's only appearance, came out of position in an end of season game. He was released by Jimmy Hill and linked up with Worcester City, his only other club, where he was a loyal servant for ten years.

BECK, John A.
Midfield
Born: Edmonton 25th May 1954
Career: Apprentice Queen's Park Rangers, pro May 1972, Coventry City June 1976 (£40,000), Fulham October 1978 (£70,000), Bournemouth September 1982, Cambridge United c/s 1986 (F/T), Retired 1989 to become Manager.

Coventry City	League	F.A.Cup	Lge.Cup
1976–77	40 – 3	2	3
1977–78	15+8s–2	1	1
1978–79	5+1s–1	–	1
Total	60+9s–6	3	5

Debut: 21/8/76 v. Middlesbrough (a) 0–1 (Mid)

After a good first season at City, injury set him back and he found it difficult to regain a regular first team place, especially when Gordon Milne produced his exciting 4–2–4 line–up which was dominated in midfield by Terry Yorath and Barry Powell. He moved on to Fulham and was a solid professional in the lower divisions for the rest of his career. It was as a manager that Beck came to prominence, taking Cambridge from the 4th Division to the brink of promotion to the newly–formed Premier Division. His long ball and intimidatory tactics were not liked but certainly brought success for his team. He is now manager of Preston.

BELL, Joseph (Joe)
Left back
Born: Sunderland 28th July 1924
Career: Stockton, Sunderland 1943, Stockton 1945, Chesterfield c/s 1946, Coventry City c/s 1949.

Coventry City	League	F.A.Cup
1949–50	4	–
1950–51	3	–
1951–52	3	–
Total	10	–

Debut: 27/8/49 v. Grimsby Town (a) 2–3 (LB)

During the war he played for Sunderland, and before arriving at City had been a first team left back at Division 2 Chesterfield. This encouraged Harry Storer to buy him, but he spent three years as a reserve in the shadows of Dick Mason. His final League game came in September 1951 in the 1–4 defeat by Hull City at Highfield Road, when he was one of four scapegoats.

BELL, William (Billy)
Left Half
Born: Manchester 9th December
Career: St.Margaret's, Manchester City 1926/7, Coventry City July 1927, Portsmouth July 1931, Chester 1932/3, Macclesfield c/s 1935.

Coventry City	League	F.A.Cup
1927–28	9	2
1928–29	40 – 1	1
1929–30	34 – 2	4
1930–31	37 – 2	3
Total	120 – 5	10

Debut: 26/11/27 v Bournemouth & B.A. (h) 2–2 (LH)

Son of ex–Scotland and Manchester United's Alec Bell. Billy Bell started at a Coventry Junior club, when his father was City's trainer, before signing for Manchester City as his father moved North. Bell was an unsung player who had been bought by James Kerr but came to prominence under James McIntyre, after playing at Maine Road as a reserve. He established himself as left half at the start of the 1928–29 season, and only lost his place through injury. His unassuming play was spotted by First Division Portsmouth who signed him, but he played only one game for Pompey before moving to Chester for the club's second season in the League.

BELLAS, John H. (Jack)
Full Back
Born: Bishop Auckland 16th September
Career: Shildon Athletic, Sheffield Wednesday September 1920, Mansfield Town June 1923, Coventry City January 1925, Heanor Town c/s 1926, Sutton Town 1927.

Coventry City	League	F.A.Cup
1924–25	19	–
1925–26	15	–
Total	34	–

Debut: 24/1/25 v Leicester C. (a) 1–5 (RB)

Bellas was a big full back who was bought from non–league Mansfield Town because of his steady play. He moved straight into the City first team being excellent at controlling the play. In the summer of 1925, the offside rule was changed, which speedened the game up and cruelly exposed the ponderous Bellas. He was dropped, and later injured. He was bought by Heanor, after refusing reduced terms by City when the club was relegated.

BENNETT, David A.
Outside Right
Born: Manchester 11th July 1959
Career: Apprentice Manchester City, pro June 1977, Cardiff City September 1981 (£50,000), Coventry City August 1983 (£100,000), Sheffield Wednesday March 1989 (£250,000), Swindon Town September 1990, Shrewsbury Town (loan) November 1991.

Coventry City	League	F.A.Cup	Lge.Cup
1983–84	32+2s–6	3	3 – 1
1984–85	29+5s–2	–	2
1985–86	34+5s–6	1	4 – 2
1986–87	31 – 7	5 – 3	5 – 2
1987–88	27+1s–4	2	3
1988–89	5+2s–0	1	–
Total	158+15s–25	12 – 3	17 – 5

Debut: 17/9/83 v Leicester C. (h) 2–1 (sub)
Full Debut: 1/10/83 v Ipswich T. (h) 1–2 (OR)
Honours: FA Cup Winners Medal 1987
FA Cup Runners–up Medal 1981

Dave Bennett had played in Manchester City's FA Cup final side of 1981 and seemed to have a bright future, but was surprisingly sold to Cardiff City four months later. His career was revived by Bobby Gould, who had an outstanding knowledge of the lower divisions. He often showed his potential in poor City sides, but it wasn't until George Curtis and John Sillett took over in 1986 that Bennett started to shine. In an attacking side he formed great partnerships with David Phillips and Cyrille Regis. His close ball control was exceptional and his goals in both the FA Cup semi-final and final were vital in City's triumphant cup run. He suffered a broken leg in March 1988 and once he was fit again he was transferred to Sheffield Wednesday. He played 30 times for the Owls. He broke his leg in his second game for Swindon, was loaned out to Shrewsbury to regain match sharpness and broke the same leg in his second game for the Shrews. On his return to Swindon he broke his leg for a fourth time in pre-season training in July 1992, and is now struggling to regain his fitness.

BENNETT, Donald (Don)
Full Back
Born: Wakefield 18th December 1933
Career: Derby County (amateur), Staines Athletic, Arsenal August 1951, Coventry City September 1959, Hereford United c/s 1962.

Coventry City	League	F.A.Cup	Lge.Cup
1959–60	26	–	
1960–61	26	–	2
1961–62	21	2	–
Total	73	2	2

Debut: 3/10/59 v Bournemouth (h) 4–0 (OL)

Bennett was a youth international who signed for Arsenal, but in his 8 years at the club, he never made a League appearance. Snapped up by City, Bennett proved to be a useful full back, who could play on either flank. Despite being the captain under Billy Frith, he was a casualty of Jimmy Hill's arrival, and was released. He was also a noted Middlesex bowler and has since become a successful cricketting coach with that county.

BENNETT, Jesse
Full Back
Born: Sheffield
Career: Dronfield Woodhouse, Sheffield United c/s 1928, Coventry City c/s 1932, Northampton Town c/s 1933, Retired 1936.

Coventry City	League	F.A.Cup
1932–33	25	4
Total	25	4

Debut: 27/8/32 v Torquay U. (a) 3–3 (RB)

Having been discarded by his local club Sheffield United, after playing 9 games, his career was revived by Harry Storer who signed him in the summer of 1932. He began solidly and soon began to impress, but later lost his way and was sold onto local rivals Northampton. He spent 3 years at the County Ground, playing 56 games before retiring through injury.

BENTLEY, Alfred (Alf)
Goalkeeper
Born: Aylesham 28th October 1931
Career: Snowdown Colliery, Coventry City October 1955, Margate 1957, Gillingham August 1958, Tunbridge Wells United c/s 1962.

Coventry City	League	F.A.Cup
1955–56	2	–
1956–57	27	–
Total	29	–

Debut: 14/4/56 v. Torquay United (h) 1–2 (Goal)

Signed from Snowdown at the same time as George Curtis, Bentley was reserve to Reg Matthews, and played through to the end of the season after the latter's sale to Chelsea in November 1956. Despite being big and agile, he was considered surplus to requirement once the experienced Charlie Ashcroft was signed. At Gillingham, he was limited to twelve appearances in four seasons.

BEST, Jeremiah (Jerry)
Goalkeeper
Born: Mickley 22nd April 1897
Career: Mickley Colliery Welfare, Coventry City May 1920, Halifax Town c/s 1926, Rotherham United 1927/8, Worksop Town c/s 1929, Newark Town c/s 1930, Worksop Town 1931.

Coventry City	League	F.A.Cup
1920–21	23	2
1921–22	40	3
1922–23	42	1
1923–24	42	2
1924–25	42	3
1925–26	35	1
Total	224	12

Debut: 25/12/20 v Cardiff C. (h) 2–4 (Goal)

Jerry Best was an outstanding goalkeeper. On many occasions it was only his sheer brilliance that saved City from severe drubbings. Best was however, an unlikely goalkeeper, for he was a slight figure, standing only 5ft 7inches. Not surprisingly he is City's shortest ever keeper and was a talking point at away games. Despite his size he was an outstanding custodian and was watched frequently by representatives of First Division clubs. After he claimed his place over Christmas 1920 he missed only seven games in six years, all through injury, and he became the first player to make 200 League & Cup appearances for City – at Southampton on the last day of the 1924–25 season. City's financial problems in 1926 resulted in all players being offered reduced wages. Best refused to sign and he surprisingly did not find a new club until the start of the new season. Ironically he joined Halifax Town from whom City had acquired Best's replacement Jimmy Newton. He only played 9 matches for The Shaymen and 26 for Rotherham.

BETT, Frederick (Fred)
Inside Forward
Born: Scunthorpe 5th December 1920
Career: Scunthorpe & Lindsey United, Sunderland c/s 1937, Coventry City May 1946, Lincoln City September 1948.

Coventry City	League	F.A.Cup
1946–47	23 – 10	–
1947–48	2	–
1948–49	2 – 1	–
Total	27 – 11	–

Debut: 31/8/46 v. Burnley (a) 1–1 (IR) 1 goal

At the outbreak of the war, Bett was a member of Sunderland's impressive First Division squad, and during the hostilities guested for Lincoln, Nottingham Forest and Chester. Bett started brightly with City, scoring four goals in his first five games. Despite injury and continual changes in team selection, he continued to score regularly. He lost his place and spent 18 months as a reserve before leaving for Lincoln where he failed to make an impression.

BETTS, Eric
Outside Left
Born: Coventry 27th July 1925
Career: Mansfield Villa, Mansfield Town February 1946, Coventry City August 1947, Nuneaton Borough, Walsall May 1949, West Ham United April 1950, Nuneaton Borough c/s 1951, Rochdale October 1951, Crewe Alexandra February 1953, Wrexham October 1953, Oldham Athletic February 1956.

Coventry City	League	F.A.Cup
1947–48	1	–

Debut: 20/9/47 v. Fulham (h) 5–2 (OL)

During the war, Betts guested for Forest and Crystal Palace. He was a tall winger who made his only appearance for City in the period between injury to George Ashall and the signing of Norman Lockhart. He was released and moved to Nuneaton, where he earned a recall to League football with Walsall. He spent his later days around the North-west.

BILLING, Peter Graham
Centre Half
Born: Liverpool 24th October 1964
Career: South Liverpool, Everton January 1986, Crewe Alexandra (loan December 1986) February 1987, Coventry City June 1989 (£120,000), Port Vale (loan February 1993) May 1993.

Coventry City	League	F.A.Cup	Lge.Cup
1989–90	16+2s	1	3+1s
1990–91	15	4	2
1991–92	17+5s–1	2	4
1992–93	3	–	–
Total	51+7s–1	7	9+1s

Debut: 25/10/89 v QPR (a) 2–1 (Sub) League Cup
Full Debut: 28/10/89 v Charlton Ath. (a) 1–1 (CH)

Billing played once for Everton, and later played with future England Internationals David Platt,

Geoff Thomas and Rob Jones at Crewe, helping the Railwayman to promotion to Division 3. Signed by John Sillett, Billing was never a regular choice at City, but showed himself to be a fierce-tackling defender with a short fuse. He was loaned out to Port Vale to help their push to promotion and was signed permanently on the eve of the club's unsuccessful Wembley 2nd Division play-off match against WBA.

BINKS, Louis
Full Back

Born: Sheffield 23rd October 1898
Died: 1969
Career: Tinsley Amateurs, Coventry City May 1919, Grimsby Town 1922, Rotherham Town 1923.

Coventry City	League	F.A.Cup
1919–20	3	–
1920–21	12	–
1921–22	–	–
Total	15	–

Debut: 24/4/20 v Lincoln C. (h) 2–0 (RB)

This strongly built full back was first blooded in the final 3 games of 1919–20 when City were in a desparate situation. He helped City obtain 5 points out of 6, and only played thereafter as cover for the injured Charlie Copeland before transferring to Grimsby. He appeared 3 times for the Mariners and moved into non-league football with Rotherham Town.

BIRD, William (Billy)
Wing Half/Forward

Born: Broughton Astley
Career: Hinckley United, Coventry City c/s 1926, Hinckley United c/s 1928, Atherstone, Nuneaton Town c/s 1930.

Coventry City	League	F.A.Cup
1926–27	12 – 5	2
1927–28	25 – 6	2 – 1
Total	37 – 11	4 – 1

Debut: 9/10/26 v Newport Co. (h) 3–1 (LH)

Billy Bird came to City as an exciting young centre half, but ironically, he only played once for City in his preferred position. During the summer of 1926, Bird chose City, refusing a considerably better offer from Chelsea. His ability to fill into most positions helped, as he made his debut at left half, had an

extended run at centre forward and a spell at outside right. He was released by new manager McIntyre and returned to his first club.

BIRTLEY, Robert J.
Outside Right

Born: Easington 1908
Career: Crook Town, Everton, Coventry City June 1934, Crystal Palace October 1935, Gateshead 1939.

Coventry City	League	F.A.Cup
1934–35	30 – 6	3 – 3
1935–36	–	–
Total	30 – 6	3 – 3

Debut: 25/8/34 v Northampton T. (h) 2–0 (OR) 1 goal

Birtley was signed in June 1934 having failed to make the first team at Everton. He scored on his debut and provided good service for his forwards, but manager Storer was looking for a winger who could offer better service and more goals. He found his man in George McNestry and Birtley was sold to Crystal Palace, where he scored 16 goals in 69 games, before returning to his native North East with Gateshead in the summer of 1939.

BISBY, Clarence Charles (Charlie)
Left Back

Born: Mexborough 10th September
Career: Denaby United, Notts County c/s 1926, Coventry City June 1932, Mansfield Town December 1935, Peterborough United c/s 1936.

Coventry City	League	F.A.Cup
1932–33	12	1
1933–34	35	–
1934–35	36	3
1935–36	17	2
Total	100	6

Debut: 27/8/32 v Torquay Utd (a) 3–3 (LB)

Harry Storer looked to the experienced Charlie Bisby to halt the alarming flow of goals that resulted in 97 being conceded in the 1931–32 season. Bisby made 207 appearances for Notts County, helping them to promotion to Division 2. He started well with City, but injury struck in his first season, when he suffered a knee injury which required the removal of a cartilage and also had an internal injury. Thereafter, he became a regular for two and a half seasons and was given the club captaincy in August 1935. In December 1935, he was guilty of breaking club rules and was immediately sold by Storer to Mansfield for whom he played only 9 games before moving into the Midland League with Peterborough.

BLAIR, Andrew (Andy)
Midfield

Born: Kirkcaldy 18th December 1959
Career: Apprentice Coventry City, pro October 1977, Aston Villa August 1981 (£300,000), Wolverhampton Wanderers (loan) October 1983, Sheffield Wednesday August 1984, Aston Villa March 1986, Barnsley (loan) March 1988, Northampton Town October 1988 (F/T), Naxaar Lions (Malta), December 1988 (F/T), Kidderminster Harriers July 1989 (F/T), Retired May 1990.

Coventry City	League	F.A.Cup	Lge.Cup
1977–78	–	–	–
1978–79	25+1s–1	2 – 1	–
1979–80	30+2s–1	2	2
1980–81	35 – 4	4 – 1	9 – 1
Total	90+3s–6	8 – 2	11 – 1

Debut: 28/10/78 v. Birmingham City (h) 2–1 (Mid)
Honours: 5 Scotland U–21 caps (2 at City)

Blair was one of the successes of City's seventies youth team. He became a first team regular in his teens and his form precipitated the departure of Terry Yorath. He was inspirational in City's League Cup run of 1980/81. In the summer of 1981, City were in need of a financial injection and champions Villa swooped for Blair. At Villa, his career stagnated and he was sold to Sheffield Wednesday where he was rejuvenated. Against Luton Town in 1985 in the Owls' 4–2 League Cup victory, he scored a hat–trick of penalties. His move back to Villa was fruitless and he picked up a knee injury which effectively ended his career. Blair was manager of Racing Club Warwick, until resigning in Spring 1993.

BLAIR, John (Jock)
Left Back

Born: Kilwinning
Career: Kilwinning Rangers, Coventry City 1919/20, Caerphilly, Kilwinning Rangers c/s 1922.

Coventry City	League	F.A.Cup
1919–20	8	–
1920–21	2	–
Total	10	–

Debut: 31/1/20 v South Shields (a) 0–1 (LB)

Jock Blair was a reserve left back, who was understudy to George Chaplin and James Lawrence. His opportunities only came when there was an injury to either of these experienced full backs. With little scope for future appearances, he moved on.

BLOCKLEY, Jeffrey Paul (Jeff)
Centre Half

Born: Leicester 12th September 1949
Career: Apprentice, Coventry City, pro June 1967, Arsenal October 1972 (£200,000), Leicester City January 1975 (£100,000), Derby County (loan) January 1978, Notts County June 1978, Gloucester City 1980.

Coventry City	League	F.A.Cup	Lge.Cup
1967–68	–	–	–
1968–69	10+2s	–	–
1969–70	39 – 3	1	1
1970–71	42 – 1	1	5 – 1
1971–72	42 – 2	1	1
1972–73	11	–	1
Total	144+2s–6	3	8 – 1

Debut: 11/1/69 v Southampton (a) 0–1 (Sub)
Full Debut: 14/3/69 v West Ham United (a) 2–5 (CH)
Honours: 1 Full England Cap
10 England U–23 Caps (6 at City)
1 appearance for Football League

Blockley was captain of City's 1968 Youth Cup final team and played with Peter Shilton for Blaby Boys before making an instant impression in the Football League. His partnership with Roy Barry was fundamental in City's qualification for Europe and the youngster proved to have outstanding talent. He was a regular throughout his time at City, but his departure was untimely. He scored an own goal against Chelsea at Highfield Road in his last game, was sold to Arsenal, and 2 days later was selected for his only full international, against Yugoslavia – City just missing out on the club's first England 'cap' since Reg Matthews. City were unable to find a satisfactory replacement for a number of years, whilst at Arsenal he became the brunt of fans' disquiet and moved on to his home town club. He was never able to reproduce the form that he had shown at City.

BLY, Terence Geoffrey (Terry)
Centre Forward

Born: Fincham 22nd October 1935
Career: Bury Town, Norwich City August 1956, Peterborough United June 1960 (£5,000), Coventry City July 1962 (£10,000), Notts County August 1963, Grantham Town October 1964 (player-manager), Retired.

Coventry City	League	F.A.Cup	Lge.Cup
1962–63	32 – 25	8 – 2	2 – 1

Debut: 18/8/62 v. Notts County (h) 2–0 (CF) 1 goal

Bly was at the centre of one of the most notorious team selections by manager Jimmy Hill. He was signed for only £10,000 in July 1962 as a big target man for wingers Humphries and Laverick. He had scored 87 goals in two seasons at London Road, including 54 in 1960/61, a record for Division 4. His scoring rate at City was excellent and he proved a great a favourite with the City fans. Bly's big frame and curly blond hair sometimes made him look cumbersome, but his looks were deceptive for he scored 27 goals in his first 41 games for City, including two hat–tricks. However with the purchase of George Hudson, also from Peterborough, in April 1963. Bly was dropped for the game against Halifax, and despite Hudson scoring a hat–trick City fans showed their disgust for the absence of Bly. He only played one more game for City before moving on. Hill's conviction proved right, for Bly's goal scoring dried up at Meadow Lane and he soon moved into non–league football. After leaving the game he established a sports shop.

BLYTH, James Anton (Jim)
Goalkeeper
Born: Perth 2nd February 1955
Career: Perth Roselea, Preston North End 1971, Coventry City October 1972 (£22,500), Hereford United (loan) March 1975, Birmingham City August 1982 (F/T), Nuneaton Borough c/s 1985, Retired 1986.

Coventry City	League	F.A.Cup	Lge.Cup
1972–73	–	–	–
1973–74	–	–	–
1974–75	–	–	–
1975–76	19	1	–
1976–77	31	2	3
1977–78	40	–	4
1978–79	6	2	–
1979–80	21	1	1
1980–81	7	–	3
1981–82	27	4	2
Total	151	10	13

Debut: 19/12/75 v. Everton (h) 1–2 (Goal)
Honours: 2 full Scotland Caps (both at City)

Blyth made his debut at Preston at the age of 16 and was quickly snapped up by Gordon Milne. He spent three years learning his trade and finally earned his chance when injury struck Bryan King.

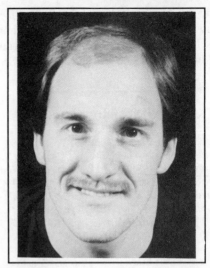

He impressed greatly and became a very accomplished goalkeeper. His best season was 1977/8 when he kept City in many a game and earned two Scotland caps. He went to Argentina with Ally McLeod's World Cup squad, but was not selected. A back injury struck in late 1978, which was to trouble him for the rest of his career. It prevented a lucrative move to Manchester United and caused a furore on 1st September 1979, when his back went in the warm–up against Norwich, which forced youth team keeper Steve Murcott to play. With his arch rival, Les Sealey in the ascendency, Blyth was released on a free transfer. He spent two and a half years in Birmingham's reserves before finishing his career at Nuneaton.

BODAK, Peter J.
Outside Right
Born: Birmingham 12th August 1961
Career: Apprentice Coventry City, pro May 1979, Manchester United July 1982 (F/T), Manchester City December 1982, Seiko (Hong Kong) October 1983, Royal Antwerp c/s 1984, Crewe Alexandra December 1986, Swansea City March 1988, Happy Valley (Hong Kong), Walsall c/s 1990, Hong Kong, Atherstone United December 1991.

Coventry City	League	F.A.Cup	Lge.Cup
1979–80	–	–	–
1980–81	21+2s–3	2	6 – 1
1981–82	9 – 2	4 – 1	–
Total	30+2s–5	6 – 1	6 – 1

Debut: 6/9/80 v. Crystal Palace (h) 3–1 (OR)

Bodak was an exciting and skilful winger, but was never able to come to terms with his precocious nature. He hit the headlines as soon as he made the first team, playing a fundamental part in City's run to the League Cup semi-finals. Dave Sexton preferred Rudi Kaiser to Bodak, and he was released on a free transfer. He never played a League game for Manchester United and left Manchester City after a breach of club discipline. After impressing at Crewe, he moved around again, including a return to Hong Kong.

BOILEAU, Henry Arthur (Harry)
Wing Half
Born: Bedworth 1910
Career: Bedworth Town, Coventry City c/s 1930, Retired 1945.

Coventry City	League	F.A.Cup
1930–31	–	–
1931–32	3	–
1932–33	23	–
1933–34	33	2
1934–35	26	3
1935–36	32	2
1936–37	7	–
1937–38	5	–
1938–39	28	1
Total	157	8

Debut: 5/9/31 v Thames (h) 2–0 (LH)
Honours: Division 3(S) Cup Winners medal 1935–36

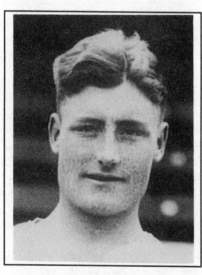

Boileau played rugby at South Street School in Coventry, but his favourite game was always football. He started as a programme seller in King Richard Street and progressed to become Harry Storer's first professional signing for City. He became a well respected member of City's team that came so close to promotion to Division 1 in 1939. During the War he guested for Notts County and Northampton Town and retired before the League restarted after the war. He was known by his team-mates as the "Old Philosopher" because of his habit of puffing long and hard on his pipe.

BOLAND, Willie John
Midfield
Born: Ennis, Co. Clare 6th August 1975
Career: Coventry City pro August 1992

Coventry City	League	F.A.Cup	Lge.Cup
1992–93	0+1s	–	–

Debut: 1/5/93 v Chelsea (a) 1–2 (Sub)

Young Irishman Boland earned his chance as substitute towards the end of the 1992–93 season as a reward for some outstanding performances for City's youth and reserve sides. He made his first team debut at the age of 17 whilst still only a first year YTS player and so still had a lot to learn. He is a product of City's increasingly successful Irish scouting system.

BOOTY, Martyn James
Right Back
Born: Kirby Muxloe 30th May 1971
Career: YTS Coventry City, pro c/s 1989, Cambridge United (trial) May 1993, Coventry City July 1993, Swindon Town (trial) June 1993.

Coventry City	League	F.A.Cup	Lge.Cup
1989–90	–	–	–
1990–91	–	–	–
1991–92	2+1s	2	1
1992–93	–	–	–
Total	2+1s	2	1

Debut: 30/10/91 v Arsenal (h) 1–0 (RB) League Cup

Young defender Martyn Booty started brightly in late 1991 as a replacement for the injured Brian Borrows. His progress was severely dented by a serious knee injury suffered against Cambridge United in January 1992, which kept him out of action until the spring of 1993. Ironically it was Cambridge who gave him a trial in May 1993, but he returned to City and signed a new contract.

BORROWS, Brian
Right Back
Born: Liverpool 20th December 1960
Career: Apprentice Everton, pro April 1980, Bolton Wanderers March 1983, Coventry City June 1985 (£80,000).

Coventry City	League	F.A.Cup	Lge.Cup
1985–86	41	1	4
1986–87	41 – 1	5	5
1987–88	32+1s	2	3
1988–89	38 – 1	1	3
1989–90	37 – 1	1	8
1990–91	38 – 6	4	5
1991–92	34+1s	2 – 1	3
1992–93	36+2s–2	1	2 – 1
Total	297+4s–11	17 – 1	33 – 1

Debut: 17/8/85 v Manchester C. (h) 1–1 (RB)
Honours: 1 England B Cap (at City)

Borrows vied with Gary Stevens, the future England full back, at Everton but was sold to Bolton in March 1983. In just over two seasons at Burnden Park he impressed greatly and was one of the best full backs in the lower divisions. He was bought by Don Mackay and established himself immediately as a skilful and intelligent right back. In his eight seasons at Highfield Road, Borrows has become one of the City's highest appearing players, primarily because he has had few injuries. Ironically it was injury that robbed him of a Wembley appearance in the 1987 Cup Final, when he suffered a knee injury in the last League game of the season against Southampton.

BOURTON, Clarence Frederick Thomas (Clarrie)
Centre Forward
Born: Paulton 30th September 1908
Died: 24th April 1981
Career: Paulton United, Bristol City 1927, Blackburn Rovers c/s 1928, Coventry City April 1931, Plymouth Argyle October 1937, Bristol City 1937, Retired 1944.

Coventry City	League	F.A.Cup
1931–32	40 – 49	2 – 1
1932–33	39 – 40	4 – 3
1933–34	30 – 25	2
1934–35	39 – 26	3 – 3
1935–36	39 – 23	2 – 2
1936–37	36 – 9	–
1937–38	5	–
Total	228– 172	13 – 9

Debut: 29/8/31 v Fulham (a) 3–5 (CF)

Harry Storer was a great judge of talent, but it is highly unlikely that even he realised what effect Bourton – his first buy for City as manager in April 1931 – would have in the following years. It was something of a coup that centre–forward Bourton even signed for Coventry, as in his first 66 first team outings for Blackburn Rovers, then well established in the top ten of Division 1, he had scored 47 goals. In his first season, Bourton established the record for the most goals scored for City in a season, including a magnificent run of 11 in consecutive games, a feat which has not been equalled since. In that first season, he also scored 7 hat–tricks, including a treble in the 8–0 crushing of high–flying Crystal Palace. Supported by Jock Lauderdale and Billy Lake, City raced to 108 goals that season and the chant of "the old five" became established at Highfield Road. Throughout the period of Division 3 (South) football, Bourton was a prolific goalscorer, indeed he was the highest scorer in the Division in the 1931–32 and 1932–33 seasons, scoring a total of 43 in the latter. It was fitting that he should score the final goal in Division 3 (South), with the winner in the 2–1 victory over Torquay illustrating Bourton's ability to poach goals.

He was there for a tap-in despite typically heavy marking, which was a burden he had to face during his spell at City. In Division 2, Bourton fared less well, and with the tighter and more efficient defences at the higher level, he scored only 9 goals in 41 games. After a short spell at Plymouth he moved back to Bristol City. His six and a half years there were mostly as player-manager, before his retirement in 1944. He will be remembered as the man who shattered City's goalscoring records, amassing 172 League goals, 9 F.A. Cup goals and 7 Division 3 (South) Cup goals in a total of 250 games; he scored 13 hat-tricks for City (all in Division 3), and perhaps it was a pity for both Bourton and City that he did not play Division 2 football until the age of 28.

BOWDEN, Frank
Outside Left

Born: Birmingham 1902
Career: Darwen (Sparkbrook), Birmingham 1925, Kidderminster Harriers 1926, Stourbridge c/s 1927, West Ham United c/s 1928, Coventry City May 1929, Evesham Town 1931, Kidderminster Harriers June 1933–1937.

Coventry City	League	F.A.Cup
1929–30	6 – 1	–
1930–31	24 – 6	3 – 2
1931–32	8 – 1	2
Total	38 – 8	5 – 2

Debut: 5/10/29 v Clapton Orient (h) 5–2 (OL) 1 goal

Bowden played one First Division match for Birmingham, before moving onto Kidderminster, Stourbridge and finally being bought by West Ham, where he failed to make the first team. Signed by City's James McIntyre, he proved an able back-up for Billy Pick and stepped into his shoes once Pick had transferred to Watford in December 1930. Bowden started in Harry Storer's team for the 1931–32 season, but was rejected by his new manager and moved on to Evesham Town.

BOWEN, Thomas George (Tommy)
Inside Right

Born: West Bromwich 1900
Career: Bush Rangers, Walsall July 1921, Wolverhampton Wanderers March 1924, Coventry City c/s 1928, Kidderminster Harriers August 1930.

Coventry City	League	F.A.Cup
1928–29	9 – 3	–
1929–30	2	–
Total	11 – 3	–

Debut: 25/8/28 v Norwich C. (h) 3–0 (IR) 2 goals

Signed by Walsall for their first season back in the League, Bowen was pushed straight into the first team. He showed himself to be an accomplished inside right, scoring 19 goals in 80 games. He then made 4 appearances in Wolves' successful run-in to the Division 3 (North) championship, and eventually scored 24 goals in 94 appearances. Surplus to requirements he moved to City, but despite scoring twice on his debut against Norwich on the opening day of the season, he was an overall disappointment.

BOWMAN, David
Midfield

Born: Tunbridge Wells, 10th March 1964
Career: Salvesen Boys Club, Heart of Midlothian c/s 1980, Coventry City December 1984 (£150,000), Dundee United May 1986 (£40,000).

Coventry City	League	F.A.Cup	Lge.Cup
1984–85	9+1s	1	–
1985–86	29 – 2	0+1s	4 – 1
Total	38+1s–2	1+1s	4 – 1

Debut: 15/12/84 v Southampton (h) 2–1 (Mid)
Honours: 4 Scotland Full Caps
      1 Scotland U–21 Caps
      Scottish Cup Runs.–up Medal 1987, 1988, and 1991

Bowman was signed as a bright prospect, but he never progressed as City had hoped and proved to be a disappointment. Curtis and Sillett allowed him to move to Dundee United, where Bowman has resurrected his career, playing in midfield and right back. He has even become a full Scottish international, which was not considered possible while he was at City.

BOXLEY, Jack
Outside Left
Born: Cradley Heath 31st May 1931
Career: Stourbridge, Bristol City October 1950 (£2,000), Coventry City December 1956, Bristol City August 1960, Chippenham Town July 1961, Welton Rovers.

Coventry City	League	F.A.Cup
1956–57	23 – 7	–
1957–58	38 – 5	1
1958–59	15 – 3	1 – 1
1959–60	16 – 2	–
Total	92 – 17	2 – 1

Debut: 29/12/56 v. Southend Utd. (a) 2–1 (OL) 1 goal

Boxley was a quick and tricky winger who was able to pitch in with his share of goals. Signed by Harry Warren, Boxley came to Highfield Road with his Ashton Gate team mate, Jimmy Rogers. Warren needed a winger to supply Ken McPherson and Boxley fitted the bill, but he often had to move to inside left to accommodate Ray Sambrook. Injuries restricted his performances and he was allowed to move back to Bristol City, the club where he had previously played consistently well for six seasons before signing for City.

BRADBURY, William (Bill)
Inside Forward
Born: Matlock 3rd April 1933
Career: Modern Machines 1949, Coventry City May 1950, Birmingham City November 1954, Hull City October 1955 (£4,000), Bury February 1960 (£5,000), Workington November 1960 (£3,000), Southport July 1961 (£1,500), Wigan Athletic June 1962, Prescot Cables c/s 1963, Kirkby Town March 1964, Retired c/s 1964.

Coventry City	League	F.A.Cup
1950–51	–	–
1951–52	1	–
1952–53	–	–
1953–54	22 – 7	–
1954–55	1	–
Total	24 – 7	–

Debut: 27/10/51 v. Nottingham Forest (h) 3–3 (LH)

Bradbury was one of a crop of good City youngsters, but like so many others in the fifties, was sold in favour of experience. He had shown glimpses of his ability in early 1954, but was sold in exchange for Ken Rowley of Birmingham. Rowley flopped and Bradbury moved to Hull, where he was a great favourite with the fans, scoring a hatful of goals in his first five years at the club.

BRADFORD, David W.
Midfield
Born: Manchester 22nd February 1953
Career: Apprentice Blackburn Rovers, pro August 1971, Sheffield United July 1974, Peterborough United (loan) October 1976, West Bromwich Albion December 1976, Detroit Express 1978, Washington Diplomats 1981, Coventry City November 1981, Tulsa Roughnecks April 1982, Seattle Sounders April 1983, Tulsa Roughnecks 1984.

Coventry City	League	F.A.Cup	Lge.Cup
1981–82	6 – 1	1	–

Debut: 21/11/81 v. West Ham United (a) 2–5 (Mid)

Bradford was a fast but small player, who went to America after his career in England was going nowhere. He had been a regular in Sheffield United's Division 1 team, but could not make the grade at The Hawthorns. The Astroturf pitches of America suited his style of play. His signing for City was a gamble and he showed he had lost the stamina necessary for the English game.

BRAZIL, Alan Bernard
Forward
Born: Glasgow 19th July 1953
Career: Apprentice Ipswich Town, pro May 1977, Detroit Express (loan) April 1978, Tottenham Hotspur March 1983 (£500,000), Manchester United June 1984 (£700,000), Coventry City January 1986 (£300,000), Queen's Park Rangers June 1986 (£200,000), Retired Spring 1987, Witham Town c/s 1987, Woolongong City (Australia) 1988, Chelmsford City July 1988, F.C. Baden (Switzerland) September 1988, Bury Town 1989–90.

Coventry City	League	F.A.Cup	Lge.Cup
1985–86	15 – 2	–	–

Debut: 1/2/86 v. Newcastle United (a) 2–3 (F) 1 goal
Honours: 13 full Scotland Caps
8 Scotland U–21 Caps
UEFA Cup Winners Medal 1980–81

Brazil emerged as a clinical striker in the Ipswich team of the late seventies and early eighties, which tasted European success and finished runners–up in the League. His partnership with Paul Mariner resulted in many goals, but his desire to better himself resulted in a move to White Hart Lane. Despite an unsettled 15 months at Spurs, Manchester United invested £700,000 for Brazil. He could not settle at Old Trafford and signed for City as part of the deal that saw free-scoring Terry Gibson move to United. Brazil scored on his debut, but in a poor side flattered to deceive. The arrival of the Curtis/ Sillett partnership saw Brazil off-loaded, and within 6 months his professional career was over due to a back injury. However he continued playing at a less demanding level.

BRESLIN, Thomas G.
Inside Left
Born: Kirkcaldy c.1906
Career: Hillhead Rovers, Glasgow Shawfield, Coventry City c/s 1925.

Coventry City	League	F.A.Cup
1925–26	11 – 2	–
1926–27	11 – 1	–
Total	22 – 3	–

Debut: 16/1/26 v Southport (h) 0–0 (IR)

Signed by Scotsman James Kerr, Breslin was a raw 19 year old inside–left when he arrived in the summer of 1925. He was considered an interesting prospect and formed a good relationship with William McGregor in the reserves. He made his debut out of position at inside–right and made 11 appearances in the first team, scoring 2 goals. The following season, he played 10 matches on the run but at outside–right. He was released at the time that Peter Ramage was signed.

BRIGGS, Thomas Henry (Tommy)
Centre Forward
Born: Chesterfield 27nd November 1923
Died: 10 February 1984
Career: Plymouth Argyle 1945, Grimsby Town May 1947, Coventry City December 1950 (£19,550), Birmingham City September 1951, Blackburn Rovers November 1952 (£15,000), Grimsby Town March 1958 (£2,000), Glentoran March 1959 (player-manager), Retired November 1960.

Coventry City	League	F.A.Cup
1950–51	7 – 3	–
1951–52	4 – 4	–
Total	11 – 7	–

Debut: 30/12/50 v. Bury (h) 5–2 (CF) 1 goal
Honours: 1 England B Cap

Tommy Briggs came to City with a goalscoring reputation, having been the Division 2 highest scorer with 39 goals in 1949/50. Signed by Harry Storer, it was anticipated that Briggs would add the firepower to push City into Division 1. But Briggs never settled at the club and failed to win over his new fans and colleagues alike. After only 11 appearances he moved on to Birmingham, before hitting a purple patch at Blackburn, scoring 143 goal in only 202 appearances. This included 7 goals against Bristol Rovers in February 1955.

BROGAN, James A. (Jim)
Left Back
Born: Glasgow 5th June 1944
Career: St. Roch's, Celtic 1963, Coventry City August 1975, Ayr United March 1977, Retired 1978.

Coventry City	League	F.A.Cup	Lge.Cup
1975–76	28	3	2
1976–77	–	–	–
Total	28	3	2

Debut: 16/8/75 v Everton (a) 4–1 (LB)
Honours: 4 Full Scotland caps
2 Scottish League appearances
European Cup Runners–up Medal 1970
Scottish League Champs. Medal 1967–68,
68–69, 69–70, 70–71, 71–72, 72–73 73–74
Scottish Cup Wins. Medal 1969, 71, 72, 74
Scottish Cup Runners–up Medal 1970, 1973
Scottish Lge. Cup Wins. Medal 1969, 1970 & 1975
Scottish Lge.Cup Runs.–up Medal 1972, 1973 & 1974

Brogan was an integral member of Celtic's dominant team of the late 1960's and early 1970's. He made his debut as a 19 year old, but it wasn't until 1968 that this tough–tackling left back made a place his own. During the next 6 years he earned many awards. He was given a free transfer and signed for City. He added some valuable experience to City's defence but his lack of speed counted against him, and he lost his place to Chris Cattin due to a hamstring injury. During the close season he suffered a calf injury and by the time he was fit again Bobby McDonald was ensconced in the first team. He signed for Ayr United and played 14 times before retiring. Outside the game he is a successful accountant, whilst his brother Frank played for Celtic, Ipswich and Halifax.

BROOK, Reginald (Reg)
Full Back

Born: Nottingham
Career: Loughborough Corinthians, Coventry City c/s 1932, Southend United 1936/7, Bristol City 1937.

Coventry City	League	F.A.Cup
1932–33	–	–
1933–34	–	–
1934–35	9	–
1935–36	–	–
Total	9	–

Debut: 19/1/35 v Watford (a) 0–2 (RB)
Honours: Division 3 (S) Cup Winners Medal 1935–36.

Full-back Brook was signed from Loughborough Corinthians and spent all his 4 seasons in the reserves. His opportunity came when first Vic Brown and then Charlie Bisby were injured. After a few steady performances he returned to the reserves, and his only other first team appearances came in the Division 3 (South) Cup, when he gained a winner's medal in April 1936. He was sold to Southend and played 3 times for the Shrimpers before transferring to Bristol City, for whom he made 71 League appearances in the 2 years before the war started. During the war he guested for both Nottingham clubs, and retired in 1942.

BROWN, Edwin (Eddy)
Centre Forward

Born: Preston 28th February 1928
Career: Preston North End September 1948, Southampton September 1950, Coventry City March 1952, Birmingham City October 1954, Leyton Orient January 1959, Scarborough c/s 1961 (player–coach), Stourbridge c/s 1964, Bedworth Town (player–manager), Wigan Athletic.

Coventry City	League	F.A.Cup
1951–52	9 – 3	–
1952–53	31 – 19	3 – 1
1953–54	33 – 20	1
1954–55	12 – 8	–
Total	85 – 50	4 – 1

Debut: 15/3/52 v. Nottingham Forest (a) 1–3 (CF)
Honours: FA Cup Runners–Up Medal 1956

Brown scored goals wherever he went. He supposedly became a professional footballer after deciding not to enter the Church. In a poor City side, Brown failed to score early on, but the following two seasons, his fast bustling style saw him score forty goals. His sale to Birmingham was to balance the books, and he showed City the shortsighted nature of their decision by scoring 90 goals in only 185 games, including a Wembley appearance in the 1956 Cup Final. He appeared in four consecutive seasons for the Blues in the newly created Fairs Cup from 1955 to 1958. After leaving football, he became a teacher and has recently retired.

BROWN, John (Jackie)
Outside Right

Born: Belfast 8th November 1914
Career: Belfast Celtic, Wolverhampton Wanderers December 1934, Coventry City October 1936 (£3,000), Birmingham September 1938, Barry Town, Ipswich Town May 1948, Retired June 1951.

Coventry City	League	F.A.Cup
1936–37	29 – 13	3 – 1
1937–38	40 – 13	1 – 2
1938–39	–	–
Total	69 – 26	4 – 3

Debut: 24/10/36 v West Ham United (h) 4–0 (OR)
Honours: 10 Northern Ireland Caps (4 at City)
　　　　　2 Republic of Ireland Caps (both at City)
　　　　　2 Irish League appearances

Signed by Harry Storer, Jackie Brown was seen as the replacement for the injured George McNestry. He had scored 7 goals in 31 League Cup games at Molineux under Major Frank Buckley and proved to be a valuable capture for only £3,000. Whilst at City he was leading scorer for two consecutive seasons and played in six internationals, four for Northern Ireland and two for the Republic of Ireland. He was a quite a character and was sold to 1st Division Birmingham in September 1938 following an unfortunate incident in a Coventry ballroom. He couldn't help the Blues stay up and the War interrupted his career. He was playing for non-league Barry Town when peace time football resumed. In May 1948 he signed for Ipswich and scored 27 goals in 103 matches before retiring aged 36 in June 1951.

BROWN, Victor Charles (Vic)
Right Back

Born: Bedford
Career: Bedford Town, Leeds United August 1929, Coventry City June 1933, Chester June 1939.

Coventry City	League	F.A.Cup
1933–34	38	2
1934–35	37	3
1935–36	23	2
1936–37	2	–
1937–38	–	–
1938–39	–	–
Total	100	7

Debut: 26/8/33 v Gillingham (h) 7–1 (RB)

Vic Brown had played only once for Leeds before signing for City in June 1933, but slotted straight in at right back. He was a regular in the side which went close to promotion in 1934 and 1935 and only injury stopped him from being part of the celebrations as City won the Division 3 (South) title in 1936. With Brown sidelined, Harry Storer bought Jack Astley and Brown was forced to be his understudy for three seasons. In June 1939 Brown moved to Chester, but the War ended his career. After guesting for Wrexham and New Brighton during this period he moved into coaching and was at Haarlem in 1948.

BROWN, William
Right Half
Born: Burnbank, Hamilton 17th November 1902
Died: Norwich 16th November 1985
Career: Bellshill Athletic, Coventry City June 1925, Wolverhampton Wanderers July 1928, Norwich City May 1929, Boulton & Paul FC May 1931 – April 1932.

Coventry City	League	F.A.Cup
1925–26	5	–
1926–27	31	3
1927–28	19	–
Total	55	3

Debut: 16/1/26 v Southport (h) 0–0 (LH)

Brown was one of the few successful Scottish signings made by James Kerr in the stormy days of the mid 1920's. It took 12 months before Brown proved himself, but he was a regular in the 1926–27 season, City's first season in Division 3 (South). He was signed by Major Frank Buckley for Wolves, the "Iron Major" not having money to spend bought players with talent and tried to mould them to his system. Brown played 34 times for the 2nd Division club, but didn't fit into the system, so moved to Norwich, before dropping the professional game and playing for the Boulton & Paul works club in the city. He spent the rest of his life in Norwich.

BRUCK, Dietmar Jurgen
Defender
Born: Denzig 19th April 1944
Career: Apprentice Coventry City, pro April 1962, Charlton Athletic October 1970 (£11,000), Northampton Town June 1972 (£4,000), Nuneaton Borough c/s 1974, Weymouth May 1975 (player–manager), Redditch United January 1976 (player–manager), Retired December 1977.

Coventry City	League	F.A.Cup	Lge.Cup
1960–61	1	–	–
1961–62	6	–	–
1962–63	24 – 1	4 – 1	2
1963–64	10	–	2
1964–65	18 – 1	1	2
1965–66	22+1s–2	4	–
1966–67	38 – 2	1	2
1967–68	33+1s–1	3	1
1968–69	12+1s	–	2+1s
1969–70	14+3s	–	–
1970–71	3+2s	–	2
Total	181+8s–7	13 – 1	13+1s

Debut: 28/4/61 v. Swindon Town (h) 1–1 (LH)

Born in Germany, Bruck was brought to England as a child and settled in Coventry. After attending Bishop Ullathorne school, he joined City and made seven appearances before signing professional forms. He came into his element under Jimmy Hill's stewardship. Despite intense competition for places, Bruck made regular appearances and the sale of Allan Harris saw Dietmar assume the left back role, to which his aggressive style of play was suited. He proved a success in City's promotion year, but struggled initially in Division 1. He was dropped to make way for Chris Cattlin. His appearances were then limited by Cattlin, the fast emerging Mick Coop, and the purchase of another German born full back, Wilf Smith.

BULL, William Harold (Harry)
Centre Forward
Born: Birmingham 1st April 1926
Career: Coventry City March 1948 – c/s 1950.

Coventry City	League	F.A.Cup
1947–48	–	–
1948–49	1	–
1949–50	–	–
Total	1	–

Debut: 7/5/49 v Luton T. (a) 0–2 (CF)

In the run–in to the end of the 1948–49 season Ted Roberts was injured. With City safely in mid–table in Division 2, a number of young reserves were given a chance. Bull was tried on the last day of the season, didn't feature again, and was given a free transfer.

BURCKITT, John D.
Full Back
Born: Coventry 16th December 1946
Career: Apprentice, Coventry City, July 1964, Bradford City (loan) March 1967, Walsall June 1968.

Coventry City	League	F.A.Cup	Lge.Cup
1964–65	5	–	1
1965–66	–	–	–
1966–67	–	–	1
1967–68	–	–	–
Total	5	–	2

Debut: 24/10/64 v. Manchester City (h) 2–2 (LB)

Burckitt was highly thought of by Jimmy Hill and made his debut whilst still only 17. He was involved in the 1–8 League Cup drubbing by Leicester and the 3–5 reverse at Rotherham. He was subsequently dropped and only made one more appearance, two years later. Sold to Walsall in June 1968, he never played for the Saddlers' first team.

BUSST, David
Centre Half
Born: Birmingham 30th June 1967
Career: Moor Green, Coventry City January 1992 (F/T).

Coventry City	League	F.A.Cup	Lge.Cup
1991–92	–	–	–
1992–93	10	0+1s	–
Total	10	0+1s	–

Debut: 13/1/93 v Norwich City (a) 0–1 (Sub) FA Cup
Full Debut: 16/1/93 v Norwich City (a) 1–1 (CH)

Insurance man Busst was playing for Moor Green when he had a trial with City under Terry Butcher. Despite the sacking of Butcher, his successor Don Howe decided to sign Busst, but it was 12 months before he made his debut. He has played as replacement for Andy Pearce at the heart of City's defence.

BUTCHER, Terence Ian (Terry)
Centre Half
Born : Singapore 28th December 1958
Career: Apprentice Ipswich Town, pro August 1976, Glasgow Rangers August 1986 (£650,000), Coventry City November 1990 (£450,000 player–manager), Halesowen Town January 1992, Sheffield Wednesday March 1992, Sunderland July 1992.

Coventry City	League	F.A.Cup	Lge.Cup
1990–91	6	–	1
1991–92	–	–	–
Total	6	–	1

Debut: 17/11/90 v Liverpool (h) 0–1 (CH)
Honours: 77 England Full cups
7 England U–21 caps
UEFA Cup Winners Medal 1980–81
Scottish Lge. Champs. Medal 1986–87, 88–89 & 89–90
Scottish Lge. Cup Winners Medal 1987
Scottish Lge.Cup Runs.–up Medal 1989 & 1990

Imposing centre half Butcher was a pillar of strength in English football in the 1980's. He played 77 times for England and appeared in three World Cup Final tournaments. His swansong was as captain in the 1990 Italy Finals. He played over 350 games for Ipswich, and in his ten years there he helped them to two consecutive runners–up positions in the League, plus a UEFA Cup final victory. When Graeme Souness took over at Rangers in 1986 Butcher was signed to steady the defence and he was part of the Rangers side that dominated Scottish football from the mid–1980's. He was suffering from a knee injury and had been involved in clashes with officials and his manager by the time John Poynton signed him as player–manager in November 1990. He played only 8 games for City and was sent off in his last comeback game against Aston Villa in the Full Members Cup in October 1991. His transfer fee of £450,000 was excessive considering his paltry input as a player and City's financial position. His time as City manager ended in January 1992 when he refused to accept a pay cut (he had retired from playing by then). He trained with Halesowen Town and played for Sheffield Wednesday reserves before making a comeback with Sunderland in July 1992. When Malcolm Crosby was sacked in 1993 Butcher was given his second chance in management.

BUTTERWORTH, Ian S.
Centre Half

Born: Nantwich 25th January 1964
Career: Apprentice Coventry City, pro August 1981, Nottingham Forest May 1985 (£200,000), Norwich City (loan September 1986), December 1986.

Coventry City	League	F.A.Cup	Lge.Cup
1981–82	13+1s	0+1s	–
1982–83	26+4s	2	3
1983–84	22+2s	3	–
1984–85	19+3s	–	2
Total	80+10s	5+1s	5

Debut: 23/1/82 v Manchester C (a) 3–1 (Sub) FA Cup
Full Debut: 17/3/82 v Manchester U (a) 1–0 (Mid)
Honours: 8 England U–21 caps (2 at City)

Tall Butterworth was groomed by Dave Sexton as a centre half of the future, but played most of his games out of position, either at right back or midfield. He overcame his initial lack of aggression to become a reliable defender. With the Kilcline/Peake partnership established, Don Mackay felt able to sell Butterworth to Nottingham Forest in May 1985 in the deal that saw Stuart Pearce move to the City Ground. At Norwich he has played over 250 matches and became captain.

BYTHEWAY, George Samuel
Outside Left

Born: Shuttlewood, near Bolsover 1902
Died: Chesterfield October 1979
Career: Mansfield Labour Club, Seymour F.C., Staveiy Town, West Bromwich Albion October 1927 (£600), Coventry City May 1933 (£100), Mansfield Town December 1933, Guildford City c/s 1936, Retired 1940.

Coventry City	League	F.A.Cup
1933–34	7 – 2	2

Debut: 14/10/33 v Charlton Ath. (h) 3–2 (OL) 1 goal

A native of the East Midlands, Bytheway only achieved a regular League first team place with Mansfield. His career prior to Field Mill was one of unfulfilled promise. He played wing–half at WBA, but only appeared 16 times in 6 seasons. Signed by Harry Storer, his 7 appearances for City came at outside–left as replacement for the injured Percy Richards. His career was hampered by a succession of serious injuries, breaking a leg three times, an ankle twice, plus his collarbone and his wrist.

CAINE, Brian
Goalkeeper

Born: Nelson 20th June 1936
Career: Burnley (amateur) 1954, Accrington Stanley c/s 1956, Blackpool February 1957, Coventry City September 1959, Northampton Town July 1961, Barrow October 1961.

Coventry City	League	F.A.Cup	Lge.Cup
1959–60	–	–	
1960–61	1		–
Total	1	–	–

Debut: 5/9/60 v. QPR (a) 1–2 (Goal)

Caine was a reserve at all of his clubs except Barrow. His only chance at City came because of injury to first choice Arthur Lightening. He moved on from City when ousted from the reserves by Bob Wesson. Whilst at Barrow, he proved to be a capable if not outstanding keeper.

CAMPBELL, Austen Fenwick
Left Half

Born: Hamsterley, Co. Durham 5th May 1901
Died: Blackburn 8th September 1981
Career: Spen Black & White, Leadgate Park, Coventry City 1919, Leadgate Park June 1921, Blackburn Rovers February 1923, Huddersfield Town September 1929, Hull City November 1935, Darwen 1936/7.

Coventry City	League	F.A.Cup
1919–20	–	–
1920–21	1	–
Total	1	–

Debut: 12/2/21 v Wolverhampton W. (a) 0–1 (LH)
Honours: 8 England Full Caps
5 Football League appearances
F.A. Cup Winners Medal 1928
F.A. Cup Runners–up Medal 1930

Austen Campbell was one of the players City missed out on after joining the Football League. With a large turnover of staff it was perhaps no surprise that City did not appreciate the talent they had on their books. He was signed from Leadgate Park in the North East on the advice of his uncle Alfred Fenwick, who was a City left half, but only played once for the club. In June 1921, he moved back to Leadgate Park where he stayed for nearly two years before he was snapped up by Blackburn Rovers. Campbell quickly established himself as one of the best left–halves in the League. He reached the semi–final of the F.A. Cup in 1925, and was an influential team member in the 1928 final

victory over Huddersfield. He soon gained the first of his eight full England caps. He moved on to Huddersfield in 1929, and played at Wembley in the 1930 F.A. Cup final defeat by Arsenal, and went on the F.A. tour of Canada. He was unable to help Hull City retain their Second Division status during his 6 months stay there. He retired after a short spell at Darwen, eventually settling in Blackburn.

CAMPLING, A. Harold (Harry)
Right Back

Born: Grimesthorpe
Career: Grimesthope Colliery, Coventry City c/s 1922.

Coventry City	League	F.A.Cup
1922–23	3	–
1923–24	3	1
1924–25	4	1
1925–26	–	–
Total	10	2

Debut: 21/4/23 v Sheffield W. (h) 1–1 (RB)

Reserve team full–back Campling, was a tough tackler who was characterised by his desperate lunging tackles. He was unable to command a regular first team place, but was considered sufficiently talented to remain a professional for 4 seasons. With the emergence of Houldey and Randle as a strong partnership, City released Campling (for financial reasons) and he was given a free transfer, and left League football.

CAPEL, Thomas A. (Tommy)
Inside Left

Born: Manchester 27th June 1922
Career: Droylsden, Manchester City November 1941, Chesterfield October 1947, Birmingham City June 1949, Nottingham Forest November 1949, Coventry City June 1954, Halifax Town October 1955, Heanor Town July 1956.

Coventry City	League	F.A.Cup
1954–55	34 – 18	4 – 4
1955–56	2 – 1	–
Total	36 – 19	4 – 4

Debut: 21/8/54 v. Bournemouth (h) 1–0 (IL)

After failing to make a significant impression with his local team, Manchester City, Capel started to score goals whilst at Chesterfield, netting 27 in two seasons. He averaged a goal every two games for the Nottingham club. It was somewhat of a coup for Jack Fairbrother to acquire the services of Forest pair Capel and Collindridge, for despite being 32, Capel continued his scoring exploits, netting 22 goals in his first season. The arrival of Jesse Carver as manager saw Capel move on to Halifax.

CARR, William McInnany (Willie)
Midfield
Born: Glasgow 6th January 1950
Career: Apprentice, Coventry City, pro July 1967, Wolverhampton Wanderers March 1975 (£100,000), Millwall August 1982, Worcester City February 1983, Willenhall Town c/s 1983, Stourbridge Town c/s 1984, Willenham Town c/s 1986.

Coventry City	League	F.A.Cup	Lge.Cup
1967–68	20+3s–1	3 – 1	0+1s
1968–69	33+3s–2	2	3
1969–70	38 – 4	2	1
1970–71	41 – 5	1	5 – 1
1971–72	42 – 8	2	1
1972–73	36 – 8	3 – 1	2 – 1
1973–74	12+1s–1	5	1
1974–75	23 – 3	3	1
Total	245+7s–32	21 – 2	14+1s–2

Debut: 2/9/67 v Arsenal (a) 1–1 (Sub)
Full Debut: 5/9/67 v Southampton (h) 2–1 (OR)
Honours: 6 Full Scotland Caps (all at City)
4 Scotland U–23 Caps (all at City)
League Cup Winners Medal 1979–80

This flame–haired Scot was a superb player, but injury ultimately ruined his career. He came to City after playing for England Schools, the result of his family moving to Cambridge when Carr was a youngster. His talent was spotted early on and enormous crowds attended reserve games to see the emerging Carr. He was thrust into the first team because of injuries and never looked back. For 7 seasons, he was a livewire in City's midfield and earned full Scottish honours, but a knee injury spelt the end of his international career. City tried to sell Carr to Wolves – for they were trying to sign Larry Lloyd – but he failed the medical although Lloyd was signed. This spelt financial strife for City, and resulted in the sale of Dennis Mortimer. Twelve months later, Carr did sign for Wolves and appeared over 200 times before a short spell at Millwall. He then ended his career with a number of non–league clubs in the West Midlands. He is well remembered as the "donkey" that allowed Ernie Hunt to score the infamous goal against Everton in 1970.

CARTWRIGHT, Leslie (Les)
Outside Right
Born: Aberdare 4th March 1952
Career: Apprentice Coventry City, pro May 1970, Wrexham June 1977, Cambridge United March 1982, Southend United (loan) September 1983, Worcester City June 1985, Coventry Sporting November 1985, Retired 1986.

Coventry City	League	F.A.Cup	Lge.Cup
1970–71	–	–	–
1971–72	–	–	–
1972–73	–	–	–
1973–74	17+6s–1	4+2s	5 – 1
1974–75	9+2s	0+1s	–
1975–76	13+2s–1	3	–
1976–77	11+8s–1	0+1s	3 – 1
Total	50+18s–3	7+4s	8 – 2

Debut: 29/9/73 v. Leicester City (a) 2–0 (sub)
Full Debut: 27/10/73 v. Stoke City (a) 0–3 (OR)
Honours: 7 full Wales Caps (5 at City)
4 Wales U–23 Caps (all at City)
Welsh Cup Winners Medal 1977–78

Cartwright took some time to break into the first team and never became a regular, despite having a talent that promised a good future.

With Tommy Hutchison on the left flank, it was difficult to find a balance with Cartwright in the team. He dropped into Division 2 with Wrexham where he enjoyed European club football by virtue of the club's success in the Welsh Cup. He spent three years at Cambridge before moving into non-league football in an attempt to protect his injured knee. After retiring, he set up business at the Wolvey Post Office just outside Coventry.

CATTLIN, Christopher (Chris)
Left Back

Born: Milnrow 25nd June 1946
Career: Milnrow 1962, Burnley (amateur) 1963, Huddersfield Town August 1964, Coventry City March 1968, Brighton & Hove Albion June 1976, Retired 1980.

Coventry City	League	F.A.Cup	Lge.Cup
1967–68	11	–	–
1968–69	32+1s	2	3
1969–70	32+1s	1	1
1970–71	14+1s	–	–
1971–72	29	2	–
1972–73	36	2	2
1973–74	5+1s	1	0+1s
1974–75	40	3	1
1975–76	14	–	–
Total	213+4s	11	7+1s

Debut: 16/3/68 v. Manchester United (h) 2–0 (LB)
Honours: 2 England U–23 Caps (both at City)

Cattlin was signed from Second Division Huddersfield when City were in a precarious position during the club's first season in Division 1. He slotted well into the team and brought vital stability to the left back position. "Spider" was a model of consistency and played a fundamental part in establishing City in the top flight. He lost his place to Jimmy Holmes in 1973, but bounced back the season after to the delight of his many fans. He was freed and went to Brighton after losing his place to Jim Brogan. He spent four years at the Goldstone Ground before establishing a rock shop in Brighton, becoming the Albion's manager in 1983. He was sacked three years later after producing a good side on a shoestring budget.

CHAPLIN, George Duncan
Full Back

Born: Dundee 26th September 1888
Died: Coventry 14th May 1963
Career: Dundee Arnott, Dundee c/s 1906, Bradford City October 1908, Coventry City May 1919, Suspended sine die May 1923.

Coventry City	League	F.A.Cup
1919–20	22	2
1920–21	32	2
1921–22	42	3
1922–23	10	–
Total	106	7

Debut: 30/8/19 v Tottenham H. (h) 0–5 (RB)
Honours: 1 Scotland Full Cap

Chaplin certainly had an eventful career! He started in his home town and earned his one and only full Scottish cap against Wales in March 1903. He played well at Bradford City helping them to reach the 1911 F.A. Cup final, but was struck down by tuberculosis. This illness took almost 3 years to clear. In May 1919, Chaplin signed for the League's new boys and was appointed captain. In the club's grey days, he was one of the few players that maintained a standard of play expected for the Football League. He was considered the best full-back ever to play for City until then. The most famous, or infamous, incident involving Chaplin, took place in April 1920. Having desperately clawed themselves to the brink of safety from virtual relegation in the club's first season in Division 2, City had to gain points in two games against Bury. Unknown to his playing colleagues, but fully condoned by his chairman David Cooke, Chaplin made arrangements with Bury players to ensure that City gained 3 points from the games. A 2–2 draw at Gigg Lane was followed by a 2–1 victory for City at Highfield Road. Rumours spread that something amiss had taken place, and an FA commission found the clubs guilty of arranging the first match, but never proved the fixing of the second. Eight Bury representatives, plus Cooke, fellow director Jack Marshall and Chaplin were all banned, sine die, in May 1923. This notorious incident was remembered for years. Chaplin remained in Coventry for the rest of his life, but never revisited Highfield Road.

CHILTON, Christopher R. (Chris)
Centre Forward

Born: Sproatley 25th June 1943
Career: Bilton 1958, Hull City August 1959, Coventry City August 1971 (£92,000), Retired 1972, Bridlington Town December 1973, Highland Park April 1974.

Coventry City	League	F.A.Cup	Lge.Cup
1971–72	26+1s–3	2 – 1	–
1972–73	–	–	–
Total	26+1s–3	2 –1	–

Debut: 11/9/71 v. Nottingham Forest (h) 1–1 (CF)

Chilton had spent 12 years at Hull banging in 224 League and Cup goals for The Tigers. His signing by Noel Cantwell was seen as an astute piece of business, but Chilton became the signing that might have been. He never really impressed and was hampered by a back injury which worsened until it forced him to retire. Twelve months later, he returned to non–league football and tried his luck in South Africa.

CHISHOLM, Kenneth McTaggart (Ken)
Inside Left

Born: Glasgow 12th April 1925
Career: Queen's Park February 1941, Partick Thistle c/s 1946, Leeds United January 1948, Leicester City December 1948, Coventry City March 1950, Cardiff City March 1952, Sunderland January 1954 (£15,000), Workington August 1956 (F/T), Glentoran February 1958, Spennymoor June 1958, Los Angeles.

Coventry City	League	F.A.Cup
1949–50	5	–
1950–51	38 – 24	1
1951–52	25 – 10	2 – 1
Total	68 – 34	3 – 1

Debut: 18/3/50 v Blackburn Rovers (h) 1–1 (IL)
Honours: 1 Scotland Victory International appearance
FA Cup Runners–Up Medal 1949

One of football's nomads, Chisholm never spent more than 2 years at a club after the war. He scored goals wherever he went and was a big, strong forward in the true British tradition. He was notorious for his love of the good life, but his answer was to train fantastically hard, including the use of tyres as rubber rings! He proved his worth by his regular goalscoring in a struggling side. Cardiff signed him in the hope of achieving promotion to Division 1. He later drifted into lower League and foreign football, eventually retiring to work in the insurance business in the North East. During the war, he guested for Chelsea, Leicester City and Portsmouth.

CHURMS, Dennis J.
Inside Left

Born: Rotherham 8th May 1931
Career: Spurley Hey, Rotherham United April 1950, Gainsborough Trinity (loan) 1952–53, Coventry City June 1956, Exeter City March 1957, Gillingham c/s 1958, Folkestone c/s 1959.

Coventry City	League	F.A.Cup
1956–57	10 – 2	–

Debut: 18/8/56 v. Exeter City (h) 1–0 (IR) 1 goal

Churms was a reserve player at both Rotherham and City. He went straight into the first team when signed and scored on his debut, but was not good enough to warrant a place. He was sold to Exeter, who were at the time the worst team in the League. Sold to Gillingham, Churms failed to make the first team and moved to Folkestone, where he was still playing at the age of 35.

CLARK, Howard W.
Midfield

Born: Coventry 19th September 1968
Career: YTS Coventry City, pro September 1986, Darlington (loan), September 1991, Shrewsbury Town December 1991, Hereford United c/s 1993 (F/T).

Coventry City	League	F.A.Cup	Lge.Cup
1986–87	–	–	–
1987–88	–	–	–
1988–89	4+5s–1	–	–
1989–90	5+5s	–	1
1990–91	0+2s	0+1s	–
1991–92	–	–	–
Total	9+12s–1	0+1s	1

Debut: 5/11/88 v West Ham United (h) 1–1 (Mid)

Clark was a fringe player who played in the successful City youth side which won the FA Youth Cup in 1987. He could not command a place, was sold, and was in and out of the Shrewsbury side, before being signed by former colleague Greg Downs, for Hereford.

CLARK, Wallace
Outside Left

Born: Jarrow 14th July 1899
Career: Durham City, Middlesbrough May 1919, Leeds United May 1921, Birmingham March 1923, Coventry City October 1924, Boston United October 1925, Barrow c/s 1926.

Coventry City	League	F.A.Cup
1924–25	8	1
1925–26	–	–
Total	8	1

Debut: 1/11/24 v Middlesbrough (h) 2–2 (OL)

Wallace Clark had been a fringe player at Middlesbrough and Leeds, playing seven and thirteen games respectively. He established himself as a regular with the Blues before being struck down by injury. City tried to sign him in the summer of 1924, but failed for undisclosed reasons. He was expected to be the missing link in the side, but proved to be a great disappointment, being replaced by local favourite, "Cute" Herbert. After Boston United his career was revived at Barrow, where he made 15 appearances.

CLARKE, George
Left Half

Born: Nottingham
Career: Redditch, Bristol City, Merthyr Town 1925, Coventry City c/s 1927, Torquay United 1928/9, Leamington Town.

Coventry City	League	F.A.Cup
1927–28	5	–

Debut: 5/9/27 v Swindon T. (h) 4–0 (LH)

Nottingham born Clarke had shown his ability at struggling Merthyr Town. He was signed for City by James Kerr as a squad player and his five appearances came when first team half backs William Brown and Jock Gardiner were injured. With Gardiner fit Clarke returned to the reserves.

CLARKE, Horace
Half Back

Born: Sheffield c. 1894
Career: Shirebrook, The Wednesday c/s 1913, Grimsby Town, Coventry City c/s 1919, Merthyr Town c/s 1920, Chesterfield c/s 1921, Exeter City 1922/3.

Coventry City	League	F.A.Cup
1919–20	17	–

Debut: 30/8/19 v Tottenham H. (h) 0–5 (RH)

A native of Sheffield, Clarke showed his ability as a versatile half–back at Grimsby during the war. The Wednesday, who held his contract, sold him to City, and he started the season at left–half, proceeding to play throughout the half back line. He was overlooked by manager Harry Pollitt. He was a regular team member with Merthyr, Chesterfield and Exeter, before leaving the League.

CLEMENTS, David
Outside Left

Born: Larne 15th September 1945
Career: Portadown, Wolverhampton Wanderers January 1963 (£5,000), Coventry City July 1964 (£6,000), Sheffield Wednesday August 1971, Everton September 1973 (£80,000), New York Cosmos 1976, Colorado Caribous 1978.

Coventry City	League	F.A.Cup	Lge.Cup
1964–65	15 – 9	–	–
1965–66	22+1s–3	2 – 1	1 – 1
1966–67	40 – 4	1	3 – 1
1967–68	40+1s–1	–	1
1968–69	37 – 3	2	4 – 1
1969–70	33 – 3	2	1
1970–71	40 – 3	1	5
1971–72	1	–	–
Total	228+2s–26	8 – 1	15 – 3

Debut: 23/1/65 v. Northampton Town (a) 1–1 (IL)
Honours: 48 full Northern Ireland Caps (21 at City)
3 Northern Ireland U–23 Caps (all at City)
1 Northern Ireland Amateur Cap
Northern Ireland Youth International

Jimmy Hill showed his ability to entice his man to City. In the summer of 1964, Clements seemed to be on the verge of signing for Bill McGarry at Watford. Hill flew to Ireland to speak to Clements and returned with his signature. This proved to be an excellent piece of business. After establishing himself in the reserves, Clements burst onto the scene with some outstanding performances.

He was able to play in any position on the left side and was one of the few players to make the transition from the Second Division to First Division immediately. This was possibly because of his great international experience. He was the equal highest capped player at City. He surprisingly moved to Sheffield Wednesday with Brian Joicey and then spent three seasons at Everton before finishing his career in the USA.

CLEWS, Alfred H.
Centre Forward
Born: Coventry
Career: Dairymen, Coventry City December 1922.

Coventry City	League	F.A.Cup
1922–23	3	–

Debut: 11/12/22 v Fulham (h) 1–0 (CF)

In normal circumstances it would be doubtful if Clews would ever have played League football, but in December 1922 City were experiencing a goal famine. Clews was on trial from Coventry Thursday League side Dairymen and scored in a reserve match . Given City's desperate need for goals, he was pushed into the side for his debut three days later. Although eager, he was sadly out of his depth and lost his place after 3 games.

COEN, R.W. Lawrence (Lol)
Outside Left/Left Back
Born: Lowestoft 4th December 1914
Died: June 1972
Career: Milford Haven 1930, West Bromwich Albion August 1932, Coventry City June 1938, South Liverpool August 1948, Dudley Town c/s 1951.

Coventry City	League	F.A.Cup
1938–39	3 – 2	–
1945–46	WWII	–
1946–47	16 – 1	2
1947–48	1	–
Total	20 – 3	2

Debut: 17/9/38 v. West Ham Utd. (a) 1–4 (OL) 1 goal

Coen was a reserve for six years at Albion, followed by a number of seasons in City's reserves. He was signed when the team was riding high in Division 2 and was never able to claim a regular place in the starting line up. After the war, Coen returned to City at the age of 32, spent two years in reserve and drifted into non–league football. During the war he guested for Wrexham, Nottingham Forest, Notts County and Stockport and was awarded the Distinguished Flying Cross.

COLLIER, Gary B.
Centre Half
Born: Bristol 4th February 1955
Career: Apprentice Bristol City, pro November 1972, Coventry City July 1979 (£325,000), Portland Timbers March 1980 (£365,000), San Diego Shockers c/s 1983.

Coventry City	League	F.A.Cup	Lge.Cup
1979–80	2	–	–

Debut: 18/8/79 v. Stoke City (a) 2–3 (CH)

Collier made headlines as the first player to move clubs through freedom of contract. He had been at Ashton Gate for seven years and was considered a dependable, if not outstanding, centre–half. He had been in conflict with manager Alan Dicks for 12 months and at the end of his contract, he moved to City for a then record fee of £325,000. Two early defeats saw the end of Collier's first team appearances. After nine months with City, he moved to the USA where he spent five seasons. Ironically, City made a profit on Collier, selling him for £365,000.

COLLINDRIDGE, Colin
Outside Left
Born: Burrough Green 15th November 1920
Career: Wombswell Main, Rotherham United c/s 1937, Sheffield United 1939, Nottingham Forest August 1950, Coventry City June 1954, Bath City July 1956.

Coventry City	League	F.A.Cup
1954–55	24 – 3	–
1955–56	10 – 3	1
Total	34 – 6	1

Debut: 21/8/54 v. Bournemouth (h) 1–0 (OL)

Characterised by his bald head, Collindridge was a crafty winger who was one of the players brought in the 1950's from higher divisions in an attempt to gain instant promotion to Division 2. His problem was that at the age of 34, the pace that he used to great benefit for The Blades and Forest was gone. He was dropped in favour of exciting prospect Ray Sambrook and moved on to Bath to end his 20 year career. During the war, he guested for Chesterfield, Notts County, Lincoln City and Oldham Athletic.

CONWELL, Laurence (Laurie)
Inside Right

Born: Aberdeen
Career: Arthurlie 1933/4, Aberdeen 1934/5, Portadown 1935/6, West Ham United 1935/6, Coventry City March 1937, Hinckley United c/s 1939.

Coventry City	League	F.A.Cup
1936–37	–	–
1937–38	2	–
1938–39	–	–
Total	2	2

Debut: 26/12/37 v Sheffield U. (h) 2–2 (IR)
Honours: 1 Irish League Representative appearance

Scotsman Conwell had to move to Ireland to achieve recognition, after 6 matches for Aberdeen. In his short time in Northern Ireland, he played in the Irish League victory over the Football League and then moved to make 8 appearances for West Ham, and scored 1 goal. He played 2 games for City as a replacement for Ted Roberts, then suffered a severe injury which forced him from the professional game. He made a short comeback with Hinckley United just before the war started.

COOK, Charles
Outside Left

Born: Glasgow 3rd June 1898
Career: Bellshill, Bradford City 1920/1, Bury 1922/3, Morton 1923, Wigan Borough January 1924, Coventry City March 1924, Bradford (P.A.) 1924/5.

Coventry City	League	F.A.Cup
1923–24	3	–

Debut: 10/3/24 v Leeds Utd (h) 2–1 (OL)

Scotsman Cook, started his professional career with 1st Division Bradford City and made 8 appearances. He played only once for the Bury before returning to Scotland with Morton. He had trials with Wigan Borough and City, but did not impress. He returned to Scotland before linking up with Bradford.

COOK, Leslie (Les)
Wing Half

Born: Blackburn, 11th November 1924
Career: Blackburn Rovers 1939, Coventry City July 1949, Rugby Town c/s 1955, Bedworth Town July 1956.

Coventry City	League	F.A.Cup
1949–50	15	–
1950–51	13	–
1951–52	27	3
1952–53	32	3
1953–54	1	–
1954–55	–	–
Total	88	6

Debut: 24/8/49 v. Luton Town (a) 0–2 (IL)

A lot was expected of Cook when he arrived from rivals Blackburn, but despite slotting straight into the first team, he did not achieve a regular first team place until Harry Barratt retired. In a transitional team, he acquitted himself well, but injury ended his League career. Once he had recovered, he was 31, which was considered old for a League player, so he was allowed to move to neighbouring Rugby Town.

COOK, Michael J.
Midfield

Born: Stroud 18th October 1968
Career: YTS, Coventry City, pro March 1987, York City (loan) September 1987, Cambridge United July 1989, York City (loan) November 1990, Wycombe Wanderers 1991, Corby Town.

Coventry City	League	F.A.Cup	Lge.Cup
1986–87	–	–	–
1987–88	–	–	0+1s
1988–89	–	–	–
Total	–	–	0+1s

Debut: 27/10/87 v Luton T. (a) 1–3 (Sub)(League Cup played at Leicester)

Cook was a leading member of City's FA Youth Cup winning side of 1987. He was however, surplus to requirements and after 2½ years as a professional he moved on to Cambridge.

COOP, Michael Anthony (Mick)

Born: Grimsby 10th July 1948
Career: Apprentice Coventry City, pro January 1966, York City (loan) November 1974, Detroit Express (loan) May 1979, Derby County July 1981 (£20,000) AP Leamington c/s 1982, Retired c/s 1983.

Coventry City	League	F.A.Cup	Lge.Cup
1965–66	–	–	–
1966–67	2+2s	–	1
1967–68	13+2s	0+1s	1
1968–69	36+1s	2	4
1969–70	41	2	1
1970–71	25	–	5
1971–72	13+2s	1	1
1972–73	42	4 – 1	2
1973–74	30 – 5	4 – 1	6 – 1
1974–75	2+4s	–	–
1975–76	42 – 4	3	2
1976–77	39 – 2	2	3 – 1
1977–78	34+1s–6	1	4
1978–79	36	2	–
1979–80	31 – 1	2	1+1s
1980–81	27	2	5
Total	413+12s–18	25+1s–2	36+1s–2

Debut: 11/9/66 v. Brighton & H.A. (h) 1–3 (RB) League Cup

Coop holds the second highest number of appearances for City behind George Curtis. For the first 14 years of City's life in Division 1, Mick Coop was a regular for all but one season. He was most comfortable at right back, but his ability to adapt to the centre half or midfield positions held him in good stead. Twice he was loaned out, but each time he bounced back to give excellent service for the club. After a miserable time at Derby, Coop moved into the antique trade in Leamington. He was wooed back to City as youth team coach in 1986 and became the first City coach to be in charge of a winning FA Youth Cup side in 1987. Coop was sufficiently fit to play for City reserves at Middlesborough in May 1987, 21 years after his League debut.

COPELAND, Charles (Charlie)
Right Back
Born: Grangetown, Middlesbrough
Career: South Bank, Leeds City August 1912, Coventry City c/s 1919, Merthyr Town c/s 1920.

Coventry City	League	F.A.Cup
1919–20	32	–

Debut: 27/9/19 v Leicester C. (a) 0–1 (RB)

Charlie Copeland was a solid right back who played either side of the Great War in professional football. He was signed by City on a free transfer from Leeds City in time for City's first season in the Football League. At the time, the deal was not particularly noteworthy, but behind the scenes, Copeland's actions were to start the process that led to the demise of the Leeds club. The Football League allowed the increase of players wages by 50% from their 1915 level, but Leeds City were not prepared to give Copeland, who was primarily a reserve, such a rise. His response was to inform the Football Association of the financial discrepancies at the club. An investigation found Leeds guilty and the club was disbanded.

CORBETT, Francis James (Frank)
Full Back
Born: Willenhall August 1903
Died: c.1970
Career: Hednesford Prims, Hednesford Town 1924, West Bromwich Albion June 1926 (£50), Coventry City May 1931, Burton Town c/s 1932, Hednesford Town 1933–1938.

Coventry City	League	F.A.Cup
1931–32	6	1

Debut: 21/11/31 v Swindon T. (a) 2–2 (RB)

After being a reserve team player at the Hawthorns for 6 seasons, playing only 12 games, Corbett came to City expecting to be a first choice full back for a struggling Division 3 (S) side. He failed to impress boss Harry Storer and moved into non–league football, and ended his career back at Hednesford Town.

COX, Ronald B. (Ron)
Centre Half

Born: Foleshill 2nd May 1919
Career: Wyken Pippin, Coventry City 1945, Atherstone Town c/s 1952, Retired c/s 1954.

Coventry City	League	F.A.Cup
1945–46	WWII	–
1946–47	10	–
1947–48	5	–
1948–49	10	1
1949–50	3	–
1950–51	–	–
1951–52	1	–
Total	29	1

Debut: 2/9/46 v WBA (h) 3–2 (CH)

The war resulted in Cox not being signed as a professional until the age of 26. Despite this, he had 7 years as deputy to George Mason, which severely restricted first team opportunities. When given his chance, he never let the side down and it was ironic that he departed the club at the same time as Mason, both of them losing out to new signing, Roy Kirk.

CRAVEN, John A.
Centre Half

Born: St. Annes 15th May 1947
Career: Apprentice Blackpool, pro 1965, Crystal Palace September 1971 (£40,000), Coventry City May 1973 (£42,000), Plymouth Argyle January 1977 (£20,000), Vancouver Whitecaps c/s 1979, California Surf c/s 1981.

Coventry City	League	F.A.Cup	Lge.Cup
1973–74	30 – 3	6	2
1974–75	25+1s–2	3	0+1s
1975–76	27+1s–3	2	2
1976–77	4+1s	1	2
Total	86+3s–8	12	6+1s

Debut: 25/8/73 v. Tottenham Hotspur (h) 1–0 (CH)

Gordon Milne signed Craven as a replacement for Roy Barry. He knew what he was signing as they were team mates at Blackpool. Craven had shown his robust style of play at Blackpool and Crystal Palace as a striker, but Milne switched him to the back four. The arrival of Larry Lloyd and departure of Dennis Mortimer saw the versatile Craven revert to a midfield position, where his competitive style was well suited. His City career ended with the arrival of Terry Yorath and he signed for Plymouth. After 18 months, he moved to the USA where he ended his playing days.

CRAWLEY, Thomas (Tom)
Centre Forward

Born: Blantyre 10th November 1911
Died: 1977
Career: Blantyre Victoria, Hamilton Academicals c/s 1932, Motherwell 1934, Preston North End c/s 1935, Coventry City February 1936, Retired 1948.

Coventry City	League	F.A.Cup
1935–36	2 – 1	–
1936–37	7	–
1937–38	5	–
1938–39	18 – 14	1
1945–46	WWII	2
1946–47	13 – 1	–
1947–48	–	–
Total	45 – 16	3

Debut: 22/2/36 v Cardiff City (h) 5–1 (CF) 1 goal
Honours: Division 3(S) Cup Winners Medal 1935–36

Crawley was reserve cover for marksman Clarrie Bourton, but established himself during 1938–39, and in a 5 game spell, he scored 9 goals. After the war, he lost his sharpness, and moved to centre–half to cover George Mason. During a war–time match, he scored 8 goals against WBA, and during this period he guested for Nottingham Forest.

CRESSWELL, Philip
Outside Right
Born: Hucknall 11th May 1933
Career: Modern Machines, Coventry City May 1950, Guildford City c/s 1955.

Coventry City	League	F.A.Cup
1950–51	–	–
1951–52	–	–
1952–53	–	–
1953–54	–	–
1954–55	2	–
Total	2	–

Debut: 18/12/54 v. Bournemouth (a) 1–2 (OR)

Cresswell came from the East Midlands area which provided City with many players during this period and was one of Harry Storer's favourite recruiting areas. He was a reserve who came into the team When Gordon Nutt was sold to Cardiff. The arrival of Alan Moore pushed Cresswell out. At the end of the season he moved to Guildford, who took the Southern League title with his help.

CRISP, George Henry
Outside Left
Born: Pontypool 30th June 1911
Career: Penrhiwceiber 27th March 1962
Career: Melbourne Stars, Llanelly 1933, Coventry City November 1933, Bristol Rovers July 1935, Newport County June 1936, Colchester United c/s 1937, Nottingham Forest c/s 1939, Merthyr Town 1946/7.

Coventry City	League	F.A.Cup
1933–34	7	–
1934–35	1	–
Total	8	–

Debut: 20/1/34 v Bristol R (a) 1–4 (OL)

Welshman Crisp was only a reserve at City, and his 8 appearances came as understudy to Percy Richards and Jim Liddle. He moved to Bristol Rovers, where he was in the team that was thrashed 12–0 by Luton in April 1936 when Joe Payne scored ten goals. He rose to prominence with the newly formed Colchester United, and during hostilities he guested for Notts County, Swansea Town, Cardiff City, Aberaman and Lovells Athletic.

CRISP, John (Jack)
Outside Right
Born: Hamstead, Birmingham 27th November 1894
Died: February 1939
Career: Aston Boys, Walsall, Aston Villa (Trial) 1910, Leicester City, Ordnance F.C. 1913/4, West Bromwich Albion May 1914, Blackburn Rovers March 1923, Coventry City February 1927, Stourbridge c/s 1928, Bromsgrove Rovers October 1929, Cheltenham Town 1933, Retired 1935.

Coventry City	League	F.A.Cup
1926–27	14 – 2	–
1927–28	8 – 1	–
Total	22 – 3	–

Debut: 12/2/27 v Bournemouth & B Ath. (a) 1–2 (OR)
Honours: League Champs. Winners Medal 1919–20
1 Football League appearance

Crisp played a large part in WBA's championship winning side of 1919–20 with his ability to outrun defenders and to pop up with useful goals; that season he represented the Football League against the Irish League. He disappointed manager Fred Everiss and was sold to Blackburn for £3125, who were rebuilding under the club's first manager Jack Carr. Crisp helped Rovers to the F.A. Cup semi-final in 1925, but he was ousted from the side, which allowed James Kerr to sign him for City. He started well, but fell away and was released at the age of 33.

CROSS, Charles Henry (Charlie)
Left Half
Born: Coventry 19th February 1901
Died: Spring 1983
Career: Sideley Deasy F.C., Coventry City September 1919, Crystal Palace 1922, Wolverhampton Wanderers 1928, Merthyr Town c/s 1929.

Coventry City	League	F.A.Cup
1919–20	6	–
1920–21	4	1
1921–22	2	–
Total	12	1

Debut: 18/10/19 v Fulham (a) 0–0 (LH)

Local lad Charlie Cross was a raw 18 year old when he was pushed into the struggling City side, but he didn't impress in a poor side and was only used briefly afterwards. Rather then keep its young talent, City chose to sell. Crystal Palace gratefully bought Cross and he proceeded to play 237 games in six seasons. He had a spell at Wolves, playing three times before finishing at Merthyr for whom he made 15 appearances.

CROSS, David
Centre Forward
Born: Heywood 8th December 1950
Career: Amateur August 1968, Rochdale pro August 1969, Norwich City October 1971 (£40,000), Coventry City November 1973 (£150,000), West Bromwich Albion November 1976 (£200,000), West Ham United December 1977 (£200,000), Manchester City August 1982 (£135,000), Vancouver Whitecaps April 1983 (£75,000), Oldham Athletic October 1983 (£20,000), Vancouver Whitecaps April 1984 (£10,000), West Bromwich Albion October 1984 (F/T), Bolton Wanderers June 1985 (F/T), Bury January 1986 (F/T), Blackpool July 1986, Cyprus 1986–87, Retired.

Coventry City	League	F.A.Cup	Lge.Cup
1973–74	26 – 8	6 – 4	–
1974–75	25 – 8	3	–
1975–76	37+1s–14	3 – 1	2 – 1
1976–77	2	–	0+1s
Total	90+1s – 30	12 – 5	2+1s – 1

Debut: 17/11/73 v Leeds United (a) 0–3 (CF)
Honours: FA Cup Winners Medal 1980
League Cup Runners–up Medal 1973 & 1981

A robust centre–forward, Cross reached his peak at West Ham, securing promotion to Division 1, winning an FA Cup winners medal in 1980, and reaching Wembley in the League Cup final in 1981. He was excellent in the air, being both powerful and accurate with his heading. Whilst at City, he formed an excellent partnership with Alan Green, but was eclipsed by Mick Ferguson, which pre-empted his departure to WBA. Cross scored 2 vital cup goals against City in his career, for Rochdale in their 2–1 victory in 1971 and for West Ham in their 2–0 victory in the League Cup semi–final at Upton Park in 1981. In 1975–76, he scored 2 hat–tricks, the first at Goodison Park on the opening day and at Turf Moor on the last day of the season.

CROWE, Francis R. (Frank)
Wing Half
Born: Birmingham
Career: Apollo Works F.C., Birmingham April 1917, Coventry City September 1919, Merthyr Town 1920/1, Chesterfield 1922/3, Rochdale 1923, Merthyr Town 1924/5, Penrhiwceiber 1925.

Coventry City	League	F.A.Cup
1919–20	2	–

Debut: 27/9/19 v Leicester C. (a) 0–1 (LH)

Crowe was bought along with Joby Godfrey and Archie Smith from Birmingham, and his 2 games were against Leicester, when he showed himself to be a vigorous half back. He was soon dropped, as City seemed to gamble over the team selection every week. He was sold to Merthyr, who were making their entry into the Football League, where he continued his style of play in a struggling side.

CROWN, Laurence (Laurie)
Right Back
Born: Sunderland 29th February 1898
Career: Furness Athletic, Sunderland November 1919, Redcar, South Shields c/s 1922, Newcastle United March 1926 (£2,750), Bury May 1927 (£750), Coventry City July 1928, Retired c/s 1931.

Coventry City	League	F.A.Cup
1928–29	41	1
1929–30	41	4
1930–31	30	–
Total	112	5

Debut: 25/8/28 v Norwich C. (h) 3–0 (RB)

Laurie Crown was a gentleman, who was considered not to have enough grit to be an effective full–back. For this reason he was released by Newcastle, who made a considerable loss on the deal, having bought him from South Shields for £2750, only to sell him for £750 just over 12 months later. He was a regular at City and became one of the few 6 foot tall full–backs to play for the club. He was made club captain and performed admirably until his retirement in 1931.

CULL, John Ernest (Jack)
Outside Right
Born: Wednesbury 18th November 1900
Career: Bloxwich Strollers, Nuneaton Town c/s 1922, Shrewsbury Town c/s 1923, Stoke City September 1925 (£1,000), Coventry City August 1931, Shrewsbury Town August 1932, Crewe Alexandra August 1933, Accrington Stanley June 1934, Gateshead July 1935, Aldershot January 1936 – May 1936.

Coventry City	League	F.A.Cup
1931/32	17 – 4	–

Debut: 19/8/31 v Fulham (a) 3–5 (OR) 1 goal

Cull came late into the professional game, and by the time he signed for Stoke, he was already 24. He never established a regular place during his 6 seasons at the Victoria Ground. Cull scored on his City debut, but injury and the impressive form of Frank White, produced only sporadic performances. Cull was released, aged 31, and rejoined non–league Shrewsbury, before reviving his Football League career.

CULPIN, Paul
Forward

Born: Kirky Muxloe 8th February 1962
Career: Apprentice Leicester City, pro May 1981, Nuneaton Borough 1982, Coventry City July 1985 (£50,000), Northampton Town October 1987 (£55,000), Peterborough United October 1989 (£40,000), Barnet (loan) March 1991, Hereford United March 1992, Kettering Town March 1992, Nuneaton Borough April 1992.

Coventry City	League	F.A.Cup	Lge.Cup
1985–86	4+3s–1	–	1
1986–87	1+1s–1	–	–
1987–88	–	–	–
Total	5+4s–2	–	1

Debut: 3/9/85 v Oxford U. (h) 5–2 (Sub)
Full Debut: 14/9/85 v Aston Villa (a) 1–1 (CF) 1 goal
Honours: 5 England Semi–Professional caps

After being rejected by Jock Wallace at Leicester, Culpin scored 131 goals in three seasons with Nuneaton Borough, and City manager Don Mackay paid what was then a record fee for an English non-League player. He scored on his full debut at Villa Park, but he didn't get the opportunities many thought he deserved. With a strong City forward line, he moved on to Northampton. After 26 goals for the Cobblers he moved to Peterborough, but couldn't command a regular place for Posh. At Barnet he helped the Bees to Football League status. Back at Nuneaton, he was the highest scorer in the Southern League in 1992/93.

CURTIS, Ernest Robert (Ernie)
Forward

Born: Cardiff 1st June 1907
Died: Cardiff late November 1992
Career: Severn Road Old Boys, Cardiff Corinthians, Cardiff City November 1925, Birmingham March 1928 (£3,000), Cardiff City November 1933, Retired c/s 1934, Coventry City February 1935, Hartlepools July 1937, Retired 1938.

Coventry City	League	F.A.Cup
1934–35	8	–
1935–36	11 – 1	–
1936–37	2 – 1	–
Total	21 – 2	–

Debut: 9/2/35 v Bristol C. (h) 1–1 (OL)
Honours: 3 Wales Full Caps
        Wales Amateur & Schoolboy International
        FA Cup Winners Medal 1927
        FA Cup Runners–Up Medal 1931
        Welsh Cup Winners Medal 1926–27

Curtis was signed by Cardiff as an amateur, whilst serving an electrician's apprenticeship with the Cardiff City Corporation. He signed professional terms in 1926, and in his first season won an FA Cup winners medal. He was at that time, the youngest player to appear in an FA Cup final and appeared in the only non-English side to win the cup. In 1931, whilst with Birmingham, he made another trip to Wembley but returned with a loser's medal. With Birmingham refusing Curtis' release for internationals (which were played on Saturday League programme days), he gained only gained 3 full caps for Wales. After returning to Cardiff, Curtis clashed with the management about wages, and decided to hang up his boots. City brought him out of retirement and he was used as cover for both wing positions. During the war, he was a prisoner of war at the hands of the Japanese from 1941 to 1945.

CURTIS, George W.
Centre Half

Born: Dover 5th May 1939
Career: Snowdown Colliery, Coventry City October 1955, Aston Villa December 1969, Retired c/s 1972

Coventry City	League	F.A.Cup	Lge.Cup
1955–56	3	–	
1956–57	19	–	
1957–58	15	1	
1958–59	43	2	
1959–60	45	2	
1960–61	46 – 1	3	2
1961–62	46	2	1
1962–63	45	9 – 1	2
1963–64	46	2	2
1964–65	41 – 1	1	4
1965–66	42 – 5	4	4
1966–67	42 – 2	1	3
1967–68	3+1s	–	–
1968–69	28+2s–2	2 – 1	3
1969–70	19+1s	–	1
Total	483+4s–11	29–2	22

Debut: 21/4/56 v Newport County (a) 2–4 (LB)
Honours: England Youth International 1956, 1957, 1958

Curtis was the 'Iron Man' around whom City's successful 1960's side was built. He holds the record for the most appearances for City, and his total of 534 full appearances will take some beating in the future. He arrived at City in October 1955 on the recommendation of Harry Barratt, the ex-City player, then manager of Snowdown Colliery.

Curtis made his debut at left back when still 16, and by the Spring of 1957 he had established himself at centre half. In the ten years that followed Curtis missed only six games. He was captain of Jimmy Hill's side that rose from Division 3 to Division 1 and his fierce tackling style was an example for his team-mates. The high point of his career, playing in Division 1, saw also his darkest hours. In only his second match he broke his leg at Nottingham Forest. He fought back to full fitness but whilst he was absent the heart had been removed from City's side. Looking to the future, manager Noel Cantwell sold him to Aston Villa for £25,000 in December 1969 and replaced him with Roy Barry. After retiring Curtis returned to City as Commercial Manager and became the club's first paid Director. He formed part of the management team with John Sillett which transformed City in 1986-87. In recent times there has been some controversy about his salary at a time when City have financial problems, but this should not tarnish the memories of Curtis' efforts and achievements for City.

DAILEY, William S. (Bill)
Wing Half

Born: Coatbridge
Career: Shieldmur Celtic, Bradford (PA) 1924/5, Coventry City c/s 1926.

Coventry City	League	F.A.Cup
1926-27	5 - 1	-

Debut: 28/8/26 v Northampton T. (h) 0-3 (RH)

Bill Dailey was another of the large number of Scots recruited by James Kerr in the summer of 1926. He was bought as a solid wing-half, but was dropped following 2 successive defeats at the start of the season. His last game was the 1-8 embarrassment at Exeter. Dailey was a teacher, playing football as an amateur. Whilst at City, he gained employment at Narrow Lane Schools.

DALEY, Alan James
Outside Left

Born: Mansfield 11th October 1927
Died: 1975
Career: Pleasley Boys Club 1944, Mansfield Town September 1946, Hull City July 1947, Bangor City c/s 1948, Worksop Town 1949, Doncaster Rovers March 1950, Peterborough United 1950, Boston United 1951, Scunthorpe United June 1952, Corby Town c/s 1953, Mansfield Town November 1953, Stockport County February 1956, Crewe Alexandra June 1958, Coventry City November 1958, Cambridge United January 1961, Burton Albion c/s 1961, Sutton Town c/s 1963.

Coventry City	League	F.A.Cup	Lge.Cup
1958-59	22 - 5	1	
1959-60	27 - 5	2 - 1	
1960-61	7	-	1
Total	56 - 10	3 - 1	1

Debut: 22/11/58 v Crystal Palace (a) 1-1 (OL)

"Digger" Daley spent 20 years flitting in and out of League football, but wherever he played he was always a first team regular. Bought by Billy Frith from Crewe, Daley was part of the side that achieved promotion from Division 4 and featured heavily in City's first season back in the 3rd. An honest player, Daley performed well until losing his place to Stewart Imlach and then finally moved out of League football. He was the father of Steve Daley, the ex-Wolves and Manchester City £1 million player.

DALTON, Reginald (Reg)
Centre Half

Born: Coventry
Career: Edgewick, Coventry City c/s 1919, Halifax Town (Trial) December 1923, Foleshill Great Heath February 1924, Nuneaton Town October 1925, Foleshill Great Heath November 1925.

Coventry City	League	F.A.Cup
1919-20	7	-
1920-21	28 - 1	-
1921-22	17 - 3	-
1922-23	2	-
1923-24	-	-
Total	54 - 4	-

Debut: 28/2/20 v Hull City (a) 1-0 (CH)

Signed with Edgewick team mate Ambrose Jarvis, Dalton had impressed in his junior side's exploits, and despite offers from other clubs, he opted for City. He took his time to settle but played his part, at centre half, in stopping City's alarming slide. He was versatile, as he also appeared at right–half. Along with George Chaplin, he became the longest serving player bought for the first season in Division 2. A serious knee cartilage injury ended his career at City. He attempted a comeback with Halifax in December 1923, but soon moved back to Coventry, signing for Foleshill Great Heath after failing to play a game for the Shaymen.

DALY, Gerard Anthony (Gerry)
Midfield
Born: Cabra, Dublin 30th April 1954
Career: Bohemians 1971, Manchester United April 1973, Derby County March 1977 (£175,000), New England Teamen (loan) May 1978, New England Teamen (loan) May 1979, Coventry City August 1980 (£300,000), Leicester City (loan) January 1983, Birmingham City August 1984, Shrewsbury Town October 1985, Stoke City March 1987 (£15,000), Doncaster Rovers July 1988, Telford United Autumn 1989.

Coventry City	League	F.A.Cup	Lge.Cup
1980–81	34+1s–8	4 – 2	7 – 1
1981–82	19 – 4	2	–
1982–83	2	–	–
1983–84	27–1s–7	3+1s	–
Total	82+2s–19	9+1s–2	7 – 1

Debut: 19/8/80 v. Liverpool (h) 0–0 (Mid)
Honours: 47 Full Republic of Ireland Caps (16 at City)
FA Cup Runners Up Medal 1976

After great success at Manchester United, Daly moved onto Derby County to end an acrimonious period under Tommy Docherty. The Doc was sacked shortly after and was appointed manager by Derby. After failing to keep the Rams in Division 1, Daly was eager to sign for City. He was brought in Gordon Milne to add class and experience to a young midfield. He did this, being instrumental in City's run to the League Cup semi final. Surprisingly, he was out of favour in Dave Sexton's reign and despite having the smallest squad in Division 1, City loaned Daly out to Leicester for five months. He returned to prominence in Bobby Gould's makeshift side, before moving for Division 2 football at Birmingham. Moved into management at the end of playing career with Telford United.

DAVIDSON, John C.
Inside Right
Born: Glenbuck
Career: Glenbuck Athletic, Solway Star, Coventry City c/s 1922, Kilmarnock July 1923, Nithsdale Wanderers November 1923, Thornhill January 1924.

Coventry City	League	F.A.Cup
1922–23	4	–

Debut: 26/8/22 v Notts County (h) 1–2 (IR)

Scotsman Davidson, earned a place in the opening line–up for the 1922–23 season after impressing in practice games. He looked out of his depth and was promptly dropped. He returned for the match against Fulham in December 1922 after a goal famine. Although keen he lacked the necessary quality, was released, and played one game for Kilmarnock.

DAVIDSON, Robert Trimming (Bobby)
Inside Forward
Born: Lochgelly 27th April 1913
Career: Bowhill Rovers, St. Bernards c/s 1930, St. Johnstone c/s 1932, Arsenal February 1935, Coventry City November 1937, Hinckley Athletic c/s 1948 (player-manager), Redditch Town c/s 1949 (player-manager).

Coventry City	League	F.A.Cup
1937–38	16 – 1	1
1938–39	28 – 8	–
1945–46	WWII	–
1946–47	1	–
1947–48	2	1
Total	47 – 9	2

Debut: 6/11/37 v. Bradford P.A. (h) 0–0 (IR)
Honours: Scottish League representative 1934

Davidson arrived at City in an exchange deal involving Les Jones. He was a good player who never achieved his potential especially at City. Never a high scorer, Davidson was the least prolific of City's forwards. His post war outings were limited to three because of the consistency of Barratt and Dearson. With little prospect of first team football, Bobby moved into local management with Hinckley Athletic. Davidson guested for Notts County, Halifax Town, Bradford City and Darlington during the war.

DAVISON, Thomas Reay (Tommy)
Centre Half

Born: West Stanley 3rd October 1901
Died: Derby 1st January 1971
Career: Tanfield Lea Rovers, Stanley United, Durham City 1921, Wolverhampton Wanderers June 1923, Derby County July 1925, Sheffield Wednesday January 1931, Coventry City July 1932, Rhyl Athletic July 1935 (player-coach), Bath City August 1936.

Coventry City	League	F.A.Cup
1932–33	36 – 2	4 – 1
1933–34	40 – 3	2
1934–35	24	2
Total	100 – 5	8 – 1

Debut: 27/8/32 v Torquay U. (a) 3–3 (CH)

Davison left the coalmine to join Durham City in their first Football League season, where he attracted the attention of Wolves. It wasn't until he joined Derby that he established himself as a top class centre half. George Jobey was the manager who signed him for both Wolves and Derby. It took some time to impress, but he played 30 games in Derby's League runners up side of 1929–30. He left for Hillsborough once future England international Jack Barker matured and in July 1932, signed for City. He played his part when City reversed the trend of conceding too many goals. As at Derby, Davison was ousted from City's centre half position by a rising star, George Mason. He signed for Rhyl Athletic as player coach.

DEARSON, Donald John (Don)
Left Half

Born: Ynysybwl 13th May 1914
Died: Birmingham 24th December 1990
Career: Llantwit, Barry Town August 1932, Birmingham April 1934, Coventry City February 1947, Walsall March 1950, Nuneaton Borough August 1951, Retired c/s 1952.

Coventry City	League	F.A.Cup
1946–47	14	–
1947–48	30 – 7	2 – 1
1948–49	24 – 2	1
1949–50	16 – 1	1
Total	84 – 10	4 – 1

Debut: 22/3/47 v. Manchester City (h) 1–1 (LH)
Honours: 3 Wales Full Caps
15 Wales War-Time Internationals
1 Wales Amateur Cap

Signed by City in 1947, Dearson immediately made an impression helping City to a safe finishing position in his first season. A strong solid player, Dearson was a vital member of City's team, being able to adapt as full back, wing half, and inside forward. Capped three times before the war by Wales, Dearson's best form was during the war. Unfortunately by the end of the war, Don's age counted against him, at the cost of more caps for his country. He signed for City at the age of 32 and moved to Walsall at the age of 36 where he had one excellent season before moving into non-league football at Nuneaton. During the war, Dearson guested for Northampton, Nottingham Forest, Wrexham and WBA.

DEEMING, Harry
Outside Left

Born: Bedworth
Career: Exhall Colliery, Coventry City October 1923, Nuneaton Town August 1925, Foleshill Great Heath August 1927.

Coventry City	League	F.A.Cup
1923–24	–	–
1924–25	1	–
Total	1	

Debut: 2/5/25 v Southampton (a) 0–3 (OR)

Local Harry Deeming was an outside left who had played in City's reserves for 18 months before making his only League appearance, playing out of position, on the final day of the 1924–25 season.

DENNISON, John S.
Wing Half

Born: Castle Douglas
Career: Amble F.C, Coventry City.

Coventry City	League	F.A.Cup
1922–23	4	1

Debut: 17/2/23 v Bradford C. (h) 2–1 (RH)

Reserve Dennison gained all his appearances following injury to captain Joe Jones and Foster Robinson. For the last 2 games of the season he was a makeshift outside left, but didn't earn a continued stay with the club.

DENTON, Peter R.
Outside Right

Born: Gorleston 1st March 1946
Career: Gorleston, Coventry City March 1964, Luton Town January 1968.

Coventry City	League	F.A.Cup	Lge.Cup
1963–64	–	–	–
1964–65	–	–	–
1965–66	9 – 1	1	–
1966–67	–	–	–
1967–68	1	–	–
Total	10 – 1	1	–

Debut: 13/11/65 v. Ipswich Town (h) 3–1 (OR)

This blond haired winger was a great success in the Football Combination side, but could not break into the first team regularly because of the form and fitness of Ronnie Rees. His opportunities were created when Dave Clements was injured and Rees was switched to outside left. Denton was originally a right half and might have been seen more regularly if he had remained in the this position. He moved out of the professional game after an unsuccessful period at Luton.

DEVLIN, William
Outside Right

Born: Belfast
Career: Belfast Celtic, Coventry City 1920/1.

Coventry City	League	F.A.Cup
1920–21	1	–
1921–22	8	–
Total	9	–

Debut: 7/5/21 v Nottingham Forest (a) 2–0 (OL)

Devlin was a reserve winger who made his debut on the final day of the season in May 1921. His lack of weight and height acted against him and he moved on.

DICKIE, Alan L.
Goalkeeper

Born: Charlton 30th January 1944
Career: Apprentice West Ham United, pro February 1962, Coventry City March 1967, Aldershot July 1968.

Coventry City	League	F.A.Cup	Lge.Cup
1966–67	–	–	–
1967–68	2	1	–
Total	2	1	–

Debut: 22/8/67 v. Nottingham Forest (a) 3–3 (Goal)

Signed from West Ham as cover for Bill Glazier. Dickie was competent, which he proved in his few first team outings for the Hammers and City, but he was not of the class to oust Glazier. After a year as understudy Dickie moved onto Aldershot in search of regular first team football. He is now in the police force.

DINSDALE, Norman
Centre Half

Born: Leeds 20th June 1898
Died: Nottingham September 1970
Career: Anston United, Notts County 1920, Coventry City March 1928, Bristol Rovers c/s 1930, Kidderminster Harriers 1931.

Coventry City	League	F.A.Cup
1927–28	12 – 5	–
1928–29	42 – 1	1
1929–30	36 – 4	4 – 2
Total	90 – 10	5 – 2

Debut: 10/3/28 v Bournemouth & B. Ath (a) 3–2 (CH)

85

Norman Dinsdale was a hard, uncompromising centre half who provided some much needed steel and experience to City's floundering side. His transfer almost didn't happen. After 300 games for Notts County he and fellow Magpie, Alf Widdowson were bought for £500 by City Director Albert Saunders in the hope of ensuring that City didn't finish bottom of Division 3 (South). The cheque bounced and it was only the intervention of former Chairman David Cooke that ensured the bill was paid. Dinsdale proved to be a good buy and was appointed club captain by new manager James McIntyre. Despite shoring up City's defence in his 95 games, he was sold to ease City's financial problems. There was constination, but he was 32 and the fee of £425 did provide a profit for City.

DIXON, Michael (Mike)
Centre Forward
Born: Willesden 14th March 1937
Career: Sundon Park, Arsenal, Brighton & Hove Albion, Hitchin Town, Luton Town April 1957, Coventry City May 1961, Cambridge United c/s 1962, Stevenage, Dunstable Town July 1965, Biggleswade.

Coventry City	League	F.A.Cup	Lge.Cup
1961–62	18 – 12	1	1

Debut: 25/8/61 v. Newport County (h) 3-0 (CF)

Brought in by Billy Frith, Mike Dixon was very successful, with an excellent strike rate in a struggling side. Injury at the wrong time in Jimmy Hill's first months, meant an end to his first team run. Dixon was part of Hill's plans but preferred to move into non–league football with Cambridge United, and later to Dunstable, where he settled. His son Kerry, also played for Dunstable before moving into Football League.

DOBBS, Eric
Right Back
Born: Forehoe 15th October 1920
Career: Coventry City August 1946, Bristol Rovers July 1948, Lockheed Leamington.

Coventry City	League	F.A.Cup
1946–47	2	–
1947–48	3	–
Total	5	–

Debut: 8/4/47 v. Swansea Town (h) 3-2 (RB)

An adequate reserve, Dobbs' first team outings were because of others' injuries. Moved from Second Division City to Third division Bristol Rovers where he could not break into the first team.

DOBSON, Anthony J. (Tony)
Defender
Born: Coventry 5th February 1969
Career: YTS Coventry City, pro May 1986, Blackburn Rovers January 1991 (£250,000).

Coventry City	League	F.A.Cup	Lge.Cup
1986–87	1	–	–
1987–88	1	–	–
1988–89	16	–	0+1s
1989–90	28+2s	–	3+2s
1990–91	5+1s– 1	–	–
Total	51+3s-1	–	3+3s

Debut: 28/3/87 v Aston Villa (a) 0-1 (LB)

Local lad Dobson had been part of City's successful 1987 FA Youth Cup side at centre half but was converted to left back by John Sillett. He established himself as a capable full back when he ousted Greg Downs. He scored one of the most spectacular goals seen at Highfield Road in August 1990. In a friendly against Banik Ostrava he ended a mazy run from his own half by hitting a fierce drive from 45 yards which flew into the back of the net. When he lost his place to Paul Edwards, Dobson languished in the reserves until former City boss Don Mackay signed him and Steve Livingstone for Blackburn in January 1991. At Blackburn he has become understudy to Alan Wright.

DORMAN, Donald (Don)
Right Half/Inside Right
Born: Birmingham 18th September 1922
Career: BSA Sports, Birmingham City May 1946, Coventry City September 1951, Walsall October 1954.

Coventry City	League	F.A.Cup
1951–52	23 – 2	–
1952–53	36 – 17	3 – 1
1953–54	30 – 8	1 – 1
1954–55	1 – 2	1
Total	90 – 29	4 – 2

Debut: 22/9/51 v Sheffield U (h) 1-1 (RH)

Dorman came to City in a player exchange, which took Tommy Briggs to Birmingham. In his first season at City he played at right half in the team which was relegated. Moving to inside right, Dorman was more successful, scoring 2 hat-tricks in consecutive games in late 1952. A good pro, Dorman proved a success at Walsall after City, beginning the revival of a very poor side. During the war, Dorman was twice wounded and was captured in the battle of Arnhem.

they would accept for his signature. The reply was that City wouldn't accept £2,000 and Manchester Town Hall! Ironically in the summer of 1926, City offered him lower terms which he rejected, and they could only recoup £555 for him from Reading. After only 12 games for the Royals he broke his leg badly which forced his retirement. He returned to Coventry to work at Morris Engines.

DOUGALL, James H. (Jimmy)
Outside Right

Born: Wishaw 1900
Career: Clelland Juniors, Motherwell, Coventry City December 1919, Reading c/s 1926 (£555), Retired 1927.

Coventry City	League	F.A.Cup
1919–20	11 – 1	2
1920–21	37 – 2	2
1921–22	32	2
1922–23	35 – 3	1
1923–24	33 – 3	–
1924–25	41 – 2	3
1925–26	38 – 2	1
Total	227 – 13	11

Debut: 10/1/20 v Luton T. (a) 2–2 (OR) (FA Cup)
Honours: Scotland Junior international

Young Scotsman Jimmy Dougall was recommended to Harry Pollitt in December 1920, and this Scottish junior international immediately made the outside right position his own. He was a tricky winger who could always be guaranteed to provide a supply of crosses for his centre forward. He was frequently watched by bigger clubs, and after mesmerising the Manchester United defenders and scoring at Old Trafford in January 1924, City were asked what fee

---

DOWNS, Gregory (Greg)
Left Back

Born: Carlton 13th December 1958
Career: Apprentice Norwich City, pro December 1976, Conneticut Bicentennials (loan) March 1977, Torquay United (loan) November 1977, Coventry City July 1985 (£40,000), Birmingham City July 1990 (F/T), Hereford United June 1991 (F/T).

Coventry City	League	F.A.Cup	Lge.Cup
1985–86	40+1s	–	4
1986–87	39 – 2	6 – 1	5
1987–88	27 – 2	2	2+1s
1988–89	20+2s	–	3 – 1
1989–90	16+1s	1	7 – 1
Total	142+4s4	9 – 1	21+1s–2

Debut: 17/8/85 v Manchester City (h) 1–1 (LB)
Honours: FA Cup Winners Medal 1987

The balding Downs had made over 200 appearances for Norwich before signing for City. He left Carrow Road under a cloud, after being omitted from the Canaries' League Cup Final side in 1985. He was signed by City as a replacement for Stuart Pearce, and suffered the barracking of the crowd in his early weeks. He won the fans over with his enthusiastic performances, which were typified by his Wembley appearance in 1987. He was given a run around by Chris Waddle in the first half but took control in the second. Once Tony Dobson began to establish himself at left back, Downs was given a free transfer and moved to Birmingham. He took over as player–coach at Hereford, with control of on–field activities in May 1992, after ex–City manager John Sillett stood down.

DRINKELL, Kevin S.
Forward

Born: Grimsby, 18th June 1960
Career: Apprentice Grimsby Town, pro June 1978, Norwich City June 1985 (£105,000), Glasgow Rangers July 1988, Coventry City October 1989 (£800,000), Birmingham City (loan) October 1991, Falkirk July 1992 (F/T).

Coventry City	League	F.A.Cup	Lge.Cup
1989–90	21+1s–5	1	3+1s–2
1990–91	11+4s	3+1s	0+2s
1991–92	2+2s	–	–
Total	34+7s–5	4+1s	3+3s–2

Debut: 4/10/89 v Grimsby T. (h) 3–0 (F) 1 goal (League Cup)
Honours: Scottish Championship Medal 1988–89
Scottish League Cup Winners Medal 1988–89
Scottish Cup Runners–up Medal 1989

Drinkell was a successful striker throughout his career, until he came to City. He had made his debut in 1977 at the age of 16 while he was still an apprentice. He scored 108 goals in 319 appearances for the Mariners and was a snip at £105,000 for 2nd Division Norwich. He continued his scoring at Carrow Road, netting 57 goals in only 150 games to establish the Canaries in Division 1. A big money move to Rangers brought him Scottish domestic honours. With City needing a striker John Sillett broke City's transfer record to buy Drinkell for £800,000. He scored in his first three games and looked sharp, but his form dipped dramatically and he failed to establish a first team place in his last two years at City. Birmingham couldn't afford to buy him after his loan spell at St. Andrew's and he was given a free transfer. After a promising start for the Bairns the goals once again dried up.

DUGDALE, Alan
Centre Half

Born: Liverpool 11th September 1952
Career: Apprentice Coventry City, pro November 1969, Charlton Athletic October 1977 (£50,000), Barnsley (loan) August 1979, Tulsa Roughnecks 1980.

Coventry City	League	F.A.Cup	Lge.Cup
1969–70	–	–	–
1970–71	–	–	–
1971–72	–	–	–
1972–73	16+3s	2	–
1973–74	39	6	6
1974–75	24	3	1
1975–76	34	3	2
1976–77	25	2	3
1977–78	1	–	–
Total	139+3s	16	12

Debut: 30/9/72 v. Chelsea (h) 1–3 (LB)

A hard centre half, Dugdale came into the side with Jeff Blockley's move to Arsenal. Not the most skilful of defenders, Dugdale did have the ability to stop forwards. He had the problem of never having a regular central defending partner, with Barry, Craven, Lloyd Holmes and Hindley taking the job in five years. He finally lost his place to Jim Holton and was allowed to move to Charlton. He went to Barnsley on loan where he was given the chance to sign, but he preferred to return to Charlton. Unfortunately, he didn't play again, moving to America.

DUNN, John
Inside Right

Born: Scotland
Career: Cambuslang, Wigan Borough 1925/6, Coventry City c/s 1926, Crewe Alexandra (Trial) November 1927, Kings Park January 1928.

Coventry City	League	F.A.Cup
1926–27	29 – 4	3 – 1

Debut: 28/8/26 v Northampton T. (h) 0–3 (IR)

Another Scotsman signed by James Kerr in the summer of 1926, Dunn had scored 6 goals in 13 games for Wigan Borough. He wasn't a high scoring inside right, but was considered a fetcher and carrier. Unfortunately his manager was not impressed with him and he lost his place in April 1927. Ironically, after scoring in the final 2 matches, he was released and his eventual trial period at Crewe was unsuccessful.

DUTTON, Charles A. (Charlie)
Centre Forward

Born: Rugeley 10th April 1934
Career: Brereton Social, Derby County (amateur) 1951, Coventry City November 1952, Rugby Town (loan) November 1952, Northampton Town March 1956, Lockheed Leamington

(loan) December 1956, Bedworth Town c/s 1957, Rugby Town c/s 1958, Hinckley Town November 1958, Brereton Social January 1963.

Coventry City	League	F.A.Cup
1952–53	–	–
1953–54	8 – 3	–
1954–55	12 – 2	1
1955–56	7 – 4	–
Total	27 – 9	1

Debut: 14/9/53 v. Bournemouth (h) 2–0 (CF) 1 goal

A favourite of the crowd because of his all action style, nonetheless, Dutton could not maintain a regular first team place, coming into the side when injury sidelined Eddy Brown and Jack Lee. Dutton was used for Jesse Carver's continental style of play, being better on the ground rather than in the air. However, injury and the need for a big man lost Dutton his place to Ken McPherson, whose arrival was soon followed by Dutton's departure for a short spell with Northampton before returning to Warwickshire with Lockheed.

DWIGHT, Roy
Forward

Born: Belvedere 9th January 1933
Career: Hastings United, Fulham June 1950, Nottingham Forest August 1958, Gravesend & Northfleet United, Coventry City January 1962, Millwall January 1964, Dartford August 1965.

Coventry City	League	F.A.Cup	Lge.Cup
1961–62	18 – 7	–	–
1962–63	13 – 1	2	–
1963–64	–	–	–
Total	31 – 8	2	–

Debut: 27/1/62 v Portsmouth (a) 2–3 (CF)
Honours: FA Cup Winners Medal 1959

A class player who could play at centre forward or on the wing. Dwight had been a success at Fulham, and at Forest picked up an FA Cup Winners medal in 1959 – scoring before breaking his leg at Wembley. A lengthy healing period greatly affected his confidence. He was allowed to drift to non-league Gravesend, from where his old team mate at Fulham, Jimmy Hill, snapped him up. He played at centre forward, moving to the wing with the arrival of Terry Bly. The successful wing partnership of Rees and Humphries limited his appearances. He is the uncle of Elton John.

DYKE, Archibald (Archie)
Outside Right

Born: Newcastle–under–Lyme
Career: Newcastle P.S.A., Stoke 1908/9, Burslem Port Vale 1912, Stoke 1913, Aston Villa 1913/4, Port Vale 1915, Stafford Rangers 1918, Coventry City 1920, Blackpool 1921, Congleton Town 1922.

Coventry City	League	F.A.Cup
1920–21	3	–

Debut: 2/10/20 v Sheffield W. (h) 2–3 (OR)

Archie Dyke was a well–known figure in the Potteries before the Great War, having had two spells at both Stoke and Port Vale. He played 9 times at outside right for Aston Villa between 1913 and 1915. He played three times for City as replacement for the injured Jimmy Dougall. He appeared once for Blackpool the following season.

DYSON, Paul Ian

Born: Birmingham 27th December 1959
Career: Apprentice Coventry City, pro June 1977, Stoke City July 1983 (£150,000), West Bromwich Albion March 1986 (£60,000) Darlington March 1989 (F/T), Crewe Alexandra c/s 1989 (F/T), Telford United c/s 1990, Solihull Borough c/s 1992.

Coventry City	League	F.A.Cup	Lge.Cup
1977–78	–	–	–
1978–79	2	–	–
1979–80	18 – 2	2	–
1980–81	41 – 2	4	9
1981–82	40 –	3	2
1982–83	39 – 1	3	3
Total	140 – 5	12	14

Debut: 23/12/78 v. Everton (h) 3–2 (CH)
Honours: 4 England U–21 Caps (all with City)

Dyson was one of the many players brought through the ranks from City's youth team in the late 1970's. He developed a good partnership with Gary Gillespie, which reached it's peak in the League Cup run in 1980–81 which ended at the semi–final stage. His final year at City proved to be traumatic and he moved to Stoke City where life was even more traumatic, as the club registered it's worst season in Division 1. After moving to WBA, he signed for Darlington, in an attempt to help prevent the club being relegated from the League, but he failed. Later, he played for his ex–City team mate Gerry Daly at Telford United.

EDWARDS, Paul R.
Left Back

Born: Birkenhead 25th December 1963
Career: Marine 1983, Altrincham 1986, Crewe Alexandra January 1988, Coventry City March 1990, Wolverhampton Wanderers (loan August 1992) October 1992 (£100,000).

Coventry City	League	F.A.Cup	Lge.Cup
1989–90	6+2s	–	–
1990–91	22+1s	2	4
1991–92	4+1s	–	2
1992–93	–		–
Total	32+4s	2	6

Debut: 17/3/90 v Sheffield Wed. (h) 1–4 (Sub)
Full Debut: 31/3/90 v Manchester Utd. (a) 0–3 (LB)

Ginger haired Paul Edwards was one of a number of Crewe players that have progressed to the 1st Division. Unlike players such as David Platt and Geoff Thomas, Edwards struggled in the top flight. He always looked clumsy and lost his place to the experienced Kenny Sansom. With the arrival of Phil Babb, Edwards was third choice left back and joined Wolves after a loan spell there.

ELLIOTT, Charles S. (Charlie)
Left Back/Centre Half

Born: Bolsover, 24th April 1912
Career: Sheffield Wednesday 1929, Chesterfield 1930, Coventry City July 1931, Retired c/s 1948.

Coventry City	League	F.A.Cup
1931–32	13	–
1932–33	20 – 1	3
1933–34	1	–
1934–35	2	–
1935–36	12 – 1	–
1936–37	4	–
1937–38	–	–
1938–39	6	–
1945–46	WWII	2
1946–47	28	1
1947–48	9	–
Total	95 – 2	6

Debut: 20/2/32 v Luton Town (a) 1–3 (LB)

Charlie Elliott was a great servant for City, but at no time during his 17 years at the club was he a regular first team choice.

Signed by fellow cricketer Harry Storer, he was a tall, solid defender who could play at either left back or centre half. Consequently, he was used as reliable cover for Charlie Bisby, George Mason and Walter Metcalf. Indeed, he performed admirably as a replacement in the final 2 games of the 1935–36 season in which City clinched promotion to Division 2. Goals were rare for Elliott, but he did score against Bournemouth in November 1935 in his only game at centre forward. During the war, Elliott guested for both Nottingham clubs and played cricket for Derbyshire, later becoming a well respected test umpire. When Jack Fairbrother resigned in October 1954, Elliott took over as City's caretaker manager until the end of the season.

EMERSON, Dean
Midfield

Born: Salford 27th December 1962
Career: Stockport County February 1982, Rotherham United July 1985 (£40,000), Coventry City October 1986 (player-exchange), Hartlepool United July 1992 (£50,000).

Coventry City	League	F.A.Cup	Lge.Cup
1986–87	19	2	–
1987–88	19+1s	–	–
1988–89	18	–	0+1s
1989–90	12	–	1
1990–91	20+4s	4	1+2s
1991–92	10+10s	–	2+1s
Total	98+15s	6	4+4s

Debut: 19/10/86 v Wimbledon (h) 1–0 (Mid)

Flame haired Emerson had impressed John Sillett in the Rotherham side that lost to City in the League Cup in 1986. He signed for City and was an immediate success, where his determined tackling and understanding with Lloyd McGrath was a great bonus to City. On a snowy afternoon in March 1987 he suffered a bad knee injury which has caused him problems ever since. Consequently he was unable to hold a regular place and was sold to Hartlepool United. He was skipper of the side that dumped Premier League Crystal Palace from the 3rd Round of the FA Cup in January 1992.

ENGLISH, Thomas S. (Tommy)
Forward
Born: Cirencester 18th October 1961
Career: Apprentice Coventry City, pro June 1979, Leicester City September 1982, Rochdale September 1984, Plymouth Argyle September 1984, Colchester United November 1984, Canberra City Olympians c/s 1985, Colchester United September 1985, Wealdstone c/s 1987, Bishop's Stortford c/s 1988, Colchester United c/s 1989, Crawley Town.

Coventry City	League	F.A.Cup	Lge.Cup
1979–80	30 – 10	2	3 – 2
1980–81	24+4s–7	1 – 1	4 – 2
1981–82	8	–	–
1982–83	–		
Total	62+4s–17	3 – 1	7 – 4

Debut: 18/8/79 v. Stoke City (a) 2-3 (IR)

English burst into the first team with the the potential to be a better player than Mark Hateley or Garry Thompson. His first 18 months in Division 1 seemed to prove that view, but the arrival of Dave Sexton saw English decline to become a reserve player. He was hampered by his off-the-field antics and it was no surprise that Sexton swapped him for Jim Melrose. At Leicester, English continued his decline and moved into the lower divisions. Whilst at Colchester and Wealdstone, he linked up with ex-City favourite, Mick Ferguson.

EVANS, Gareth J.
Forward
Born: Coventry 14th January 1967
Career: Apprentice Coventry City, pro January 1985, Rotherham United October 1986 (player-exchange), Hibernian February 1988 (£50,000).

Coventry City	League	F.A.Cup	Lge.Cup
1984–85	–	–	–
1985–86	5+1s	–	1 – 1
1986–87	0+1s–1	–	–
Total	5+2s	–	1 – 1

Debut: 2/11/85 v Manchester United 0-2 (CF)
Honours: Scottish League Cup Winners Medal 1990-91

After being overawed in his early days at City, Evans appeared to improve in 1986. He never had the chance to prove himself however, since he was sold to Rotherham in the deal that brought Dean Emerson to City. Having scored 18 goals for the Merry Millers in 18 months he was sold to Hibernian where he ultimately teamed up with ex-City striker Keith Harchen. He has not been a heavy scorer in a traditionally low-scoring side, but achieved success in the League Cup in 1990-91. He has tried to return South, but to no avail.

EVANS, John J. (Jack)
Centre Forward
Born: Coventry 11th March 1926
Career: Modern Machines, Coventry City 1942, Nuneaton Borough 1952, Banbury Spencer, Lockhead Leamington.

Coventry City	League	F.A.Cup
1945–46	WWII	–
1946–47	–	–
1947–48	–	–
1948–49	1 – 1	–
1949–50	3	–
1950–51	4	–
1951–52	–	–
Total	8 – 1	–

Debut: 2/4/49 v Fulham (h) 1-0 (CF) 1 goal

A local lad whose first team opportunities were severely limited by the form of Ted Roberts. When in the team however, Jack Evans was disappointing, although he was playing in a struggling team. He scored his only goal on his debut, and it was no surprise that City released him.

FARMER, Ronald J. (Ron)
Left Half
Born: Guernsey 6th March 1936
Career: North Athletic Club 1951, Nottingham Forest 1952, Coventry City November 1958, Notts County October 1967, Grantham Town April 1969, Retired 1970.

Coventry City	League	F.A.Cup	Lge.Cup
1958–59	26 – 1	–	
1959–60	33 – 5	2	
1960–61	36 – 3	3 – 2	2
1961–62	26 – 7	1	1
1962–63	22 – 6	5 – 1	1
1963–64	44 – 11	2	1
1964–65	25 – 3	–	1
1965–66	34+1s–9	4 – 1	4
1966–67	32+2s–2	1	2 – 1
1967–68	3+1s	–	
Total	281+4s–47	18 – 4	12 – 1

Debut: 20/11/58 v Chester (h) 5-1 (LH)

Ron and his brother Bill, came to England from Guernsey in the 1950's to play for Nottingham Forest. Billy Frith swooped in November 1958 for Farmer and Lightening, both of whom proved to be excellent buys. City were in Division 4 at the time and the emergence of the half back line up of Farmer, Curtis and Kearns, was the lynch pin for City's surge to Division 1 in the 1960's. Farmer was a specialist penalty taker, but was also a prolific scorer in open play. Indeed, he is the only player to have scored a hat–trick from the half back line – in City's 5–1 victory over Crystal Palace in August 1963. Injury and the signing of Brian Lewis, saw Farmer unable to gain a regular place in Division 1. He moved to Notts County on a free transfer and retired after a short spell at Grantham. A short coaching spell at City, was followed by Farmer working for Massey Ferguson.

FENWICK, Alfred Randolph
Left Half
Born: Hamsterley, Co. Durham 26th March 1891
Died: 1975
Career: Blyth Spartans, Hull City 1910, West Ham United c/s 1914, Coventry City December 1919, Craghead United 1921, Lincoln City 1921, Notts County 1923, Ashington 1924/5, Lincoln City 1924/5, Shirebrook c/s 1926, Newark Town c/s 1927, Horncastle Town September 1928, Shildon Athletic 1928/9.

Coventry City	League	F.A.Cup
1919–20	24	2
1920–21	26 – 1	1
Total	50 – 1	3

Debut: 20/12/19 v Clapton Orient (h) 0–0 (LH)

Fenwick was a useful left half who was one of Harry Pollitt's first signings as he attempted to move City off the bottom of Division 2 in December 1919. He and George Hadley battled for the left half position and in the summer of 1921 he moved back North. He encouraged Notts County to sign him and he played 6 games for the Magpies, 3 of them in Division 1. He was still playing for Shildon Athletic aged 39, and was the uncle of England International Austen Campbell, arranging for his nephew to sign for City when he was a youngster. After one game the young Campbell was released and City lost another star!

FERGUS, Alexander (Alex)
Right Back
Born: Bathgate
Career: Kirkintilloch Rob Roy, Bathgate February 1922, Burnley 1924, Coventry City March 1927.

Coventry City	League	F.A.Cup
1926–27	12	-
1927–28	18	1
Total	30	1

Debut: 12/3/27 v Brentford (h) 3–1 (RB)

Scotsman Fergus was signed by 1st Division Burnley in 1924 after figuring prominently in the Bathgate side that finished high in the Scottish Second Division. In his 38 games at Turf Moor he showed himself to be a strong full back and it was James Kerr's knowledge of Scottish players that enabled him to sign the experienced Fergus. He was replacement for the injured Charlie Houldey and was himself troubled with injury. He was released in the summer of 1928.

FERGUSON, David
Outside Left
Born: Bonnybridge 11th March 1929
Career: Alloa Athletic, Coventry City October 1956.

Coventry City	League	F.A.Cup
1956–57	4	1

Debut: 13/10/56 v. Millwall (h) 1–2 (OL)

Signed by City in October 1956, Ferguson was selected immediately for the first team. After five sporadic games, he was dropped and didn't play again. He is one of many Scottish players that did not last long at City.

FERGUSON, Michael John (Mick)

Centre Forward

Born: Newcastle–Upon–Tyne 3rd October 1954

Career: Apprentice Coventry City, pro December 1971, Everton August 1981 (£280,000), Birmingham City (loan November 1982) c/s 1983, Coventry City (loan) March 1984, Brighton & Hove Albion October 1984, Colchester United March 1986, Wealdstone c/s 1987, Retired 1988.

Coventry City	League	F.A.Cup	Lge.Cup
1971–72	–	–	–
1972–73	–	–	–
1973–74	–	–	–
1974–75	12 – 2	–	–
1975–76	11+4s–3	–	0+2s–1
1976–77	32 – 13	–	3 – 2
1977–78	30 – 17	1	4
1978–79	16+2s–6	–	1
1979–80	17 – 10	1	2
1980–81	3	1	–
1983–84	7 – 3	–	–
Total	128+6s–54	3	10+2s–3

Debut: 1/2/75 v. Leeds United (a) 0–0 (CF)

The impact that Mick Ferguson had on Coventry City's fortunes during the late 1970's was immense. He was a first team regular for only two seasons, but he will be remembered for his part in transforming City from being nervous and relegation-haunted into an attractive and high scoring side that was liable to steam–roller any opposition. Ferguson made his City debut in February 1975, over three years after being signed as a professional by Noel Cantwell in December 1971. His early appearances were limited by the presence of David Cross in the side. His sale to WBA in August 1976, was the herald for Ferguson's impact upon Division One. 1976/77 was a bad season for City. At the end, there was a desperate dog fight for survival, which of course, City achieved by drawing with Bristol City in the last game of the season. Despite chronic injuries to the squad, Ferguson had scored 13 goals in 32 League games and towards the end of the season, had worked up a good partnership with Ian Wallace. Few could have anticipated season 1977–78. City were a revelation, with Ferguson at the forefront. By March he had scored 17 goals, including 3 hat-tricks, when injury struck. He played only 3 more games in the last two and a half months of the season, which surely cost City a place in Europe. Ian Wallace will always be remembered as the more prolific scorer of the partnership, but more credit should go to Ferguson. He not only scored more hat-tricks in Division 1 than any other player for City (four), but he created many of Wallace's goals by perfect flick-on headers. His City career was curtailed by injury and the introduction of younger players like Garry Thompson, Mark Hateley and Tom English, but his departure to Everton was not the last City saw of him. In March 1984 with City once more in relegation trouble, Bobby Gould loaned Fergie from Birmingham's reserves for the final few games. He played 7 times, scoring 3 vital goals. The most significant was in the final game, a 2–1 victory over Norwich. This saved City and relegated his own team, Birmingham City! After several years in the lower division and non–league football, Ferguson retired in 1988 to become a community development officer in Sunderland.

FERGUSON, Robert L.

Outside Left

Born: Stewarton c.1900

Career: Stewarton Thistle, Fulham c/s 1925, Coventry City c/s 1926, Fulham January 1928 (£50).

Coventry City	League	F.A.Cup
1926–27	40 – 4	3
1927–28	–	–
Total	40 – 4	3

Debut: 28/8/26 v Nothampton T. (h) 0–3 (OL)

Ferguson's first appearance for City was in a practice match in August 1926 under the name of "White". He impressed with his pace and excellent ball control and was duly signed from Fulham where he had made 17 appearances. His form was patchy but he retained his place, until his game deteriorated and his speed faded. He was overlooked at the start of the 1927–28 season and moved back to Fulham for £50 in January 1928, making 4 more appearances for the Cottagers.

FINDLAY, Norman
Goalkeeper
Born: Walker–on–Tyne
Career: Newcastle City 1913/4, Blyth Spartans 1913/4, Heart of Midlothian c/s 1914, Walker Celtic, Coventry City May 1921.

Coventry City	League	F.A.Cup
1921–22	2	–
1922–23	–	–
1923–24	–	–
1924–25	–	–
1925–26	7	–
Total	9	–

Debut: 17/11/21 v Derby Co. (h) 1–2 (Goal)

Signed as cover for Jerry Best, Findlay showed himself to have splendid judgement and anticipation whilst in the reserves. He could not get into the team, and had to content himself with appearing only when Best was injured. He was released in May 1926 and whilst at City, was the tallest goalkeeper at the club – at 5 feet 9 inches!

FITTON, George Arthur (Arthur)
Outside Left
Born: Melton Mowbray May 1902
Died: Worcester September 1984
Career: Kinver Swifts, Cookley St. Peters, Kidderminster Harriers c/s 1922, West Bromwich Albion October 1922 (£400), Manchester United March 1932 (£1,000), Preston North End December 1932, Coventry City c/s 1935, Kidderminster Harriers 1938, Retired 1939.

Coventry City	League	F.A.Cup
1935–36	24 – 12	2
1936–37	25 – 8	2
1937–38	5 – 2	–
Total	54 – 22	4

Debut: 31/8/35 v Reading (a) 1–2 (OL)

Arthur Fitton was one of a number of players that served City after playing most of their early years in WBA's reserves. He made a total of 99 first team appearances for the Baggies – but only once in his last 18 months as they achieved promotion to Division 1. He dropped down to 2nd Division Manchester United, but only played 12 times in his 9 months with the club. He moved on to Preston and helped them to return to Division 1. Signed by Harry Storer, Fitton added a bit of sparkle to City's forward play, to help them rise from Division 3(S). Prior to his death, he was game warden at Kinver National Trust Park near Kidderminster.

FLEMING, Terence Maurice (Terry)
Outside Right/Right Back
Born: Marston Green 5th January 1973
Career: YTS Coventry City, pro c/s 1991, Northampton Town July 1993 (F/T).

Coventry City	League	F.A.Cup	Lge.Cup
1990–91	0+2s	–	–
1991–92	–	–	–
1992–93	8+3s	–	0+1s
Total	8+5s	–	0+1s

Debut: 2/2/91 v Wimbledon (a) 0–1 (Sub)
Full Debut: 15/8/92 v Middlesbrough (h) 2–1 (RB)

Youth team winger Fleming was pushed into the first team as substitute in February 1991 as City were short of forwards, just a couple of weeks after manager Terry Butcher had sold Steve Livingstone. He was out of his depth and didn't play again until August 1992. With injuries to Brian Borrows and Martyn Booty, Fleming was converted to right back and equipped himself well until Borrows returned. He didn't progress as expected and was given a free transfer.

FLYNN, Sean
Midfield
Born: Birmingham 13th March 1968
Career: Halesowen Town, Coventry City November 1991 (£20,000).

Coventry City	League	F.A.Cup	Lge.Cup
1991–92	21+1s–2	–	–
1992–93	4+3s	–	–
Total	25+4s–2	–	–

Debut: 26/12/91 v Sheffield Utd (a) 3–0 (Mid) 1 goal

Birmingham–born Flynn was signed by Terry Butcher, made a dream debut – scoring at Bramhall Lane – and showed himself to be a highly competitive midfielder. He was still learning and was kept in the reserves by new boss Bobby Gould as City changed the style for the 1992–93 season. His best assets are his determination and heading ability.

FOSTER, Samuel Bernard (Sam)
Centre Forward
Born: Southwell
Career: Southwell Federation, Lincoln City 1919/20, Mansfield Town c/s 1920, Coventry City October 1920, Mansfield Town 1921, Newark Town c/s 1922

Coventry City	League	F.A.Cup
1920–21	10 – 4	–

Debut: 25/12/20 v Cardiff C. (h) 2–4 (CF) 1 goal

Signed from Midland League Mansfield, Foster was pushed into the first team when Bert Millard was moved back to centre half. He started well, scoring on his debut at Ninian Park and scored some useful goals – including one against Wolves in City's 4–0 victory best League victory to that time. He lost his place to Sammy Stevens and his only other League appearance was for Lincoln.

FRANCIS, Gerald C.J. (Gerry)
Midfield

Born: Chiswick 6 December 1951
Career: Apprentice Queen's Park Rangers, pro June 1969, Crystal Palace July 1979, Queen's Park Rangers February 1981 (£150,000), Coventry City January 1982 (£150,000), Exeter City August 1983 (F/T) (Player–Manager), Cardiff City August 1984, Swansea City October 1984, Portsmouth November 1984, Wimbledon c/s 1985, Bristol Rovers September 1985, Wimbledon 1986, Bristol Rovers July 1987 (Player–Manager).

Coventry City	League	F.A.Cup	Lge.Cup
1981–82	18 – 1	2	–
1982–83	32 – 1	2	1
Total	50 – 2	4	1

Debut: 16/1/82 v. Ipswich Town (h) 2–4 (Mid)
Honours: 12 full England Caps
        6 England U–23 Caps

Francis came to City a highly experienced midfielder, who would provide a wealth of experience in City's promising, but very inexperienced side. His desire to move from his native London to City was twofold, for he respected Dave Sexton's coaching and the Loftus Road pitch was causing problems with his knees. The fee of £150,000 seemed excessive at the time, and this proved to be the case when Francis was later given a free transfer by Bobby Gould. He moved around the lower divisions, including management at Exeter, before managing Bristol Rovers and then QPR. Probably the greatest moment of Francis' career, came in May 1975 when he scored two goals for England in the 5–1 victory over Scotland at Wembley.

FRITH, William (Billy)
Wing Half

Born: Sheffield 9th June 1912
Career: Worksop Town, Mansfield Town 1930, Chesterfield 1931, Coventry City May 1932, Port Vale 1945, Coventry City c/s 1946, Retired February 1947.

Coventry City	League	F.A.Cup
1932–33	3 – 1	–
1933–34	8	–
1934–35	22	1
1935–36	30 – 2	2
1936–37	28 – 1	3
1937–38	32	–
1938–39	39	1
1946–47	7	1
Total	169 – 4	8

Debut: 17/9/32 v Newport County (h) 3–1 (IL) 1 goal

Brought in by Harry Storer as a promising youngster, Billy Frith became a vital member of City's successful 1930's side. He was a solid and dependable attacking wing half, who was highly admired in the game. During the war, he guested for Leicester City before taking a management position at Port Vale in 1945. After 12 months, League football recommenced and Frith returned to City as a player. The resignation of Dick Bayliss in February 1947, because of ill health, saw Frith become City manager. He twice became City manager, but was sacked after each period, feeling that he had been made the scapegoat; City were the only League club that he managed. Frith turned to teaching in Coventry, which he enjoyed until his retirement in 1977.

FURLONG, Paul Anthony
Forward

Born: Wood Green 1st October 1968
Career: Enfield 1986, Coventry City July 1991 (£100,000), Watford July 1992 (£250,000).

Coventry City	League	F.A.Cup	Lge.Cup
1991–92	27+9s–4	1+1s	4 – 1

Debut: 17/8/91 v Manchester C (h) 0–1 (Sub)
Full Debut: 24/8/91 v QPR (a) 1–1 (F)

Striker Furlong had played for five years at Enfield before signing for City for a considerable fee for a non–League player. He started well, but as the side declined so Furlong's form dipped. He had talent but was often played out of position on the left wing. He was sold to Watford, and has scored goals regularly in a side that could provide him with good service.

GAFFNEY, Peter
Centre Half

Born: Edinburgh c.1899
Career: Loanhead Mayflower, Bo'ness February 1920, Hamilton Academicals April 1920, Alloa Athletic c/s 1921, Dunfermline Athletic 1922/3, Doncaster Rovers c/s 1923, Denaby United February 1924, Barrow June 1924, New Brighton April 1925, Coventry City c/s 1926, Ashington 1927, Torquay United c/s 1927, Aldershot November 1927.

Coventry City	League	F.A.Cup
1926–27	2	1 – 1

Debut: 28/8/26 v Northampton T. (h) 0–3 (CH)

The experienced Gaffney was signed as a centre half around which City's new Division 3(S) side could be built. After a shocking performance on his debut, in the 0–3 defeat by Northampton at Highfield Road, he was immediately replaced by the former Birmingham centre half Alec McClure. Gaffney played twice more, scoring against Lincoln in the FA Cup defeat in December 1926, before being released. After moving to Ashington he moved onto Torquay for the club's first season in the Football League.

GALLACHER, Kevin William
Forward

Born: Clydebank 23rd November 1966
Career: Duntocher Boys Club, Dundee United 1983, Coventry City January 1990 (£900,000), Blackburn Rovers March 1993 (player–exchange & £1.5 million).

Coventry City	League	F.A.Cup	Lge.Cup
1989–90	15 – 3	–	2
1990–91	32 – 11	2	3 – 5
1991–92	33 – 8	1	4 – 2
1992–93	19+1s–6	1	2
Total	99+1s–28	4	11 – 7

Debut: 3/2/90 v Chelsea (h) 3–2 (OR)
Honours: 17 Scotland Full Caps (10 at City)
2 Scotland B Caps
7 Scotland U–21 Caps
UEFA Cup Runners–up Medal 1987
Scottish Cup Runners–up Medal 1987 & 1988

Gallacher came to City in January 1990 for a record £900,000 fee. He had started brightly at Dundee United and showed his electrifying pace and great finishing in the side that reached two Scottish Cup finals and the 1987 UEFA Cup final. He was languishing at Tannadice when signed by John Sillett and after a period of transition he proved to be a terrier–like forward who could score excellent goals, but injuries hampered his performances at times. He resurrected his Scotland career and played in the 1992 European Championships. In a bid to keep City's finances in check he was sold to Blackburn Rovers for a fee of £1.5 million and Roy Wegerle. His value of £2.5 million is the highest ever for a City player. His father William and his grandfather Patsy both played for Celtic.

GALLAGHER, Thomas H.
Centre Half

Born: Oldbury
Career: Oldbury Town, Coventry City 1917.

Coventry City	League	F.A.Cup
1919–20	1	–

Debut: 17/1/20 v Rotherham Co. (a) 3–4 (CH)

Centre half Gallagher had played once for City, in the English League Midland Section in 1918–19, and stayed with the club as it moved into the Football League. His only League appearance came when the much respected Edward Hanney was injured.

GALLOWAY, Septimus Randolph (Randolph)

Centre Forward

Born: Sunderland 22nd December 1896

Died: 10th April 1964

Career: Sunderland Tramways F.C., Derby County October 1922, Nottingham Forest November 1924 (£2,500), Luton Town June 1927, Coventry City January 1928, Tottenham Hotspur September 1928, Grantham F.C. c/s 1929, ?, Royal Ordnance, Nottingham 1937/8.

Coventry City	League	F.A.Cup
1927–28	4 – 1	–
1928–29	–	–
Total	4 – 1	–

Debut: 14/1/28 v Torquay U. (h) 5–1 (CF) 1 goal

Galloway arrived late into the professional game, being 3 weeks short of his 26th birthday when he made his debut for Derby. He scored 30 goals in only 76 games for the Rams, including 21 in 1923–24 when the club narrowly missed promotion to Division 1. After unimpressive periods with Forest and Luton and City, and finally a season of reserve team football at Spurs, he disappeared for 7 years and was playing works football in 1937.

GARDINER, John G. (Jack)

Left Half

Born: Hamilton

Career: Blantyre Victoria, Motherwell October 1925, Coventry City May 1926, Wolverhampton Wanderers June 1928, Norwich City (Trial) November 1928, Kettering Town July 1929, Workington January 1930, Barrow August 1932, Lancaster Town October 1932.

Coventry City	League	F.A.Cup
1926–27	36	3
1927–28	15	–
Total	51	3

Debut: 28/8/26 v Northampton T. (h) 0–3 (LH)

Another Scottish player to be signed by James Kerr, Gardner proved to be a successful acquisition to start with, but he lost his way in his second season. He was snapped up by Major Frank Buckley and started the 1928–29 season in the first team at Molineux. He only played 3 games before receiving a knee injury. This threatened his career and he was released by Wolves. He had a trial at Norwich, but played only once. He spent the rest of his career playing non–league football, except for a short period at Barrow in 1932, when he played 2 games in Division 3(N).

GARDNER, Frederick Charles (Fred)

Outside Right

Born: Coventry 4th June 1922

Died: Coventry 12th January 1979

Career: Birmingham 1939, Coventry City 1945, Newport County May 1949, Rugby Town August 1950, Lockheed Leamington.

Coventry City	League	F.A.Cup
1945–46	WWII	–
1946–47	4 – 1	–
1947–48	3 – 1	–
1948–49	6 – 1	–
Total	13 – 3	–

Debut: 16/9/46 v. Newcastle United (h) 1–1 (IR)

Gardner was signed by Birmingham as a promising youngster in 1939, but never had the opportunity to show his worth. During the war, he guested for Northampton and Port Vale before signing for City, where his first team chances were limited. He later played only 4 games for Newport County. He was better known as a cricketer and regularly appeared as an opening batsman for Warwickshire.

GAY, James

Left Back

Born: Birmingham

Career: Perth Celtic, St. Bernards November 1920, Lochgelly United c/s 1921, East Fife c/s 1924, St. Bernards November 1924, Rhyl Athletic c/s 1925, Coventry City c/s 1926, Clapton Orient c/s 1928, Watford c/s 1930, Raith Rovers 1931/2.

Coventry City	League	F.A.Cup
1926–27	17	–
1927–28	13	2
Total	30	2

Debut: 28/8/26 v Northampton T. (h) 0–3 (LB)

Birmingham born Gay moved to Scotland in early life and started his professional career with St Bernards. He was captain of Rhyl, before being bought by James Kerr to add experience to the new look side. City conceded a lot of goals and Gay was made the scapegoat for the 1–8 thrashing by Exeter in December 1926. He lost his place to Jackie Randle and only regained it 11 months later, when Randle was injured. He made 44 appearances for Clapton Orient and 4 for Watford, before moving back to Scotland.

GIBSON, Frederick T.B. (Fred)
Outside Left

Born: South Africa 1888

Career: Bedworth Town, Sunderland Royal Rovers, Sunderland c/s 1909, Raith Rovers July 1910, Dunfermline Athletic c/s 1911, Raith Rovers c/s 1912, Heart of Midlothian 1917, Coventry City c/s 1919, Nuneaton Town c/s 1922, Atherstone Town.

Coventry City	League	F.A.Cup
1919–20	28 – 2	–
1920–21	21 – 2	–
1921–22	5 – 1	–
Total	54 – 5	–

Debut: 30/8/19 v Tottenham H (a) 0–5 (OL)
Honours: Scottish Cup Runners-up Medal 1913

The Gibson family settled in Bedworth in 1899, after moving from South Africa. Young Fred attended Bablake School in Coventry and later Lichfield Grammar School, both of which were rugby playing schools. In the holidays, however, Gibson played football for Bedworth Town. He moved to Sunderland to start an engineering apprenticeship, and whilst playing with non-league Royal Rovers he was spotted by First Division Sunderland. He spent a season at Roker Park without playing for the first team. He moved to Scotland and in his second spell at Raith, played in the 1913 Scottish Cup Final. He made some impressive performances at City, but injury curtailed his career and he moved back to Nuneaton. In 1906, Gibson won a bronze medal for shooting at Bisley.

'Gibbo' was a great favourite with the City fans, and it was no coincidence that his 2 best seasons, 1966–67 and 1969–70, saw City gain promotion and qualify for Europe. After his arrival he found problems adapting to the City style of play. He was dropped and demanded a transfer after a clash with Jimmy Hill. A series of poor results forced Hill to pick Gibson and the team took off, a run which culminated in promotion. Knee injuries restricted his appearances thereafter, but he showed great form in helping City to a Fairs Cup place. He was surprisingly sold to Cardiff and helped that club to the brink of promotion to Division 1. In 1983, Gibson could be found in the Falkland Islands, working on major contracts for the Government.

GIBSON, Ian S.
Midfield

Born: Newton Stewart 30th March 1943

Career: Accrington Stanley July 1958, Bradford (PA) c/s 1959, Middlesbrough March 1962, Coventry City July 1966, Cardiff City July 1970, Bournemouth October 1972, Gateshead Utd 1974.

Coventry City	League	F.A.Cup	Lge.Cup
1966–67	31 – 8	1 – 1	2
1967–68	14+1s	2	1
1968–69	17+1s–3	–	4 – 1
1969–70	28+1s–2	–	1
Total	90+3s–13	3 – 1	8 – 1

Debut: 20/8/66 v Hull City (h) 1–0 (IR)
Honours: 2 Scotland U-23 Caps
　　　　Welsh Cup Winners Medal 1971
　　　　Welsh Cup Runners-up Medal 1972

GIBSON, Terence Bradley (Terry)
Forward

Born: Walthamstow 23rd December 1962

Career: Apprentice Tottenham Hotspur, pro January 1980, Coventry City August 1983 (£70,000), Manchester United January 1986 (£600,000), Wimbledon August 1987 (£200,000), Swindon T. (loan) March 1991, Charlton Ath. (trial) c/s 1993.

Coventry City	League	F.A.Cup	Lge.Cup
1983–84	35+1s17	3 – 2	2
1984–85	38 – 15	2 – 3	2 – 1
1985–86	24 – 11	1	3 – 2
Total	97+1s43	6 – 5	7 – 3

Debut: 27/8/83 v Watford (a) 3–2 (F) 1 goal
Honours: FA Cup Winners Medal 1988

A bargain buy from Spurs, Gibson was one of Bobby Gould's best signings. Standing at 5'5" Gibbo is one of the shortest strikers around, but his

strike rate of 51 goals in only 111 games was remarkable considering City were such a struggling side. In the Autumn of 1985 Gibbo scored in seven consecutive matches to create a Division One record for a City player. He was often the subject of transfer speculation and he finally left in a deal that brought Alan Brazil to Highfield Road. Gibbo had a nightmare 18 months at Old Trafford, scoring only once in 23 appearances and his career was revived by Bobby Gould when Gibbo signed for Wimbledon. He appeared in the 1988 Cup Final but his time with the Dons was not a complete success, and was given a free transfer in April 1993. His greatest moment must have been his sensational hat-trick for City in December 1983 in the 4–0 defeat of Liverpool. Whilst on loan at Charlton, Terry suffered a long term knee injury.

GILBERT, William A. (Billy)
Goalkeeper
Born: Newcastle–upon–Tyne 7th November 1925
Career: Murton Colliery Welfare, Coventry City September 1948, Snowdown Colliery 1953, Stockport County July 1954, Bedworth Town August 1956.

Coventry City	League	F.A.Cup
1948–49	–	–
1949–50	–	–
1950–51	–	–
1951–52	5	–
1952–53	9	–
Total	14	–

Debut: 22/3/52 v Brentford (h) 2–1 (Goal)

Gilbert came to City aged 23 and spent over three years as third choice goalkeeper. When Alf Wood

moved to Northampton in December 1951, Gilbert was still behind Peter Taylor in the pecking order. He took his opportunity in March 1952 when Taylor was injured and was a reliable replacement until he too was injured. He started the following season in the first team but lost out to Taylor, Derek Spencer and the rising star Reg Matthews. With such strength in depth, Gilbert was released and moved to Snowdown Colliery to team up with ex–City colleague Harry Barratt.

GILLESPIE, Gary Thomson
Centre Half
Born: Stirling 5th July 1960
Career: Apprentice Falkirk, semi–pro c/s 1977, Coventry City March 1978, Liverpool July 1983 (£325,000), Glasgow Celtic August 1991 (£1 million).

Coventry City	League	F.A.Cup	Lge.Cup
1977–78	–	–	–
1978–79	14+1s	–	1
1979–80	38 – 1	2	3
1980–81	37 – 1	4	7
1981–82	40 – 2	4	2
1982–83	42 – 2	3	3
Total	171+1s–6	13	16

Debut: 19/8/78 v Middlesbrough (a) 2–1 (CH)
Honours: 13 Scotland Full Caps
8 Scotland U–21 Caps (all at City)
League Champs. Medal 1985–86, 87–88 & 88–89
European Cup Runners–up Medal 1984–85
FA Cup Runners–up Medal 1987–88
League Cup Runners–up Medal 1986–87

When Gillespie was signed in March 1978 as a 17 year old from Falkirk he had to give up his job in a bank and the captaincy of the Bairns. He was slowly groomed for Division 1 football, and by Christmas 1979 he had shown himself to be one of the most consistent and stylish defenders in the country. He only missed a handful of games for City in four years before signing for Liverpool. At the time of the mass exodus, he was one of the few who were reluctant to move on. It took a year for Gillespie to make his Anfield debut. Despite bad injury problems whilst with the Reds it is surprising that he only gained 13 full caps whilst with them. With the arrival of Mark Wright at Anfield, Gillespie returned to Scotland with Celtic, but his run of injury has continued with the Bhoys, therefore limiting his appearances.

GITTOS, John E.
Centre Forward

Born: Chesterfield 1901
Career: Staveley Town, Scunthorpe & Lindsey United c/s 1922, Coventry City c/s 1923, Frickley Colliery c/s 1924.

Coventry City	League	F.A.Cup
1923–24	5 – 1	–

Debut: 25/8/23 v Barnsley (h) 2–3 (CF) 1 goal

Youngster Gittos had impressed Albert Evans in practice games in August 1923 and was pushed straight into the League side, scoring on his debut. He was a quick and agile striker, but his inexperience let him down. He was replaced by Hugh Richmond and was released after the free scoring Albert Pynegar was signed up.

GLAZIER, William James (Bill)
Goalkeeper

Born: Nottingham 2nd August 1943
Career: Brighton Boys Brigade, Torquay United 1959, Crystal Palace 1960, Coventry City October 1964 (£35,000), Brentford July 1975 (£12,500), Retired c/s 1976.

Coventry City	League	F.A.Cup	Lge.Cup
1964–65	24	1	–
1965–66	7	–	–
1966–67	41	1	3
1967–68	40	2	1
1968–69	42	2	5
1969–70	40	2	1
1970–71	40	1	5
1971–72	37	2	1
1972–73	28	4	2
1973–74	40	6	6
1974–75	7	–	1
Total	346	21	25

Debut: 17/10/64 v. Portsmouth (a) 2–0 (Goal)
Honours: 3 England U–23 Caps
1 Football League appearance

When Jimmy Hill bought Glazier in October 1964, he paid a world record fee for a goalkeeper of £35,000. This was for a man arriving from Crystal Palace, who had only just been promoted with City from Division Three the previous May. Glazier had a lot to live up to, but he did more than repay Hill's investment. In his eleven years at City, he became not only a great favourite, but also an England U–23 international, with three appearances in 1964–65. In fact, Bill's first cap came in a 5–0 trouncing of Romania at Highfield Road. In all three games, he did not concede a goal, and in March 1970, he

represented The Football League versus the Scottish League, played again at Highfield Road. Indeed his early career consistency made many people view him as Gordon Banks' understudy for the 1966 World Cup. However this was to count for little, as during the Easter 1965 match at Maine Road, Glazier collided with Glyn Pardoe and broke his leg, which resulted in a year long lay off. Happily, Glazier was fit again for the glorious championship season of 1966–67, and was the first team regular for eight more seasons. During the early days in Division One, it often seemed that Bill was single handedly preventing City's return to Division Two with a series of quite outstanding performances. His reward was to see City become established and he made three appearances in the Fairs Cup in 1970–71. He missed only one game during City's European exploits, the disastrous 1–6 defeat by Bayern Munich in Germany. Glazier was a first team regular until the summer of 1974, when Neil Ramsbottom took over. However his final season at City was not a poor one as it was his testimonial year, which culminated in November 1974, when 15,205 saw the 1966 World Cup winning team play the City. When he was transferred to Brentford in July 1975 for £12,500, Glazier had played 402 times in all competitions for the City. He was a great servant of the club who shared in one of the most exciting periods of Coventry City's history.

GLOVER, Benjamin D. (Benny)
Half Back

Born: Birmingham 30th November 1946
Career: Apprentice Coventry City, pro October 1966.

Coventry City	League	F.A.Cup	Lge.Cup
1966–67	0+1s	–	–
1967–68	–	–	–
Total	0+1s	–	–

Debut: 26/11/66 v Cardiff City (h) 3–2 (Sub)

Glover was a young professional who made his only appearance as a substitute, when City were forced into a shake up because of injury. He returned to the reserves and was released once players like Willie Carr started to emerge from the youth side.

GODFREY, Joby (Joe)
Centre Forward
Born: Sheffield 1894
Career: Beighton Recreation, Nottingham Forest October 1916, Birmingham 1918, Coventry City October 1919, Manchester City November 1919, Merthyr Town c/s 1920, Rotherham Town c/s 1921, Denaby United c/s 1923, Mexborough, Denaby United April 1925.

Coventry City	League	F.A.Cup
1919–20	6	–

Debut: 4/10/19 v Leicester C. (h) 1–2 (CF)

Godfrey was signed in October 1919 with Frank Crowe and Archie Smith from Birmingham, for whom he had played 3 times that season. He played 6 consecutive games for City and was considered to be the best forward at the club. However, it seemed that any player of quality was quickly on his way, and was sold only a month after arriving at Highfield Road. He played 9 times for 1st Division Manchester City, scoring once before being sold to 3rd Division Merthyr, for whom he played 9 times.

GOODING, Raymond (Ray)
Midfield
Born: Hartlepool 16 February 1959
Career: Apprentice Coventry City June 1976, Bristol City (loan) March 1982, Plymouth Argyle August 1982, Retired 1983.

Coventry City	League	F.A.Cup	Lge.Cup
1976–77	5	–	–
1977–78	5 – 1	1	–
1978–79	2+2s	–	–
1979–80	23+1s–2	2	1
1980–81	10 – 2	–	1
1981–82	1	–	1
Total	46+3s–5	3	3

Debut: 23/3/77 v. Newcastle United (a) 0–1 (Mid)

Gooding's career was continually hampered by serious knee injuries. It was only during 1979–80 that he was able to string a series of games together and reach some good form. In an attempt to prove his fitness, he moved to Bristol City, but they were prevented from buying him by the receiver during the club's financial traumas. He moved to Plymouth, where he retired after another knee injury. He is now City's Football Development Officer.

GOODWIN, Ian D.
Midfield
Born: Irlam 14 November 1950
Career: Apprentice Oldham Athletic 1968, Apprentice Coventry City 1969, pro 1970, Brighton & Hove Albion October 1970, Nuneaton Borough 1974.

Coventry City	League	F.A.Cup	Lge.Cup
1969–70	–	–	–
1970–71	4	–	–
Total	4	–	–

Debut: 18/8/70 v. Ipswich Town (a) 2–0 (Mid)

Goodwin signed for City by accident. He drove his brother to a trial match and as the team was a player short, he played and was promptly signed up! He played 4 games in August 1970, but was not considered good enough.

GOUGH, Claude W.M.
Outside Left
Born: Llandrindrod Wells 17th October
Career: Llandrindrod Wells, Swansea Town 1920/1, Coventry City 1921, Swansea Town c/s 1922.

Coventry City	League	F.A.Cup
1921–22	15 – 1	3 – 1

Debut: 26/11/21 v Leicester C. (a) 1–1 (OL)

Youngster Gough had been bought from Swansea, for whom he played twice in the club's first League season, and a great deal was expected of him. He was given an extended run in the team, but his form was sporadic. Manager Albert Evans released him as he preferred Arthur Wood. Gough returned to Swansea where he played ten further games.

GOULD, Jonathan Alan
Goalkeeper

Born: London 18th July 1968
Career: Derby County 1988, Napier City Rovers (New Zealand), Clevedon Town 1990, Halifax Town July 1990, West Bromwich Albion January 1992 (F/T), Coventry City c/s 1992 (£7,500).

Coventry City	League	F.A.Cup	Lge.Cup
1992–93	9	–	–

Debut: 19/12/92 v Liverpool (h) 5–1 (Goal)

The son of the manager Bobby Gould, Jonathan had a tortuous route to the Premier League. He started as a right back and was rejected by Bristol Rovers. He converted to goalkeeper and appeared for Derby's reserves, later showing himself to be a dependable keeper at Halifax Town. His father signed him for WBA, but he didn't play a first team game there, and he moved to City with Bobby Gould in the summer of 1992. He made his debut against Liverpool after Steve Ogrizovic was injured and impressed in City's 5–1 victory. He kept his place for two more games before returning to the reserves. He has shown speed around his box that is valuable for the current back pass rule and ousted Ogrizovic from the first team in April 1993.

GOULD, Robert Alfred (Bobby)
Centre Forward

Born: Coventry 12th June 1946
Career: Apprentice Coventry City, pro June 1964, Arsenal February 1968 (£90,000), Wolverhampton Wanderers June 1970 (£55,000), West Bromwich Albion September 1971 (£66,666), Bristol City December 1972 (£70,000), West Ham United November 1973 (£80,000), Wolverhampton Wanderers December 1975 (£30,000), Bristol Rovers October 1977 (£10,000), Hereford United September 1978 (£10,000), Retired 1980.

Coventry City	League	F.A.Cup	Lge.Cup
1963–64	2	–	–
1964–65	8 – 3	–	1 – 1
1965–66	17+2s–5	1	–
1966–67	38+1s–24	1	3 – 1
1967–68	13+1s–8	–	1
Total	78+4s–40	2	5 – 2

Debut: 30/10/63 v Shrewsbury T. (a) 0–0 (CF)
Honours: FA Cup Winners Medal 1975
Texaco Cup Winners Medal 1970–71

Gould was almost lost to City when Billy Frith originally released him. Fortunately Jimmy Hill revived his career and placed considerable confidence in the young bustling forward when he sold George Hudson to Northampton. Despite facing the initial angry reaction of the crowd, Gould was the highest scorer in Division 2 as City won promotion in 1967. He scored City's first hat–trick in Division 1 in the 5–1 victory over Burnley in December 1967. He was sold to Arsenal for City's record fee received at that time, a move which started a nomadic tour around the Football League. Since taking up management his roaming has continued with two spells at Bristol Rovers, a FA Cup winning period at Wimbledon, a controversial time at West Brom and now two stays at City. His first period of management at City from May 1983 to December 1984 saw an incredible 45 transfer deals. His return to Highfield Road has brought some stylish football and a pride in Coventry City which was so patently missing before.

GOULD, Trevor R.
Outside Right

Born: Coventry 5th March 1950
Career: Apprentice Coventry City, pro July 1967, Northampton Town October 1970, Bedford Town c/s 1973, Rushden Town c/s 1982, Retired 1983.

Coventry City	League	F.A.Cup	Lge.Cup
1967–68	–	–	–
1968–69	–	–	–
1969–70	9	–	–
1970–71	–	–	–
Total	9	–	–

Debut: 12/8/69 v. W.B.A. (h) 3–1 (OR)

Trevor had the problem of trying to emulate his brother Bobby's achievements at City and never did so. All of his appearances were in the season that City achieved a place in Europe, and the team lost only one game in which he pe, and the teamcame a well respected manager at Aylesbury before returning to City in the summer of 1992 as youth coach.

GRAHAM, Robert (Bobby)
Inside Forward

Born: Motherwell 22nd November 1944
Career: Apprentice Liverpool, pro November 1961, Coventry City March 1972 (£70,000), Tranmere Rovers (loan) January 1973, Motherwell September 1973, Hamilton Academicals July 1977 (£15,000), Retired 1981.

Coventry City	League	F.A.Cup	Lge.Cup
1971–72	13 – 2	–	–
1972–73	6 – 1	–	–
1973–74	–	–	–
Total	19 – 3	–	–

Debut: 11/3/72 v. Leeds United (a) 0–1 (IF)

Graham was a fringe player at Liverpool, but proved dependable whenever called upon. In his ten years at the club, he made over 100 appearances, including games in all three European club tornaments, and was an ever–present in season 1969–70, when he scored 21 goals in all competitions. Graham was Cantwell's final signing and played his first game the day before his manager's sacking. He never fitted in at City and moved to his native Scotland. Whilst at Motherwell, Graham helped 'Well beat City in both legs of the Texaco Cup.

GRAY, William H. (Billy)
Right Half

Born: Binley 3rd December 1931
Career: Binley Youth Club 1944, Morris Motors FC 1946, Coventry City December 1948, Kettering Town 1954, Morris Motors 1955.

Coventry City	League	F.A.Cup
1948–49	–	–
1949–50	–	–
1950–51	–	–
1951–52	2	–
1952–53	–	–
1953–54	–	–
Total	2	–

Debut: 13/10/51 v Birmingham C. (h) 1–1 (RH)

Local wing half Gray spent six years with City but only made two appearances in that time, these coming when he replaced Don Dorman. He moved to Kettering Town in 1954 before returning to Morris Motors in Coventry, the team from whom City acquired his services.

GRAYDON, Raymond J. (Ray)
Outside Right

Born: Bristol 21st July 1947
Career: Apprentice Bristol Rovers, pro September 1965, Aston Villa June 1971 (£25,000), Coventry City c/s 1977, Washington Diplomats March 1978, Oxford United November 1978, Retired 1981.

Coventry City	League	F.A.Cup	Lge.Cup
1977–78	17+3s–5	0+1s	2+1s–1

Debut: 20/8/77 v. Derby County (h) 3–1 (OR)
Honours: Lge.Cup Winners Medal 1974/75 & 1976/77

Prior to playing for City, Graydon was instrumental in Aston Villa's rise from Division 3 to Division 1 and their victory in 2 League Cup finals. He stayed for only 6 months at City, but nevertheless, played a major part in the resurgence of the City in 1977–78. His arrival allowed Gordon Milne to play the 4–2–4 formation which proved to be so effective. His speed and trickery provided great service to Ferguson and Wallace, and it was only when he moved to the USA in March 1978, that his true value was realised. After retiring, he moved into coaching at Oxford.

GREEN, Alan Paul
Forward

Born: Worcester 1st January 1954
Career: Apprentice Coventry City, pro January 1971, Washington Diplomats (loan) c/s 1977; Washington Diplomats April 1979 (£150,000), Worcester City 1979–80, Washington Diplomats April 1980, Jacksonville Tea Men April 1981, Team America April 1983, New York Cosmos April 1984

Coventry City	League	F.A.Cup	Lge.Cup
1970–71	–	–	–
1971–72	0+1s	–	–
1972–73	5+3s	0+1s	–
1973–74	14+3s–4	–	3 – 2
1974–75	20+2s–7	–	–
1975–76	29+2s–9	3	2 – 1
1976–77	14+3s–4	2	1+1s
1977–78	10 – 5	–	–
1978–79	6+5s–1	0+2s–1	–
Total	98+19s–30	5+3s–1	6+1s–3

Debut: 22/4/72 v Leicester City (a) 0–1 (Sub)
Full Debut: 12/8/72 v. Tottenham H. (a) 1–2 (OL)

Green was an exciting young prospect who promised much, but in the end he never quite lived up to his potential. He was a great favourite with the fans, loved for his explosive running. Injury problems throughout his career limited his appearances, and the emergence of the Ferguson/Wallace partnership ended his stay at City. He was a great success in America, where he finally took up residence. Despite playing for City for eight seasons, it is surprising that Green left the English game at 25.

GREEN, Thomas (Tommy)
Inside Right

Born: Droitwich May 1913
Career: Droitwich Spa, Droitwich Comrades, West Bromwich Albion October 1931, West Ham United December 1936 (£3,000), Coventry City March 1939, Worcester City 1941, Bromyard, Retired 1949.

Coventry City	League	F.A.Cup
1938–39	9 – 2	–

Debut: 18/3/39 v Millwall (a) 0–0 (CF)
Honours: England Junior International

The son of Tommy Green senior, who played for WBA and Aston Villa in the 1880's, Tommy junior followed his father to The Hawthorns. He played a major role in the club's successful reserve side, but only played 10 first team games in 5 years. A move to West Ham did not prove to be successful, but Harry Storer saw him as a useful signing to help City to Division 1. He was only at City for a few months when war broke out, and guested for Notts County and WBA during this period. He ended at Bromyard, where he still lives.

GREENMAN, Christopher (Chris)
Centre Half

Born: Bristol 22nd December 1968
Career: YTS Coventry City, pro c/s 1989, Peterborough United (trial February 1993) March 1993 (F/T).

Coventry City	League	F.A.Cup	Lge.Cup
1989–90	–	–	–
1990–91	–	–	–
1991–92	4	–	–
1992–93	1+1s	–	–
Total	5+1s	–	–

Debut: 10/10/91 v Crystal Palace (h) 1–2 (LB)

The tall and thin Greenman came into the game late, having taken his 'A' levels at school before taking up a trainee position at 18. He never looked as if he would break into the first team on a regular basis and moved to Peterborough after a trial period.

GRICE, Michael J. (Mike)
Outside Right

Born: Woking 3rd November 1931
Career: Lowestoft Town, Colchester Utd June 1952, West Ham Utd March 1956, Coventry City August 1961, Colchester Utd June 1962.

Coventry City	League	F.A.Cup	Lge.Cup
1961–62	37 – 6	1	–

Debut: 19/8/61 v Reading (a) 0–4 (OR)

Mike Grice played impressively for Colchester United before West Ham stepped in to sign him for £10,000. He played an important part in The Hammers' promotion to Division 1 and was an ever-present in the club's first season back in the top flight, 1958/59. At the age of 30, Grice was signed by Billy Frith. He only lasted one year, because he did not feature in Jimmy Hill's long-term plans. He returned to his first League club, Colchester, where he retired.

GRIFFITHS, Vernon
Wing Half

Born: Birmingham 14th June 1936
Career: South Birmingham Boys 1950, WBA 1951, Sheldon Town 1953, Coventry City 1954, Rugby Town July 1959.

Coventry City	League	F.A.Cup
1954–55	–	–
1955–56	–	–
1956–57	–	–
1957–58	13 – 1	2
1958–59	2	–
Total	15 – 1	2

Debut: 28/9/57 v Brentford (a) 3–1 (RH)

Griffith's early promise, never resulted in a long-term first team position. Appearances were initially limited because of Jamieson, Nicholas and Harvey, but even when in the team, Vernon could never maintain the necessary level of consistency required. The arrival of Ron Farmer, meant Griffiths was surplus to requirements.

GRIMES, Augustine Ashley (Ashley)
Midfield

Born: Dublin 2nd August 1957
Career: Villa United, Bohemians 1975, Manchester United March 1977 (£20,000), Coventry City August 1983 (£200,000), Luton Town August 1984 (£100,000), Osasuna (Spain) c/s 1989, Stoke City January 1992, Retired c/s 1992.

Coventry City	League	F.A.Cup	Lge.Cup
1983–84	29+3s–1	–	3–1

Debut: 27/8/83 v Watford (a) 3–2 (Mid)
Honours: 19 Republic of Ireland Full Caps (2 at City)
  League Cup Winners Medal 1987–88
  League Cup Runners–up Medal 1988–89
  Full Membs. Cup Runs.–up Medal 1987–88
  FA Cup Winners Medal 1976

Ashley Grimes was bought from Manchester United in August 1983 by Bobby Gould to be the play-maker of the side. He started well but faded badly and after one season, he was sold to Luton Town in a deal that bought Kirk Stephens to City. He made 3 Wembley appearances for The Hatters before being sold to Osasuna, and later Stoke, before taking up coaching duties with The Potters. His early career mirrored fellow Dubliner Gerry Daly, having appeared for his country after playing for Bohemians, Manchester United and City.

GRUNDY, William
Right Half

Born: Kirkby–in–Ashfield
Career: Annesley Colliery Welfare, Coventry City c/s 1933, Mansfield Town 1935/6.

Coventry City	League	F.A.Cup
1933–34	–	–
1934–35	1	–
Total	1	–

Debut: 30/3/35 v Brighton & H.A. (a) 0–2 (RH)

Young right half Grundy spent two years at City, making 2 consecutive appearances against Brighton and then Watford in the Division 3(South) Cup. He disappointed and was replaced. This fair haired half–back moved to Mansfield for whom he made 5 appearances in 1935–36, before leaving the professional game.

GYNN, Michael
Midfield

Born: Peterborough 19th August 1961
Career: Apprentice Peterborough United, pro April 1979, Coventry C. August 1983(£60,000), Stoke C. August 1993 (F/T)

Coventry City	League	F.A.Cup	Lge.Cup
1983–84	20+3s–2	2+1s	2
1984–85	32+7s–4	2	2
1985–86	6+6s–1	–	1+1s
1986–87	16+6s–5	3+1s–2	0+3s
1987–88	19+6s–3	2	3 – 2
1988–89	8 – 1	–	2 – 3
1989–90	31+3s–3	1	6 – 1
1990–91	35 – 8	4 – 2	5 – 1
1991–92	21+2s–3	1	1
1992–93	18+2s–2	0+1s	–
Total	206+35s–32	15+3s–4	22+4s–7

Debut: 27/8/83 v Watford (a) 3–2 (Mid)
Honours: FA Cup Winners Medal 1987

Diminutive Michael Gynn is a quick and skilful midfielder who came to City, after he had been watched by Dave Sexton, and his successor Bobby Gould decided to sign him. He suffered injury on his debut and his career has been plagued by injury ever since. In the 1987 FA Cup run, Gynn scored vital goals at Stoke and against Leeds in the semi-final and he played his part in the final. He has the distinction of holding the highest number of appearances for City as a substitute. At London Road he was a free scoring midfielder but his goals tally for City was somewhat disappointing. After ten years service at Highfield Road he was given a free transfer in May 1993.

HACKETT, Ernest
Goalkeeper

Born: Royston
Career: Monckton Athletic, Frickley Colliery c/s 1929, Wolverhampton Wanderers November 1930, Coventry City c/s 1931, Newport County July 1932, Frickley Colliery c/s 1933.

Coventry City	League	F.A.Cup
1931–32	4	1

Debut: 14/11/31 v Clapton Orient (h) 4–2 (Goal)

Signed as cover for Tommy Allen and Joe Hewett, Yorkshireman Hackett got his chance when he proved to be an able stand-in. But without experience and a touch of class, manager Storer only chose him when Allen was injured. His last appearance was in goal in the 5–5 draw against Fulham in January 1932. He moved onto Newport where he played 4 times.

HADLEY, George A.
Left Half
Born: West Bromwich 5th June 1893
Career: Willenhall Swifts, Southampton July 1913, Aston Villa March 1919, Coventry City July 1920.

Coventry City	League	F.A.Cup
1920–21	28 – 2	2
1921–22	41 – 1	3
1922–23	3	–
Total	72 – 3	5

Debut: 28/8/20 v Rotherham Co. (a) 3–2 (LH) 1 goal

Hadley was a stocky centre half who emerged as a member of Southampton's Southern League side just before the Great War. He signed for Villa, but failed to establish himself in a powerful squad and made only 4 appearances. He was a regular member of City's line up for 2 seasons, but retired in 1922 following a seriously broken collarbone.

HAGAN, James (Jim)
Defender
Born: Monkstown 10th August 1956
Career: Larne, Coventry City November 1977, Torquay United (loan) September 1979, Detroit Express February 1980, Coventry City September 1980, Seiko October 1980, Coventry City July 1981, Birmingham City May 1982, Real Celta April 1987, Colchester United November 1989 (F/T).

Coventry City	League	F.A.Cup	Lge.Cup
1977–78	–	–	–
1978–79	12+1s	2	–
1979–80	–	–	–
1980–81	–	–	–
1981–82	3	1	–
Total	15+1s	3	–

Debut: 7/10/78 v Ipswich Town (h) 2–2 (CH)

Hagan's first team appearances were limited by the consistency of Holton, Dyson and Gillespie. He holds the distinction, along with Fred Jones, of being signed three times for City – twice by Gordon Milne and once by Dave Sexton. Hagan lacked sufficient height to be a commanding centre-half and adapted as a right back at Birmingham. Following a successful time in Spain, Hagan finished with a short spell at Colchester in the club's Football League relegation season.

HALE, Kenneth Oliver (Ken)
Inside Forward
Born: Blyth 18th September 1939
Career: Everton 1955, Newcastle United October 1956, Coventry City December 1962 (£10,000), Oxford United March 1966 (£5,000), Darlington May 1968 (£5,000), Halifax Town January 1973 (£500), Retired c/s 1974.

Coventry City	League	F.A.Cup	Lge.Cup
1962–63	15 – 2	2 – 1	–
1963–64	39 – 16	2 – 1	2
1964–65	32 – 9	–	3 – 3
1965–66	12+1s	–	3 – 1
Total	98+1s–27	4 – 2	8 – 4

Debut: 15/12/62 v Notts County (a) 1–1 (IR)

Jimmy Hill signed Hale from Newcastle, where his first team outings were limited, but 15 goals in 30 games for the Magpies showed his potential. Hale took time to settle into City's style of play, but his 16 goals in his first full season proved to be vital in securing the 3rd Division championship for City. His partnership with George Hudson proved that Hill's decision to sell Terry Bly was right. Hale was finally replaced by Ray Pointer. Hale took over as manager of Halifax after retiring as a player at the age of 34.

HALL, Derek R.
Midfield
Born: Aston-under-Lyne 5th January 1965
Career: Apprentice Coventry City, pro c/s 1982, Torquay United March 1984, Swindon Town July 1985, Southend United August 1986, Halifax Town c/s 1989 (F/T), Hereford United July 1991 (F/T).

Coventry City	League	F.A.Cup	Lge.Cup
1982–83	1	–	–
1983–84	–	–	–
Total	1	–	–

Debut: 18/9/82 v Birmingham City (a) 0–1 (Mid)

Hall made his only first team appearance in September 1982 at St Andrew's, when City had the smallest squad in the First Division. He remained at City under Bobby Gould and despite appearing in pre-season matches, he didn't play another league match. He has since moved around the lower divisions, and is now the influential captain of the Hereford United side, which is managed by ex-City full back Greg Downs.

HALL, George W.E.
Wing Half

Born: Worksop 1912
Career: Worksop Town, Sheffield United c/s 1932, Coventry City c/s 1935, Newport County c/s 1936, Bristol City May 1937, Retired 1939.

Coventry City	League	F.A.Cup
1935–36	–	–

Debut: 21/10/35 v Millwall (a) 1–0 (RH) (Div. 3 South Cup)

George Hall was a strong wing half who had the misfortune to join City when the likes of Frith, McCaughey, Mason and Boileau were helping City to promotion from Division 3(S). His only first team appearance came in the first round of the Division 3(S) Cup as a replacement for Billy Frith. He played a further part as City went on to win the cup. Earlier, he had played 22 League games with Sheffield United, mostly in Division 1. He stayed a season with City and later performed well at Somerton Park, which attracted Bristol City to buy him. He played 13 games for the Ashton Gate club, before hanging up his boots in 1939.

HALL, Thomas L. (Tom)
Right Back

Born: Crawcock, Newcastle–upon–Tyne
Career: Crawcock Albion, Coventry City February 1932.

Coventry City	League	F.A.Cup
1931–32	2	–
1932–33	–	–
1933–34	–	–
Total	2	–

Debut: 30/4/32 v Watford (h) 5–0 (RB)

Tom Hall was signed from North–East side Crowcock Albion in February 1932. He was given his chance in the last 2 games of the 1931/32 season. He was a regular choice for the reserves, but was not able to oust Jesse Bennett or Vic Brown from the right back spot and was released in 1934.

HANN, James
Inside Left

Born: Birtley
Career: Birtley F.C., Coventry City 1920, Leadgate Park c/s 1921, Birtley F.C., Workington c/s 1927.

Coventry City	League	F.A.Cup
1920–21	1	–

Debut: 6/9/20 v Port Vale (a) 0–0 (IL)

North–Easterner James Hann, was signed in the summer of 1920 and made an unexpected debut in September 1920 when Harold Nash was injured. He was replaced by the much more experienced Nash for the next game. He spent the rest of the season in the reserves and was released, moving to Leadgate Park with Austen Campbell, the future England international.

HANNEY, Edward T. (Ted)
Centre Half

Born: Reading
Career: Wokingham F.C., Reading 1911, Manchester City November 1913, Coventry City November 1919 (£2,000), Reading c/s 1921, Northfleet c/s 1922.

Coventry City	League	F.A.Cup
1919–20	20	2
1920–21	12	2 – 1
Total	32	4 – 1

Debut: 22/11/19 v Blackpool (h) 0–0 (CH)
Honours: G. Britain Olympic Gold Medal Winner 1912
2 England Amateur Caps
1 Southern League appearance

The highly experienced Ted Hanney was the centre half Harry Pollitt wanted to reverse City's shocking slide in 1919, spending a massive amount for his services. He certainly did what was required and helped City to stay up. Injury restricted his appearances the following season, and he moved on to Reading. Prior to The Great War, Hanney had an illustrious career, gaining an Olympic Gold medal from the football tournament at the 1912 Stockholm games, two England amateur caps and he represented The Southern League whilst at Reading in 1913. His First Division career at Manchester City seemed set up, only for the Great War to intervene.

HANNIGAN, Ernest (Ernie)
Outside Right

Born: Glasgow 23rd January 1943
Career: St. Roch's, Queen of the South 1961, Preston North End August 1964 (£10,000), Coventry City November 1967 (£50,000), Torquay United (loan) December 1969, Morton c/s 1970, Queen of the South c/s 1971, Raith Rovers 1972.

Coventry City	League	F.A.Cup	Lge.Cup
1967–68	23 – 5	3 – 1	–
1968–69	13+3s–1	0+1s	2
1969–70	7+1s	–	–
Total	43+4s–6	3+1s–1	2

Debut: 11/11/67 v Fulham (h) 0–3 (OR)

Hannigan provided a settled look to the outside right position during the second half of the 1967/68 season, scoring 5 goals in vital matches. After this initial good period, he lost out to Ernie Hunt, but was an important squad man. Hannigan was allowed to move back to Scotland with Morton. After retiring, he moved into coaching and was last heard of coaching in Australia.

HARRIS, Allan J.
Left Back

Born: Hackney 28th December 1942
Career: Chelsea June 1960, Coventry City November 1964 (£35,000), Chelsea May 1966, Q.P.R. July 1967, Plymouth Argyle March 1971, Cambridge United July 1973.

Coventry City	League	F.A.Cup	Lge.Cup
1964–65	20	1	–
1965–66	40	4	4 – 1
Total	60	5	4 – 1

Debut: 28/11/64 v Norwich City (a) 0–1 (LB)

When Harris lost his way at Chelsea, Jimmy Hill had no hesitation in bringing him to City. His 18 months at City saw him influential in City's Division 3 championship side, and impressive performances in Division 2 saw many clubs take an interest. The move back to Chelsea was not successful, and Harris drifted down the divisions after two good seasons at QPR. He has made his name in management as Terry Venables' right hand man, at Crystal Palace, QPR, Barcelona and Tottenham.

HARRISON, James Charles (Jim)
Left Back

Born: Leicester 12th February 1921
Career: Wellington Victoria, Leicester City December 1940, Aston Villa July 1949, Coventry City July 1951, Corby Town July 1953, Hinckley Town August 1956, Banbury Spencer c/s 1957

Coventry City	League	F.A.Cup
1951–52	12	3 – 1
1952–53	8 – 2	–
Total	20 – 2	3 – 1

Debut: 22/12/51 v Q.P.R. (a) 4–1 (LB)
Honours: F.A. Cup Runners Up Medal 1949

After reaching Wembley with 2nd Division Leicester, Harrison's career seemed to be about to flourish at Aston Villa, but first team opportunities were limited to 8 in 2 seasons. His was a career of ill-fortune, as the war (during which he guested for Reading) prevented a League debut until the age of 25. Injuries were a problem and his transfers to both Villa and City came at inopportune moments. The move to City provided the opportunity for him to regain a regular position, but injury and the consistency of Dick Mason limited his outings. In his first season, City were relegated. His 2 League goals were both scored against QPR on 30/8/52, when Harrison played at centre forward.

HART, Harold (Harry)
Inside Left

Born: Sheffield 29th September 1926
Career: Rotherham United 1945, Coventry City June 1950, Grimsby Town December 1952, Frickley Colliery July 1953, Gainsborough, Stocksbridge August 1956.

Coventry City	League	F.A.Cup
1950–51	4 – 1	–
1951–52	6	–
1952–53	–	–
Total	10 – 1	–

Debut: 23/3/51 v Grimsby Town (a) 2–1 (IL)

Understudy to the popular Ken Chisholm, Hart never had the opportunity of an extended run in the City side. He had only played 10 times in 4 seasons at Rotherham prior to joining City and never looked any more than a Division 3 player. Moving to Division 3(N) Grimsby didn't produce regular appearances. He was one of many players City used fleetingly in a decline period, from Division 2 to 3.

HARVEY, Laurence (Lol)
Left Back/Wing Half
Born: Heanor 25th July 1934
Career: Modern Machines, Coventry City July 1951.

Coventry City	League	F.A.Cup	Lge.Cup
1951–52	3	–	
1952–53	20	–	
1953–54	3	–	
1954–55	20	4 – 1	
1955–56	24 – 1	1	
1956–57	–	–	
1957–58	26	1	
1958–59	41	2	
1959–60	2	–	
1960–61	1	–	–
Total	140 – 1	8 – 1	–

Debut: 3/11/51 v Brentford (a) 0–1 (RH)

Harvey made his debut at the age of 17 and proved to be one of the most consistent players during the turbulent 1950's. He was a solid, no–nonsense defender that could play either at left back or wing half. Despite being plagued by injury, Harvey could always be relied upon. His most impressive season was the 1958–59 promotion campaign from Division 4. After this, only 3 more games were played and Harvey ended his League career aged 27. In recent years, he has been involved in part–time scouting for City at a local level.

HATELEY, Anthony (Tony)
Centre Forward
Born: Derby 13th June 1941
Career: Normanton Sports, Notts County June 1958, Aston Villa August 1963 (£22,000), Chelsea November 1966 (£100,000), Liverpool July 1967 (£100,000), Coventry City September 1968 (£80,000), Birmingham City August 1969 (£72,500), Notts County October 1970 (£20,000), Oldham Athletic June 1972, Boston Minuteman c/s 1974, Bromsgrove Rovers August 1974, Prescot Town c/s 1975, Keyworth United.

Coventry City	League	F.A.Cup	Lge.Cup
1968–69	17 – 4	1	2 – 1

Debut: 21/9/68 v Everton (h) 2–2 (CF)
Honours: FA Cup Runners Up Medal 1967

The attraction of Hateley to clubs was his proven ability to score goals. His most prolific period was at Aston Villa when he averaged a goal every other game. This was fundamental in Chelsea's decision to buy Hateley – the first six figure fee paid between British clubs for a player. Hateley arrived at City expecting to score goals, but for the first time in his career he didn't excel, although he was in a struggling side. His second spell at Meadow Lane was fruitful with 35 goals in 68 matches.

HATELEY, Mark W.
Centre Forward
Born: Liverpool 7th November 1961
Career: Apprentice Coventry City, pro December 1978, Detroit Express (loan) April 1980, Portsmouth June 1983 (£190,000), A.C. Milan c/s 1984 (£1 million), Monaco June 1987, Glasgow Rangers June 1990 (£500,000).

Coventry City	League	F.A.Cup	Lge.Cup
1978–79	1	–	–
1979–80	2+2s	1	–
1980–81	17+2s–3	2+1s	6 – 2
1981–82	31+2s13	4 – 4	2 – 1
1982–83	35 – 9	3 – 2	–
Total	86+6s–25	10+1s–6	8 – 3

Debut: 5/5/79 v Wolves (h) 3–0 (CF)
Honours: 32 England Full Caps
 10 England U–21 (5 at City)
 Scottish Champs. Medal 1991, 1992 & 1993
 Scottish Cup Winners Medal 1992 & 1993
 Scottish Lge. Cup Wins. Medal 1991 & 1993

The son of Tony Hateley, Mark had been patiently groomed by Gordon Milne and Dave Sexton, from being a poor finisher to a good Division 1 striker. He had played under Sexton in the England U–21 side. When he left City in 1983, under the freedom of contract, he joined 2nd Division Portsmouth. Pompey offered £50,000 and a transfer tribunal settled the fee at £190,000. This was shown to be inadequate only 12 months later when he moved to AC Milan for £1 million. This transformation in his career came about after he graduated from the U–21 side to become a full international. His game improved whilst on the continent but injury hampered his appearances for Monaco. He joined Rangers, and has formed a partnership with Ally McCoist, which has resulted in Scottish League Championship medals in his first 3 seasons at Ibrox and an exciting European Cup run in 1992–93.

HAWKINGS, Barry
Forward
Born: Birmingham 7th November 1931

Career: Modern Machines 1948, Coventry City January 1949, Rugby Town (loan) November 1952, Lincoln City March 1956, Northampton Town June 1957, Gravesend & Northfleet c/s 1959, Wisbech Town 1959-60, Brierley Hill Alliance 1960, Abergavenny Thursdays c/s 1961, Retired c/s 1962.

Coventry City	League	F.A.Cup
1948-49	-	-
1949-50	-	-
1950-51	-	-
1951-52	-	-
1952-53	-	-
1953-54	4	
1954-55	15 - 6	-
1955-56	15 - 6	-
Total	34 - 12	-

Debut: 26/12/53 v Ipswich Town (a) 1-4 (IL)

Hawkins took some time to establish himself in the City first team, because of established forwards such as Eddy Brown and Peter Hill, together with Ronnie Waldock. Once established, in the run up to the end of the 1955/56 season, he scored a hat-trick in the 6-0 victory against Swindon. However, the general lack of penetration brought in Ken McPherson and Dennis Uphill, and Hawkins was allowed to move to Lincoln. He is now a potter, living near Worcester.

HAWLEY, Frederick (Fred)
Half Back
Born: Ripley 28th October 1890

Career: Ripley Athletic, Sheffield United 1912/3, Coventry City May 1919, Birmingham 1920, Swindon Town c/s 1920, Bristol City 1923, Brighton & Hove Albion c/s 1925, Queen's Park Rangers c/s 1926, Loughborough Corinthians January 1928.

Coventry City	League	F.A.Cup
1919-20	14	-

Debut: 30/8/19 v Tottenham H. (h) 0-5 (CH)

Hawley had been a commanding centre half in Sheffield United's 1st Division side before the war. City had to pay a "pretty stiff figure" for his services. He played 14 times for City and never appeared in a winning side. He was bought by Birmingham however, as they knew his potential given a place in a good side, since he had played for the Blues during the Great War. Whilst at City, the local press made mention of his age, 28, and so it is testimony to Hawley's fitness that he continued to produce sterling performances for another eight years, after his brief stay at St. Andrew's. He was still playing at the age of 37 for Loughborough Corinthians, following 97 appearances for Swindon, 71 games for Bristol City, 37 League games for Brighton and 29 for QPR.

HAYWOOD, Clive
Outside Right
Born: Ramsgate 1st November 1960

Career: Apprentice Coventry City August 1978, Seiko (loan) 1980-81, Washington Diplomats c/s 1981.

Coventry City	League	F.A.Cup	Lge.Cup
1978-79	-	-	-
1979-80	-	-	-
1980-81	1	-	-
Total	1	-	-

Debut: 30/8/80 v Aston Villa (a) 0-1 (OR)

Injury to Roger Van Gool gave Haywood a chance in the first team. After one game, he was replaced by fellow youngster Peter Bodak, who established himself as a first team regular, and no more chances in England came Haywood's way. He now lives in Bromley in his native Kent.

HEALD, Paul
Goalkeeper
Born: Wath-on-Dearne 20th August 1968

Career: YTS Sheffield United, pro 1987, Leyton Orient December 1988, Coventry City (loan) March 1992, Crystal Palace (loan) August 1992.

Coventry City	League	F.A.Cup	Lge.Cup
1991-92	2	-	-

Debut: 21/3/92 v Oldham Athletic (h) 1-1 (Goal)

With injury to Steve Ogrizovic and Clive Baker, Don Howe borrowed Heald from Leyton Orient. He was recovering from a serious back injury, and his 2 games in March were his first of the season. But City needed a more experienced keeper for the relegation fight and he returned to London. His career was put in doubt by another serious injury in the summer of 1993.

HEALEY, Ronald (Ron)
Goalkeeper
Born: Manchester 30th August 1952
Career: Apprentice Manchester City, pro October 1969, Coventry City (loan) December 1971, Preston North End (loan) December 1973, Cardiff City March 1974, Retired April 1982.

Coventry City	League	F.A.Cup	Lge.Cup
1971–72	3	–	–

Debut: 27/12/71 v Manchester United (a) 2–2 (Goal)
Honours: 2 full Republic of Ireland Caps
Welsh Cup Winners Medal 1974 & 1976
Welsh Cup Runners–up Medal 1977

Injury to regular keepers Glazier and McManus, forced Noel Cantwell to look for someone to bridge the gap. Manchester City's reserve keeper, Healey, was available and stayed with City for a month until Glazier was fit again. Healey never had many opportunities at Manchester City due to the emergence of Joe Corrigan and he moved to Cardiff, where he achieved international honours with Ireland through his parental qualification. Injury forced Healey to retire at the premature age of 29.

HEATHCOTE, James (Jimmy)
Centre Forward
Born: Bolton 17th January 1894
Career: Bolton Wanderers WW1, Blackpool 1919, Notts County 1922, Pontypridd 1923, Lincoln City 1924, Mansfield Town 1925, Coventry City c/s 1926, Accrington Stanley January 1929, Retired March 1929.

Coventry City	League	F.A.Cup
1926–27	40 – 21	3
1927–28	23 – 15	2
1928–29	–	–
Total	63 – 36	5

Debut: 28/8/26 v Northampton T. (h) 0–3 (IL)

Heathcote scored 33 goals in 95 games for Blackpool, which encouraged Notts County to spend the large figure of £1200 for his services. He struggled at Meadow Lane, scoring only 1 goal in 12 games, and was given a free transfer. Lincoln revived his career and after a season in The Midland League with Mansfield, he signed for City in 1926 and immediately recaptured his scoring touch. Injury stopped his run and he tried to regain his form at Accrington Stanley, but he didn't last long, for he returned to The City in March 1929 as steward for the Howitzer Club at Highfield Road.

HEIGH, Robert
Centre Forward
Born: Bathgate c.1908
Career: Bathgate (trial) August 1925, Tranent Juniors, Coventry City c/s 1926, Arbroath c/s 1928, Armadale August 1929, Grimsby T. 1929/30, Carlisle U. c/s 1930, Armadale c/s 1931.

Coventry City	League	F.A.Cup
1926–27	5	–
1927–28	3	–
Total	8	–

Debut: 1/9/26 v Watford (a) 0–1 (CF)

Heigh came to City as a raw 18 year old and was pushed straight into the first team. He was seen as a prospect for the future by James Kerr but didn't develop as expected at a time when the club was at a very low ebb. He was surplus to requirement for new boss James McIntyre and moved back to his native Scotland. He returned to England but didn't appear in Grimsby's first team and played only 6 matches for Carlisle.

HEINEMANN, George Henry
Left Half
Born: Stafford 17th December 1905
Career: Stafford Rangers, Manchester City October 1928, Coventry City May 1931, Crystal Palace August 1934, Clapton Orient August 1935, Wellington Town c/s 1938.

Coventry City	League	F.A.Cup
1931–32	39 – 1	2
1932–33	11	4
1933–34	2	–
Total	52 – 1	6

Debut: 19/8/31 v Fulham (a) 3–5 (LH)
Honours: Welsh Cup Winners Medal 1939–40

Harry Storer acquired Heinemann from Manchester City to the dismay of many of the Maine Road faithful who felt that he had a bright future. He was a strong left half who was a regular for his first season at City, but he lost his place to the up and coming Harry Boileau. He showed his value at Selhurst Park and later for Clapton Orient. He scored only 2 goals in his career, but the one for City was notable for it was the fifth in the 5–5 draw against Fulham, in January 1932.

HENDERSON, William James
Outside Right

Born: Carlisle 11th January 1899
Died: 18th January 1934
Career: Carlisle United, Arsenal October 1921 (£1,000), Luton Town March 1923, Southampton December 1923 (£500), Coventry City June 1938 (£200), Carlisle United c/s 1929.

Coventry City	League	F.A.Cup
1928–29	15 – 1	–

Debut: 25/8/28 v Norwich C. (h) 3-0 (OR)

Signed by James McIntyre, together with fellow Saint Tommy Allen, Henderson was bought for £200 for his renowned trickery down the right wing. A mixture of injury and frustrating play restricted his appearances at City. He started and finished his career at Carlisle United and early in his career, played 7 games for Arsenal in Division 1. After retiring, he became a tobacconist in his home town.

HENDRIE, John Grattan
Forward

Born: Lennoxtown, 24th October 1963
Career: Apprentice Coventry City, pro May 1981, Hereford United (loan) January 1984, Bradford City July 1984 (F/T), Newcastle United June 1988 (£500,000), Leeds United June 1989 (£600,000), Middlesbrough July 1990 (£500,000).

Coventry City	League	F.A.Cup	Lge.Cup
1981–82	6	–	–
1982–83	8+4s–2	–	1
1983–84	1+2s	–	1
Total	15+6s–2	–	2

Debut: 5/12/81 v Tottenham H. (a) 2-1 (OR)

Under Dave Sexton, the young Scot Hendrie was being groomed for the first team, but lost out to Terry Gibson when Bobby Gould took over. In his first season at Bradford City, he helped them to promotion from Division 3. This achievement was tarnished by the awful fire at Valley Parade on the final day of the 1984–85 season. He scored 57 goals in 212 appearances and attracted the attention of Newcastle, for whom he signed for £500,000 in June 1988, after Bradford failed to gain promotion to Division One through the play–offs. He spent an unsuccessful season at St James' Park, as The Magpies were relegated. In his season at Leeds, he helped them to promotion, but was sold before the start of the 1990–91 season. Since he moved to Ayresome Park, he has been involved in the play-offs and promotion to and relegation from the FA Premier League.

HERBERT, Frederick (Fred)
Inside Left

Born: Bedworth
Career: Foxford United, Bedworth Town, Exhall Colliery, Coventry City 1922, Brierley Hill Alliance 1929, Retired c/s 1930.

Coventry City	League	F.A.Cup
1922–23	13 – 2	–
1923–24	33 – 12	2
1924–25	30 – 5	3 – 2
1925–26	37 – 22	1
1926–27	38 – 24	3 – 2
1927–28	31 – 13	2
1928–29	5 – 4	1
Total	187 – 82	12 – 4

Debut: 18/11/22 v Stockport Co. (a) 1-5 (CF)

Fred Herbert, nicknamed "Cute", was the local lad who made good. He arrived at City after a highly successful career in local football whilst employed at Exhall Colliery. He was a bustling forward who was characterised by his close–cropped, slicked–back hair. He was used along the forward line, but was mostly played at inside left – his preferred position and from where he scored the vast majority of his goals – or on the left wing. Towards the end of his days at City, he suffered from injury and was allowed to move to Brierley Hill Alliance, becoming a publican in Bedworth 12 months later. He set a scoring record at City, which was subsequently eclipsed by Clarrie Bourton.

HEWETT, Joseph T. (Joe)
Goalkeeper

Born: Coventry
Career: Coventry Motor Sundries, Watford 1927, Coventry City c/s 1931.

Coventry City	League	F.A.Cup
1931–32	5	–

Debut: 14/9/31 v Cardiff C. (a) 1–6 (Goal)

Big goalkeeper Joe Hewett was a Coventry kid, but only joined City after four years at Watford, for whom he played 110 games. He was often called on to save the day and didn't let the side down, but lost his place at Vicarage Road, and was set back by a broken collar bone. He was signed by James McIntyre as the replacement for Tommy Allen. His first game was a 1–6 defeat at Cardiff, but he played a blinder! New manager Harry Storer released him in 1932.

HEWITT, Ronald (Ron)
Inside Forward

Born: Flint 21st June 1928
Career: Wolverhampton Wanderers 1946, Walsall (loan) November 1949, Darlington May 1950, Wrexham July 1951, Cardiff City May 1957 (£7,000), Wrexham July 1959 (£2,000), Coventry City March 1960 (£4,500), Chester March 1962, Hereford United August 1963 (£3,000), Retired 1964 to go to Australia to coach, Caernavon Town 1966–7.

Coventry City	League	F.A.Cup	Lge.Cup
1959–60	14 – 5	–	
1960–61	25 – 11	1	
1961–62	20 – 7	2 – 1	1
Total	59 – 23	3 – 1	1

Debut: 5/3/60 v Barnsley (a) 0–1 (IL)
Honours: 5 full Wales Caps
Welsh Cup Winners Medal 1957

Hewitt spent most of his career in his native North Wales with Wrexham, but his best moments were with Cardiff City in Division 1, as he appeared in Wales' quarter final 0–1 defeat to Brazil in the 1958 World Cup finals. When at City, Hewitt was providing experience in a team which was establishing itself in Division 3. The arrival of Jimmy Hill resulted in a move, along with Bill Myerscough, to Chester.

HIBBITT, Kenneth (Ken)
Midfield

Born: Bradford 3rd January 1951

Career: Apprentice Bradford (P.A.) 1967, Wolverhampton Wanderers November 1968 (£6,000), Seattle Sounders (loan) May 1982, Coventry City July 1984 (F/T), Bristol Rovers August 1986, Retired 1988.

Coventry City	League	F.A.Cup	Lge.Cup
1984–85	31+2s–3	2	1
1985–86	11+3s–1	–	0+1s
Total	42+5s–4	2	1+1s

Debut: 25/8/84 v Aston Villa (a) 0–1 (sub)
Full Debut: 4/9/84 v. West Ham Utd. (a) 1–3 (Mid)
Honours: 1 England U–23 Cap
League Cup Winners Medals 1974 & 1980

Hibbitt came to City after giving fine service to Wolves for 16 years. He was brought by Bobby Gould to provide experienced back–up, but Hibbitt became a regular in his first season at City, in the team that avoided relegation by winning the last three games. He left City, after failing to get a coaching job at the club, to take a similar post at Bristol Rovers. His career was ended following a broken leg and he has now moved into management at Walsall.

HICKMAN, William
Centre Half

Born: Wolverhampton
Career: Burton Town, Coventry City c/s 1927, Oakengates Town 1928.

Coventry City	League	F.A.Cup
1927–28	9 – 2	–

Debut: 3/9/27 v Charlton Ath. (h) 3–3 (CH)

Hickman was a well thought of youngster who was surprisingly pushed into the first team after 2 successive defeats. He started well but was replaced by William Hunter. He was recalled in November 1927, but played his final League game against Millwall in the 1–9 disaster at the Den. With the arrival of Norman Dinsdale, Hickman was surplus to requirement and was released.

HIGHAM, Frank
Right Half

Born: Daventry September 1905
Career: Daventry, Walsall 1924/5, Wolverhampton Wanderers May 1925, Coventry City June 1928, Lincoln City July 1930, Worcester City July 1931, Nuneaton Town 1933/4, Evesham Town c/s 1934, Hereford United c/s 1935.

Coventry City	League	F.A.Cup
1928–29	30 – 2	1
1929–30	5	–
Total	35 – 2	1

Debut: 25/8/28 v Norwich C. (h) 3–0 (RH)

Higham made his League debut at the age of 20, making 2 appearances for The Saddlers before signing for Wolves. He made 38 appearances at Molineux, primarily as cover, before being bought by City. He was an impressive right half in his first season, establishing a half back partnership with Norman Dinsdale and Billy Bell, in City's best season since joining the League. The arrival of Jimmy Baker from Wolves, pushed Higham into the reserves. Consequently, his appearances in his second season came only as a replacement for the injured Dinsdale. Higham was able to fit into the centre half position as he stood 6ft 1inch tall and weighed 12½ stone. He made no first team appearances at Lincoln.

HILL, Brian W.
Midfield

Born: Bedworth 31st July 1941
Career: Apprentice Coventry City, pro August 1958, Bristol City (loan) March 1971, Torquay United October 1971, Bedworth United.

Coventry City	League	F.A.Cup	Lge.Cup
1957–58	1 – 1	–	
1958–59	10	–	
1959–60	8 – 1	1	
1960–61	10 – 1	–	1
1961–62	9	2	1
1962–63	37 – 1	9	1
1963–64	40 – 2	2	1 – 1
1964–65	28	1	1
1965–66	22	3	4
1966–67	15+1s	–	1
1967–68	16+2s–1	2+1s	–
1968–69	31	2	5
1969–70	8+1s	–	–
1970–71	5	–	1
1971–72	–	–	–
Total	240+4s–7	22+1s	16–1

Debut: 30/4/58 v Gillingham (a) 2–3 (1R) (1 goal)

When Brian Hill made his debut at the age of 16 years 273 days, he became both City's youngest player and goalscorer. This was City's last game in Division 3(S), enabling Hill to play in five divisions for City and in European competition during his 13

years at Highfield Road. He only became a regular after the arrival of Jimmy Hill, but injury limited his appearances. He was a vital member of the "Sky Blue Era", because of his ability to play in any defensive or midfield position.

HILL, James (Jimmy)
Outside Left

Born: Wishaw 19th August 1931
Career: Modern Machines, Coventry City August 1948, Millwall June 1956, Wisbech Town March 1957, Shrewsbury Town 1957–58.

Coventry City	League	F.A.Cup
1948–49	–	–
1949–50	1	1
1950–51	4 – 1	–
1951–52	–	–
1952–53	11 – 2	–
1953–54	31 – 3	–
1954–55	3	–
1955–56	17 – 2	–
Total	67 – 8	1

Debut: 12/11/49 v Hull City (a) 1–2 (OL)

When Hill moved up to the professional ranks in 1948, a lot was expected of him. Yet his first team appearances were very limited in his 8 years at City. Being understudy to Norman Lockhurst, an Irish international, restricted his outings. 1953–54 was by far Hill's most successful season, but the emergence of exciting Ray Sambrook led Hill to look elsewhere for first team football, which he was unable to achieve regularly at either Millwall or Shrewsbury.

HILL, Peter
Forward

Born: Heanor 8th August 1931
Career: Rutland United, Modern Machines 1946, Coventry City August 1948, Retired 1962.

Coventry City	League	F.A.Cup	Lge.Cup
1948–49	3	–	
1949–50	5 – 2	–	
1950–51	1	–	
1951–52	5	1	
1952–53	34 – 12	2 – 1	
1953–54	17	–	
1954–55	35 – 8	4	
1955–56	31 – 5	–	
1956–57	24 – 10	1	
1957–58	38 – 10	2 – 1	
1958–59	25 – 6	2 – 2	
1959–60	25 – 7	2	
1960–61	33 –12	3	–
1961–62	9 – 1	1	–
Total	285 – 73	18 – 4	–

Debut: 5/2/49 v Sheffield W. (a) 1–2 (IR)

During the bleak days of the 1950's when the movement of City staff was considerable, one thing remained constant, Peter Hill. He was a regular for 9 consecutive seasons in his 14 year spell at City, his only professional club. Hill was never a high goalscorer, but could be relied upon to provide his share, and his consistency has resulted in his total of 78 goals only being bettered for City by 5 other players. He retired in 1962, aged only 30. He became trainer for 5 years during the Sky Blue revolution. He returned to the club as kit man, a position he has held since 1988.

HILL, Raymond W. (Ray)
Forward

Born: Stourbridge 15th February 1936
Career: Redditch Town, Coventry City November 1957, Rugby Town July 1959.

Coventry City	League	F.A.Cup
1957–58	11 – 5	–
1958–59	3	–
Total	14 – 5	–

Debut: 14/12/57 v Plymouth Argyle (a) 0–4 (IL)

Hill did not stay for a long period at City, but his adaptability was a bonus for him, for he played when Ray Straw or Peter Hill were injured. When he, together with Peter Hill and Brian Hill, lined up in April 1958 at Gillingham, this was the first time that three players with the same surname had appeared together for City – playing at centre forward and the two inside forward positions.

HINDLEY, Peter
Defender

Born: Worksop 19th May 1944
Career: Apprentice Nottingham Forest, pro June 1961 Coventry City February 1974 (£35,000), Peterborough United July 1976.

Coventry City	League	F.A.Cup	Lge.Cup
1973–74	9	–	–
1974–75	23	–	–
1975–76	1	–	–
Total	33	–	

Debut: 9/2/74 v Newcastle United (a) 1–5 (CH)
Honours: 1 England U–23 Cap

After 13 years service for Nottingham Forest in Division 1, and latterly Division 2, Hindley was given the opportunity by City to play once more in Division 1. His start was inauspicious as City were thrashed 5–1 at Newcastle. Season 1974–75 saw Hindley form a defensive partnership with Larry Lloyd, but the return from injury of Alan Dugdale resulted in Hindley dropping into the reserves, where he regularly played until his transfer to Peterborough.

HOLDER, Colin W.
Forward

Born: Cheltenham 6th January 1944

Career: Coventry City 1959, Chelmsford City 1963, Weymouth February 1964, Nuneaton Borough 1964, Stourbridge May 1964, Deal Town August 1964, Margate c/s 1965, Cheltenham Town c/s 1968, Banbury c/s 1969, Rugby c/s 1971, Kidderminster Harriers 1971–72, Salisbury 1971–72, Gloucester City c/s 1972, Hednesford Town c/s 1974, Armitage c/s 1976 (Player Manager), Coleshill Town c/s 1979 (Player Manager), Retired c/s 1982.

Coventry City	League	F.A.Cup	Lge.Cup
1959–60	–	–	
1960–61	7 – 3	–	–
1961–62	2 – 1	–	–
1962–63	–	–	–
Total	9 – 4	–	–

Debut: 20/3/61 v Newport County (a) 3–3 (IL)

Holder never had a long run in the first team and was unable to show his potential. He was allowed to move into the Southern League by Jimmy Hill at the end of the 1962–63 season. During his non-league career, Holder became something of a nomad, playing for a total of 15 clubs.

HOLMES, James Paul (Jimmy)
Defender
Born: Dublin 11th November 1953
Career: St. John Bosco, Coventry City November 1970, Tottenham Hotspur March 1977 (£120,000), Vancouver Whitecaps March 1981, Leicester City October 1982, Brentford February 1983, Torquay United March 1983, Peterborough United November 1983, Nuneaton Borough December 1985, Leicester United c/s 1987, Hitchin Town 1987–88, Bedworth United October 1988, Nuneaton Borough c/s 1989, Retired c/s 1990.

Coventry City	League	F.A.Cup	Lge.Cup
1970–71	–	–	–
1971–72	3	–	–
1972–73	1	–	–
1973–74	41 – 1	6	6
1974–75	18+4s–5	1+1s	–
1975–76	34+1s	3	1
1976–77	25+1s	1	3
Total	122+6s–6	11+1s	10

Debut: 4/12/71 v Leicester City (a) 1–1 (LB)
Honours: 30 full Republic of Ireland caps (17 at City)

Spotted by Noel Cantwell playing for St John Bosco in Dublin, Holmes was signed for City. He made his international debut before playing for City's first team and became Eire's youngest international at the age of 17½. Holmes was a regular for 3½ seasons at left back or central defence before moving onto

Spurs. His first Division career was wrecked by a broken leg which resulted in complications. This injury occurred during his 29th international appearance, versus Bulgaria in Sofia in 1979. He was unable to play for 2 seasons, and then moved to Vancouver before returning to a series of clubs on a non-contract basis. He became assistant manager at Peterborough and manager at both Nuneaton and Bedworth. He had the honour of a testimonial game at Lansdowne Road between the Republic of Ireland and a Tottenham X1.

HOLMES, W. Harold (Harry)
Outside Right
Born: Ambergate 1908
Career: Heanor Town, Coventry City 1931/2, Heanor Town 1933, Notts County 1933/4, Heanor Town 1934/5, Birmingham 1934/5, Heanor Town 1934/5.

Coventry City	League	F.A.Cup
1931–32	8 – 5	–
1932–33	14 – 7	–
Total	22 – 12	–

Debut: 6/2/32 v Crystal Palace (h) 8–0 (OR) 1 goal

Harry Holmes was an amateur outside right who was based in the East Midlands. He played twice for Notts County and once for Birmingham, but his notable spell was with City. He scored on his debut and bagged a hat-trick in his second game against Gillingham. His scoring rate was remarkable for a winger and he scored another hat-trick against Torquay in December 1932.

HOLTON, James Allan (Jim)
Centre Half
Born: Lesmahagow 11th April 1951
Career: Celtic 1967, West Bromwich Albion April 1968, Shrewsbury Town June 1971, Manchester United January 1973 (£80,000), Miami Toros (loan) c/s 1976, Sunderland September 1976 (£75,000), Coventry City March 1977 (£50,000), Detroit Express (loan) April 1980, Sheffield Wednesday c/s 1981, Coventry Talbot c/s 1982, Retired c/s 1983.

Coventry City	League	F.A.Cup	Lge.Cup
1976–77	8	–	–
1977–78	25	–	3 – 1
1978–79	34	2	1
1979–80	24	–	3
1980–81	–	–	–
Total	91	2	7 – 1

Debut: 19/4/77 v W.B.A. (h) 1–1 (CH)
Honours 15 full Scotland Caps
1 Scotland U–23 Cap

"Big Jim" was a feared centre–half. His no–nonsense style meant that he was a great favourite with the fans. He was at his peak with Manchester United, when he played in the 1974 World Cup finals, although he broke his leg twice and lost his place. A short spell at Sunderland ended with a move to City, where he played an important part in keeping City in Division 1, and then establishing the club in the late 1970's. After losing his place to Paul Dyson, Holton moved to 2nd Division Sheffield Wednesday, but retired from the first class game without making the first team. He became a publican at the Rising Sun in the Coventry.

HOPPER, Matthew
Outside Right
Born: Co. Durham
Career: Percy Main Colliery Welfare, Ashington, Lincoln City 1920/1, Millwall Athletic April 1921, Percy Main Colliery Welfare, Ashington, Catford South End, Sittingbourne, Coventry City August 1926, Ashington August 1927, Annfield Plain November 1928.

Coventry City	League	F.A.Cup
1926–27	15 – 1	2

Debut: 28/8/26 v Northampton T. (h) 0–3 (OR)

North–East product Matt Hopper, played 47 times for Millwall in the early 1920's, but was then released. City revived his League career as James Kerr was looking for players with experience that City could afford to pay cheaply! He started in the first team, but lost his place once Kerr decided to

blood Scottish youngster Tommy Breslin. His move to Ashington became his third spell with the club.

HORMANTSCHUK, Peter
Full Back
Born: Coventry 11th September 1962
Career: Apprentice Coventry City, pro September 1980, Nuneaton Borough 1985, Coventry Sporting 1986, Nuneaton Borough 1988, Retired 1989.

Coventry City	League	F.A.Cup	Lge.Cup
1980–81	–	–	–
1981–82	0+5s	1+1s	–
1982–83	10+1s–1	2	1
1983–84	8	–	–
1984–85	–	–	–
Total	18+6s–1	3+1s	1

Debut: 2/1/82 v Sheffield W. (h) 3–1 (Sub) FA Cup 3rd Rd.
Full Debut: 23/1/82 v Man. C. (a) 3–1 (RB) FA Cup 4th Rd.

After spending the first three years at City as cover for Roberts and Thomas, it looked as if "Chukkie" could expect to establish himself in the 1st team with the arrival of Bobby Gould. After playing eight games, he was the scapegoat for two successive defeats and didn't play again. A knee injury in a reserve game was said by doctors to be too serious to continue playing. He played infrequently in local non–league football before calling it a day.

HOUCHEN, Keith M.
Centre Forward
Born: Middlesbrough 25th July 1960
Career: Chesterfield 1977, Hartlepool United February 1978, Orient March 1982 (£25,000), York City March 1984, Scunthorpe United March 1986, Coventry City June 1986 (£50,000), Hibernian March 1989 (£300,000), Port Vale c/s 1991, Hartlepool United c/s 1993 (F/T).

Coventry City	League	F.A.Cup	Lge.Cup
1986–87	20 – 2	5 – 5	–
1987–88	13+8s–3	–	2
1988–89	10+3s–2	0+1s	0+1s
Total	43+11s7	5+1s–5	2+1s

Debut: 23/8/86 v West Ham Utd (a) 0–1 (CF)
Honours: FA Cup Winners Medal 1987

When signed for City in June 1986, Houchen was a journeyman striker who had tasted FA Cup glory at York, where he scored the winning penalty against Arsenal in 1985, but then struggled at Scunthorpe. Despite his low strike rate in the League, Houch came into his element in the FA Cup, and in his

five cup matches in 1987, he scored five vital goals. His diving header in the 1987 Final was one of the best goals seen at Wembley. With the profits of the cup run, City bought David Speedie. Houch was out in the cold and only made 25 full appearances in 18 months before signing for Hibernian, where he teamed up with Gareth Evans, and later helped Port Vale in their unsuccessful push for promotion in 1993.

HOULDEY, Charles Arthur
Full Back

Born: Birmingham 1902
Career: Barbel F.C., Harbourne Lynwood F.C., Coventry City April 1925, Walsall October 1928 (£400), Oswestry Town c/s 1931, Evesham Town, Halesowen Town October 1934, Shirley Town 1935/6.

Coventry City	League	F.A.Cup
1925–26	28 – 2	1
1926–27	13	–
1927–28	14	–
1928–29	3	–
Total	58 – 2	1

Debut: 5/9/25 v Southport (a) 2–1 (RB)

Charles Houldey staked his claim for a regular right back place in the only season (1925–26) that City spent in Division 3(N). He made his City debut when Jack Bellas was dropped following a 1–5 thrashing at Wigan Borough. He impressed his manager and was the only player in the line-up on the opening day of the 1926–27 season to have previously appeared for City. He played well, but a broken leg in November 1926 ruled him out for 16 months and he didn't regain his place until February 1928. With the departure of manager James Kerr, new boss James McIntyre signed Laurie Crown, who made the right back spot his own. Whilst an amateur, in his early days, he worked at Birmingham Fish Market. City players could often be seen waiting at the station, some chatting to the driver and guard, and others looking for the taxi bringing Houldey from work! Houdley was signed by Walsall (whose manager was Kerr) where he established a regular place for 3 seasons. In total, he made 112 appearances for the Saddlers, including an eventful FA Cup 3rd Round replay at Middlesbrough in January 1929. Walsall's goalkeeper Harry Wait, was suffering from a boil on the leg which was sufficient to force him out of the match at short notice. Having no reserve keeper in the party, Houldey played in goal, but couldn't save The Saddlers from a 1–5 defeat.

HOWE, Frederick (Fred)
Wing Half

Born: Rotherham c. 1895
Career: Kimberworth Old Boys, Coventry City 1919, Brentford 1920/1, Peterborough & Fletton United, Wellingborough Town, Peterborough & Fletton United c/s 1925.

Coventry City	League	F.A.Cup
1919–20	5	–

Debut: 6/9/19 v Tottenham H. (a) 1–4 (LH)

Spotted by manager William Clayton playing in a junior final at Bramall Lane in 1919, Howe was snapped up and plunged straight into City's struggling side. He played in 5 consecutive games, but was a casualty of City's poor performances. He signed for Brentford and played 3 times in 2 seasons before signing for Peterborough & Fletton United.

HOWELL, Albert
Forward

Born: Birmingham
Career: Hednesford Town, Coventry City 1920/1, Jarrow 1921.

Coventry City	League	F.A.Cup
1920–21	4 – 1	–

Debut: 24/2/21 v Wolverhampton W. (h) 4–0 (IR) 1 goal

Howell seemed to have made the perfect start when he scored on his debut in the vital victory over Wolves in February 1921, as City tried to escape the relegation zone in the club's second season in the League. He played just 3 more matches, and was overlooked in the season's end in favour of experienced Sammy Stevens.

HUDSON, George A.
Centre Half

Born: Manchester 14th March 1937

Career: Blackburn Rovers December 1957, Accrington Stanley June 1960 (F/T), Peterborough United October 1961 (£5,000), Coventry City April 1963 (£22,000), Northampton Town March 1966, Tranmere Rovers January 1967, Altrincham.

Coventry City	League	F.A.Cup	Lge.Cup
1962–63	15 – 6	–	–
1963–64	32 – 24	2 – 3	2 – 1
1964–65	38 – 19	1	4 – 5
1965–66	28 – 13	3 – 2	4 – 2
Total	113 – 62	6 – 5	10 – 8

Debut: 6/4/63 v Halifax Town (h) 5–4 (CF) (3 goals)

In April 1963, Jimmy Hill dropped a bombshell by dropping Terry Bly, who had scored 24 goals in 31 league games, replacing him with George Hudson. Not even a Hudson hat–trick seemed to satisfy the critics. This started however, a purple patch of City scoring, and in the next three seasons Hudson netted a remarkable 75 goals in 129 games. It was fitting that he scored the winner against Colchester in 1964 to clinch the Division 3 championship. Just as it was a shock to include Hudson originally, there was outrage when he was sold to Northampton. He could never reclaim the same scoring touch, and the following season City took the Second Division title. After retiring, Hudson became employed in Manchester at the Daily Mirror printing presses.

HUMPHRIES, William M. (Willie)
Outside Right

Born: Belfast 8th June 1936

Career: Ards, Leeds United September 1958, Ards December 1959, Coventry City April 1962, Swansea Town March 1965 (£14,000), Ards 1968.

Coventry City	League	F.A.Cup	Lge.Cup
1961–62	1	–	–
1962–63	41 – 10	9	1
1963–64	40 – 10	2	2 – 1
1964–65	27 – 3	1	2
Total	109 – 23	12	5 – 1

Debut: 28/4/62 v Hull City (h) 0–2 (OR)

Honours: 14 N.Ireland full caps (10 at City)
8 Irish League appearances
Irish Cup Winners Medal 1969
Irish Cup Runners–up Medal 1960
Welsh Cup Runners–up Medal 1966

When Jimmy Hill bought Humphries over from Ards, he was taking a big risk, for Willie was very reluctant to move to the mainland after experiencing an unhappy time whilst at Leeds. But whilst with City he was superb, and his dashing runs down the right flank were a key weapon in City's rise out of Division 3. Humphries played for his country on 10 occasions while he was at City, 9 of which were while the club was in Division 3. He was a prolific scorer for a winger, but was sold to Swansea once Jimmy Hill had found another Northern Irish winger, Dave Clements. Humphries spent 3½ successful seasons at Swansea before moving back to Ards, and later became their Manager.

HUNT, Roger P. (Ernie)

Forward

Born: Swindon 17th March 1943

Career: Apprentice Swindon Town, pro March 1960, Wolverhampton Wanderers September 1965 (£40,000), Everton September 1967 (£80,000), Coventry City March 1968 (£70,000), Doncaster Rovers (loan) January 1973, Bristol City December 1973, Atherstone 1975.

Coventry City	League	F.A.Cup	Lge.Cup
1967–68	6+1s–1	–	–
1968–69	39 – 11	2	5 – 2
1969–70	30+1s–9	2	1
1970–71	29+2s10	1 – 1	4 – 1
1971–72	26+1s12	1+1s	1
1972–73	7 – 2	–	–
1973–74	3+1s	–	–
Total	140+6s–45	6+1s–1	11 – 3

Debut: 16/3/68 v Manchester United (h) 2-0 (IR)
Honours: 3 England U–23 Caps

"Ernie" Hunt signed for his home town club Swindon and emerged in their young and exciting team of the early 1960's. Whilst at The County Ground, he earned the first of his England U–23 caps. After scoring 88 goals in 237 League & Cup games, he transferred to Wolves and netted 35 goals, including 21 in season 1966–67 when they fought with City for promotion from Division 2. He played 6 Division 1 matches before signing for Everton. At Highfield Road, he was a great favourite and scored some vital goals in keeping City in Division 1 and earning a place in Europe. His most famous goal was the "Donkey Kick" against Everton in October 1970. Willie Carr flicked the ball into the air with his heels and as the ball was in the air, Hunt volleyed from 20 yards straight past the stranded keeper. He is the fourth highest scorer for City in Division 1, but injury limited his appearances and he was loaned to Doncaster and sold to Bristol City once Colin Stein was signed. After leaving the game, Hunt ran a pub in Ledbury and coached the Gloucester City youth team. His arthritis now prevents him from working, and his image was tarnished by his press allegations of match–fixing at City, but this should not overshadow his contribution to City and the game in general.

HUNT, Stephen K. (Steve)

Midfield

Born: Birmingham 4th August 1956

Career: Apprentice Aston Villa, pro January 1974, New York Cosmos February 1977 (£30,000), Coventry City August 1978 (£40,000), New York Cosmos (loan) May 1982, West Bromwich Albion March 1984 (£100,000), Aston Villa March 1986 (£30,000) Willenhall Town 1988 (player–manager), Retired 1989.

Coventry City	League	F.A.Cup	Lge.Cup
1978–79	20+4s–5	–	–
1979–80	34+1s–1	–	3
1980–81	40 – 6	3	9 – 2
1981–82	36 – 9	4 – 3	1
1982–83	35 – 4	3	3 – 1
1983–84	13+2s–1	4 – 1	1
Total	178+7s–26	14 – 4	17 – 3

Debut: 2/9/78 v Derby County (a) 2-0 (OR) 1g
Honours: 2 full England Caps.

Steve Hunt was a great success at City. Initially, he was discarded by his home team, Aston Villa, and he tried his luck with NY Cosmos, playing with

Pele and Franz Beckenbauer. He gave up the possibility of immense riches to return to play for City, and he soon impressed everybody with his skilful left foot. He had the ability to score some outstanding goals. During his time at City, he represented an England X1 versus the London FA, but it was only after an acrimonious departure that he received his two caps. He had been restless for several years and it was a great surprise that Hunt didn't leave in the summer of 1983 when City suffered a mass exodus. Whilst at Albion and Villa, he played in struggling sides, but still showed his cultured football. A back injury forced him out of the game, and Hunt is now coaching at Leicester City.

HUNTER, William
Centre Half

Born: Falkirk 16th August 1900
Career: Bowhill, Birmingham early 1921, Grimsby Town January 1927, Coventry City October 1927, Walsall October 1928, Torquay United 1929/30.

Coventry City	League	F.A.Cup
1927–28	31 – 1	2
1928–29	–	–
Total	31 – 1	2

Debut: 15/10/27 v Southend United (h) 6–1 (CH)

Scotsman Hunter made his League debut for Birmingham in season 1921–22 and was considered to be a good prospect for the future, despite being primarily a reserve. After 5 seasons in the wings, he played 20 matches for the Blues during the 1925–26 season. Although expecting to hold down his place he was pushed back into the reserves, and moved to Grimsby, where he made only 6 appearances. After a disappointing start to the season City manager James Kerr bought Hunter, and one of the 2 games he missed before the season's end was the 1–9 drubbing by Millwall. Despite being a versatile left footed player, Hunter didn't figure in the plans of the new manager James McIntyre and teamed up with Kerr at Walsall. After only 10 games, he ended his professional career with 6 appearances for Torquay.

HURST, Lee Jason
Midfield

Born: Nuneaton 21st September 1970
Career: YTS Coventry City, pro May 1989.

Coventry City	League	F.A.Cup	Lge.Cup
1989–90	–	–	–
1990–91	3+1s	0+1s	–
1991–92	8+2	1	2+1s
1992–93	35 – 2	–	1
Total	46+3s–2	1+1s	3+1s

Debut: 29/1/91 v Southampton (a) 0–2 (Sub) FA Cup
Full Debut: 2/2/91 v Wimbledon (a) 0–1 (LB)

Local youngster Lee Hurst made his first appearances for City at left back, as a replacement for Paul Edwards and Kenny Sansom. He had the distinction of scoring a remarkable own goal at Cambridge in the FA Cup in January 1992. When Steve Ogrizovic saved an injury time penalty, Hurst following up the kick, shot into his own net, for City to lose 0–1. In the summer of 1992 he was pushed into midfield and never looked back. He has shown himself to be a tough–tackling and creative midfielder who can move back into defence if needed.

HUTCHISON, Thomas (Tommy)
Outside Left

Born: Cardenden 22nd September 1947
Career: Dundonald Bluebell, Alloa Athletic 1965, Blackpool February 1968, Coventry City October 1972 (£140,000 & player–exchange), Seattle Sounders (loan) April 1980, Manchester City October 1980 (£47,000), Bulova (H/K) July 1982, Burnley August 1983, Swansea City c/s 1985, Merthyr Tydfil March 1991

Coventry City	League	F.A.Cup	Lge.Cup
1972–73	30 – 2	4 – 1	–
1973–74	41 – 3	6 – 1	6
1974–75	42 – 4	3	1
1975–76	42 – 1	3	2
1976–77	31+2s–3	2 – 1	–
1977–78	40 – 3	1	4 – 1
1978–79	42 – 6	2	1
1979–80	40 – 1	2 – 1	3
1980–81	4 – 1	–	1 – 1
Total	312+2s24	23 – 4	18 – 2

Debut: 14/10/72 v Manchester City (a) 3–2 (OL)
Honours: 17 Full Scotland Caps (all at City)
1 Scotland U–23 Cap
FA Cup Runners–up Medal 1981

Hutch was one of the most exciting players to play for City. He had breathtaking skill and was a great favourite at City. He began with Alloa in 1965 and played with Gordon Milne at Blackpool. His former colleague signed him for City in October 1972, in a deal which saw Billy Rafferty move to Bloomfield

Debut: 22/10/60 v Bury (h) 1–2 (OL)
Honours: 4 full Scotland caps

Imlach was a proven talent. Having played for Scotland and gained an FA Cup winner's medal, it was a shrewd piece of business by Billy Frith to gain Imlach's signature for £8000 from Luton. During his time at City, he missed only 1 game and brought some skill and guile to a middle–of–the–table Division 3 side. The arrival of Jimmy Hill meant the end of Stewart's City career, for the manager was looking to establish a team for the future and at the age of 30, Imlach did not figure in those plans. His son Gary, is a sports presenter with independent television.

Road. For eight seasons, Hutch was a great club man, being captain in 1979–80. His close ball play was outstanding and provided tremendous service for a whole series of City forwards. Despite very heavy marking, Hutch missed very few games until 1980, when he was sold to Manchester City with Bobby McDonald. He was 33 and with wingers Bodak and Bannister and the impressive Steve Hunt at Coventry, it seemed to be a reasonable decision by Milne, but nobody could have anticipated the longevity of Hutch's career. He had the distinction of scoring at both ends in the 1981 FA Cup final and moved to Hong Kong in July 1982. Since returning in August 1983, he has spent his time in the lower divisions and even appeared in the European Cup Winners Cup in 1989–90. He now works as a community liaison officer with Taff–Ely Council and is still playing with Vauxhall Conference Merthyr, at the age of 45.

IMLACH, James John Stewart (Stewart)
Outside Left

Born: Lossiemouth 6th January 1932
Career: St. James' Youth Club, Lossiemouth, Lossiemouth United, Lossiemouth, Bury May 1952, Derby County May 1954, Nottingham Forest July 1955 (£5,000), Luton Town June 1960 (£8,000), Coventry City October 1960 (£8,000), Crystal Palace July 1962, Dover December 1964, Chelmsford City February 1965, Crystal Palace February 1966, Retired March 1967.

Coventry City	League	F.A.Cup	Lge.Cup
1960–61	28 – 4	3	–
1961–62	45 – 7	2	1
Total	73 – 11	5	1

JACOBS, Stephen Douglas (Steve)
Defender/Midfield

Born: West Ham 5th July 1961
Career: Apprentice Coventry City, pro November 1978, Brighton & Hove Albion June 1984 (F/T), Charlton Athletic August 1986 (F/T), Gillingham December 1986.

Coventry City	League	F.A.Cup	Lge.Cup
1978–79	–	–	–
1979–80	1	–	–
1980–81	8+3s	1+1s	1+3s
1981–82	37+2s	1+1s	2
1982–83	30+2s	1	2
1983–84	18	–	1
Total	94+7s	3+2s	6+3s

Debut: 3/5/80 v Arsenal (h) 0–1 (LB)

During Dave Sexton's reign at City, Jacobs was a first team regular in midfield and proved more than able in an attack minded team. Under Bobby Gould, Jacobs started in the first team but lost his place to Sam Allardyce, and only when Trevor Peake was injured did he return. Jacobs was often unsettled at City and was twice sent off in matches. Gould allowed him to move to Brighton, where he stayed for 2 years, before short spells at Charlton and Gillingham.

JAMIESON, Ian Wallace
Wing Half

Born: Dumbarton 14th October 1928
Career: Aberdeen 1946, Oswestry Town (loan) 1947–49, Coventry City January 1949, Rugby Town November 1958 (player-manager).

Coventry City	League	F.A.Cup
1948–49	9 – 1	–
1949–50	9 – 2	–
1950–51	2	–
1951–52	14 – 2	–
1952–53	3	–
1953–54	38 – 1	1
1954–55	28	–
1955–56	17	–
1956–57	25	1
1957–58	36	1
1958–59	–	–
Total	181 – 6	3

Debut: 15/1/49 v Leeds United (h) 4–1 (IR) 1 goal

Jamieson, whilst in the army, was spotted by Harry Storer playing for Oswestry Town . Once free from military duties, his signature was obtained from Aberdeen, who held his registration. Early in his career at City, Jamieson struggled to oust Bryn Allen or Don Dorman, but later became a strong, dependable wing half in a struggling City side. During the latter stages of his career, he played part-time, combining football with a job at Courtaulds. In 1973, he joined the board and became chairman in 1983. His one year reign saw a return to the City's roots, from a club unconcerned about the views of the people of Coventry. Unfortunately, this attitude did not continue after his departure.

JARVIS, Ambrose W.
Goalkeeper

Born: Coventry
Career: Edgewick, Coventry City c/s 1919, Nuneaton Town December 1920.

Coventry City	League	F.A.Cup
1919–20	3	–
1920–21	–	–
Total	3	–

Debut: 22/11/19 v Blackpool (h) 0–0 (Goal)

Signed in the summer of 1919, Jarvis was a local lad who was cover for the experienced Albert Lindon. Injury to Lindon gave Jarvis his chance in November 1919, and in his 3 consecutive games he conceded only 2 goals and achieved 2 clean sheets. He stayed in City's reserves for 18 months, but the arrival of Jerry Best triggered the sale of Jarvis to Nuneaton Town.

JENKINS, Walter
Left Back

Born: Chesterfield
Career: Staveley Town, Coventry City 1928, Staveley Town February 1929.

Coventry City	League	F.A.Cup
1928–29	6	–

Debut: 1/12/28 v Plymouth Argyle (a) 0–3 (LB)

Young full back Jenkins came to City on trial and was picked for the first team following injury to Adam Plunkett. He was not considered worthy of retention and moved back to Staveley soon after Plunkett was fit.

JENKINSON, Leigh
Outside Left

Born: Moorends, nr. Thorne 9th July 1969
Career: YTS Hull City, pro July 1987, Rotherham United (loan) September 1990, Coventry City March 1993 (£200,000).

Coventry City	League	F.A.Cup	Lge.Cup
1992–93	2+3s	–	–

Debut: 13/3/93 v Arsenal (h) 0–2 (OL)

Yorkshire-born Jenkinson started with Hull City where he took some time to establish himself, but in 1991 he made the left wing position his own. He showed himself to be fast, with an ability to cross well, which encouraged Bobby Gould to sign him when David Smith moved to Birmingham. With Peter Ndlovu on international duty he was pushed straight into the team against Arsenal. He struggled to make his mark and was dropped to the subs' bench while he adjusted to City's style of play.

JOHNSON, Arthur
Outside Left

Born: Atherstone 1902
Career: Atherstone Town, Barnsley October 1925, Birmingham May 1927, Bristol City c/s 1928, Coventry City c/s 1931.

Coventry City	League	F.A.Cup
1931–32	5 – 1	–

Debut: 5/9/31 v Thames (h) 2–0 (OL)

Johnson was a tall outside left who had shown his excellent play at Bristol City. He came to City in the summer of 1931, when the club had a number of talented wingers such as Frank Bowden, Frank White and Fred Lee. Consequently he played infrequently and left at the end of the season.

JOHNSON, Eric
Outside Left

Born: Moulton 25th May 1927
Career: Winsford United, Coventry City September 1952, Torquay United July 1957.

Coventry City	League	F.A.Cup
1952–53	25 – 2	3 – 1
1953–54	13 – 1	1
1954–55	22 – 2	4
1955–56	20	1
1956–57	10 – 1	1
Total	90 – 6	10 – 1

Debut: 25/9/52 v Newport Co. (a) 4–4 (OL)

Johnson had a lot to live up to when he replaced Irish international Norman Lockhart. He certainly proved his point, for in his first season his form was excellent. A great future was predicted, but things never worked out. Injury and loss of form resulted in limited first team outings. There was great competition for the outside left position and Johnson was allowed to move to Torquay, where he spent two fruitful seasons.

JOHNSON, George Henry
Outside Right

Born: Darnall, Sheffield 1903

Career: Swansea Town 1922/3, Southend United c/s 1923, Newport County c/s 1926, Coventry City c/s 1927, Torquay United 1928.

Coventry City	League	F.A.Cup
1927–28	14 – 2	–

Debut: 27/8/27 v Watford (a) 1–3 (OR)

Johnson was a stocky, speedy outside right, who was signed by James Kerr after a successful season at Newport County. He disappointed at City and couldn't command a regular place in the team, despite being Kerr's preferred choice for the number 7 shirt. He left after less than 12 months at Highfield Road, linking up with Torquay, and later playing 62 League games for Southend.

JOHNSON, Henry Edward (Harry)
Centre Forward

Born: Birmingham 1897
Career: The Army, Coventry City September 1919, Darlaston 1920/1, Southampton April 1921, Queen's Park Rangers February 1924, Cradley Heath c/s 1926.

Coventry City	League	F.A.Cup
1919–20	2	–
1920–21	–	–
Total	2	–

Debut: 11/9/19 v Leeds City (h) 0–4 (CF)

Johnson was one of a number of players brought into the City team early in the club's first season in the Football League, in an attempt to break the habit of losing. After 2 games, he was dropped and moved onto Darlaston, before signing for Southampton where he started well, but faded badly.

JOHNSTONE, Walter
Centre Forward

Born: Glasgow c.1909
Career: Shawfield, Falkirk (trial) 1927, Coventry City August 1927, Walsall November 1928, Morton c/s 1929.

Coventry City	League	F.A.Cup
1927–28	23 – 7	2
1928–29	6 – 5	–
Total	29 – 12	2

Debut: 3/9/27 v Charlton Ath. (h) 3–3 (CF)

Another of Kerr's signings from the Shawfield club of Glasgow, Johnstone had been impressive in a trial for Falkirk and it was seen as a coup that City signed him. He was a speedy 18 year old when he arrived in August 1927 and he was being talked of as the second Hughie Gallagher. He was thrown into the team after 2 successive defeats at the start of the season and equipped himself well, scoring twice against Southend in the 6–1 victory and twice against Luton (4–2). He produced a hat–trick against Merthyr in September 1928, but was sold shortly after to Walsall, teaming up with former manager James Kerr. He played only 3 times at Fellows Park, before returning to Scotland, never achieving the heights expected of him.

JOICEY, Brian
Forward
Born: Winlaton 19th December 1945
Career: North Shields, Coventry City June 1969, Sheffield Wednesday August 1971, Barnsley July 1976, Frickley Athletic 1979, Matlock Town 1980.

Coventry City	League	F.A.Cup	Lge.Cup
1969–70	13+6s–7	–	–
1970–71	16+2s–1	1	2
1971–72	2 – 1	–	–
Total	31+8s–9	1	2

Debut: 8/10/69 v Derby Co. (a) 3–1 (Sub)
Full Debut: 11/10/69 v. West Ham U.(h) 2–2 (IR) 1 goal

For a prolific goalscorer it was surprising that Joicey was not spotted until he was almost 24 years of age. He was an immediate success in Division 1 and his 7 goals in 1969–70 were vital in the push for a European place. Indeed, it was his goal in the 1–0 victory at Wolves, that made certain of a top six finish. Unfortunately, he was unable to follow up this initial success, and he moved to Sheffield Wednesday with Dave Clements. At Wednesday and Barnsley, he was a prolific scorer. He moved out of the professional game when his health began to fail.

JOL, Maarten Cornelius (Martin)
Midfield
Born: Den Haag 16th January 1956
Career: Den Haag, Bayern Munich, Twente Enschede, West Bromwich Albion October 1981, Coventry City July 1984, Den Haag January 1985.

Coventry City	League	F.A.Cup	Lge.Cup
1984–85	15	–	–

Debut: 25/8/84 v Aston Villa (a) 0–1 (Mid)

Jol arrived at City with a reputation as a tough tackling midfielder in the Yorath role, but his stay at City was too short for this to be appreciated. Signed by Bobby Gould to add steel to the team, Jol was a disappointment. It was halfway through his first season that his father fell ill. He was allowed to move back to his native Holland and did not return.

JONES, David R.
Defender
Born: Liverpool 17th August 1956
Career: Apprentice Everton, pro May 1974, Coventry City June 1979 (£250,000), Seiko (loan) 1981, Seiko 1982, Preston North End August 1983.

Coventry City	League	F.A.Cup	Lge.Cup
1979–80	7	–	–
1980–81	1+3s	–	1
1981–82	–	–	–
Total	8+3s	–	1

Debut: 18/8/79 v Stoke City (a) 2–3 (RB)
Honours: 1 England U–21 Cap.

Jones left Everton because he was being used as a utility player, rather than a regular centre half. Of his 9 starts at City, only 2 were in that position, the rest being at right back. He came to City when the Gillespie/Dyson partnership began to bear fruit. His move to City was a backward step, which was unfortunate for a player that had been capped at U/21 level only 2 years before. As the squad had to be rationalised, he was allowed to move.

JONES, Eric J.
Half Back
Born: Dover 5th March 1938
Career: Snowdown Colliery, Coventry City May 1955, Nuneaton Borough c/s 1962.

Coventry City	League	F.A.Cup	Lge.Cup
1955–56	–	–	
1956–57	5	1	
1957–58	–	–	
1958–59	3	–	
1959–60	1	–	
1960–61	5	–	1
1961–62	–	–	
Total	14	1	1

Debut: 10/11/56 v Brentford (h) 1–1 (CH)

In the summer of 1955, 3 players moved from Snowdown Colliery to City; Jones was accompanied by Alf Bentley and George Curtis. Despite staying 7 years, Jones was limited to only 18 first team games. It is inconceivable now, that a struggling lower division side could hold onto such a peripheral squad player for so long. He was finally released by Jimmy Hill in the summer of 1962.

JONES, Fred
(See 'Southern League' section)

JONES, Joseph Thomas (Joe)
Centre Half

Born: Rhosymedre, Nr. Wrexham 1887
Died: Stoke 23rd July 1941
Career: Cefn Albion, Wrexham July 1910, Stoke September 1910, Crystal Palace June 1920, Coventry City July 1922, Crewe Alexandra May 1924, Retired c/s 1925.

Coventry City	League	F.A.Cup
1922–23	36 – 1	1
1923–24	14	2
Total	50 – 1	3

Debut: 26/8/22 v Notts Co. (h) 1–2 (CH)
Honours: 15 Wales Full Caps
2 Wales Victory Internationals

Jones was an effective stopper but not noted for having airs and graces to his game. He made his name at Stoke in the club's Southern League days and earned the first 7 of his full caps before the Great War. During the hostilities, Jones was employed as a coalminer and sacrificed a day's pay every time he turned out for Stoke. He helped Crystal Palace to the Division 3 championship during their first season in the Football League, before signing for City. His only goal for City came in the 7–1 thrashing of Wolves on Christmas Day 1922. He had a short spell afterwards at Crewe, but retired in 1925 following a bad eye injury. He returned to Stoke and worked in a bookshop for the blind before his death in 1941.

JONES, Leslie Jenkin (Les)
Inside Forward

Born: Aberdare 1st July 1913
Died: Brighton 1983

Career: Aberdare Athletic, Cardiff City 1929, Coventry City January 1934, Arsenal November 1937 (player–exchange), Swansea Town May 1946 (player–coach), Barry Town 1947/8 (player–manager), Brighton & Hove Albion August 1948 (player–coach), Retired 1949.

Coventry City	League	F.A.Cup
1933–34	17 – 9	–
1934–35	41 – 28	3 – 3
1935–36	32 – 19	–
1936–37	37 – 9	3 – 1
1937–38	12 – 4	–
Total	139–69	6 – 4

Debut: 20/1/34 v Bristol R. (a) 1–4 (IL)
Honours: 11 Wales Full Caps (5 at City)
5 Wales war–time Internationals
League Champ. Winners Medal 1937–38

Welsh international Les Jones signed for City after manager Harry Storer had been impressed by his performances for Cardiff against City at Christmas 1933. He was an instant hit with the Highfield Road crowd, scoring a hatful of goals and helping City to promotion to Division 2. His tally of goals was attracting the attention of bigger clubs and City rejected a £7,000 bid from Spurs. But after 73 goals in 145 games, City accepted an offer from Arsenal of £2,000 plus Bobby Davidson in November 1937. Jones gained a League Championship medal in his first season with The Gunners, whilst City failed to gain promotion. During the War, he guested for 13 clubs and played in 5 war–time internationals, including one in May 1942 where he was marked by ex team–mate George Mason. After he retired, he moved into management with Scunthorpe.

JONES, Richard Kenneth (Ken)
Full Back

Born: Llanelly 16th April 1926
Career: Llanelly, Coventry City November 1949, Lockheed Leamington July 1956,

Coventry City	League	F.A.Cup
1949–50	–	–
1950–51	–	–
1951–52	2	–
1952–53	1	–
1953–54	26	1
1954–55	37	4
1955–56	17	–
Total	83	5

Debut: 15/9/51 v Barnsley (a) 0–1 (RB)

Jones' transfer fee from Llanelli was a record fee for a player from the Welsh League. The transition of Martin McDonnell from right back to centre half allowed him to have a regular first team place, which he grabbed. He was strong and dependable, forming a good partnership with Roy Kirk. Jones' injury allowed Frank Austin and Charlie Timmins to establish first team places, thus Jones was allowed to move to Leamington.

JONES, Robert (Bobby)
Centre Half

Born: Glasgow

Career: Saltcoats Victoria, Glasgow Celtic April 1924, Dumbarton (loan) 1924/5, Coventry City c/s 1925, Stourbridge September 1926, Workington October 1927, Marseilles, Nithsdale Wanderers, Brechin City July 1929.

Coventry City	League	F.A.Cup
1925–26	7	–

Debut: 29/8/25 v Lincoln C. (h) 3–2 (CH)

Jones was manager Kerr's star signing. Bought from Celtic in 1925, he was made club captain. A sturdily built centre half, he came with a reputation as a dependable defender, but he was awful! He was dropped after the second game of the season, a 1–5 drubbing at Wigan Borough, failed to show any constructive play and was too slow. He lasted only 12 months and moved to Stourbridge.

KAISER, Rudi
Outside Right

Born: Amsterdam 26th December 1960

Career: Ajax, Royal Antwerp, Coventry City August 1981, Nice May 1982.

Coventry City	League	F.A.Cup	Lge.Cup
1981–82	11+5s–3	1	2

Debut: 2/9/81 v Stoke City (a) 0–4 (Sub)
Full Debut: 5/9/81 v. Notts County (a) 1–2 (OR)

Of all City's foreign signings, Kaiser seemed to settle in best and produced some good football. He was a great favourite with the fans because of his willingness to take on his man. This was his downfall, for against Sheffield Wednesday in the FA Cup he fell into a hoarding and broke his collarbone. By the time he was fit again, he was a forgotten man. He was part of the rationalisation programme and was released on a free transfer.

KEARNS, Michael D. (Mick)
Defender

Born: Nuneaton 10th March 1938

Career: Stockingford Villa 1953, Coventry City September 1955, Retired c/s 1968.

Coventry City	League	F.A.Cup	Lge.Cup
1955–56	–	–	
1956–57	–	–	
1957–58	3	–	
1958–59	32 – 2	2	
1959–60	31 – 3	–	
1960–61	40 – 1	3	1 – 1
1961–62	26 – 2	–	–
1962–63	36 – 2	9	1
1963–64	42	2	1
1964–65	36	1	4
1965–66	40 – 2	4	4
1966–67	41 – 1	1	3
1967–68	17	2	–
Total	344 – 13	24 – 1	14 – 1

Debut: 9/9/57 v Bournemouth (h) 0–3 (LH)

Mick was a great servant of the club and only four players have appeared more times for City. Never a player in the limelight, Kearns nevertheless, was a vital member of the team that moved from Division 3 to Division 1. Indeed, he played in five divisions for City. Kearns was continually hampered by injury, particularly his knees, and it is a testimony to his commitment and his importance to the team that he often played with pain killing injections. He was granted a well merited testimonial, with George Curtis. After one season in Division 1, Kearns retired to run the family's bingo hall in Nuneaton. He returned to City as a coach in 1986, but was sacked in 1992.

KELLEY, Stanley R. (Stan)
Left Back
Born: Foleshill 14th June 1920
Career: Herberts Athletic, Coventry City 1942–1948.

Coventry City	League	F.A.Cup
1945–46	WWII	–
1946–47	4	–
1947–48	–	–
Total	4	–

Debut: 2/9/46 v W.B.A. (H) 3–2 (LB)

Locally born Kelley signed for the City during the War and played regularly during hostilities. With the return of League football, however, players such as Lol Coen, Charlie Elliott, Dick Mason and Dennis Tooze were ahead of him and so his first team appearances were limited to only four.

KEMP, Gilbert
Forward
Born: Wallasey 1888
Died: 1951
Career: Wallasey Rovers, Oldham Athletic December 1911 (£150), Bradford City July 1919, Coventry City October 1919, Grimsby Town January 1920, Doncaster Rovers c/s 1920.

Coventry City	League	F.A.Cup
1919–20	3 – 2	–

Debut: 1/11/19 v Bristol C. (a) 0–1 (IL)

Gilbert Kemp was a prolific centre forward who took Oldham to the brink of the Division 1 Championship in 1915, with his 19 goals. Post-war he played once for Bradford City before signing for Coventry. After 3 games, which included 2 goals against Rotherham, he was sold to Grimsby.

KEY, John P.
Outside Right
Born: Chelsea 5th November 1937
Career: Fulham May 1956, Coventry City May 1966 (F/T), Orient March 1968, Retired 1969.

Coventry City	League	F.A.Cup	Lge.Cup
1966–67	21+1s–6	1	1
1967–68	6 – 1	–	1
Total	27+1s–7	1	1

Debut: 20/8/66 v Hull City (h) 1–0 (OR)

It was a surprise when Fulham gave Key a free transfer in the summer of 1966, but Jimmy Hill acted quickly to acquire his signature. He was a known property as Hill played with Key in the late 1950's. Key provided the necessary experience in attack which took the City into Division 1. He holds the distinction of scoring the first Division 1 goal for the City at Highfield Road. When he retired from the game he became a London cabbie.

KEYWORTH, Kenneth (Ken)
Centre Forward
Born: Rotherham 24th February 1934
Career: Wolverhampton Wanderers 1950, Rotherham United January 1952, Leicester City May 1958, Coventry City December 1964 (F/T), Swindon Town August 1965.

Coventry City	League	F.A.Cup	Lge.Cup
1964–65	7 – 3	–	–

Debut: 5/12/64 v Rotherham Utd. (h) 3–5 (CF) 1 goal.
Honours: FA Cup runners-up medals 1961 & 1963

Keyworth arrived at City in the club's first season back in Division 2, at a time when the team were 15th and looking for a fillip. Despite being past his peak, Keyworth scored in his first two games and was essentially a squad man to provide back-up for Hudson. It was a sign of City's rising stature that Keyworth, a renowned Division 1 striker chose to come to Highfield Road rather than nine other clubs.

KILCAR, Stephen P.
Inside Forward
Born: Bo'ness 22nd December 1907
Career: Linlithgow Rose, East Stirlingshire April 1927, Bradford (PA) May 1929, Coventry City May 1932, Mansfield Town 1933, Chester November 1934, Burnley 1935/6, Bournemouth & Boscombe Athletic 1936/7, Watford c/s 1937.

Coventry City	League	F.A.Cup
1932–33	4	–

Debut: 27/8/32 v Torquay U. (a) 3–3 (IL)

Kilcar was a journeyman professional who never stayed long at any club. He was signed by City after 29 games for Bradford (PA), but was upstaged by Billy Lake and moved to Mansfield. This was the best time of his career, scoring 15 goals in 32 League games. After a later move, to Watford, he suffered a severe knee injury in pre-season training and this forced him to retire.

KILCLINE, Brian
Centre Half
Born: Nottingham 7th May 1962
Career: Apprentice Notts County, pro 1979, Coventry City June 1984 (£60,000), Oldham Athletic July 1991 (£400,000), Newcastle United March 1992 (£250,000).

Coventry City	League	F.A.Cup	Lge.Cup
1984–85	26 – 2	2	1+1s
1985–86	32 – 7	1 – 1	4 – 1
1986–87	29 – 3	6	2 – 1
1987–88	28 – 8	2 – 1	–
1988–89	33 – 4	1	3 – 1
1989–90	11 – 1	–	4 – 1
1990–91	14 – 3	3 – 1	2
Total	173–28	15 – 3	16+1s–4

Debut: 25/8/84 v Aston Villa (a) 0–1 (CH)
Honours: 2 England U–21 Caps
FA Cup Winners Medal 1987

When signed by Bobby Gould, Killer came with a reputation as a hard man with a point to prove. He started badly and was sent off in his sixth match against Manchester United at Highfield Road. He lost weight and began to establish a fine partnership with Trevor Peake. Standing at 6 feet 2 inches tall and 13 stone in weight, with long hair and moustache, Kilcline certainly showed himself to be a fierce competitor who was outstanding in the air. Whilst at City, he became a regular penalty and free kick expert and became the first City captain to hold aloft the FA Cup. After suffering injury in his last two seasons with City, he was sold to Oldham. He only played 10 times for The Latics before becoming Kevin Keegan's first signing for Newcastle in March 1992.

KING, Michael Bryan (Bryan)
Goalkeeper
Born: Bishops Stortford 18th May 1947
Career: Chelmsford Town, Millwall July 1967, Coventry City August 1975 (£57,000), Retired 1977.

Coventry City	League	F.A.Cup	Lge.Cup
1975–76	23	2	2
1976–77	–	–	–
Total	23	2	2

Debut: 16/8/75 v Everton (a) 4–1 (Goal)

It appeared that King's career was set in 1975 when he joined City. For seven years he had probably been the best goalkeeper outside the First Division, and in five years he missed only one game for Millwall. Signed by Gordon Milne, it was envisaged that King would be the natural successor to Bill Glazier, but this was never to be. After an excellent start, his form became inconsistent and he picked up injuries. In his last game, the 5–0 thrashing by Newcastle in the FA Cup, King picked up a groin injury. His comeback in August 1976 in a friendly saw his knee give way, which finally forced him out of the game.

KIRBY, George A.
Centre Forward
Born: Liverpool 20th December 1933
Career: Everton June 1952, Sheffield Wednesday March 1959, Plymouth Argyle January 1960, Southampton September 1962 (£17,000), Coventry City March 1964 (£12,500), Swansea Town October 1964, Walsall May 1965, New York Generals 1967, Brentford October 1968, Worcester City 1969, Retired 1969.

Coventry City	League	F.A.Cup	Lge.Cup
1963–64	9 – 5	–	–
1964–65	9 – 5	–	–
Total	18 –10	–	–

Debut: 21/3/64 v Bournemouth (a) 1–2 (CF)

Kirby was signed from Southampton close to the transfer deadline in March 1964 in an attempt to regain City's scoring touch. City went eleven games without victory and certain promotion from Division 3 was in doubt. Kirby provided the goals with a home debut hat–trick versus Oldham. He started the next season, the first back in Division 2, in the first team, but lost his place and quickly moved onto Swansea. Kirby was a successful goalscorer right up to the end of his career, when he moved into management with Halifax Town.

KIRK, Roy
Defender

Born: Bolsover 11th June 1929
Career: Bolsover Colliery, Luton Town, Leeds United August 1948, Coventry City March 1952, Cambridge United c/s 1960 (player–coach).

Coventry City	League	F.A.Cup
1951–52	9	–
1952–53	40 – 1	3
1953–54	46 – 2	1
1954–55	46	4 – 1
1955–56	45	1
1956–57	39	–
1957–58	33	2
1958–59	46 – 3	2
1959–60	26	2
Total	330 – 6	15 – 1

Debut: 15/3/52 v Nottingham Forest (a) 1-3 (CH)

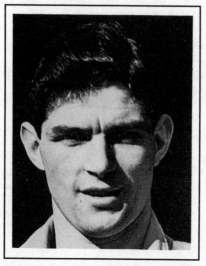

In a period of unrest, Kirk was one of the few consistent players in the 1950s. As a centre half he was originally John Charles' understudy at Leeds, and was signed by City as a replacement for George Mason. He couldn't prevent relegation in 1951–52, but proved to be a most impressive performer in Division 3. The early part of 1954–55 season was Kirk's most dramatic, for in September he scored 2 own goals against Clapton Orient in the 2-2 home draw, and then in November he scored with an 80 yard shot against Northampton in the FA Cup.

KIRTON, William John (Billy)
Inside/Outside Right

Born: Newcastle–Upon–Tyne 2nd December 1899
Died: Sutton Coldfield 27th September 1970
Career: Pandon Temperance, Leeds City May 1919, Aston Villa October 1919 (£500), Coventry City September 1928, Kidderminster Harriers c/s 1930, Leamington Town October 1930.

Coventry City	League	F.A.Cup
1928–29	13	1
1929–30	3	–
Total	16	1

Debut: 8/9/28 v Exeter C. (h) 1-1 (IR)
Honours: 1 England Full Cap
FA Cup Winners Medal 1920
FA Cup Runners–up Medal 1924

Billy Kirton achieved what most players could only dream of. For he scored the winning goal in an FA Cup final (for Aston Villa in 1920), and was capped for England, scoring in his only game – against Ireland in October 1921. These highlights came however, only after the ignominy of watching himself being auctioned in October 1919. He had made only one appearance for Leeds City before the club was disbanded on the instructions of the FA. All the players were auctioned off and Kirton was bought by Villa for £500. He played 261 times for Villa, but had not played for over 12 months when signed by City in September 1928. The fee of £1700 was large and he only played 17 games for City in 2 injury troubled seasons.

KLETZENBAUER, Carl Frank (Frank)
Full Back

Born: Coventry 21st July 1936
Career: Municipal Sports, Coventry City January 1953, Walsall March 1964, Retired 1966.

Coventry City	League	F.A.Cup	Lge.Cup
1952–53	–	–	
1953–54	–	–	
1954–55	–	–	
1955–56	–	–	
1956–57	15	–	
1957–58	–	–	
1958–59	–	–	
1959–60	2	–	
1960–61	44 – 1	3	2
1961–62	33 – 1	1	1
1962–63	19	–	2
1963–64	9 – 1	–	1
Total	122 – 3	4	6

Debut: 19/1/57 v QPR (a) 1-1 (LB)

For two seasons, Kletzenbauer was a first team regular, operating primarily at right back, but could also fill in at left back. He took his time to become established as Lol Harvey and Roy Kirk were first team regulars, but Frank kept to his task and played some good games for City. The establishment of John Sillett and Mick Kearns as the full back partnership resulted in Kletzenbauer moving to Walsall. Unfortunately, he broke his leg twice, which ended his career.

KNAPP, Anthony (Tony)
Centre Half
Born: Newstead 13th October 1936
Career: Newstead Colliery, Nottingham Forest 1952, Bentinck 1953, Leicester City December 1953, Southampton August 1961, Coventry City August 1967, Los Angeles Wolves March 1968, Bristol City March 1969, Tranmere Rovers October 1969, Poole Town July 1971.

Coventry City	League	F.A.Cup	Lge.Cup
1967–68	11	–	1

Debut: 26/8/67 v Sheffield United (h) 2–2 (CH)
Honours: 1 Football League appearance

When George Curtis broke his leg in August 1967, City needed an experienced centre half. Noel Cantwell decided upon Knapp, who had been at the heart of Southampton's rise to Division 1. However, he only played in eleven League games. City struggled to establish themselves and it appeared that someone with more steel was required. Maurice Setters arrived from Stoke in 1968 and Knapp moved to the USA.

KNOX, James (Jimmy)
Inside Forward
Born: Brechin 26th November 1935
Career: Raith Rovers 1956, Coventry City May 1957, Rugby Town November 1958, Lockheed Leamington August 1964, Corby Town c/s 1966.

Coventry City	League	F.A.Cup
1957–58	2	–
1958–59	–	–
Total	2	–

Debut: 9/9/57 v Bournemouth (h) 0–3 (IL)

A speculative signing from Raith, Knox was limited to two appearances. He later found his level in local non–league football and is more noted for his successful management career, particularly at V.S. Rugby. His brother Archie, is assistant manager at Glasgow Rangers.

L

LAGER, Ellis Walter
Centre Forward
Born: Mansfield 14th January 1918
Career: Sutton Junction, Coventry City August 1934, Retired 1943.

Coventry City	League	F.A.Cup
1934–35	–	–
1935–36	1 – 1	–
1936–37	6 – 3	–
1937–38	17 – 8	–
1938–39	26–13	–
Total	50–25	–

Debut: 18/4/36 v Bournemouth & B.A. (h) 2–0 (CF) (1 goal)
Honours: England Junior International

Lager was signed as a 16 year old in August 1934 and learned his trade quickly. His goalscoring record was excellent, but it wasn't until 1938–39 that he made a regular place for himself. He played twice for England Juniors whilst at City. The war came at an unfortunate time for Lager as he was at his prime. He guested for Watford and both Nottingham clubs during the War and retired in 1943.

LAKE, Willian Henry (Billy)
Forward
Born: Birmingham 1908
Career: Yardley White Star, Walsall September 1926, Coventry City November 1928, Retired September 1939.

Coventry City	League	F.A.Cup
1928–29	8 – 2	–
1929–30	36–16	4 – 2
1930–31	40–22	3 – 1
1931–32	27–14	2 – 1
1932–33	35–18	4 – 2
1933–34	31–16	2 – 1
1934–35	12 – 9	–
1935–36	18 – 4	1 – 1
1936–37	2 – 2	3 – 2
1937–38	7 – 7	–
1938–39	9 – 3	–
Total	225–113	19–10

Debut: 15/12/28 v QPR (a) 1–3 (IL)
Honours: Division 3 (S) Cup Winners Medal 1935–36

Billy Lake was the longest serving City player prior to the War. His 123 goals in 244 games, is second only to Clarrie Bourton in City's all-time goal-scoring records. He became a professional as a fresh-faced 18 year old with Walsall, for whom his father was a director. After 27 appearances at Fellows Park, he signed for City and was an instant success, always scoring at an average of a goal every other game. His purple patch came in 1930–31 when he netted 23 goals, and when he was joined by Clarrie Bourton and Jock Lauderdale City's front line was devastating. He lost out to Welsh international Les Jones, but was always able to score whenever he was called up to the first team. He retired in September 1939 at the outbreak of hostilities.

LANE, Martin J.
Left Back

Born: Altrincham 12th April 1961
Career: Apprentice Manchester United, pro May 1979, Chester August 1982, Coventry City January 1987 (£27,500), Wrexham (loan) October 1988, Chester City January 1989, Walsall c/s 1991, Shepshed Albion c/s 1992, Worcester City February 1993, Hinckley Town February 1993.

Coventry City	League	F.A.Cup	Lge.Cup
1986–87	0+1s	–	–
1987–88	0+2s	–	–
1988–89	–	–	–
Total	0+3s	–	–

Debut: 3/5/87 v Southampton (h) 1–1 (sub)

Lane had left Old Trafford after failing to make the first team in 3 years as a professional. He played

---

209 games for Chester and established himself as a respected left back in the lower divisions. His record attracted John Sillett to sign him, but he was unable to depose Greg Downs from the left back position. After making 120 appearances in his second spell at Chester, mainly at centre half, he moved to Walsall, where he made 11 full appearances for The Saddlers before moving into non-League football.

LANGLEY, Thomas W. (Tommy)
Centre Forward

Born: Lambeth 8th February 1958
Career: Apprentice Chelsea, pro April 1974, Queen's Park Rangers August 1980 (£400,000), Crystal Palace March 1981 (£200,000), AEK Athens 1983, Coventry City March 1984, Wolverhampton Wanderers June 1984, Aldershot March 1985 (loan), South China 1985, Aldershot August 1986, Exeter City c/s 1988, Slough Town c/s 1989, Aylesbury September 1991, Basingstoke Town 1991, Wokingham Town c/s 1992.

Coventry City	League	F.A.Cup	Lge.Cup
1983–84	2	–	–

Debut: 24/3/84 v Tottenham H. (h) 2–4 (IL)
Honours: 3 England B Caps
1 England U–21 Cap

Langley had a sparkling early career with Chelsea and QPR, but his move to Crystal Palace was not so successful as the team struggled in Division Two. He moved to Greece in an attempt to revitalise his form, which it failed to do. In dire need of goals, Bobby Gould brought Langley back to England. After two disappointing performances Langley was dropped and was released at the end of the season. He is still playing in non-league football.

LATCHFORD, Robert D. (Bob)
Centre Forward

Born: Birmingham 18th January 1951
Career: Birmingham City August 1968, Everton February 1974 (£350,000), Swansea City July 1981 (£125,000), NAC Breda January 1984 (F/T), Coventry City June 1984 (F/T), Lincoln City August 1985 (F/T), Newport County January 1986, Hamrun Spartans August 1986, Merthyr Tydfil October 1986.

Coventry City	League	F.A.Cup	Lge.Cup
1984–85	11+1s–2	1+1s	–

Debut: 28/8/84 v Norwich City (h) 0–0 (CF)
Honours: 12 full England Caps
6 England U–23 Caps
League Cup Runners Up Medal 1977

Before arriving at City, Latchford had been renowned as a great goalscorer. At Everton he gained his full caps, and scored 30 League goals in season 1977–78, before helping Swansea to the top six in Division 1. He arrived at City at the age of 33 and had clearly lost his sharpness. He played regularly to start with, but the goals had dried up, so Bobby Gould brought in Cyrille Regis.

LATHAM, Leslie (Les)
Centre Half
Born: Foleshill 31st December 1917
Career: Aston Villa 1938, Coventry City October 1946, Banbury Spencer 1949.

Coventry City	League	F.A.Cup
1946–47	1	–

Debut: 3/5/47 v WBA (a) 1–1 (CH)

Latham's only first–team appearance came when regular centre–half George Mason and his under-study Roy Cox were both injured. This game was at the age of 29 and like many players the War destroyed Latham's professional career. During the War Latham guested for Exeter City and Plymouth Argyle. He later moved into management with Lockheed Leamington and Bedworth.

LAUDERDALE, John Herbert (Jock)
Forward
Born: Dumfries 27th November 1908
Career: Parkhead F.C., Third Lanark December 1925, Sten-housemuir August 1926, Queen of the South October 1928, Blackpool October 1929, Coventry City c/s 1931, Northampton Town November 1936, Nuneaton Borough c/s 1939.

Coventry City	League	F.A.Cup
1931–32	42–19	2
1932–33	41–15	4
1933–34	40–11	2 – 1
1934–35	21 – 4	1 – 2
1935–36	23–11	2
1936–37	5	–
Total	172–60	11 – 3

Debut: 29/8/31 v Fulham (a) 3–5 (IR) 1 goal
Honours: Division 3 (South) Cup Winners Medal 1935–36

Jock Lauderdale was an excellent fetch–and–carry inside right who was able to provide great service for Clarrie Bourton and score his fair share of goals. He had been bought from First Division Blackpool and established a magnificent partnership with

Bourton. He was loved by City fans and the City board were determined to hold on to him, which paid off as City gained promotion to Division 2. He only played 5 Division 2 games before losing his place to Bill McDonald and moved to Northampton. He continued to live in Coventry and returned to the area when he signed for Nuneaton in the summer of 1939. During the war, he guested 9 times for City.

LAVENDER, Horace A.
Winger
Born: Dudley
Career: Dudley Town, Coventry City 1926/7.

Coventry City	League	F.A.Cup
1926–27	3 – 1	–
1927–28	6	–
Total	9 – 1	–

Debut: 19/4/27 v Aberdare (h) 1–0 (OL)

Youngster Lavender was a bright prospect in the reserves who didn't quite transmit his second eleven form to the first team. He was well regarded and was selected for a Birmingham FA X1 versus a Scottish Junior X1. He was overtaken by the outstanding Ernie Toseland to the extent that Lavender couldn't even claim a place in the reserve side and was released.

LAVERICK, Robert M. (Bobby)
Outside Left
Born: Trimdon 11th June 1938
Career: Chelsea June 1955, Everton February 1959, Brighton & Hove Albion June 1960, Coventry City July 1962, Corby Town 1963, King's Lynn September 1964.

Coventry City	League	F.A.Cup	Lge.Cup
1962–63	4	–	1 –1

Debut: 18/8/62 v Notts Co. (h) 2–0 (OL)

Laverick was the left–winger in City's new look forward line in Jimmy Hill's first full season. However, his early form was poor and so he was replaced by Roy Dwight and then young Ronnie Rees. Laverick had no future at City and moved into non–league football.

LAWRENCE, James
Full Back

Born: Earlestown
Career: Earlestown, Aston Villa 1919, Coventry City August 1920, Retired 1925.

Coventry City	League	F.A.Cup
1920–21	36	2
1921–22	40 – 1	3
1922–23	36 – 1	1
1923–24	12	–
1924–25	4	–
Total	128–2	6

Debut: 28/8/20 v Rotherham Co. (a) 3–2 (LB)

James Lawrence made 14 appearances for Aston Villa in 1919–20, before signing for City. He slotted straight into the left back position, which he established as his own. He was a good full back, but every so often missed a match or his perform–ance was hampered by his being unwell. He suf–fered injury in 1923 and his appearances were restricted thereafter. He finally retired through injury in 1925.

LEE, Frederick (Fred)
Outside Left

Born: Yardley, Birmingham
Career: Yardley White Star, Coventry City 1930/1, Walsall c/s 1932, Blackpool c/s 1935, Mansfield Town March 1936.

Coventry City	League	F.A.Cup
1930–31	4	–
1931–32	3	–
Total	7	–

Debut: 18/4/31 v Brighton & H.A. (h) 0–0 (OL)

Fred Lee was a young prospect who was not able to command a place ahead of Frank Bowden and later Frank White. He signed for Walsall in the summer of 1932 and impressed greatly, in total scoring 28 goals in 94 games, a more than respectable total for a winger. He linked up with ex–City players Alsop, Sheppard and Ball, all four playing in the epic 2–0 FA Cup victory over Arsenal in January 1933. In 1934, Lee suffered a bad injury which threatened his career, and Second Division Blackpool took a gamble when they signed him. He didn't play a game during his spell at Bloomfield Road.

LEE, John (Jackie)
Centre Forward

Born: Sileby 4th November 1920
Career: Quorn Methodists, Leicester City December 1940, Derby County July 1950, Coventry City November 1954 (£10,000), Retired 1955.

Coventry City	League	F.A.Cup
1954–55	15 – 8	3 – 2

Debut: 27/11/54 v Crystal Palace (h) 4–1 (CF) 1 goal
Honours: 1 full England Cap
FA Cup Runners Up Medal 1950

Lee was a big, strong centre forward who scored goals throughout his career, and at a good rate at City. But aged 34, he arrived at City in the twilight of his career, and it was 4 years since his solitary England cap. He left at the end of his first season due to injury. This summed up City's policy of the time, the selling of young talent and the buying players at the end of their careers. He was an able Leicestershire cricketer.

LEITCH, William (Billy)
Inside Forward

Born: Glasgow
Career: Port Glasgow, Partick Thistle c/s 1915, Coventry City September 1920, Bournemouth & BoS. Athletic July 1923.

Coventry City	League	F.A.Cup
1920–21	20 – 2	1
1921–22	4	1
1922–23	3	–
Total	27 – 2	2

Debut: 4/10/20 v West Ham Utd. (h) 0–1 (IL)

Scotsman Leitch was bought from Partick in September 1920 and showed himself to be a wholehearted player who always tried very hard. However, he failed to score the goals that City desperately needed and was consequently dropped, making sporadic appearances thereafter at half back. He played 81 League games in Bournemouth's first 3 seasons in the Football League.

LEWIS, Brian
Midfield

Born: Woking 29th January 1943
Career: Crystal Palace April 1960, Portsmouth July 1963, Coventry City January 1967, Luton Town July 1968, Oxford United January 1970, Colchester United December 1970, Portsmouth April 1972, Hastings United 1975.

Coventry City	League	F.A.Cup	Lge.Cup
1966–67	13	–	–
1967–68	20+2s–2	1	1
Total	33+2s–2	1	1

Debut: 11/2/67 v Preston North End (h) 2–1 (Mid)

Brian Lewis was brought in by Jimmy Hill to ensure that Division 1 football came to Highfield Road, and this was achieved with Lewis playing his part. He was a grafter rather than an outstanding midfielder, but this was required as games became very competitive. He lost his place during 1967–68, in Division 1, to Ernie Hannigan.

LEWIS, Idris
Outside Left

Born: Cardiff
Career: Longford St. Thomas, Coventry City 1937–46.

Coventry City	League	F.A.Cup
1937–38	–	–
1938–39	1	–
1945–46	WWII	–
Total	1	–

Debut: 4/3/39 v Chesterfield (a) 0–3 (OL)

Young Welshman Lewis, made his only appearance when both first team wingers George Ashall and George Taylor were injured. He was still a youngster learning his trade and was dropped when Ashall was fit. After the outbreak of War, Lewis played a handful of matches each season until 1946, when he was released. He is not the same 'Idris Lewis' as the former Bristol Rovers and Newport County player.

LEWIS, Trevor
Outside Right

Born: Bedwelty 6th January 1921
Career: Catherine-de-Barnes, Redditch Town January 1948, Coventry City February 1948, Gillingham February 1953, Banbury Spencer 1955, Rugby Town July 1956.

Coventry City	League	F.A.Cup
1947–48	3	–
1948–49	–	–
1949–50	4	–
1950–51	–	–
1951–52	3	–
1952–53	1	–
Total	11	–

Debut: 10/4/48 v Sheffield Wednesday (a) 1–1 (OR)

Signed as a speedy winger, Lewis' first team outings were limited to 10 in 5 years as he was understudy to "Plum" Warner. He moved onto Gillingham, but regular football was limited there also. His move into non-League football achieved some success.

LIDDLE, James Frederick (Jim)
Outside Left

Born: Mickley, Co. Durham
Career: Crawcock Albion, Queen's Park Rangers, Huddersfield Town c/s 1929, Rotherham United October 1929, Newcastle United, Gillingham c/s 1932, Coventry City May 1934, Exeter City c/s 1937.

Coventry City	League	F.A.Cup
1934–35	32 – 6	3 – 1
1935–36	14 – 4	–
1936–37	16 – 2	1
Total	62 – 12	4 – 1

Debut: 25/8/34 v Northampton T. (h) 2–0 (OL)
Honours: Division 3 (S) Cup Winners Medal 1935–36.

Jim Liddle was an ex-miner and professional sprinter who had failed to make the grade at QPR, Huddersfield and Newcastle, before signing for

Gillingham. His 17 goals in 79 League games enticed Harry Storer to sign him. He shared the outside left duties with Arthur Fitton and was sold to Exeter City in the summer of 1937, where he stayed until the outbreak of the war.

LIGHTENING, Arthur D.
Goalkeeper

Born: Durban, South Africa 1st August 1936
Career: Railway & Queen's Park, Nottingham Forest December 1956, Coventry City November 1958, Middlesbrough August 1962 – May 1963.

Coventry City	League	F.A.Cup	Lge.Cup
1958–59	25	–	
1959–60	46	2	
1960–61	33	3	2
1961–62	42	2	1
1962–63	4	–	–
Total	150	7	3

Debut: 13/12/58 v Hartlepools (h) 4–1 (Goal)

In an astute piece of business, Billy Frith bought Lightening and Ronnie Farmer from Nottingham Forest in November 1958 for £6000. For the next 3 seasons Lightening proved to be a great success, being a popular player with the fans because of his exuberant goalkeeping style. It was a surprise when he was sold in 1962 by Jimmy Hill, but he lasted only until the end of that season, before moving out of the professional game.

LINDLEY, Richard
Inside Forward

Born: Bolton
Career: Bolton Wanderers, Burnley 1908, Bradford City May 1920, Coventry City c/s 1921.

Coventry City	League	F.A.Cup
1921–22	15 – 1	–

Debut: 27/8/21 v Fulham (a) 0–5 (IL)

Lindley made 138 appearances for Burnley, scoring 43 League goals from the inside forward positions. He helped The Clarets to promotion to Division 1 in 1913. Albert Evans bought him for City from Bradford City. He started well, forming a partnership with "Mollie" Morgan, but faded and was released after scoring only 1 goal in 15 matches.

LINDON, Albert E.
Goalkeeper

Born: Aston 24th January 1891
Died: Dowlais 1st October 1976
Career: Vaughan United, Delta Metal Works 1907, Birmingham Fruiterers, Birmingham June 1910, Aston Villa August 1911, Barnsley September 1912, Huddersfield Town 1915, Birmingham 1916, Coventry City March 1918, permanent May 1919 (£1,000), Merthyr Town c/s 1920, Charlton Athletic December 1927, Retired c/s 1931.

Coventry City	League	F.A.Cup
1919–20	29	2

Debut: 30/8/19 v Tottenham H. (h) 0–5 (Goal)
Honours: Welsh Cup Runners–up Medal 1923–24

Before the Great War Lindon had been a reserve at Birmingham, Villa and Barnsley, making 7,1 and 0 appearances respectively. During the war he played for Huddersfield and Birmingham. He was attracted to Highfield Road by manager William Clayton who had known Lindon at St Andrew's. He impressed in the Midland League and was signed for City's assault on the League. He must have felt punch drunk, for in 31 games he conceded 61 goals and lost his place to Joe Mitchell. He was sold to Merthyr where he was a loyal servant, later becoming the player/manager there and also at Charlton. At six foot and 13½ stone, Lindon was considered the right size for a goalkeeper and was well respected throughout the game.

LIVINGSTONE, Stephen (Steve)
Centre Forward

Born: Middlesbrough 8th September 1968
Career: YTS Coventry City, pro July 1986, Blackburn Rovers January 1991 (£450,000), Chelsea March 1993 (player-exchange).

Coventry City	League	F.A.Cup	Lge.Cup
1986–87	1+2s	–	–
1987–88	3+1s	–	0+1s
1988–89	1	–	–
1989–90	6+7s–3	–	4+1s–5
1990–91	6+4s–2	–	4 – 5
Total	17+14s5	–	8+2s–10

Debut: 18/4/87 v Luton Town (a) 0–2 (Sub)
Full Debut: 9/5/87 v Southampton (h) 1–1 (CF)

Livingstone came through City's youth team and scored the winning goal in the 1987 Youth Cup final. His opportunities in the first team were limited by Cyrille Regis, David Speedie and Keith Houchen, but whenever called upon he did well. With the arrival of Terry Butcher, Livingstone was considered surplus to requirements and was sold to Blackburn with Tony Dobson when Don Mackay was in charge at Ewood Park. He lost his place to Kenny Dalglish's big money signings and was sold to Chelsea in March 1993 in a deal which took Graeme Le Saux to Blackburn.

LLOYD, Laurence Valentine (Larry)
Centre Half
Born: Bristol 6th October 1948
Career: Apprentice Bristol Rovers, pro July 1967, Liverpool April 1969 (£60,000), Coventry City August 1974 (£240,000), Nottingham Forest December 1976 (£60,000), Wigan Athletic March 1981 (player–manager), Retired c/s 1983.

Coventry City	League	F.A.Cup	Lge.Cup
1974–75	34 – 5	3 – 1	1
1975–76	11	–	–
1976–77	5	–	–
Total	50 – 5	3 – 1	1

Debut: 21/8/74 v Derby County (a) 1–1 (CH)
Honours: 4 full England caps
     8 England U–23 caps
     2 European Cup Winners Medals 1979 & 80
     UEFA Cup Winners Medal 1973
     2 League Champ. Medals 1972–73 & 77–78
     2 League Cup Winners Medals 1978 & 1979
     FA Cup Runners–up Medal 1971

Lloyd's career was glittered with honours, but his time at City was a nightmare for both player and club. He had impressed sufficiently at Liverpool to acquire 3 England caps. Gordon Milne saw Lloyd as the linchpin around which City would develop a championship winning side. In order to buy Lloyd, City's transfer record was broken, and in order to overcome the burden of a £240,000 fee, Willie Carr

was to be sold to Wolves. This fell through and City were in dire financial straits. To make matters worse, Lloyd suffered injury and a complete lack of form. When Second Division Forest made a bid of £60,000, it was gladly accepted by City. At Forest, he became what City had hoped he would be, the centre–half of a championship winning side. He had a great Indian summer with Forest before entering management with Wigan and Notts County. He is now a publican in Nottingham.

LOCKHART, Norman H.
Outside Left
Born: Belfast 4th March 1924
Career: Windsor Star, Distillery 1940, Linfield 1942, Swansea Town October 1946, Coventry City October 1947, Aston Villa September 1952, Bury November 1956.

Coventry City	League	F.A.Cup
1947–48	31 – 6	2 – 1
1948–49	31 – 5	1
1949–50	32 – 7	–
1950–51	38 – 7	1
1951–52	42 – 15	3 – 2
1952–53	8 – 1	–
Total	182 – 41	7 – 3

Debut: 11/10/47 v Bury (h) 0–0 (OL)
Honours: 8 Northern Ireland full Caps (3 with City)
     Irish Cup Wins. Medals 1945 & 1946
     Irish Cup Runners–up Medal 1944

Lockhart was a superb outside left with the ability to cross on the run with accuracy, and also scored his fair share of goals. His spell at City marked the team's period of struggle in Division 2 immediately after the War. He had injury problems at City – he broke his ankle – but he greatly impressed and he moved onto First Division Aston Villa where he played 73 games in 4 seasons.

LOUGHLIN, James (Jimmy)
Centre Forward

Born: Darlington 9th October 1905
Career: Darlington Railway Athletic, Newcastle United 1923 (£125), West Ham United May 1927 (£650), Coventry City January 1929, Dolphins F.C. c/s 1931, Bray Unknowns, Worcester City October 1931, Northwich Victoria c/s 1932, Darlington July 1933.

Coventry City	League	F.A.Cup
1928–29	19 – 8	–
1929–30	31 – 23	4 – 6
1930–31	11 – 1	–
Total	61 – 32	4 – 6

Debut: 5/1/29 v Brighton & H.A. (h) 3–0 (CF)

Despite scoring 5 goals in 12 games, Newcastle's squad was too strong for Loughlin to play regularly. He moved to First Division rivals West Ham, and ten games and 4 goals later he signed for City. He came into his element at City and scored at a rate of a goal every other game. Despite his 29 goals in 1929–30, he lost his place to John Phillips. New manager Harry Storer brought in Clarrie Bourton and loaned Loughlin out. He scored proficiently at both Worcester and Northwich. He was sold by City to his home club, Darlington in July 1933, where he spent a season.

LOVERING, Johnny
Left Half

Born: Nuneaton, 10th December 1922
Career: Nuneaton Griff, Holbrook Old Boys, Coventry City WWII, Birmingham 1945, Coventry City c/s 1946, Bedworth Town c/s 1949, Atherstone Town 1949, Nuneaton Borough c/s 1951, Retired c/s 1953.

Coventry City	League	F.A.Cup
1946–47	1	–
1947–48	5	–
1948–49	–	–
Total	6	–

Debut: 7/9/46 v Barnsley (h) 1–1 (CH)

Lovering was basically a reserve team player who was drafted in when first team men such as Dick Mason and Don Dearson were injured. City had a strong half back line in the late forties, with Noel

Simpson also playing left half and so Lovering was released and joined up with Bedworth.

LOWES, Barry T.
Outside Right

Born: Barrow 16th March 1939
Career: Holker C.O.B., Barrow January 1960, Blackpool November 1961 (£6,000), Workington August 1962, Bury February 1966, Coventry City March 1967, Swindon Town August 1967.

Coventry City	League	F.A.Cup	Lge.Cup
1966–67	3	–	–

Debut: 11/3/67 v Northampton Town (a) 0–0 (OR)

Signed by Jimmy Hill with 11 games of the 1966–67 Division 2 championship season remaining, Lowes was there to ensure promotion. In his 3 games, he ably filled in for regulars Lewis and Key. After that, there was no place for him in Division 1. He was basically a good lower Division player, which was highlighted by his spells at Workington and Bury.

LOWES, Thomas (Tommy)
Inside Right

Born: Newcastle–Upon–Tyne
Career: Walker, Wallsend Park Villa, Newcastle United September 1910 (£25), Coventry City June 1914 (£50), Nuneaton Town c/s 1920, Caerphilly c/s 1921, Newport County c/s 1922, Yeovil Town c/s 1926, Retired.

Coventry City	League	F.A.Cup
1914–15	7 – 3	–
1919–20	10 – 2	–
Total	17 – 5	–

Debut: 5/9/14 v Brentford (a) 1–3 (IR) 1 goal

In his 4 years at St James' Park, Lowes made 16 appearances, but he was then released – such was the strength of The Magpies' squad. Lowes was one of the very few City players to appear for the club before and after the Great War. In City's eventful 1919–20 season, Lowes' appearances were few in number and he only scored 2 goals, but 1 was vital, when he netted the second in the 2–2 draw at Bury in the penultimate game of the season. This helped the club retain it's Second Division status. He moved into non–League football, before playing 109 times for Newport. He started his managerial career at Yeovil after finishing his playing days with the

Somerset side. He later managed Barrow and Walsall and scouted for Arsenal and Norwich.

LOWRIE, George
Centre Forward

Born: Tonypandy 19th December 1919
Died: South Wales 4th May 1989
Career: Tonypandy 1933, Swansea Town 1935, Preston North End December 1937, Coventry City June 1939, Newcastle United March 1948, Bristol City September 1949 (£10,000), Coventry City February 1952, Lovells Athletic July 1953.

Coventry City	League	F.A.Cup
1945–46	WWII	–
1946–47	34 – 26	2 – 3
1947–48	22 – 18	–
1951–52	12 – 3	–
1952–53	15 – 9	–
Total	83 – 56	2 – 3

Debut: 2/9/46 v WBA (h) 3–2 (IL)
Honours: 4 Wales Full Caps (3 with City)
4 Wales War Time Internationals (all with City)

When the war stared, Lowrie was 19, so the best years of his career were lost. During the war, he guested for Bristol City, Nottingham Forest and Northampton Town. He was a great goalscorer, gaining 9 hat–tricks for City; in January 1947, he netted 3 goals in 2 consecutive games, both against

Newport County. His strike rate at City was phenomenal, which encouraged Newcastle to pay the vast fee of £18,500, a City record. In the great Newcastle side, Lowrie could only force his way into the team for 12 games in two and a half years. Lowrie returned to City via Bristol City, when he was past his best, but he proved that he could still score.

McCAIG, Alexander (Alex)
Inside Right

Born: Stirling
Career: Larbert Central, Stenhousemuir, Falkirk March 1919, Alloa Athletic c/s 1919, Stenhousemuir c/s 1920, Coventry City c/s 1921, Reading c/s 1922, Cowdenbeath c/s 1923, Stenhousemuir October 1923, St. Bernards c/s 1928, Stenhousemuir December 1928.

Coventry City	League	F.A.Cup
1921–22	10 – 2	–

Debut: 27/8/21 v Fulham (a) 0–5 (IR)

Scotsman McCaig was a big and burly inside right who was instantly recognisable by his bald head. He started the 1921–22 season brightly, scoring in his second and third games and was dropped following a run of 4 scoreless City games in 5 played. He played 17 games for Reading before returning to Scotland. He had four spells with Stenhousemuir.

McCANN, Albert
Inside Forward

Born: Maidenhead 1st November 1941
Career: Luton Town April 1959, Coventry City August 1961, Portsmouth September 1962 (£6,000), South Africa 1974.

Coventry City	League	F.A.Cup	Lge.Cup
1961–62	22 – 3	–	–
1962–63	–	–	–
Total	22 – 3	–	–

Debut: 16/9/61 v Shrewsbury T. (a) 1–1 (IR)

When signed by Billy Frith, McCann was a reserve team player at Luton. He played half of the League matches in season 1961–62, primarily as cover for more experienced players. The sacking of Frith and the arrival of Jimmy Hill, resulted in McCann becoming out of favour. As the transfer merry–go–round started in the Sky Blue Revolution, McCann was sold to Portsmouth, where he was a stalwart for 12 seasons, and played a total of 379 games for Pompey.

McCAUGHEY, Cecil
Wing Half

Born: Bootle
Career: Burscough Rangers, Blackburn Rovers 1932, Coventry City c/s 1935, Cardiff City c/s 1937, Southport c/s 1939.

Coventry City	League	F.A.Cup
1935–36	20	–
1936–37	11	–
Total	31	–

Debut: 5/10/35 v Watford (h) 2–0 (IR)
Honours: Division 3 (South) Cup Winners Medal 1935–36

McCaughey came to City after spending 3 years in Blackburn's reserves. He was a combative half back who was used as cover for Billy Frith, as City won the Division 3 (South) championship. He was bought by Cardiff City in order to strengthen their Division 3(South) team and he played 64 League games before returning to his native North West, and retired during the war.

McCLURE, Alec
Centre Half

Born: Workington 3rd April 1892
Died: August 1973
Career: Grangetown, Birmingham 1911, Aston Villa December 1923, Stoke City 1924, Coventry City c/s 1926, Walsall March 1928, Retired c/s 1928, Market Harborough Town 1929, Retired 1931.

Coventry City	League	F.A.Cup
1926–27	35 – 6	1
1927–28	14 – 1	1
Total	49 – 7	2

Debut: 1/9/26 v Watford (a) 0–1 (CH)
Honours: 1 Football League appearance

McClure was a loyal servant of Birmingham and in 1928 joined the coaching staff. In his 4 years of coaching, he helped to establish Birmingham's 3rd team and a youth trials system. As a player McClure made his debut at the age of 19, and he came into his own as a solid centre half, missing only 2 games in The Blues' 1920–21 Second Division championship side. After 2 successful seasons in Division 1, he moved to Aston Villa and then Stoke. At City, he provided some much needed experience for a team in turmoil, where he made 51 appearances and chipped in with 7 goals. When Norman Dinsdale was signed from Notts County, McClure was sold to Walsall. Whilst coaching at Birmingham he helped out non–League Market Harborough Town.

MacDONALD, Kevin Duncan
Midfield

Born: Inverness 22nd December 1960
Career: Apprentice Inverness Caledonian 1978, Leicester City May 1980 (£40,000), Liverpool November 1984 (£450,000), Leicester City (loan) December 1987, Glasgow Rangers (loan) 1988, Coventry City July 1989 (F/T) Cardiff C. (loan) March 1991, Walsall July 1991 (F/T), Retired c/s 1993.

Coventry City	League	F.A.Cup	Lge.Cup
1989–90	19+3s	1	4+1s–1
1990–91	7+2s	2+2s	2+2s
Total	26+5s	3+2s	6+3s–1

Debut: 9/9/89 v Millwall (a) 1–4 (Sub)
Full Debut: 19/9/89 v Grimsby T. (a) 1–3 (Mid) (League Cup)
Honours: FA Cup Winners Medal 1986

After over 150 appearances for Leicester, Joe Fagan signed MacDonald and he began to show his stylish play at Anfield. But he broke his leg and had recurrent injuries that restricted him to only 55 appearances in 5 years. John Sillet signed him in July 1989 on a free transfer and it looked as if it might revive his career, but he faded badly. He ran with a limp and was not up to Division 1 football. He retired in May 1993 and joined the coaching staff at Leicester City

McDONALD, Robert Wood (Bobby)
Left Back

Born: Aberdeen 13th April 1955
Career: Apprentice Aston Villa, professional September 1972, Coventry City August 1976 (£40,000) Manchester City October 1980 (£250,000), Oxford United September 1983, Leeds United February 1987 (£20,000) Wolverhampton Wanderers (loan) February 1988, V.S. Rugby c/s 1988, Burton Albion c/s 1989, Nuneaton Borough September 1989, Worcester City October 1990, Sutton Coldfield Town January 1991, Armitage c/s 1991, Redditch United c/s 1992.

Coventry City	League	F.A.Cup	Lge.Cup
1976–77	39 – 1	2 – 1	3
1977–78	42 – 5	1	4
1978–79	42 – 4	2	1
1979–80	37 – 4	2	3
1980–81	1	–	0+1s
Total	161 – 14	7 – 1	11+1s

Debut: 31/8/76 v Bristol C. (a) 1–0 (Mid) League Cup
Honours: League Cup Winners Medal 1975
FA Cup Runners–up Medal 1981

Despite winning a League Cup winners medal with Villa, McDonald could not hold down a regular first team place. After joining City, Bobby played 178 consecutive games before being dropped. His spell at City coincided with an upturn in the team's performances. McDonald was a strong tackler and also had the ability to make good runs into the opposition penalty area. He left under a cloud, after accusing the club of lacking ambition. He moved with Tommy Hutchison to Manchester City, where he reached Wembley, but a breach of club discipline preceded his move to Oxford. Bobby is still playing non–league football with Redditch.

MacDONALD, William (Bill)
Forward

Born: Coatbridge
Career: Law Scotia, Airdrionians c/s 1928, Manchester United 1932, Tranmere Rovers c/s 1934, Coventry City June 1936, Plymouth Argyle, June 1939 (£800), Retired 1940.

Coventry City	League	F.A.Cup
1936–37	36 – 8	3
1937–38	36 – 12	1
1938–39	19 – 3	1
Total	91 – 23	5

Debut: 7/9/36 v Swansea T. (a) 0–2 (IR)
Honours: Welsh Cup Winners Medal 1934–35

Experienced Scotsman MacDonald, was bought to give some knowledge of 2nd Division football to City's forward line, having earlier played 27 games for Manchester United. The blond schemer started well, forming a partnership with Clarrie Bourton and Les Jones. He lost his way in 1939 and was replaced by Ellis Lager. With Storer looking to gain transfer income, MacDonald was sold to Plymouth as George Lowrie arrived at City. MacDonald retired after only 12 months at Home Park.

McDONNELL, Martin
Defender

Born: Newton–le–Willows 27th April 1924
Died: Coventry 13th April 1988
Career: Everton August 1942, Southport August 1946, Birmingham City May 1947 (£3,500) Coventry City October 1949, Derby County July 1955, Crewe Alexandra July 1958.

Coventry City	League	F.A.Cup
1949–50	28	1
1950–51	42	1
1951–52	39	3
1952–53	42	3
1953–54	44	1
1954–55	37	4
Total	232	13

Debut: 22/10/49 v Cardiff City (h) 2–1 (RB)

McDonnell's spell at City was the most successful of his career. Signed in October 1949, he was equally adept at right back or centre–half. During this turbulent period in City's history, he proved to be an adequate replacement for George Mason. Whilst the team struggled, he showed himself to be an able defender. After ending his career, McDonnell became an estate agent in Coventry.

McGRATH, Lloyd A.
Midfield

Born: Birmingham 24th February 1965
Career: Apprentice Coventry City, pro December 1982.

Coventry City	League	F.A.Cup	Lge.Cup
1982–83	–	–	–
1983–84	1	–	–
1984–85	22+1s	2	–
1985–86	32	1	4
1986–87	30 – 3	4	5
1987–88	17	2	3
1988–89	6+2s	1	–
1989–90	12+1s	1	2
1990–91	12+2s	2	1
1991–92	38+2s–1	2	4 – 1
1992–93	20+5s	1	2
Total	190+13s–4	16	21 – 1

Debut: 28/4/84 v Southampton (a) 2–8 (CH)
Honours: 1 England U–21 Cap (at City)
FA Cup Winners Medal 1987

McGrath overcame serious collarbone injuries whilst an apprentice, and made his debut in City's heaviest post–War defeat. In his second game he suffered from concussion against Sheffield Wednesday and took part in the 2–6 defeat by Chelsea in his third

match. He was still thought of as a centre half but made a midfield place his own before the end of the 1984/5 season. His best role is as a man–marker, which was epitomised by his tremendous performance against Glenn Hoddle in the 1987 FA Cup final and it was his cross that Gary Mabbutt put into his own net. It wasn't until 1991 that McGrath was free from injury, the worst being a broken leg which occurred in a Full Members' Cup match against Ipswich. Niggling injuries have restricted his appearances to just over 200 in 10 years as a professional. He was granted a testimonial in 1993.

McGREGOR, William (Bill)
Winger
Born: Levenbank 1903
Career: Levenbank Amateurs, Dumbarton Harps c/s 1924, Duntocher Hibs May 1925, Coventry City c/s 1925, Burton Town 1926/7, Stourbridge c/s 1927, Hinckley Athletic, Leamington Town.

Coventry City	League	F.A.Cup
1925–26	9 – 1	–
1926–27	–	–
Total	9 – 1	–

Debut: 17/3/26 v Chesterfield (a) 3–4 (OL)

Scotsman McGregor was signed by fellow Scot James Kerr, who had a reputation for raiding Scottish junior sides to find talent for City. McGregor had been spotted in a junior cup final for Duntocher Hibs in 1925. He was kept out of the first team by fellow Scot Jimmy Dougall. He made his debut in March 1926 in a bizarre match at Chesterfield. City

lost 3–4 in a game in which 3 players were injured, having only 8 fit players at the end. He suffered a motor cycle accident in which he badly damaged his thigh. The injury curtailed his professional career and he was released by City and joined Burton Town. He spent the rest of his footballing days locally, before settling in Coventry.

McGUIRE, Douglas (Dougie)
Winger
Born: Bathgate 6th September 1967
Career: YTS Glasgow Celtic, pro 1986, Dumbarton (loan) February 1988, Sunderland (loan) March 1988, Coventry City August 1988 (£40,000), (F/T) November 1990, Queen Of The South c/s 1991.

Coventry City	League	F.A.Cup	Lge.Cup
1988–89	–	–	–
1989–90	1+3s	–	–
1990–91	–	–	–
Total	1+3s	–	–

Debut: 22/8/89 v Arsenal (a) 0–2 (Sub)
Full Debut: 16/9/89 v Luton Town (h) 1–0 (OL)

McGuire was signed from Celtic after a week's trial in August 1988, when he was outstanding during a friendly at Gloucester. It was not until later that the club discovered that he was suffering from glandular fever during the match. His disease ruled him out for the whole of the 1988–89 season, so it was not until August 1989 that he made his first team debut. His only first team appearance came as a replacement for David Smith, but his progress was not as expected and he was released in November 1990.

McGUIRE, Michael James (Mick)
Midfield
Born: Blackpool 4th September 1952
Career: Apprentice Coventry City, pro November 1969, Norwich City January 1975 (£60,000), Tampa Bay Rowdies (loan) c/s 1978, Barnsley March 1983 (£30,000), Oldham Athletic January 1985, Blackpool (loan) August 1987, Mossley 1987, Grantham c/s 1988, Retired c/s 1989.

Coventry City	League	F.A.Cup	Lge.Cup
1969–70	–	–	–
1970–71	–	–	–
1971–72	23+3s–1	–	1
1972–73	13+4s	1+1s	–
1973–74	19+5s	3	4
1974–75	5	–	1
Total	60+12s–1	4+1s	6

Debut: 21/8/71 v WBA (a) 1–1 (Mid)

At City, McGuire was regarded as an important squad player who could adequately fill in for first team players such as Willie Carr and Dennis Mortimer. Allowed to move to Norwich, McGuire quickly established himself, but a broken leg cost him a layoff lasting almost 2 years. He regained his place, but was allowed to move to Barnsley as fresh talent developed at Carrow Road. He played a significant part in Oldham's attempts at promotion to Division 1 and has worked for the PFA since retiring from the game.

MACHIN, Ernest T. (Ernie)
Midfield
Born: Little Hulton 26th April 1944
Career: Nelson January 1962, Coventry City March 1962, Plymouth Argyle December 1972, Brighton & H.A. August 1974–76.

Coventry City	League	F.A.Cup	Lge.Cup
1961–62	–	–	–
1962–63	6	–	–
1963–64	17 – 3	–	1 – 1
1964–65	14 – 4	1	2
1965–66	38+1s–4	2	3 – 2
1966–67	34 – 11	1	1
1967–68	40 – 4	3	1 – 1
1968–69	41 – 5	2 – 1	4
1969–70	15+1s–1	2	1
1970–71	24	1	1 – 1
1971–72	15 – 1	1	–
1972–73	11	–	2
Total	255+2s–33	13 – 1	16 – 5

Debut: 8/4/63 v Millwall (h) 2–0 (IL)

Ernie Machin was Jimmy Hill's "Blue Eyed Boy" (because he "liked the colour of his eyes"), and was a fundamental member of the Sky Blue Revolution. His non-stop exuberance and tigerish play were essential ingredients in City's climb to Division 1. His ability to score vital goals was a great asset. Although playing over 280 games for City, Machin missed out on many because of his recurring knee injuries. By 1972, his injuries were affecting his play and he lost his place to newcomers like John Craven and Dennis Mortimer. It may surprise many City fans, that Ernie was only 28 when he moved to Plymouth.

McILVANNEY, Michael
Wing Half
Born: Glasgow
Career: Kirkintilloch Rob Roy, Broxburn United October 1924, Coventry City October 1925 – c/s 1927, Thames c/s 1928.

Coventry City	League	F.A.Cup
1925–26	19 – 1	1
1926–27	5 – 1	–
Total	24 – 2	1

Debut: 10/10/25 v Barrow (a) 4–1 (RH)

McIlvanney was signed by James Kerr in October 1925 from Scottish 2nd Division side Broxburn United, in order to team up with his former colleague Jimmy Walker. This partnership never really materialised and McIlvanney's reputation as a constructive player was dented. The club was in financial trouble and offered reduced terms to the staff. McIlvanney refused to re-sign and returned to Scotland. When he couldn't find a club, he returned to City, but after only 5 further appearances, he was released. He was out of the professional game for 12 months before linking up with Thames.

McINALLY, James E. (Jim)
Full Back/Midfield
Born: Glasgow 19th February 1964
Career: Celtic Boys, Celtic pro 1982, Dundee (loan) 1983, Nottingham Forest June 1984, Coventry City January 1986 (£80,000), Dundee United May 1986 (£90,000).

Coventry City	League	F.A.Cup	Lge.Cup
1985–86	5	–	–

Debut: 19/3/86 v WBA (a) 0–0 (Mid)

Honours: 10 Scotland Full Caps
        UEFA Cup Runners–up Medal 1987
        Scottish Cup Runs.–up Medal 1987 & 1991

McInally started with Celtic but was sold to Nott-ingham Forest in June 1984 after only making 3 appearances for the Bhoys. He impressed at right back and was surprisingly sold to City. He spent only five months at Highfield Road and played only five games because of injury. He even scored an own goal at Arsenal in one of those appearances. He was sold to Dundee United with Davie Bowman in May 1986 and moved into midfield. He returned to form and showed himself worthy of appearing for his country.

McINTOSH, Alexander (Alex)
Inside Forward

Born: Dunfermline 14th April 1916
Career: St. Mirren, Folkestone, Wolverhampton W. October 1937, Birmingham City January 1947, Coventry City February 1948, Kidderminster Harriers c/s 1949, Bilston United c/s 1951.

Coventry City	League	F.A.Cup
1947–48	13 – 3	–
1948–49	7	–
Total	20 – 3	–

Debut: 21/2/48 v Newcastle (h) 1–1 (IL)
Honours: FA Cup Runners–up Medal 1939

McIntosh certainly lost the best part of his career to the war. In 1938–39, at the age of 22, he was a regular in the Wolves League runners–up and FA Cup finalists team. During the war he guested for Newcastle United, Watford and Cardiff City. He was 31 when City signed him as experienced cover for Peter Murphy. After 18 months, McIntosh moved into non–league football.

MACKAY, James
Winger

Born: Ryton–on–Tyne
Career: Newburn Colliery, Coventry City 1920/1, Carlisle United c/s 1922, Notts County 1923, Lincoln City late 1923, Luton Town 1924, Crewe Alexandra c/s 1925, West Stanley 1926, Torquay United c/s 1927, Dartford c/s 1929, Sheppey United c/s 1930.

Coventry City	League	F.A.Cup
1920–21	6	–
1921–22	6	–
Total	12	–

Debut: 19/3/21 v Clapton Orient (h) 1–1 (OR)

In City's early days in the Football League, there was little stability in the side, but the one depend-able figure was Jimmy Dougall. It was therefore bad luck for any reserve in his position that Dougall seldom received an injury. Mackay found this out. He played several games out of position on the left wing and was well regarded, even if surplus to requirements. He proved that he was worthy of a League place, for after playing for Carlisle, he had 3 games for First Division Notts County. He returned to his native North East in 1926, before helping Torquay in the club's first 2 League seasons.

MACKRILL, Percy
Full Back

Born: Bradford 19th October 1892
Career: Bradford (P.A.), Rotherham County 1915, Coventry City c/s 1919, Halifax Town, Pontypridd 1923/4, Torquay United 1925, Retired c/s 1928.

Coventry City	League	F.A.Cup
1919–20	1	–

Debut: 20/9/19 v Birmingham (h) 1–3 (RB)

Mackrill had been an impressive right back at Rotherham. He was considered to be a robust character and a lot was expected of him, but he only made 1 appearance, as Dick Roberts and then Charlie Copeland, commanded the right back posi-tion. He helped Torquay to Football League status and was player–manager in the club's first season in Division 3 (S). He retired in 1928 to take on the manager's job full time.

MacLACHLAN, Frederick (Fred)
Centre Half

Born: Kirkcudbright 21st August 1899
Career: Aberdeen, Partick Thistle 1920, Maidstone United 1922, Coventry City July 1923, Grimsby Town December 1925 (£250), Bury May 1927, Halifax Town c/s 1928.

Coventry City	League	F.A.Cup
1923–24	42	2
1924–25	24	3
1925–26	1	–
Total	67	5

Debut: 25/8/23 v Barnsley (h) 2–3 (CH)

Fred MacLachlan was not a big man, standing 5 feet 9 inches tall, but was a strong centre half who was very popular with the Highfield Road side. He spent a successful first season at centre half and was ever-present, but was switched to right half for the 1924–25 season. He was not as impressive in the wider position and was dropped. In November 1925, he was transfer listed and signed for Grimsby, where he helped The Mariners gain promotion to Division 2 and attracted the attention of First Division Bury. He only played twice for The Shakers, before signing for Halifax Town, for whom he appeared 94 times in the League.

McMANUS, Charles Eric (Eric)
Goalkeeper
Born: Limavady 14th November 1950
Career: Coleraine 1966, Coventry City August 1968 (£8,000), Notts County May 1972 (£3,000), Stoke City October 1979 (£35,000), Lincoln City (loan) December 1979, Bradford City August 1982 (£15,000), Middlesbrough (loan) January 1986, Peterborough United (loan) March 1986, Tranmere Rovers July 1986, Boston United September 1986, Retired c/s 1987.

Coventry City	League	F.A.Cup	Lge.Cup
1968–69	–	–	–
1969–70	2	–	–
1970–71	2	–	–
1971–72	2	–	–
Total	6	–	–

Debut: 16/12/69 v Ipswich (h) 3–1 (Goal)

Eric McManus will always be remembered by City fans as the keeper that conceded 6 goals against Bayern Munich in Germany. It was an atrocious night, with torrential rain and Eric could do no right. During his time at City, he was reserve to Bill Glazier, who restricted McManus to 7 first team games in total. The arrival of Jim Blyth meant a move and a drop to the lower divisions, where he proved to be a reliable performer.

McNAB, David
Half Back
Born: Cleland 2nd December 1897
Career: Newarthill Thistle, Portsmouth March 1923, Fulham July 1925, Coventry City c/s 1930 (£500), Llanelly c/s 1931, Retired 1936.

Coventry City	League	F.A.Cup
1930–31	9	–

Debut: 30/8/30 v Notts Co. (h) 1–2 (CH)

McNab was signed from Fulham in the summer of 1930, to give an experienced backbone to City's side. He had fine credentials, playing 169 games

for Fulham in 5 seasons and scoring 21 goals from the centre half position. The fee was £500, a considerable sum for a 32 year old and McNab was to take over from the well respected Norman Dinsdale. Unfortunately, McNab had a dreadful debut against Notts County and was dropped. He never regained his place except at a time of injury and was released.

McNESTRY, George
Outside Right
Born: Chapwell 7th January 1908
Career: Chapwell Institute, Bradford (P.A.) 1926, Doncaster Rovers c/s 1927, Leeds United November 1928, Sunderland November 1929, Luton Town August 1930, Bristol Rovers May 1932, Coventry City June 1935, Retired 1937.

Coventry City	League	F.A.Cup
1935–36	39 – 20	2
1936–37	7 – 1	–
Total	46 –21	2

Debut: 31/8/35 v Reading (a) 1–2 (OR)
Honours: Division 3 (S) Cup Winners Medal 1935 & 1936.

Harry Storer signed McNestry to add extra ammunition for Les Jones and Clarrie Burton, to help the club to promotion from Division 3(S). He achieved this and scored his fair share of goals. He had been a fringe player for First Division sides Leeds United and Sunderland, before making his mark at Luton and Bristol Rovers. He scored 26 goals in 2 seasons at Kenilworth Road and 47 in 3 years at Eastville. Many of his City goals came from the penalty spot, but ironically, he missed the most important one when City were drawing in the final game of the 1935–36 season against Torquay United. Needing a victory for promotion, he put his spot kick straight at the keeper; fortunately, City still won and gained promotion. After only 7 appearances in Division 2, McNestry was forced to retire due to a knee injury.

MacPHEE, Magnus George (Tony)
Centre Forward
Born: Edinburgh 30th April 1914
Died: 1960
Career: Wellington Rovers, Edina, Heart of Midlothian 1932, Bangor August 1935, Belfast Celtic September 1935, Workington August 1936, Bradford (P.A.) October 1936, Coventry City June 1937, Reading May 1938, Banbury Spencer c/s 1949.

Coventry City	League	F.A.Cup
1937–38	12 – 6	1

Debut: 28/8/37 v Tottenham H. (a) 0–0 (CF)

MacPhee failed to establish himself at his home town club Hearts, and was forced to move to Ulster to gain a regular place, but was attracted back to the mainland by Workington before Bradford Park Avenue snapped him up in October 1936. 18 goals in 31 games encouraged Harry Storer to sign him for City. He never settled at City despite scoring a hat–trick in the 4–3 victory at Fulham. At Reading he achieved an excellent scoring rate either side of the War, scoring 85 goals in 4 seasons. During the War, he made regular appearances for Reading and guested briefly for Crystal Palace. He ended his playing days with a short spell at Banbury, before coaching at Reading and managing Walsall. McPhee died aged 46, after spending his last years in charge of The George Hotel in Basingstoke.

McPHERSON, Kenneth (Ken)
Centre Forward
Born: West Hartlepool 25th March 1927
Career: Hartlepools United (amateur), Notts County August 1950, Middlesbrough July 1953 (£15,000), Coventry City December 1955, Newport County June 1958, New York Americans June 1961, Swindon Town August 1961 (£2,550), Retired c/s 1965.

Coventry City	League	F.A.Cup
1955–56	25 – 14	–
1956–57	40 – 21	1 – 1
1957–58	23 – 3	1 – 1
Total	88 – 38	2 – 2

Debut: 10/12/55 v Newport Co. (h) 3–0 (CF) 1 goal

McPherson was a big, strong centre forward in the traditional English mould. He had been a para-trooper and his physique was perfect for the game in the 1950's. He had been understudy to Tommy Lawton at Notts County before moving to Middles-brough. Jesse Carver signed him for City as the manager changed from push–and–run football. He scored on his debut and continued getting goals for 18 months, but they then dried up and Ray Straw replaced him. At Newport he continued his scoring spree, and after he signed for Swindon he reverted to centre half. He retired in 1965 to run a grocery business.

McSEVICH, Peter
Goalkeeper
Born: Stevenston 1908
Career: Shieldmuir Celtic, Glasgow Celtic August 1924, Aberdeen July 1925, Bournemouth & Boscombe Athletic c/s 1928, Coventry City August 1932, Walsall June 1933, Wellington Town c/s 1936.

Coventry City	League	F.A.Cup
1932–33	34	4

Debut: 27/8/32 v Torquay U. (a) 3–3 (Goal)
Honours: 2 Scotland Junior Caps

In the summer of 1932, Harry Storer needed to solve a problem. His defence was leaky and goal-keeper Tommy Allen was past his peak, but the latter's natural replacement – Bill Morgan – was not quite ready to be blooded as the regular choice. Storer needed a reliable, experienced keeper who could breach the gap. McSevich was an obvious choice. After a spell in Celtic's reserves and 36 games for Aberdeen, he had signed for Bourne-mouth and had impressed in the 4 years he had spent there. Although Steve Ogrizovic is the only keeper to score for City, McSevich experienced the delight of this feat when he netted for Bournemouth in the 4–1 victory over Brighton in October 1931. He was however, playing at outside right after being injured earlier in the match. McSevich lost his place to Morgan, and was sold to Walsall shortly after. He eventually returned to Fellows Park as a backroom boy and stayed for many years.

MARSH, John Kirk (Jack)
Forward
Born: Mansfield 8th October 1922
Career: Mansfield Boys Club, Notts County August 1942, Coventry City September 1948, Leicester City March 1950, Chesterfield September 1950, Worksop Town c/s 1951.

Coventry City	League	F.A.Cup
1948–49	11 – 4	–
1949–50	9 – 3	–
Total	20 –7	

Debut: 30/10/48 v Nottingham Forest (h) 1–2 (IR)

Marsh came to City after showing great potential at Notts County, but he could not command a regular first team place at City during the club's struggle to stay in Division 2. A move to Leicester was quick-ly followed by a short stay at Chesterfield before moving into non–league football.

MARTIN, Neil
Centre Forward
Born: Tranent 20th October 1940
Career: Tranent Juniors, Alloa Athletic 1959, Queen of the South c/s 1961 (£2,000), Hibernian July 1963 (£6,000), Sunderland October 1965 (£50,000), Coventry City February 1968 (£90,000), Nottingham Forest February 1971, Brighton & H.A. July 1975, Crystal Palace March 1976, St. Patrick's Athletic 1976, Retired 1978.

Coventry City	League	F.A.Cup	Lge.Cup
1967–68	15 – 8	–	–
1968–69	25 – 9	2	2
1969–70	40 – 14	2 – 1	1
1970–71	26 – 9	1	5 – 2
Total	106 – 40	5 – 1	8 – 2

Debut: 10/2/68 v Chelsea (h) 2–1 (CF)
Honours: 3 Scotland Caps
1 Scotland U–23 Cap
1 Scotland XI appearance
2 Scottish League appearances

In February 1968, City were languishing at the foot of Division 1 and needed a goalscorer, Martin fitted the bill and was most prolific in his spell at City. It was his goals that kept City in Division 1 and ensured a place in Europe in 1970. Martin was a prolific goalscorer throughout his career, which earned him 3 full Scotland caps before arriving at City. His departure to Forest was a surprise, but his form suffered in a struggling side. He formed an exciting managerial partnership with Alan Buckley at Walsall, before taking a coaching job in the Middle East.

MASKILL, Thomas (Tommy)
Half Back

Born: York 1903
Career: York City, Coventry City c/s 1923, Caernarvon Town c/s 1926, Rhyl Town 1927, Coventry City c/s 1928, Scarborough Town c/s 1929, Carlisle United c/s 1930, Barnsley c/s 1931, York City c/s 1932, Selby Town 1933.

Coventry City	League	F.A.Cup
1923–24	15	–
1924–25	26 – 1	1
1925–26	18	–
1928–29	10	–
Total	69 – 1	1

Debut: 8/12/23 v Hull City (a) 2–3 (RH)

Signed from his home town club, Maskill was a useful right half who was highly thought of by Albert Evans, but once James Kerr had settled in as manager, Michael McIlvanney was preferred. When City were transferred to Division 3(South), all players were offered reduced terms. Maskill rejected them and linked up with his former team mate George Thompson who was player–manager of Caernarvon Town, where he won a Welsh National League Championship medal. He was re–signed for City by James McIntyre, but left for Scarborough after an unsuccessful time.

MASON, George William
Centre Half

Born: Birmingham 5th September 1913
Died: Coventry 12th August 1993
Career: Redhill Amateurs, Coventry City November 1931, Nuneaton Borough c/s 1952 (F/T).

Coventry City	League	F.A.Cup
1931–32	3	–
1932–33	6	–
1933–34	2	–
1934–35	24	3
1935–36	40	2
1936–37	42 – 3	3 – 2
1937–38	38 – 1	1
1938–39	42 – 1	1
1945–46	WWII	2
1946–47	28	2
1947–48	34	2
1948–49	35	1
1949–50	28 – 1	1
1950–51	–	–
1951–52	8	2
Total	330 – 6	20 – 2

Debut: 12/3/32 v Bristol Rovers (a) 1–3 (CH)
Honours: 2 England War–time Caps (both at City)

George Mason epitomised the City team of the 1930's under the management of Harry Storer. He was courageous, solid and totally committed to the cause, becoming the captain and linchpin of the side which passed from Division 3 (South) mediocrity, to promotion challengers in the 2nd Division. He was signed at the age of 18, in November 1931 from Redhill Amateurs in Birmingham. For his first three seasons, Mason's first team outings were limited by the consistent form of Tommy Davison. Although he made his debut on the 12th OF March 1932, in a 3–1 defeat at the hands of Bristol Rovers at Eastville, it was not until January 1935 that Mason became the regular centre half. Following an incident which involved goalkeeper Hubert Pearson, Davison was dropped for disciplinary reasons and Mason never looked back, taking over the captaincy in the middle of the championship season of 1935–36, following the sale of Charlie Bisby to Mansfield Town. Mason then led City through an exciting 3 year period in Division 2, but the hopes and promises of high achievement from such a skilful side, were never quite fulfilled. Storer had anticipated great things from Mason, and his prediction came true when Mason became the first City player to appear for England, albeit in the 1942 war time internationals against Scotland and Wales, in the latter game of which, he marked City forward George Lowrie. When League football resumed in 1946, Mason was 33 years old, but he continued to captain his side in his own indomitable way, until October 1949, when he handed over the reins to the more youthful Martin McDonnell. Mason was to play only another eight games for the City – during the disastrous 1951–52 relegation season– before joining non–league Nuneaton Borough in the summer on a free transfer. Later in life, Mason became a popular publican in the City, but above all, he will be remembered for his unstinting loyalty to Coventry City over a twenty year period.

MASON, Richard J. (Dick)
Defender
Born: Arley 2nd April 1918
Died: Arley October 1992
Career: Arley Miners Welfare, Nuneaton Borough, Coventry City May 1946, Bedworth Town February 1955 (player-manager), Retired 1958.

Coventry City	League	F.A.Cup
1946–47	24	2
1947–48	36	2
1948–49	39	1
1949–50	37	1
1950–51	36	–
1951–52	36 – 1	1
1952–53	39 – 1	3
1953–54	6	–
1954–55	–	–
Total	253 – 2	10

Debut: 11/9/46 v Newcastle Utd (a) 1–3 (LH)

During the torrid upheaval after the Second World War, Mason proved to be one of the few consistent performers in the City squad. It was an ageing team and Mason was bought from Nuneaton at the age of 28 and left to become player–manager of Bedworth at 36. In his spell at City, he proved to be a strong tackler and good header of the ball, despite his lack of inches. He finally lost his place to Roy Kirk, and eventually retired at the age of 40.

MATTHEWS, Horace
Outside Left
Born: Coventry c.1913
Career: Gosford Street Baptists, AWA Baginton, Newdigate Colliery, Coventry City 1945.

Coventry City	League	F.A.Cup
1945–46	WWII	2

Debut: 5/1/46 v Aston Villa (h) 2–1 (IL)

Horace Matthews, was well known in local league football before joining City in 1945. He was in his thirties and was brought in to help in a time when many players were unavailable. His only recognised games came in the FA Cup in 1946, as the League was still suspended. He played twice in the 2-legged tie against Aston Villa when Villa won 3–2 on aggregate. His son Johnny Matthews played in City's reserves in the 1960's, before moving to Waterford, with Peter Thomas, where he made a name for himself.

MATTHEWS, Reginald Derrick (Reg)
Goalkeeper
Born: Coventry 20th December 1931
Career: Modern Machines 1947, Coventry City May 1950, Chelsea November 1956 (£22,500), Derby County October 1961, Rugby Town c/s 1968 (player–manager).

Coventry City	League	F.A.Cup
1950–51	–	–
1951–52	–	–
1952–53	10	–
1953–54	5	–
1954–55	36	4
1955–56	43	1
1956–57	17	–
Total	111	5

Debut: 21/3/53 v Southend United (a) 0–1 (Goal)
Honours: 5 Full England Caps (all with City)
        3 England B Caps (all with City)
        4 England U–23 Caps (all with City)
        2 Football League appearances (with City)
        2 Division 3 (S) appearances (with City)

Looking back, it is very difficult to comprehend quite what happened to Reg Matthews in a glorious 3 year spell whilst at City. He made his debut in March 1953, in a struggling City side, but by April 1956, he was still playing in the same division and was a full England international. He was a tremendous goalkeeper, certainly more agile than the average keeper of the 50's, and attracted attention from major clubs very early in his career. After 15 Division 3 (S) games, he played for the Football League and England U–23 teams, and full Caps quickly followed. He thus became the first City player to play for England (and remains the most capped), and became the first Division 3 keeper to achieve this distinction. In his five games, England did not lose, but after being dropped from the international side the pressure was on him to move from lowly City. Matthews finally accepted the inevitable and signed for Chelsea for a goalkeeping record fee of £22,500. He spent the next 12 years playing in Division 1, but received no further honours. After leaving Derby, he became player-manager of Rugby Town. He now lives in Coventry.

MEADOWS, Frank
Forward

Born: Maltby 27th June 1933
Career: Rotherham United April 1952, Coventry City June 1956, Bath City 1957.

Coventry City	League	F.A.Cup
1956–57	8	–

Debut: 10/5/56 v Norwich City (h) 3–2 (IR)

Meadows was signed from 2nd Division Rotherham, and his spell with City was short with few appearances. He was a squad man, given an opportunity when Noel Simpson was sold to Exeter, but whose place was quickly taken by Iain Jamieson.

MEESON, David J.
Goalkeeper

Born: Oxford 6th July 1934
Career: Oxford City, Wolverhampton W. February 1952, Reading August 1954, Coventry City August 1962 (£4,000), Wisbech Town c/s 1965.

Coventry City	League	F.A.Cup	Lge.Cup
1962–63	15	–	2
1963–64	5	–	–
1964–65	4	–	2
Total	24	–	4

Debut: 1/9/62 v Southend United (h) 3–4 (Goal)

Meeson was a big named replacement for the fans' favourite Arthur Lightening. He turned out to be a bad buy for Jimmy Hill, for after indifferent performances he was replaced by youth recruit, Bob Wesson. During his spell at Reading, Meeson had been well respected, but his move to City didn't work. After the arrival of Bill Glazier, Meeson moved into non–League football with Wisbech Town.

MELROSE, James Millsopp (Jim)
Forward

Born: Glasgow 7th October 1958
Career: Eastercraigs, Partick Thistle 1975, Leicester City June 1980 (£250,000), Coventry City September 1982 (player-exchange), Celtic August 1983 (£100,000), Wolverhampton W. (loan) September 1984, Manchester City November 1984, Charlton Athletic March 1986, Leeds United September 1987 (£50,000), Shrewsbury Town February 1988, Macclesfield Town August 1990 (F/T), Curzon Ashton October 1990 (F/T), Halesowen Harriers c/s 1991 (F/T).

Coventry City	League	F.A.Cup	Lge.Cup
1982–83	21+3s–8	1+1s	3 – 2

Debut: 18/9/82 v Birmingham City (a) 0–1 (F)
Honours: 8 Scotland U–21 Caps
Scottish FA Cup Runners–up Medal 1984

Melrose made a great impression with City when he scored a hat-trick on his home debut versus Everton. He netted 6 goals in total in his first 3 games, but as the team struggled towards the relegation zone, he found scoring difficult. His goalscoring had been apparent at his previous clubs, but was beginning to struggle, and consequently Leicester's manager Gordon Milne was eager to swap him for Tom English. When Bobby Gould arrived, Melrose was sold to Celtic, from whence he started his time as a football nomad. At Shrewsbury, Melrose became the first player to successfully sue a fellow professional for damages following an on-the-field incident with Chris Kamara.

MERCER, Alec
Inside Forward

Born: Tamworth 12th September
Career: Kettlebrook, Bury October 1912, Coventry City August 1919 – May 1923.

Coventry City	League	F.A.Cup
1919–20	27 – 6	–
1920–21	19 – 2	–
1921–22	26 – 4	3 – 1
1922–23	29 – 4	1
Total	101 –16	4 – 1

Debut: 30/8/19 v Tottenham H. (h) 0–5 (IR)

Mercer was a stocky forward in the "fetch and carry" mould, who proved his worth for City by playing along the whole of the forward line. He had scored 10 goals in 29 games for Bury before The Great War, but his goal scoring was limited for City. Two of his most important goals came against his former club on the 1st of May 1920. With City needing to win and a goal down, Mercer scored a brace to secure victory. This game was, of course, to come in for a great deal of scrutiny. He left the game in May 1923, tarred with the same brush as club captain George Chaplin, who had instigated the "Bury Scandal".

METCALF, Walter Frederick
Left Back

Born: Scarborough 15th December 1910
Died: Autumn 1981
Career: Scarborough, Sunderland October 1932, Brentford c/s 1934, Coventry City July 1937, Retired 1946.

Coventry City	League	F.A.Cup
1937–38	42	1
1938–39	34 – 1	1
1945–46	WWII	2
Total	76 – 1	4

Debut: 28/8/37 v Tottenham H. (a) 0–0 (LB)

Big left back Walter Metcalf had been sold by Sunderland before making the first team, and had only played 7 league games for Brentford when the Bees sold him to City in July 1937. Metcalf made the transition from a First Division reserve to Division 2 with ease. Standing at 6 feet and weighing 15½ stone, Metcalf was a fearless left back who was able to keep even the trickiest of wingers at bay. He formed a fine full back partnership with Jack Astley and missed only 8 League games before the war. During the war, he guested for Nottingham Forest and Northampton Town. In 1946, Metcalf was 35 and stationed in Singapore. These factors combined to precipitate his retirement from the game.

MIDDLETON, Craig D.
Midfield

Born: Nuneaton 10th September 1970
Career: YTS Coventry pro May 1989, Cambridge United July 1993 (F/T).

Coventry City	League	F.A.Cup	Lge.Cup
1989–90	0+1s	–	–
1990–91	–	–	–
1991–92	1	–	1
1992–93	1	–	
Total	2+1s	–	1

Debut: 14/4/90 v Tottenham H. (a) 2–3 (Sub)
Full Debut: 4/12/91 v Tottenham H. (h) 1–2 (Mid) League Cup

The twin brother of Lee Middleton, Craig is a midfield player who was part of City's FA Youth Cup winning side of 1987, as centre forward. He played only a handful of times for the first team and each time City lost!

MIDDLETON, Lee W.
Centre Half

Born: Nuneaton 10th September 1970
Career: YTS Coventry City, pro May 1989, Swindon Town (trial) c/s 1992, Corby Town 1992.

Coventry City	League	F.A.Cup	Lge.Cup
1989–90	0+2s	–	–
1990–91	–	–	–
1991–92	–	–	–
Total	0+2s	–	–

Debut: 23/9/89 v Chelsea (a) 0–1 (sub)

Middleton was a promising centre half who was expected to step into Trevor Peake's shoes. Unfortunately, a severe back injury forced Middleton from the professional game. He had an unsuccessful trial with Swindon in the summer of 1992 before teaming up with Michael Cook at Corby Town. He and Craig are the only twin brothers to play for City's first team.

MILLARD, Albert E. (Bert)
Centre Half

Born: West Bromwich 1st October 1898
Career: Barry Town 1914, Birmingham 1919, Coventry City October 1920, Crystal Palace July 1922, Charlton Athletic October 1924, Leamington Town.

Coventry City	League	F.A.Cup
1920–21	30 – 4	2 – 1
1921–22	33 – 4	3
Total	63 – 8	5 – 1

Debut: 30/10/20 v Stoke (h) 1–0 (CF)

Millard had been a centre forward at St Andrew's, but made a transition to centre half after a few games with City. His partnership with Sammy Stevens often disappointed, because of Millard's poor distribution. He was a useful goalscorer, scoring 7 of his goals from the centre half position. In the summer of 1922, he and Joe Jones of Crystal Palace exchanged clubs. He played 36 matches before joining Charlton Athletic. He ended his playing days with Leamington Town and became a publican in the town.

MILLER, James
Outside Right

Born: Tynemouth 1889
Career: South Shields Albion, Wallsend Park Villa, Newcastle United May 1912 (£25), Grimsby Town April 1913 (£50), Everton c/s 1919, Coventry City December 1919 (£1,500), Preston North End January 1920, Darlington October 1920, Pontypridd c/s 1921, Chesterfield May 1922, Bournemouth & Boscombe Athletic June 1923, Swansea Town c/s 1924, Luton Town May 1925.

Coventry City	League	F.A.Cup
1919–20	7	–

Debut: 13/12/19 v West Ham United (a) 0–2 (OR)

Born in the North–east, Miller failed to break into Newcastle's side before moving to Grimsby. He impressed during the War and signed for Everton. City needed to escape from the bottom of Division 2 and spent the massive sum of £1500 for Miller. Whilst at City, he established a successful but brief partnership with Peter Quinn, and played 7 successive games, proving to be sufficiently spritely that First Division Preston snapped him up. He didn't last long at Deepdale before moving to non-league Darlington. He spent the rest of his playing days as a useful winger at each of his clubs.

MITCHELL, Joseph T. (Joe)
Goalkeeper

Born: Sheffield
Career: Sheffield United 1909, Luton Town c/s 1913, South Shields 1919, Coventry City February 1920, Chesterfield March 1921.

Coventry City	League	F.A.Cup
1919–20	10	–
1920–21	19	–
Total	29	–

Debut: 21/2/20 v Hull C. (h) 0–1 (Goal)

The experienced Mitchell was signed by Harry Pollitt in February 1920 to help City escape from relegation. He provided some stability as City achieved the impossible. He continued the season after, but lost his place to Jerry Best who went on to make the place his own. Before the war, he played 37 League games for 1st Division Sheffield United and 61 for Southern League Luton.

MITE, Robert (Bob)
Wing Half
Born: Details unknown
Career: Rotherham United, Coventry City September 1919, Rotherham Town, Mansfield Town December 1921.

Coventry City	League	F.A.Cup
1919–20	7	–

Debut: 20/9/19 v Birmingham (h) 1–3 (RH)

Bob Mite was one of a number of players that were used by manager Will Clayton in an attempt to stop City's drastic run at the start of the club's first League season. He played in the first 2 games in which City achieved a point – 0–0 draws against Fulham and Bristol City. New manager Harry Pollitt, brought in new players and Mite returned to Rotherham.

MITTEN, John
Outside Left
Born: Manchester 30th March 1941
Career: Mansfield Town January 1958, Newcastle United September 1958, Leicester City October 1961 (F/T), Manchester United April 1963 (F/T), Coventry City July 1963 (F/T), Plymouth Argyle January 1967 (£5,000), Exeter City June 1968, Bath City August 1971, Tiverton Town.

Coventry City	League	F.A.Cup	Lge.Cup
1963–64	4	–	–
1964–65	10 – 1	–	2 – 1
1965–66	12 – 3	1	1
1966–67	8+2s–1	–	0+1s
Total	34+2s–5	1	3+1s–1

Debut: 12/10/63 v Wrexham (h) 3–0 (OL)

John's father was Charlie Mitten, who had also played for both Newcastle and Manchester United, but with more success. Charlie caused a stir when as manager of Newcastle, he signed and picked his son for the first team at the age of 17. He was never a regular first team choice in his career, until his move to Plymouth. While at City, Mitten was understudy to Dave Clements, and his first team outings were therefore limited. He was also a wicket keeper with Leicestershire.

MOKONE, Steve V.
Outside Right
Born: South Africa 23rd March 1932
Career: Pretoria, Coventry City October 1956, P.S.V. Eindhoven 1957, Cardiff City July 1959, Benfica 1960, Barnsley August 1961–October 1961.

Coventry City	League	F.A.Cup
1956–57	4 – 1	–

Debut: 13/10/56 v Millwall (h) 1–2 (OR)

"Kalamazoo" Mokone was City's first ever black player. His time at City was short as he had disagreements with manager Harry Warren about tactics. He was immensely popular wherever he went, particularly in Portugal when with Benfica. At Barnsley he made only one League Cup appearance, before drifting out of the professional game.

MOORE, Alan
Winger
Born: Hebburn 7th March 1927
Career: Sunderland May 1946, Spennymoor United 1948, Chesterfield December 1948, Hull City June 1951 (£7,000), Nottingham Forest January 1952, Coventry City December 1954 (£10,500), Swindon Town June 1957, Rochdale November 1958, Wisbech Town June 1959, Cambridge United 1960 (player–manager).

Coventry City	League	F.A.Cup
1954–55	17 – 3	2 – 1
1955–56	25 – 7	1
1956–57	15 – 3	–
Total	57 – 13	3 – 1

Debut: 25/12/54 v Southampton (h) 1–1 (OR) 1 goal

Moore's stay at City coincided with one of the worst periods of their history, however, throughout his stay he gave total commitment. Therefore it was a shock in early 1957 when manager Warren suspended him for "gross insubordination", at a time when the players and management were at loggerheads. He earned a recall at the end of the season, but was quickly sold to Swindon. The most fruitful spell of his career, came at Forest, where he scored 39 goals from the wing, in 101 games.

MORGAN, William A. (Bill)
Goalkeeper
Born: Ryton-on-Tyne 1914
Died: Coventry February 1993
Career: Mickley Colliery, Chopwell Institute October 1931, Coventry City March 1932, Retired 1944.

Coventry City	League	F.A.Cup
1931–32	–	–
1932–33	8	–
1933–34	4	–
1934–35	2	1
1935–36	12	–
1936–37	42	3
1937–38	41	1
1938–39	41	1
Total	150	6

Bill Morgan was a highly regarded keeper, whose career was cruelly ended by the War and a shoulder injury. He had made his debut as a replacement for Peter McSevich at the age of 18. He had impressed Harry Storer whilst playing in the North-east, and his manager was prepared to be patient with his find. It wasn't until March 1936 that he made the keeper's jersey his own. From then up to the war, he missed only 2 games and helped City to the brink of Division 1. At the outbreak of war, Morgan joined the local fire service (an essential function for a city so vulnerable to air attack). He continued to play for City and guested for Nottingham Forest and Leicester City. It was at Filbert Street that he ended his career, when, on September 26th 1942, he dislocated his shoulder in the 0-0 draw against Leicester. Despite 18 months recuperation, he took medical advice and retired. He continued at the club, coaching the nursery team, Modern Machines, and later the first team, before working at Standard Triumph.

MORGAN, William Albert L.

Forward

Born: Cradley Heath 1891
Career: Cradley Heath St. Luke's, Birmingham 1912, Coventry City 1920, Crystal Palace July 1922, Cradley Heath St. Luke's June 1925, Shrewsbury Town 1927.

Coventry City	League	F.A.Cup
1920-21	29 - 7	2
1921-22	24 - 7	2
Total	53 - 14	4

Debut: 6/11/20 v Notts Co. (a) 1-1 (OL)

William "Mollie" Morgan was a constructive left sided forward who could play at either outside or inside left. He was bought to provide experience to a struggling side, having scored 13 goals in 67 games for Birmingham. He scored some useful goals for City and made some impressive performances, but was sold to Crystal Palace in the summer of 1922 as Arthur Wood came to City. He continued his good form with The Glaziers.

MORRIS, Frederick (Fred)

Inside Forward

Born: Tipton 27th August 1893
Died: Great Bridge 4th July 1962
Career: Bell Street Primitives, Tipton Victoria, Redditch Town 1910, West Bromwich Albion May 1911, Coventry City August 1924 (£625), Oakengates Town c/s 1925, Retired 1930.

Coventry City	League	F.A.Cup
1924-25	22 - 8	2 - 1

Debut: 30/8/24 v Chelsea (a) 0-1 (IL)
Honours: 2 England Full Caps
England Junior International
League Championship Medal 1919-20
1 Football League appearance

Morris reached the height of his career immediately after the Great War. He scored 37 goals in WBA's Football League championship campaign of 1919-20, and his reward was 2 England caps, including a goal on his international debut against Scotland in the 5-4 victory in April 1920. He was a regular right up to the end of his time at The Hawthorns, and it was considered something of a coup that Morris signed for City. He started off brightly, showing his typically aggressive style, but in City's struggling side he faded badly. At the end of the 1924-25 season, City were relegated to Division 3 (N) and as part of the club's cost cutting, Morris was released. He moved onto Oakengates Town, the forerunner of Telford United.

MORRISSEY, Patrick J. (Pat)

Midfield

Born: Enniscorthy 23rd February 1948
Career: Apprentice Coventry City, pro July 1965, Torquay United July 1968, Crewe Alexandra July 1969, Chester October 1971, Watford December 1971 (£7,000), Aldershot November 1974, Swansea City (loan) October 1977, Dartford 1977, Hayes 1978, Slough Town 1979, Carshalton Athletic 1980, Hendon 1981, Chesham United 1982 (player-manager), Dunstable 1985 (player-manager), Buckingham Town, Chesham United.

Coventry City	League	F.A.Cup	Lge.Cup
1965–66	–	–	–
1966–67	0+1s	0+1s	–
1967–68	6+3s	1	–
Total	6+4s	1+1s	–

Debut: 9/12/66 v Ipswich Town (h) 5–0 (sub)
Full Debut: 23/9/67 v West Brom. Albion (h) 4–2 (IR)
Honours: 1 Republic of Ireland U–23 Cap (with City)

Morrissey had a fruitful career with lower division teams and in non–League football. At the age of 41, he was still player–manager of Chesham. His stay at City was short and his progress limited by the arrival of Ernie Hunt. While at City, he gained an U–23 cap, 6 months before his first team debut, when aged 18!

MORTIMER, Dennis G.
Midfield
Born: Liverpool 5th April 1952
Career: Apprentice Coventry City, pro September 1969, Aston Villa December 1975 (£175,000), Sheffield United (loan), December 1984, Brighton & Hove Albion c/s 1985, Birmingham City August 1986 (F/T), Kettering Town July 1987 (F/T), Redditch United 1988 (player–manager).

Coventry City	League	F.A.Cup	Lge.Cup
1969–70	6+3s	1	–
1970–71	24+3s	–	2
1971–72	26+8s–4	1+1s	1
1972–73	39 – 1	4	2
1973–74	33 – 1	3	3
1974–75	29 – 3	–	1
1975–76	22 – 1	–	2
Total	179+14s–10	9+1s	11

Debut: 11/10/69 v West Ham United (h) 2–2 (sub)
Full Debut: 7/1/70 v Liverpool (h) 1–1 (Mid) FA Cup
Honours: 3 England B caps
6 England U–23 caps (all with City)
European Cup Winners Medal 1982
League Championship Medal 1980–81
League Cup Winners Medal 1977

Mortimer's departure was one of the most controversial incidents to occur since City's arrival in Division 1. With City, he had developed from a bright youngster to an outstanding talent that would form the basis for City's push towards honours in the mid– 1970's. However, the arrival of Larry Lloyd forced Gordon Milne to sell to balance the books. He chose to sell Willie Carr, but a proposed move to Wolves fell through. With the wolf at the door, City gave it's fans the worst Christmas present possible in 1975, with the sale of Mortimer to arch rivals, Villa. Whilst with Villa, he achieved most of his ambitions, skippering the club to the League Championship and the European Cup, but never winning the full England caps he deserved. Now he is coaching at WBA, but City fans still believe his departure gave the true picture of City's ambitions.

MURCOTT, Steven (Steve)
Goalkeeper
Born: Streetley 17th January 1961
Career: Apprentice Coventry City, pro November 1978, Worcester City c/s 1981, Retired August 1981.

Coventry City	League	F.A.Cup	Lge.Cup
1978–79	–	–	–
1979–80	1	–	–
1980–81	–	–	–
Total	1	–	–

Debut: 4/9/79 v Norwich City (h) 2–0 (Goal)

Murcott's only appearance came as a surprise. Jim Blyth was warming up when he injured his back and Murcott was summoned from the bar to get changed. He played a "blinder", but was replaced the following week by Les Sealey who had been at an away reserve game on the day of the Norwich game. Murcott was released because of his off the field behaviour and moved to Worcester City, where, returning after his first appearance, he was involved in a serious car crash which ended his career.

MURPHY, Donal P.
Forward
Born: Dublin 23rd February 1955
Career: Apprentice Coventry City, pro August 1972, Shamrock Rovers late 1973, Coventry City early 1975, Millwall (loan) October 1977, Torquay United May 1978, Plymouth Argyle June 1980 (£65,000), Torquay United (loan) December 1981, Blackburn Rovers February 1982, Drogheda United (loan) October 1982, Bohemians (loan) March 1983, Drogheda United c/s 1983, University College Dublin c/s 1984.

Coventry City	League	F.A.Cup	Lge.Cup
1972–73	–	–	–
1973–74	–	–	–
1974–75	–	–	–
1975–76	19+3s–4	3 – 1	–
1976–77	13+5s–6	2	2 – 1
1977–78	1+2s	–	–
Total	33+10s–10	5 – 1	2 – 1

Debut: 8/11/75 v West Ham Utd (a) 1–1 (IL)
Honours: FAI Cup Runners–up Medal 1984

Murphy was essentially a squad player, acting as back–up for strikers Alan Green and Ian Wallace, but the success of the latter resulted in Murphy being surplus to requirements. It was no surprise that he returned to Ireland to finish his career, for whilst in his early City days, he moved to Shamrock Rovers due to home sickness, only to return to Highfield Road to start his League career.

MURPHY, Peter
Inside Forward
Born: West Hartlepool 7th March 1922
Died: 7th April 1975
Career: Dunlop, Birmingham, Coventry City 1943, Tottenham Hotspur May 1950 (£18,000), Birmingham City January 1952 (£20,000), Rugby Town c/s 1960, Retired 1961.

Coventry City	League	F.A.Cup
1945–46	WWII	–
1946–47	11 – 2	1
1947–48	29 – 7	2
1948–49	36 – 13	1
1949–50	39 – 15	1
Total	115 –37	5

Debut: 7/12/46 v Fulham (h) 1–0 (IL)
Honours: League Championship Medal 1950–51
FA Cup Runners–up Medal 1956

During the War, Murphy moved from the North East to Coventry, was spotted by Harry Storer playing in local football and joined City. He was very talented and he prospered in City's Division 2

side just after the War. In early 1950, City spent to avoid relegation and in order to recoup some money they accepted Spurs' offer of £18,000 for him. In his first season, he won a Championship medal, but soon moved to Birmingham, following his failure to settle in London. At the Blues he played in the 1956 Cup Final. He was involved in the unfortunate incident at Wembley, which resulted in Bert Trautmann breaking his neck. He died in 1975 aged 53.

MYERSCOUGH, William H. (Bill)
Centre Forward
Born: Bolton 22nd June 1930
Died: 1977
Career: Manchester City (amateur), Ashfield, Walsall June 1954, Aston Villa July 1955, Rotherham United July 1959, Coventry City July 1960, Chester March 1962, Wrexham July 1963, Macclesfield 1964.

Coventry City	League	F.A.Cup	Lge.Cup
1960–61	40 – 13	3 – 3	1 – 1
1961–62	18 – 3	–	1
Total	58 – 16	3 – 3	2 – 1

Debut: 20/8/60 v Barnsley (a) 1–4 (CF)
Honours: FA Cup Winners Medal 1957

Myerscough didn't play League football until he was 24, but his early performances for Walsall convinced Villa to buy this skilful centre forward. Whilst there he gained a Cup Winners medal, before moving to 2nd Division Rotherham. Billy Frith bought Myerscough and he scored regularly, but became a victim of Jimmy Hill's shake–up of the club. He was only 47 when he died in 1977.

NARDIELLO, Donato
Outside Right

Born: Cardigan 9th April 1957
Career: Apprentice, Coventry City, pro April 1974, Detroit Express March 1980, Washington Diplomats 1981, Nuneaton Borough 1981, West Midlands Police 1982.

Coventry City	League	F.A.Cup	Lge.Cup
1974–75	–	–	–
1975–76	–	–	–
1976–77	–	–	–
1977–78	12+1s–1	–	2
1978–79	16	2	–
1979–80	4	1	–
Total	32+1s–1	3	2

Debut: 22/10/77 v Ipswich Town (h) 1–1 (OR)
Honours: 2 full Wales Caps (both with City)
1 Wales U–21 Cap (with City)

Nardiello was a tricky, skilful winger, but he never seemed to have the confidence to be a successful player. He emerged in the City team thanks to Gordon Milne's exciting 4–2–4 strategy. 25 days after making his League debut, Donato made his first full Wales appearance. He was never a City regular and was allowed to move to America. On his return to England, he became a policeman in the city and became a regular on duty at Highfield Road.

NASH, Harold E. (Harry)
Forward

Born: Fishponds c.1893
Career: Brislington United, Mardy, Aberdare c/s 1910, Abertillery c/s 1913, Pontypridd c/s 1914, Aston Villa February 1915, Coventry City August 1920, Cardiff City February 1921, Merthyr Town May 1923, Aberbargoed c/s 1925, Ystrad Mynach c/s 1926.

Coventry City	League	F.A.Cup
1920–21	15 – 3	2

Debut: 28/8/20 v Rotherham Co. (a) 3–2 (IL)
Honours: Welsh Cup Runners–up Medal 1923–24

Plucked from the obscurity of the Southern League Division 2, Bristolian Nash scored a hat-trick on his League debut for Aston Villa in April 1915, against Liverpool. Unfortunately for him, hostilities soon ended the league programme. On the return to League action in 1919, Nash struggled to find a place in the Villa side. After 12 games and 5 goals, he moved to City. In 15 games he scored 3 goals

and attracted the attention of Cardiff, helping The Bluebirds to promotion to Division 1 in the club's first League season, scoring 6 goals in 29 games.

NDLOVU, Peter
Forward

Born: Bulawayo, 25th February 1973
Career: Highlanders (Zimbabwe), Coventry City July 1991 £10,000.

Coventry City	League	F.A.Cup	Lge.Cup
1991–92	9+14s–2	–	2
1992–93	27+5s–7	1	1
Total	36+19s–9	1	3

Debut: 24/8/91 v QPR (a) 1–1 (sub)
Full Debut: 21/9/91 v Everton (a) 0–3 (F)
Honours: 30 Zimbabwe Full Caps (19 at City)

The young Zimbabwe international was spotted by John Sillett when City played against that country in 1990. He came over for a trial and was signed by Terry Butcher in July 1991, at 18 years of age. He was gradually brought into the team and scored vital goals in victories against Arsenal and Aston Villa. The latter was a tremendous shot from 20 yards, after he had dummied the Villa centre halves. An ankle injury slowed his progress, but under Bobby Gould he has flourished. His great pace, close ball control and incredible body swerve make him one of the most exciting players to have played for City, yet despite being a full international for 5 years he is still learning the game. He was capped at 15 and has two brothers who also play professional football, Madinda who plays in Germany and Adam who has had trials with City and Manchester United.

NELSON, Alfred
Forward

Born: Coventry
Career: Foleshill Albions, Coventry City 1919, Foleshill Albions.

Coventry City	League	F.A.Cup
1919-20	2	-

Debut: 8/11/19 v Huddersfield T. (h) 0-2 (IR)

Local lad Nelson was pushed into the struggling City side when injury hit Alec Mercer and Fred Gibson. Not surprisingly Nelson didn't shine, given the circumstances, and he returned to Foleshill Albions, who at the time were one of Coventry's leading junior sides.

NEWMAN, Ronald (Ron)
Outside Right

Born: Pontypridd 1st May 1933
Career: Ynysbwl, Northampton Town October 1953, Coventry City March 1956 (player exchange), Torquay United July 1957, Bedford, Rugby Town, Rushden Town.

Coventry City	League	F.A.Cup
1956-57	6 - 2	-
1957-58	7	-
Total	13 - 2	-

Debut: 17/3/56 v Southampton (h) 2-0 (OR) 1 goal

Throughout his time in the Football League, Newman was never more than a fringe player. After 18 games for the Cobblers, he came to City in a straight swap for Charlie Dutton. He scored on his debut, but could not secure a regular place in a struggling side and his spell at Torquay was brief.

NEWSOME, Robinson (Bobbie)
Inside Right

Born: Hebden Bridge 25th May 1919
Career: Willington Boys Club, Congleton Town 1937, West Bromwich Albion March 1939, Coventry City May 1947, Hereford United 1948, Brierley Hill Alliance c/s 1949, Dudley Town c/s 1950, Gornal Wood c/s 1953, Retired c/s 1955.

Coventry City	League	F.A.Cup
1947-48	7 - 2	-

Debut: 18/10/47 v Southampton (a) 1-3 (IR)

During the war, Newsome played for WBA and guested for Walsall, Burnley, Chester, Norwich City and once for Manchester United. Bobbie made his

League debut for City at the age of 28, some 8 years after signing professional forms with his first League club. His stay at Highfield Road, after being signed from WBA's reserves, lasted only six months. He failed to impress and moved on to non-league Hereford United, before moving to the Black Country.

NEWTON, Graham W.
Forward

Born: Bilston 22nd December 1942
Career: Wolverhampton Wanderers July 1959, Blackpool August 1961, Walsall February 1962, Coventry City January 1964, Bournemouth December 1964, Atlanta Chiefs 1967, Port Vale November 1968, Atlanta Chiefs 1969, Reading 1971, Worcester City 1971, Stourbridge 1975, Worcester City 1976.

Coventry City	League	F.A.Cup	Lge.Cup
1963-64	8 - 3	-	-
1964-65	-	-	1
Total	8 - 3	-	1

Debut: 15/2/64 v Brentford (h) 2-2 (IR)

Jimmy Hill had a habit of buying players to perform a task and once the task was achieved, sell them. Newton was one of these. Signed in the hope of helping City gain promotion from Division 3 as a capable squad player, he played well when selected and scored 3 essential goals. He was soon sold to Bournemouth and later became one of the first English players to play in the latterday North American Football League, with Atlanta Chiefs.

NEWTON, James (Jimmy)
Goalkeeper

Born: Horsforth
Career: Horsforth, Queen's Park 1921, Bradford City June 1923, Halifax Town May 1925, Coventry City July 1926, Brighton & Hove Albion May 1929.

Coventry City	League	F.A.Cup
1926-27	42	3
1927-28	28	2
1928-29	-	-
Total	70	5

Debut: 28/2/26 v Northampton T. (h) 0-3 (Goal)

When Jerry Best failed to agree terms with City, a replacement was needed for this excellent goalkeeper. James Kerr swooped for Newton, who had surprisingly been given a free transfer by Halifax.

He was a giant, who could command his area well and made some impressive performances during his time at City. He lost out to the experienced and well respected Tommy Allen. After spending a season in City's reserves, he was released. During his first season with City, Newton didn't miss a game, but his debut against Northampton on the opening day of the season was put in jeopardy by an accident a couple of weeks beforehand. Whilst using a chopper, he damaged his hand, which was somewhat careless for a goalkeeper! He made the match, only to pick the ball out of the net 3 times in the 3–0 drubbing by the Cobblers at Highfield Road.

NICHOLAS, Charles Brian (Brian)
Half Back
Born: Aberdare 20th April 1933
Career: Queen's Park Rangers 1949, Chelsea July 1955, Coventry City February 1958, Rugby Town July 1962.

Coventry City	League	F.A.Cup	Lge.Cup
1957–58	20	–	–
1958–59	26	2	–
1959–60	35	2	–
1960–61	8	–	1
1961–62	24	2	1
Total	113	6	2

Debut: 1/2/58 v Torquay United (a) 0–1 (RH)

Nicholas made his debut for QPR at the age of 16, and it took him a while to make an impression, but by the early 1950's he was a first team regular. This encouraged First Division Chelsea to invest in his services, but the lack of first team football encouraged him to sign for City. Nicholas was only 24 years of age, despite having a distinctive balding pate, and gave five years excellent service.

NUTT, Gordon E.
Outside Right
Born: Birmingham 8th November 1932
Career: Sheldon Town, Coventry City November 1949, Cardiff City December 1954, Arsenal September 1955, Southend United October 1960, PSV Eindhoven c/s 1961, Hereford United c/s 1962, Rugby Town c/s 1963, Bexley United February 1964.

Coventry City	League	F.A.Cup
1949–50	–	–
1950–51	–	–
1951–52	3 – 1	3
1952–53	10 – 1	–
1953–54	42 – 6	1
1954–55	21 – 3	2
Total	76 – 11	6

Debut: 29/12/51 v Blackburn R. (h) 1–2 (OR) 1 goal.

Gordon Nutt was one of the many young City players groomed at the beginning of the 1950's. The future of the club was to be based upon them, however, as soon as a good offer came in, Nutt was sold to Cardiff City. Soon afterwards, Arsenal bought him. He spent 6 seasons with the Gunners, mainly as a fringe player, before moving to Southend. He later emigrated to Australia where he still lives.

OAKEY, Graham
Right Back
Born: Worcester 5th October 1954
Career: Apprentice Coventry City, pro October 1972, Swindon Town (loan) December 1979, Worcester City September 1980, Stourport Swifts late 1980, Retired 1981.

Coventry City	League	F.A.Cup	Lge.Cup
1972–73	–	–	–
1973–74	–	–	–
1974–75	31	3	1
1975–76	22+1s	0+1s	2
1976–77	13	–	–
1977–78	21	–	4
1978–79	–	–	–
1979–80	–	–	–
1980–81	–	–	–
Total	87+1s	3+1s	7

Debut: 7/9/74 v Manchester City (h) 2–2 (RB)

Oakey was one of the greatest full backs that City ever had. His pace was lightning and his tremendous enthusiasm was greatly appreciated by the City fans. In his first season in the first team, he was voted the Supporters Club player of the year. Unfortunately, his career was dogged by injury which finally curtailed it. On an awful day at Villa Park, he twisted badly and the rupture of his knee was so bad that he was unable to play League football again. His short spells in non-league football lasted 6 months during which time each game was played after a painkilling injection. His injury was a tremendous blow to City, as players of his calibre are few and far between. In recent years, he has been a delivery man in his native Worcester and continues to have the great enthusiasm that typified his game.

O'BRIEN, Ronald Victor (Ron)
Half Back

Born: Coventry
Career: Morris Motors, Coventry City, Watford June 1934, Bedworth Town c/s 1947.

Coventry City	League	F.A.Cup
1930-31	3	–
1931-32	29	1
1932-33	17	–
1933-34	8 – 3	–
Total	57 – 3	1

Debut: 7/4/31 v Watford (h) 2-2 (OL)

Local youngster O'Brien came through City's local scouting system and impressed Harry Storer with his hard working displays. He played his first 3 games out of position and took his chance to make the right half place his own in September 1931. After losing his place to Jimmy Baker, he played his last games at outside right, from which position he scored all of his goals for City. He made 193 appearances for Watford before the War, and guested for City during hostilities whilst he lived and worked in Coventry.

OGRIZOVIC, Steven (Steve)
Goalkeeper

Born: Mansfield 12th September 1957
Career: Old Newark Road Youth Club, Chesterfield July 1977, Liverpool November 1977 (£75,000), Shrewsbury Town August 1982 (player-exchange), Coventry City June 1984 (£72,500).

Coventry City	League	F.A.Cup	Lge.Cup
1984-85	42	2	2
1985-86	42	1	4
1986-87	42 – 1	6	5
1987-88	40	2	3
1988-89	38	1	3
1989-90	37	1	7
1990-91	37	4	5
1991-92	38	2	3
1992-93	33	1	2
Total	349 – 1	20	34

Debut: 25/8/84 v Aston Villa (a) 0-1 (Goal)
Honours: FA Cup Winners Medal 1987
1 Football League appearance

Oggy started as a policeman in Nottingham alongside ice-skater Christopher Dean. He received his break at Chesterfield and continued the Spireites' tradition of grooming top goalkeepers. After only 16 appearances at the Recreation Ground Oggy signed for Liverpool. He played only five times for the Reds in his five years, but received a European Cup Winners medal as non-appearing substitute. He moved to Shrewsbury in a swap deal that sent Bob Wardle to Anfield. He impressed greatly at Gay Meadow and was snapped up by Bobby Gould for only £72,500. He played 241 consecutive games for City – which is a record for the club – before being injured at Millwall in September 1989. Oggy is one of the biggest keepers in the League and one of the most reliable. He has the distinction of being the first keeper to score in City colours. This happened at a wet and windy Hillsborough in October 1986. With a gale behind him, Oggy punted the ball downfield and as Wednesday keeper

Martin Hodge ran from his line, the ball hit the deck and skidded over his head into the net. Oggy has now played over 400 games for City in all competitions which makes him the third highest appearing City player, behind George Curtis and Mick Coop. In August 1987 his outstanding record was rewarded with a substitute appearance for the Football League against the Rest of the World in the 3–0 victory at Wembley.

ORMSTON, Arthur
Centre Forward

Born: Alnwick 3rd June 1900
Died: Oldham 13th October 1947
Career: Radcliffe Borough, South Shields October 1919 (£25), Chesterfield August 1921, Durham City September 1922, Coventry City March 1923, Barrow August 1923, Wigan Borough March 1924 (£30), Oldham Athletic June 1925 (£25), Bradford City October 1926 (£650), Bristol Rovers June 1927 (£300), Oldham Athletic November 1928 (£425), Stalybridge Celtic October 1930, Macclesfield August 1931.

Coventry City	League	F.A.Cup
1922–23	2	–

Debut: 17/3/23 v Leicester C. (a) 1–2 (CF)

Ormston was a happy wanderer who spent most of his career in the North and his time at City was short. He came on a trial from Durham City and played twice before being suspended, with William Toms, for an undisclosed breach of club conduct. His most successful period came when with Oldham. He cost The Latics only £25, but in his first 2 games he scored 8 times, netting 23 goals in 37 games in the season 1925–26. Ormston's 15 month spell at Boundary Park earned Oldham a hefty profit. Despite scoring 6 goals in 15 games, he couldn't prevent The Bantams from being relegated to Division 3 (N).

O'ROURKE, John
Centre Forward

Born: Northampton 11th February 1945
Career: Arsenal 1961, Chelsea April 1962, Luton Town December 1963, Middlesbrough July 1966, Ipswich Town February 1968, Coventry City November 1969, Queen's Park Rangers October 1971 (£70,000), Bournemouth January 1974 (£45,000).

Coventry City	League	F.A.Cup	Lge.Cup
1969–70	20 – 11	2	–
1970–71	27+1s–5	–	4 – 2
1971–72	5+1s–1	–	1
Total	52+2s–17	2	5 – 2

Debut: 22/11/69 v Newcastle Utd (h) 1–0 (IL)
Honours: 1 England U–23 Cap

In his early career, O'Rourke was unable to make either the Arsenal or Chelsea first team, so he dropped down to 4th Division Luton, where he scored 64 League goals in only 84 matches. This provided the springboard for better things and O'Rourke earned his reward for 29 goals in 43 games for Middlesbrough in 1966–67, with an England U–23 appearance against Turkey in which he scored. He stayed with City for only 2 years, but his contribution was immeasurable. He came during City's push for Europe, and quickly worked up an understanding with Neil Martin that created some vital goals. It was O'Rourke's hat–trick in Bulgaria that enabled City to beat Trakia Plovdiv 4–1. His League goals dried up and he was sold to 2nd Division QPR.

OSGOOD, Keith
Defender

Born: Isleworth 8th May 1955
Career: Apprentice Tottenham Hotspur May 1972, Coventry City January 1978 (£130,000), Derby County October 1979 (£150,000), Orient December 1981 (£20,000), HJK Helsinki May 1984, Cambridge United November 1984, Burton Albion February 1986, Stapenhill March 1986, Retired c/s 1986.

Coventry City	League	F.A.Cup	Lge.Cup
1977–78	13+1s–1	–	–
1978–79	11	–	1
1979–80	–	–	–
Total	24+1s–1	–	1

Debut: 14/1/78 v Chelsea (h) 5–1 (CH)

Osgood was bought as a centre–half, but was capable of playing anywhere in the back four. His appearances were limited by the emergence of Gary Gillespie in 1978. He was only called on during 1978–79 when injury forced out others. It was no surprise therefore, when City accepted Derby's £150,000 offer for Osgood, during the Rams slide into Division 2. After playing for lower division clubs, Osgood was forced to retire with a back injury.

OWEN, William
Goalkeeper

Born: Coventry 1906
Career: Nuneaton Town, Birmingham c/s 1926, Fulham c/s 1929, Coventry City c/s 1930, Stourbridge c/s 1931, Nuneaton Town c/s 1934.

Coventry City	League	F.A.Cup
1930–31	5	–

Debut: 15/11/30 v Bristol R. (a) 0–1 (Goal)

Local boy Owen came to City via a number of clubs. He made his First Division debut for Birmingham as a 20 year old, after impressing for Nuneaton Town. After playing 5 games for The Blues, he failed to regain his place and moved to Fulham, but in his 12 months at Craven Cottage, he didn't appear for the first team. After joining City, Owen was given his chance following a series of impressive reserve performances. City wanted Owen to re-sign for the club, but he rejected terms. He couldn't find a League team to join and was snapped up by Stourbridge.

PADDON, Graham Charles
Midfield
Born: Manchester 24th August 1950
Career: Apprentice Coventry City, pro May 1968, Norwich City October 1969 (£25,000), West Ham United December 1973 (£160,000), Norwich City November 1976 (£110,000), Tampa Bay Rowdies (loan) c/s 1978, Millwall (loan) December 1981, Hong Kong c/s 1982, Retired.

Coventry City	League	F.A.Cup	Lge.Cup
1968–69	0+1s	–	–
1969–70	3+1s–1	–	–
Total	3+2s–1	–	–

Debut: 25/2/69 v QPR (h) 5–0 (Sub)
Full Debut: 13/9/69 v. Crystal Palace (h) 2–2 (Mid)
Honours: 1 England U–23 cap
  FA Cup Winners Medal 1975
  Cup Winners Cup Runners up Medal 1975–76
  League Cup Runners-up Medal 1972–73
  Texaco Cup Runners-up Medal 1972–73

Paddon was a solid and dependable midfield schemer. As a young professional, his chances at City were limited, but his potential was sufficiently evident for 2nd Division Norwich to pay £25,000 for him, and he was influential in The Canaries rise into Division 1. At West Ham, Paddon was part of the 1975 FA Cup winning team with Bobby Gould, gained a Cup Winners Cup medal and appeared for England U–23 as an over age player. He moved

back to Norwich where he struggled with injury. After leaving the professional game, Paddon became coach at Portsmouth where he remains to this day.

PAINTER, Ian J.
Forward
Born: Wombourne 28th December 1964
Career: Apprentice Stoke City 1982, Coventry City July 1986 (£80,000), Retired c/s 1987

Coventry City	League	F.A.Cup	Lge.Cup
1986–87	0+3s	–	1+1s

Debut: 19/10/86 v Wimbledon (h) 1–0 (Sub)
Full Debut: 19/11/86 v. Liverpool (h) 0–0 (F) Lge.Cup
Honours: 1 England U–21 Cap

Painter's short stay at City was a nightmare. He had a persistent injury which meant that he was never able to force his way into the team. His only full appearance was against Liverpool in the League Cup 0–0 draw. At the end of the season, he was released. It was Painter that missed the last gasp penalty for Stoke City in May 1985, in Coventry's 1–0 win on their way to a miraculous escape from relegation; if he had scored, the Sky Blues would have been down. Painter eventually retired because of his back injury.

PARKER, Richard
Centre Forward
Born: Stockton-on-Tees 14th September 1894
Died: 1969
Career: Stockton F.C., Sunderland June 1919, Coventry City January 1920, South Shields October 1920, Wallsend September 1921, Queen's Park Rangers c/s 1922, Millwall Athletic c/s 1924, Watford 1927, Merthyr Town 1928, Tunbridge Wells Rangers 1930.

Coventry City	League	F.A.Cup
1919–20	16 – 9	–
1920–21	10 – 2	–
Total	26 – 11	–

Debut: 31/1/20 v South Shields (a) 0–1 (CF)

Richard Parker didn't stay long at City, but his goalscoring was essential in ensuring City escaped the almost certain drop from Division 2 in 1920. Nine goals in his 16 games was a great scoring rate considering City had only managed 16 in 26 previous games. His goals earned City vital points and included both in City's 2–0 victory against Lincoln in April 1920 in the relegation battle. After 2 matches against South Shields in October 1920, he moved to the North East side. He dropped down to Wallsend before scoring 30 times in 63 games for QPR and 61 goals in only 89 games for Millwall.

PARKER, Robert (Bobby)
Centre Half
Born: Coventry 11th November 1952
Career: Apprentice Coventry City, pro May 1970, Carlisle United June 1974 (£60,000), Retired c/s 1984.

Coventry City	League	F.A.Cup	Lge.Cup
1969–70	1+1s	–	–
1970–71	18+1s	–	–
1971–72	27	2	1
1972–73	24	4	1
1973–74	7+1s	–	3
Total	77+3s	6	5

Debut: 28/3/70 v Burnley (h) 1–1 (CH)

Parker is one of the few players to appear for Coventry in Division 1 that were actually born in the City, the others being Gareth Evans, Tony Dobson and Howard Clark, who all followed much later. Parker was a solid, but not outstanding player, who was sold in the Summer of 1974. He moved to Carlisle, who were just about to embark on Division 1 football for the first time. Parker was an ever–present in that season (1974–75), which saw Carlisle top the League before being relegated. For the rest of his career, he was a consistent performer for Carlisle before retiring in 1984.

PARKIN, Thomas (Tommy)
Inside Forward
Born: Byker, Newcastle–upon–Tyne 5th February 1902
Died: April 1984
Career: Preston Colliery, Coventry City 1924, Durham City November 1925, Exeter City c/s 1926, Merthyr Town c/s 1928, Yeovil Town September 1929.

Coventry City	League	F.A.Cup
1924–25	20 – 2	–
1925–26	–	–
Total	20 – 2	–

Debut: 25/12/24 v South Shields (h) 0–1 (IL)

Tommy Parkin played 20 games in City's relegation season of 1924–25. He made a place in the team once the vastly experienced Danny Shea left. He

also played at outside left following injury to "Cute" Herbert. With City experiencing financial problems, Parkin was transfer listed in October 1925 and was sold to Durham City. He played 19 League games for Durham, 5 for Exeter and 24 for Merthyr, before joining Yeovil where he stayed until at least 1935.

PATERSON, William
Centre Forward
Born: Hill O'Beath
Career: White Rose, Cowdenbeath c/s 1914, Glasgow Rangers (loan) September 1916, Derby County January 1921 (£3,500), Armadale (loan) 1923/4, Cowdenbeath June 1924, Coventry City August 1925, Springfield (USA), Fall River (USA), Providence (USA) August 1929 (player–manager), Gold–Bugs (USA), New York Nationals (USA).

Coventry City	League	F.A.Cup
1925–26	40 – 25	1
Total	40 – 25	1

Debut: 29/8/25 v Lincoln C. (h) 3–2 (CF) 1 goal

Paterson was one of the first, and most successful, of James Kerr's Scottish signings. Kerr was notorious for buying Scots and at least Paterson was known to City fans, having played for Derby County for 3 years. He served Cowdenbeath well and even played 5 times for Glasgow Rangers during a loan spell in 1916. In his season at City, Paterson bagged 25 goals, which was the highest tally in a season for a City player since joining the League. But Paterson was attracted to the United States, where he spent the rest of his career.

PATRICK, William C.G. (Bill)
Full Back
Born: Lochgelly 12th March 1932
Career: Snowdown Colliery, Coventry City November 1954, Gillingham June 1958, Folkestone July 1960.

Coventry City	League	F.A.Cup
1954–55	–	–
1955–56	9	–
1956–57	17	1
1957–58	18 – 6	1
Total	44 – 6	2

Debut: 3/9/55 v Colchester Utd (h) 2–0 (LB)

Bill Patrick was Scottish, but his family moved to the Kent coalfield. It was while playing for the Snowdown Colliery that Harry Barratt recommended him to City. Patrick was followed 12 months later by Alf Bentley and George Curtis. He started as a full back, but in an emergency became a forward. It was in the front line that he scored a hat-trick against Exeter in November 1957.

PEAKE, Trevor
Centre Half
Born: Nuneaton 10th February 1957
Career: Nuneaton Borough, Lincoln City June 1979 (£25,800), Coventry City July 1983 (£100,000), Luton Town August 1981 (£100,000).

Coventry City	League	F.A.Cup	Lge.Cup
1983–84	33 – 3	4 – 1	3
1984–85	33+1s–1	1	2
1985–86	37 – 1	1	4
1986–87	39	6	4
1987–88	31	1	2
1988–89	32	1	2
1989–90	33	1	8
1990–91	36 – 1	2	5
1991–92	2	–	–
Total	276+1s–6	17 – 1	30

Debut: 23/8/83 v Tottenham H. (a) 1–1 (CH)
Honours: FA Cup Winners Medal 1987
2 England Semi–Professional Caps

Peake was one of Bobby Gould's first signings after taking over from Dave Sexton in 1983. Unlike many of Gould's buys, Peake was not a gamble. He was, at 26, an experienced centre half who had taken Lincoln to the brink of promotion to Division 2. He soon established himself as one of the best centre halves in Division 1 and possessed a cool head that was badly needed by City. He established

a partnership with Brian Kilcline which helped City turn the corner from being relegation candidates. Despite this, his only international recognition was a call–up to the England B team, only for injury to rob him of his chance. When Terry Butcher took over, he began to look to the future, but his treatment of Peake appeared nothing short of shabby. Peake, Lloyd McGrath and Kenny Sansom, were transfer listed for drinking on a tour of Scotland. His colleagues were excused, but Peake, who was a loyal servant of the club, was sold to Luton Town against his will. He couldn't help The Hatters escape relegation in his first season at Kenilworth Road. Gould made an unsuccessful bid to bring him back to City in late 1992.

PEARCE, Andrew John (Andy)
Centre Half
Born: Bradford–on–Avon 20th April 1966
Career: Wednesbury Town, Stourbridge, Halesowen Town, Coventry City May 1990 (£15,000), Sheffield Wednesday June 1993 (£500,000).

Coventry City	League	F.A.Cup	Lge.Cup
1990–91	11 – 1	–	–
1991–92	36 – 2	2	4
1992–93	21+3s–1	1	2
Total	68+3s–4	3	6

Debut: 9/3/91 v Leeds United (a) 0–2 (CH)

Tall, blond–haired centre half Andy Pearce came late into League football, being signed by John Sillett at the age of 24. He established his place in the first team and this encouraged Terry Butcher to sell Brian Kilcline. Pearce continued his good form in 1991–92 and he contributed to City's particularly mean defence. His form dipped in 1992–93 which resulted in David Busst getting his chance, and Phil Babb moving to centre half. He was allowed to move to Sheffield Wednesday in the summer of 1993, as Bobby Gould began his campaign for the next season. The fee of £½ million made a considerable profit for City who bought him for only £15,000.

PEARCE, Stuart
Left Back
Born: Shepherd's Bush 24th April 1961
Career: Wealdstone 1977, Coventry City November 1983 (£50,000), Nottingham Forest May 1985 (£250,000).

Coventry City	League	F.A.Cup	Lge.Cup
1983–84	23	–	–
1984–85	29 – 4	2	–
Total	52 – 4	2	–

Debut: 12/11/83 v QPR (h) 1–0 (LB)
Honours: 53 England Full Caps
1 England U–21 Cap
League Cup Winners Medal 1989 & 1990
FA Cup Runners–Up Medal 1991
Full Membs. Cup Wins. Medal 1989 & 1992

Pearce was signed from non–League Wealdstone and was pushed straight into the first team. He became an instant success and his tough tackling style made him a fans' favourite. His stay at City was less than 2 years, but it was an eventful time. In both seasons City just avoided relegation and it was his penalty that ensured a 1–0 victory at Stoke, as City won the last 3 games of the season in May 1985 to stay up. Pearce showed his inexperience by stating publicly that he would sign a new contract if City stayed up. The impossible was achieved but Pearce was determined to move, and signed for Nottingham Forest, where he has played over 300 games. The international career that all City fans expected for him began in May 1987, and he has now played over 50 times for England. Despite many excellent appearances, it is his penalty shoot-out miss against West Germany in the semi–final of The 1990 World Cup that has been his most notorious moment in an England shirt.

PEARSON, Harold (Harry)
Outside Left
Born: Birkenhead

Career: Shaftesbury F.C., Tranmere Rovers 1932/3, Bournemouth & Boscombe Athletic, Prescot Cables, Northwich Victoria c/s 1936, Coventry City November 1936, Queen's Park Rangers c.1938, Barrow c/s 1939.

Coventry City	League	F.A.Cup
1936–37	–	–
1937–38	3	–
Total	3	–

Debut: 28/8/37 v Tottenham H. (a) 0–0 (OL)

Merseysider Pearson started his career in his native Birkenhead with Tranmere Rovers, appearing 30 times before trying his luck with Bournemouth. After failing to appear for The Cherries' first team, he returned to the North West with Prescot Cables. Signed by Northwich Victoria in the summer of 1936, Pearson played so well that City came in with a record fee for the Cheshire League side, in November 1936. His 3 appearances came at the start of the 1937–38 season, but he was dropped, being replaced by Arthur Fitton. He played 11 times for QPR, before signing for Barrow for the illfated 1939–40 season.

PEARSON, Herbert
Forward
Born: Brierley Hill 7th January 1901
Died: Dudley late 1972
Career: Brierley Hill Alliance, Southampton c/s 1923, Coventry City c/s 1924, Nuneaton Town c/s 1925.

Coventry City	League	F.A.Cup
1924–25	5 – 1	1

Debut: 6/12/24 v Hull C. (a) 1–4 (IR) 1 goal

Signed by Albert Evans as understudy to Albert Pynegar in the summer of 1924, Pearson's opportunities were scarce, for despite City being relegated, Pynegar continued to score goals. Pearson scored on his debut at Anlaby Road, but failed to shine thereafter. With the team relegated, the club decided to lower costs and Pearson was one of the players not retained.

PEARSON, Horace
Goalkeeper
Born: Tamworth 6th April 1907
Career: Nuneaton Town, Luton Town c.1928, Blackpool May 1929, Oldham Athletic November 1931, Coventry City May 1933, Newport County May 1937, Barry Town c/s 1938, Bristol City September 1938, Retired WWII.

Coventry City	League	F.A.Cup
1933–34	38	2
1934–35	40	2
1935–36	30	2
1936–37	–	–
Total	108	6

Debut: 9/9/33 v Bristol R. (h) 5–3 (Goal)

No relation to the other Pearsons to play for City, Horace was however, part of the Pearson goalkeeping family. Horace's uncle Hubert and cousin Harold both played in goal for WBA. Horace helped Blackpool to promotion to Division 1 and impressed at Oldham, before signing for City in May 1933. He proved to be a fine custodian, despite being only 5 feet 9 inches tall and formed part of the best defence seen at Highfield Road, as the side won the Division 3 (S) Championship in 1936. A breach of club discipline lost him his place in early 1935, but his replacement Bill Morgan wasn't ready for a long run. In March 1936, Morgan did however take over, and Pearson didn't play for the first team again. He ended his playing days during the war with Bristol City and settled in that city.

PERDOMO, Jose T.
Midfield

Born: Uruguay 6th January 1965
Career: Uruguay, Genoa, Coventry City (trial) August 1990, Betis Seville (loan) January 1991.

Coventry City	League	F.A.Cup	Lge.Cup
1990–91	4	–	2

Debut: 8/9/90 v Aston Villa (a) 1–2 (Mid)

Uruguay international Perdomo had come to the attention of City fans when he scored a tremendous goal from a thirty yard free kick at Wembley for Uruguay against England in May 1990 and appeared in the 1990 World Cup Finals. It came as a shock therefore, when it was announced that he was signing for City. He came on trial from Genoa, but there were mitigating circumstances, for the Italian club could only field 2 foreign players and Perdomo was surplus to requirement. In addition he had a long term ankle injury. In his time at City, he showed great vision and passing ability, but there were misgivings about the deal. His agent was pressing for a permanent move, but City were not happy with his ankle injury. In one of his last acts as manager, John Sillett withdrew from the deal and Perdomo returned to Italy.

PERRY, Eric
Full Back

Born: West Bromwich
Career: Solihull School, West Bromwich Albion, Willenhall, Brierley Hill Alliance, West Bromwich Albion, Coventry City November 1932, Dudley Town c/s 1935.

Coventry City	League	F.A.Cup
1932–33	26 – 3	1
1933–34	14 – 1	2
1934–35	–	–
Total	40 – 4	3

Debut: 17/12/32 v Brighton & H.A. (a) 0–1 (RB)

Perry had not played for the first team at WBA, but proved to be a versatile defender with City. He was able to play at right back or right half, but his appearances at City were restricted by his cricket commitments. He played for West Bromwich C.C. in The Staffordshire League, and represented his County in minor counties cricket. With City's strong squad, he was released in 1935.

PHILLIPS, David O.
Midfield

Born: RAF Wegberg, Germany 29th April 1963
Career: Apprentice Plymouth Argyle, pro August 1981, Manchester City August 1984, Coventry City June 1986 (player–exchange), Norwich City July 1989 (£500,000).

Coventry City	League	F.A.Cup	Lge.Cup
1986–87	39 – 4	6	5
1987–88	32+3s–2	2	2
1988–89	22+4s–2	1 – 1	1
Total	93+7s–8	9 – 1	8

Debut: 23/8/86 v West Ham Utd (a) 0–1 (Mid)
Honours: 46 Wales Full Cap (9 at City)
3 Wales U–21 Caps
FA Cup Winners Medal 1987

Phillips made an impression in the Plymouth side that reached the FA Cup semi–final in 1984, which attracted Manchester City to sign him. At Maine Road he acquired a reputation for spectacular goalscoring, but in his time at City he only scored nine goals, although he proved to be a useful midfield player who could fill in at full back if necessary. This he did successfully in the 1987 FA Cup Final when Brian Borrows was injured. After three years at City, Phillips wanted to play in a central midfield role and signed for Norwich expecting to adopt this position. However, in his four years since his £500,000 move Phillips has played the vast majority of his games on the flanks.

Coventry City	League	F.A.Cup	Lge.Cup
1978–79	–	–	–
1979–80	4+1s	–	–
1980–81	–	–	–
Total	4+1s	–	–

Debut: 1/3/80 v Brighton & H.A. (a) 1–1 (Mid)

Phillips was a member of City's great youth policy that produced players in the late 1970's such as Mark Hateley, Danny Thomas and Garry Thompson. At the tail end of 1979–80, Phillips was given his chance, but he could not force either Andy Blair or Gerry Daly from the first team. As part of City's pruning of surplus players in 1981, Phillips moved on, to Hong Kong.

PHILLIPS, John
Centre Forward

Born: Barry
Career: Barry Brooklands F.C., West Bromwich Albion October 1923, Southend United c.1924, Merthyr Town c.1925, Brentford c/s 1927, Bristol Rovers September 1928, Coventry City July 1930, Merthyr Town September 1931.

Coventry City	League	F.A.Cup
1930–31	25 – 17	3 – 1

Debut: 6/9/30 v Clapton Orient (a) 3–3 (CF) 1 goal

Welshman Phillips had come to Highfield Road with a reputation for scoring goals. After being rejected by WBA and playing 8 games at Southend, Phillips scored 32 goals in 57 league games for a struggling Merthyr side. He continued his scoring at Brentford, notching 22 goals in 29 games. Transferred to Bristol Rovers in September 1928, Phillips scored 39 goals in 68 games. Despite his scoring record, Phillips came to City as back-up for Jimmy Loughlin. After great displays in the reserves, Phillips forced his way into the first team, scoring on his debut and bagging 18 in 28 league and cup games. At the end of the season, Harry Storer released Phillips. This proved to be sound judgement as his replacement was Clarrie Burton.

PHILLIPS, Nicholas (Nicky)
Midfield

Born: West Ham 29th November 1960
Career: Apprentice Coventry City, pro August 1978, Hong Kong February 1981, Barking c.1983–86.

PHILPOTTS, David R.
Centre Half

Born: Bromborough 31st March 1954
Career: Apprentice Coventry City, pro October 1971, Southport (loan) January 1974, Tranmere Rovers September 1974, Carolina Lighting April 1979, Tranmere Rovers October 1983, Retired c/s 1985.

Coventry City	League	F.A.Cup	Lge.Cup
1971–72	–	–	–
1972–73	–	–	–
1973–74	3	–	1
1974–75	–	–	–
Total	3	–	1

Debut: 27/10/73 v Stoke City (a) 0–3 (CH)

Philpotts received his chance in October 1973 after waiting 2 years, through an injury to John Craven. City lost all 3 games in which Philpott played and he was dropped in favour of Bobby Parker. An injury later forced him to play in the less competitive NASL with Carolina. Philpotts is currently first team coach at Wigan Athletic.

PICK, William Edward (Billy)
Outside Left

Born: Danesmoor 5th June 1903
Died: Clay Cross 27th August 1981
Career: Danesborough Rovers, Bury c/s 1925, Lincoln City 1925/6, Portsmouth c/s 1926, Newport County July 1927, Coventry City November 1928, Watford December 1930, Barrow July 1932, Stockport County c/s 1933.

Coventry City	League	F.A.Cup
1928–29	27 – 5	–
1929–30	37 – 17	4 – 1
1930–31	10 – 3	–
Total	74 – 25	4 – 1

Debut: 1/12/28 v Plymouth Argyle (a) 0–3 (OL)

It was at City that Billy Pick's career blossomed. He had failed to make the grade at either Bury of Portsmouth and played twice for Lincoln and 19 times for Newport, before James McIntyre bought him in a deal which involved David Ward moving to South Wales. His sparkling wing play was a significant factor in helping City move out of their 'Stormy Period'. He set up a fine partnership with Jimmy Loughlin and scored a remarkable amount of goals for a winger in the 1929–30 season. This included the dubious distinction of scoring both goals for City in the 2–10 drubbing against Norwich, which is still City's heaviest league defeat. He was surprisingly sold to Watford.

PICKERING, Nicholas (Nick)
Left Midfield

Born: South Shields 4th August 1963
Career: Apprentice Sunderland, pro August 1981, Coventry City January 1986 (£125,000), Derby County July 1988 (£300,000), Middlesbrough (loan) July 1991, Darlington November 1991 (F/T), Burnley March 1993 (£15,000).

Coventry City	League	F.A.Cup	Lge.Cup
1985–86	15 – 4	–	–
1986–87	35+1s–5	6	5
1987–88	26+1s	–	2 – 1
Total	76+2s–9	6	7 – 1

Debut: 1/2/86 v Newcastle United (a) 2–3 (LH)
Honours: 1 England Full Cap
           15 England U–21 Caps (2 with City)
           FA Cup Winners Medal 1987
           League Cup Runners–up Medal 1984–85

Pickering burst onto the scene at the start of the 1981–82 season, aged 18. He established his place in the Sunderland side, making over 200 appearances, playing in a Wembley final and gaining an England cap on the tour to Australia in 1983. He signed at the same time for City as Alan Brazil and Jim McInally and his fee was a scoop at £120,000. He played wide left in midfield rather than left back where he had played at Roker Park. Pickering played a fundamental part in City's Cup winning side of 1987, but was pushed into the left back

position when David Smith emerged. His time at The Baseball Ground was torrid, for he suffered from injury and loss of form, and was given a free transfer.

PLATNAUER, Nicholas R. (Nicky)
Midfield

Born: Leicester 10th June 1961
Career: Bedford Town, Bristol Rovers August 1982, Coventry City July 1983 (£10,000), Birmingham City December 1984 (£50,000), Reading (loan) January 1986, Cardiff City September 1986 (F/T), Notts County July 1989, Port Vale (loan) January 1991, Leicester City July 1991 (F/T), Scunthorpe United March 1993 (F/T), Mansfield Town c/s 1993 (F/T).

Coventry City	League	F.A.Cup	Lge.Cup
1983–84	29+5s–6	4	3
1984–85	9+1s–1	–	2
Total	38+6s–7	4	5

Debut: 27/8/83 v Watford (a) 3–2 (sub)
Full Debut: 29/8/83 v. Tottenham H. (a) 1–1 (Mid)

Bobby Gould made a huge gamble in July 1983 when signing Platnauer from his old club Bristol Rovers. 12 months earlier, he had been a bank clerk in Bedford, and was pushed immediately into Division 1 after being only a squad player with Rovers. The gamble paid off. Platnauer was not skilful but he was determined, enthusiastic and always gave 100% effort. He typified that City season – a nobody thrown into the lion's den who came out fighting. It came as a surprise when he was sold to 2nd Division Birmingham. The everlasting memory of Platnauer must be his goal against Liverpool in December 1983. He scored after 39 seconds, with his head, as he lay on his hands and knees! (City won 4–0).

PLUMMER, Arthur
Right Back

Born: Sheffield
Career: Welton Rovers, Bath City c/s 1929, Coventry City December 1929, Boston United c/s 1932, Walsall c/s 1933, Dundalk, France, Bristol Rovers c/s 1937, Gloucester City c/s 1938.

Coventry City	League	F.A.Cup
1929–30	–	–
1930–31	11	–
1931–32	14	–
Total	25	–

Debut: 20/12/30 v Torquay U. (h) 6–1 (RB)

Youngster Arthur Plummer first played at Highfield Road on the 14th of December 1929 in the FA Cup for Bath City. He didn't fare well and his side lost 1–7, but he showed sufficient talent for City's manager James McIntyre to immediately sign him up. He spent most of his time in the reserves learning his trade, whilst Laurie Crown and Ted Watson were in the first team. He played whenever there was an injury, but was released when Jesse Bennett arrived. He later appeared 3 times for Walsall. He made no appearances for Bristol Rovers, before moving to Gloucester.

PLUNKETT, Adam
Full Back

Born: Newton c.1901
Career: Blantyre Celtic, Bury c/s 1922, Queen's Park Rangers July 1925, Guildford City August 1926, Walsall June 1927, Coventry City June 1928, Crystal Palace August 1929, Southend United September 1929, Oswestry Town October 1929, Hinckley 1930, Loughborough Corinthians August 1930, Rochdale March 1931, Stalybridge Celtic 1932, Hinckley c/s 1933.

Coventry City	League	F.A.Cup
1928–29	23	1

Debut: 25/8/28 v Norwich C. (h) 3–0 (LB)

Plunkett was a footballing nomad, never staying too long at any club. His longest spell at a club was 3 years at Bury, his first club, where he failed to gain a first team place. He played 15 times for QPR, before being released. He was later signed by James McIntyre for City and played inconsistently, frequently becoming the subject of the crowd's barracking. He lost his place to Ted Watson and was sold to Crystal Palace. His only other League appearances were with Rochdale, where he played 18 games in 18 months.

POINTER, Raymond (Ray)
Centre Forward

Born: Cramlington 10th October 1936
Career: Dudley Welfare Juniors 1952, Burnley 1954, Bury August 1965, Coventry City December 1965, Portsmouth January 1967, Retired c/s 1973, Blackpool Rangers 1976–77.

Coventry City	League	F.A.Cup	Lge.Cup
1965–66	19 – 11	4	–
1966–67	7 – 2	–	2
Total	26 – 13	4	2

Debut: 27/12/65 v Norwich City (a) 1–1 (IL) 1 goal
Honours: 3 England Full Caps
5 England U–23 Caps
Football League Champs. Medal 1959–60
FA Cup Runners–up Medal 1962
2 Football League appearances

The blond haired Pointer will be remembered for his spectacular goalscoring feats for Burnley, which helped them to win the 1959–60 championship and reach the 1962 FA Cup final. In his 3 England appearances in 1961, he scored 2 goals but was then dropped. Pointer came to City, hoping his career would return to the top flight, as City pushed towards promotion from Division 2. He was a proven goalscorer at the highest level, but injury had severely restricted his appearances for Burnley from 1963 to 1965. His move to Bury enable him to recapture his touch, which continued at City. In his first game, he scored and followed this up with a hat–trick in the 5–1 defeat of Preston on New Year's Day 1966. He couldn't command a regular place in 1966–67 and moved to Portsmouth in exchange for Brian Lewis.

POINTON, Thomas
Outside Left

Born: Coventry
Career: Redditch Town, Birmingham c/s 1913, Walsall c/s 1914, Nuneaton Town 1919, Coventry City c/s 1920, Redditch, Tamworth Castle 1921/2.

Coventry City	League	F.A.Cup
1920–21	2	–

Debut: 6/9/20 v Port Vale (a) 0–0 (OL)

Coventry born Pointon was signed from Nuneaton Town in the summer of 1920 for the reserve side, but injury to Fred Gibson gave him his chance. The leap from Southern League to Football League was considerable and Pointon didn't make the grade.

POOLE, William A.
Inside Forward
Born: Handsworth
Career: Kidderminster Harriers 1920, Merthyr Town c/s 1921, Stoke 1921/2, Watford c/s 1923, Coventry City c/s 1925, Kidderminster Harriers c/s 1926, Yeovil Town c/s 1927, Merthyr Town c/s 1928, Wellington Town, Stourbridge United, Walsall February 1932, Dudley Town c/s 1932.

Coventry City	League	F.A.Cup
1925–26	17 – 6	–

Debut: 19/9/25 v Wrexham (a) 1–3 (IR)

Before signing for Watford, Poole played 12 games for Stoke, 6 of them in Division 1. The tall forward was signed from Watford and started with several impressive performances, chipping in with 6 goals in 17 games. He was injured and didn't stay with City. He later drifted in and out of the League, returning for a second spell at Merthyr and playing 2 games for Walsall.

POUNDER, John A.
Outside Right
Born: Sheffield 16th March 1935
Career: Atlas Sports, Luton Town December 1955, Coventry City June 1957, Yeovil Town, Crewe Alexandra December 1957, Yeovil Town August 1959.

Coventry City	League	F.A.Cup
1957–58	6 – 1	–

Debut: 24/8/57 v. Reading (h) 1–0 (OR)

Signed as a young winger from 1st Division Luton Town, Pounder was pushed straight into the first team. He scored in his 2nd game, but played only 6 matches. He was soon released, and moved to Yeovil Town. Son Tony plays for Bristol Rovers.

POWELL, Barry Ivor
Midfield
Born: Kenilworth 29th January 1954
Career: Wolverhampton Wanderers January 1972, Portland Timbers (loan) April 1975, Coventry City September 1975 (£75,000), Derby County October 1979 (£350,000), Portland Timbers (loan) April 1981, Bulova (Hong Kong) August 1982, Burnley July 1984, Swansea City February 1985, Bulova July 1985, South China (Hong Kong) July 1986, Wolverhampton Wanderers November 1986, Retired 1988.

Coventry City	League	F.A.Cup	Lge.Cup
1975–76	32+2s–7	1+1s	1
1976–77	40 – 4	2	1
1977–78	42 – 4	1	4 – 2
1978–79	38 – 9	2	1
1979–80	10 – 4	–	2
Total	162+2s–28	6+1s	9 – 2

Debut: 10/9/75 v Bolton W (a) 3–1 (Mid) Lge. Cup
Honours: 4 England U–23 Caps
League Cup winners Medal 1973–74

Gordon Milne proved his astute recognition for a bargain when buying Barry Powell. He had been a regular in the successful Wolves side of the early 1970's and was restless after failing to break into the first team in August 1975. City snapped him up and for 4 seasons he proved to be an essential member of City's midfield. His non-stop creative game blended well with Terry Yorath's stern tackling to provide the basis for City's run of success from 1977 to 1979. City's need for finance and Powell's wish to better himself, saw him move to Derby who were soon relegated to Division 2. At Burnley and Swansea he played with Tommy Hutchison, and later moved into coaching at Wolves. He is now City's Football & Community Officer.

PRITCHARD, Harvey John (John)
Outside Right
Born: Meriden 30th January 1918
Career: Exhall Colliery, Coventry City October 1935, Crystal Palace June 1937, Manchester C. March 1938, Southend Utd. February 1947, Folkestone c/s 1952.

Coventry City	League	F.A.Cup
1935–36	–	–
1936–37	5 – 2	–
Total	5 – 2	–

Debut: 14/9/36 v Fulham (h) 1–1 (OR)

Local lad Pritchard played 5 matches when George McNestry was injured, and despite scoring twice, manager Harry Storer preferred to sign Irish international Jackie Brown to fill the right wing role. He was sold to Crystal Palace in June 1937 and showed such skill at Selhurst Park that Manchester City bought him. At the outbreak of War, Pritchard was a 21 year old establishing his place in a top Division 1 side, but his career was halted by the hostilities. He guested for City, Leicester and Northampton. He made 72 post–war League appearances for Southend United.

PROVERBS, Roy J.
Right Half
Born: Wednesbury 8th July 1932
Career: Stratford Town, Coventry City May 1956, Bournemouth July 1957, Gillingham February 1958, Canterbury City 1962, Tunbridge Wells United November 1962, King's Lynn 1964.

Coventry City	League	F.A.Cup
1956–57	10	1

Debut: 29/8/56 v Southampton (a) 1–1 (RH)

Proverbs moved into the Football League at the relatively late age of 24. He spent a season at City, but couldn't establish himself in a struggling Division 3(S) side. At the end of 1956–57, he moved to Bournemouth, then a much better side than City. He failed to make the first team and moved to struggling Gillingham. He only played two games towards the end of 1957–58, before he became a regular for four seasons.

PYNEGAR, Albert E.
Centre Forward
Born: Basford 24th September 1895
Died: Basford 1978
Career: Sutton Town, Leicester City May 1920, Coventry City January 1924, Oldham Athletic July 1925 (£1,200), Port Vale January 1929 (player–exchange), Chesterfield November 1930, Rotherham United August 1932.

Coventry City	League	F.A.Cup
1923–24	17 – 9	–
1924–25	37 – 18	3
Total	54 – 27	3

Debut: 26/1/24 v Port Vale (a) 1–1 (CF) 1 goal

Albert Pynegar was a goalscorer wherever he went, scoring at a rate of a goal every other game throughout his career. Whilst at City, he played in a very poor side, but still scored 27 goals in 54 League games. At Oldham, he notched up 55 goals in 138 games, but at Port Vale, despite 10 goals in 18 league games, he couldn't prevent Vale from being relegated from Division 2. They bounced straight back as he scored 20 goals in only 29 games. He was bought by Chesterfield and netted 26 times in 29 games. He was later released by Rotherham after only one season.

QUINN, Michael (Mick)
Centre Forward
Born: Liverpool 2nd May 1962
Career: Apprentice Derby County 1977, Wigan Athletic pro September 1979, Stockport County July 1982 (F/T), Oldham Athletic January 1984 (£52,000), Portsmouth March 1986 (£150,000), Newcastle Utd. August 1989 (£680,000), Coventry City (loan November 1992) December 1992 (£250,000).

Coventry City	League	F.A.Cup	Lge.Cup
1992–93	26 – 17	1	–

Debut: 21/11/92 v Manchester C. (h) 2–3 (CF) 2 goals

Quinn is one of the characters in today's game. He completed his apprenticeship at Derby, began to show his scoring prowess at Wigan, but was surprisingly sold to Stockport. Wigan manager Larry Lloyd announced that he wouldn't part with Quinn, but actually paid £2,000 for County to take him off his hands! In his 18 months at Edgeley Park he scored 41 goals before signing for Oldham, and after scoring 37 goals he was sold to Portsmouth to help the Latics balance the books. He continued his great scoring record with Pompey as he helped them to Division 1. His best season for goals came in 1989–90, his first for Newcastle, netting four on his debut and racing to 34 in the season. Despite scoring 69 goals in just over three seasons for the Magpies, manager Kevin Keegan felt that Quinn was not the man to lead his attack. A move to Aston Villa fell through and Quinn came to City initially on loan. He scored two goals on his debut against Manchester City and continued his tremendous run, scoring 10 goals in his first six games. His fee of £250,000 was a steal, and he will be particularly remembered for scoring two goals against both Liverpool (5–1) and Aston Villa (3–0) in consecutive home games. He was involved in a strange incident in April 1993, when he was sent off against Manchester United, but after the referee had watched the video of the game the dimissal was rescinded.

QUINN, Peter
Forward

Born: North Shields
Career: Jarrow Blackett F.C. 1913, North Shields Athletic c/s 1914, Bradford City July 1919, Coventry City November 1919.

Coventry City	League	F.A.Cup
1919–20	15 – 3	–

Debut: 29/11/19 v Blackpool (a) 0–2 (IL)

When Harry Pollitt took over as manager in November 1919, he was given £5000 to spend. One of his signings was Peter Quinn from 1st Division Bradford City. He had only played 4 games and scored 1 goal for the Valley Parade club, but was a revelation at City. He scored in 3 consecutive matches, including City's first League victory on Christmas day – only 20 games into the season! He struggled afterwards, losing his place to Dick Parker, and was released by new manager Albert Evans.

QUINNEY, John
Full Back

Born: Bulkington 2nd October 1932
Career: Modern Machines, Coventry City November 1949, Cheltenham Town c/s 1954.

Coventry City	League	F.A.Cup
1949–50	–	–
1950–51	–	–
1951–52	–	–
1952–53	3	–
1953–54	–	–
Total	3	–

Debut: 3/4/53 v Colchester United (a) 1–0 (LB)

Like many City players of the 1950's, Quinney progressed through the City's junior team, Modern Machines, before signing as a professional. His

---

early career was restricted by Dick Mason's consistent form and then National Service intervened. In January 1953, he was demobbed because of an injury received in Korea, yet 3 months later, he made his League debut at Colchester. His 3 matches were all played away from home, and at the end of 1953–54, he was released.

R

RAFFERTY, William Henry (Billy)
Centre Forward

Born: Glasgow 30th December 1950
Career: Port Glasgow Rovers 1967, Coventry City September 1969, Blackpool October 1972, Plymouth Argyle March 1974 (£25,000), Carlisle United May 1976 (£30,000), Wolverhampton Wanderers March 1978 (£125,000), Newcastle United October 1979 (£175,000), Portsmouth December 1980 (£80,000), Bournemouth February 1984.

Coventry City	League	F.A.Cup	Lge.Cup
1969–70	1	–	–
1970–71	9 – 1	–	–
1971–72	13 – 2	1 – 1	1
1972–73	4	–	2
Total	27 – 3	1 – 1	3

Debut: 14/4/70 v Newcastle United (a) 0–4 (CF)

Rafferty never established himself in the first team, for players like Neil Martin, John O' Rourke and Ernie Hunt were always ahead of him. When the opportunity for City to sign Tommy Hutchison appeared, Rafferty was used as part of the deal. This started a 12 year period in which Rafferty played for 7 clubs, primarily in Division 2. At that level, he proved to be a consistent goalscorer who was often bought to get a team out of trouble or to push them towards promotion.

RAMAGE, Jock
Full Back

Born: Edinburgh
Career: Bonnybridge Rose Athletic, Heart Of Midlothian September 1919, Coventry City November 1926 (£1,250), Luton Town January 1928, Heart Of Midlothian c/s 1928, Ross County c/s 1931, Chirnside United c/s 1934.

Coventry City	League	F.A.Cup
1926–27	8 – 1	3 – 1
1927–28	3 – 1	1
Total	11 – 2	4 – 1

Debut: 6/11/26 v Norwich C. (a) 0–3 (CH)

Jock Ramage, the older brother of Peter Ramage, was a centre half who had spent a successful 7 years at Tynecastle, before being brought south by James Kerr. Despite his time at City being un–distinguished, he was a very popular player. Whilst playing for City at The Den, Ramage scored the opening goal against Millwall – unfortunately, The Lions went on to score 9 goals without further reply! He was forced to switch to right back, and broke his leg whilst playing in that position in December 1926 against Swindon. He only played 3 more times in 12 months, before signing for Luton. He played just 9 matches before moving back to Hearts, and then moved into the Highland League.

RAMAGE, Peter
Forward

Born: Bonnyrigg 26th March 1908
Died: Ballydare 17th December 1982
Career: Tranent Juniors, Newtowngrange Star, Coventry City June 1927, Derby County August 1928 (£1,500), Chesterfield August 1937, Chelmsford City c/s 1939, Heanor Town 1939, Atherstone T. 1946, Ilkeston F.C. 1947. Retired October 1948.

Coventry City	League	F.A.Cup
1927–28	26 – 5	2 – 1

Debut: 5/9/27 v Swindon T. (h) 4–0 (IL) 1 goal

The younger brother of Jock Ramage, Peter Ramage was a stylish inside forward who proved to be a good link man between the defence and centre forward, particularly at Derby. His stay at City was short, but he helped to breathe fresh life into the club at a time of great despair. Unfortunately, he was sold to Derby for £1500. Whilst City needed the money, Ramage could have helped City to better things. He proved his worth with The Rams, scoring 60 goals in 255 games. He was still playing non–League football after the war.

RAMSBOTTOM, Neil
Goalkeeper

Born: Blackburn 25th February 1948
Career: Apprentice Bury, pro July 1964, Blackpool February 1971, Crewe Alexandra (loan) January 1972, Coventry City March 1972 (£10,000), Sheffield Wednesday August 1975, Plymouth Argyle July 1976, Blackburn Rovers January 1978, New Jersey Americans c/s 1979, Sheffield United October 1979, New Jersey Americans c/s 1980, Bradford City August 1980, Bournemouth August 1983, Chorley.

Coventry City	League	F.A.Cup	Lge.Cup
1971–72	–	–	–
1972–73	14	–	–
1973–74	2	–	–
1974–75	35	3	–
Total	51	3	–

Debut: 28/10/72 v Birmingham City (h) 0–0 (Goal)

When Bob Dennison sold Eric McManus to Notts County, he needed a reliable understudy to Bill Glazier, and Ramsbottom fitted the bill. Before signing for City, he had been a regular at Bury and understudy at Blackpool. His first team appearances at City were limited until 1974. Glazier played the first 7 games of the season before injury and Ramsbottom kept him out for the rest of the season. Ramsbottom moved due to the signing of Bryan King, although due to the latter's injury problems if he had stayed he would probably have maintained his first team place.

RANDLE, John (Jackie)
Full Back

Born: Bedworth 23rd August 1902
Died: Bournemouth 1990
Career: Exhall Colliery, Coventry City early 1922, Birmingham November 1927, Bournemouth & Boscombe Athletic October 1933, Guildford City c/s 1934, Newdigate.

Coventry City	League	F.A.Cup
1923–24	38	2
1924–25	28	1
1925–26	42	1
1926–27	29	3
1927–28	12	–
Total	149	7

Debut: 27/8/23 v Bradford C. (a) 0–0 (LB)

In the "Stormy Period" of the early 1920's, there were very few stabilising influences in the City team. One of the few reliable and long serving players was full back Jackie Randle. A local lad, he took over from Jimmy Lawrence at left back at the start of the 1923–24 season. He was a revelation and kept his more experienced colleague out of the side. This stocky, tough tackling full back was as adept at right back as on the left. Possibly his most memorable game for City was at Ashton Gate on 18th September 1926. He scored a noteworthy hat-trick – all of them in his own net – as City lost 0-3! In November 1927, Randle was sold to 1st Division Birmingham, which eased City's money problems and he quickly settled down in the top flight. He played 116 games for The Blues, but missed his chance of a Wembley appearance in the 1931 FA Cup final. In his last two and a half seasons at St Andrews, he only played 10 matches and was sold to Bournemouth for whom he made 28 appearances.

RAYNOR, Harold A.
Centre Forward
Born: Hipperholme
Career: Selby Town, Halifax Town 1925/6, Coventry City c/s 1926, Colwyn Bay c/s 1929, Lancaster Town c/s 1930.

Coventry City	League	F.A.Cup
1926–27	3	–
1927–28	5	–
1928–29	4	–
Total	12	–

Debut: 28/8/26 v Northampton T. (h) 0-3 (CF)

Raynor came to City as a centre forward, but failed to impress in that position. He was considered to be a good passer of the ball but did not have a strong shot, so he was moved back to the half back line. He only played 9 more games before being released.

REAY, George T.
Outside Right
Born: East Howden
Career: Percy Main Colliery Welfare, South Shields 1922/3, Blyth Spartans 1922/3, Reading 1923/4, Kettering Town 1924, Raith Rovers December 1925, Bristol Rovers c/s 1928, Coventry City July 1930, Burton Town c/s 1931, Rushden Town c/s 1934.

Coventry City	League	F.A.Cup
1930–31	11 – 3	3

Debut: 11/10/30 v Northampton T. (h) 0-1 (OR)

North-eastern winger Reay had struggled to establish himself before joining Bristol Rovers, having played twice for South Shields and four times at Reading. He scored 11 goals in 72 games for The Pirates which encouraged James McIntyre to sign him for City. He became a reserve player, who played only when Percy Richards was injured. He was released by new manager Harry Storer and moved to Burton Town.

REES, Ronald Raymond (Ronnie)
Winger
Born: Ystradgynlais 4th April 1944
Career: Apprentice Coventry City, pro May 1962, West Bromwich Albion March 1968 (£65,000), Nottingham Forest February 1969 (£60,000), Swansea City January 1972, Retired c/s 1975.

Coventry City	League	F.A.Cup	Lge.Cup
1962–63	33 – 4	8	1 – 1
1963–64	46 – 13	2 – 1	2 – 1
1964–65	41 – 7	1	4 – 2
1965–66	41 – 7	3 – 2	4
1966–67	39 – 3	1 – 1	3 – 1
1967–68	30 – 8	2 – 1	1
Total	230 – 42	17 – 5	15 – 5

Debut: 15/9/62 v Shrewsbury Town (h) 0-0 (OL)
Honours: 39 Full Wales caps (21 with City)
7 Wales U–23 caps (all with City)

Jimmy Hill's first season in charge of City was to be an eventful one for Rees. Hill had bought Bobby Laverick as outside left and had Roy Dwight as reserve. However, poor form forced Hill to push the skinny 18 year old into the first team. How he shone! He immediately made the place his own and during 6 years at City, missed a total of only 11 games. His wing play was magnificent, for being so short and fleet footed, he was able to race past big full backs and created many a goal for forwards such as Terry Bly, George Hudson and Bobby Gould. Rees was able to play at the highest level, but City needed to recoup money in order to offset the buying of Maurice Setters, Neil Martin, Ernie Hannigan, Ernie Hunt and Chris Cattlin. Noel Cantwell therefore sold the Welsh Wizard to WBA. He soon moved onto Forest, who were relegated to Division 2, before finally moving back to Wales.

REEVE, Frank D.
Forward

Born: Nuneaton
Career: Rugby Town, Nuneaton Town c/s 1925, Rugby Town, Coventry City September 1927, Walsall November 1927, Rugby Town c/s 1928, Market Harborough Town c/s 1930, Rugby Town 1933–35.

Coventry City	League	F.A.Cup
1927–28	2	–

Debut: 24/9/27 v Merthyr Town (a) 2–3 (IL)

Frank Reeve came to City on trial from Rugby Town. He was selected for the first team in 2 consecutive matches, but disappointed at both inside left and outside right, in the defeats against Merthyr and Walsall. He was given a free transfer, but only played for Walsall once, in a 1–7 defeat at Millwall.

REGAN, James (Jim)
Right Half

Born: Hemsworth 7th December 1927
Career: Moorthorpe Colliery, Rotherham United August 1949, Bristol City June 1953, Coventry City March 1956, Yeovil Town July 1957.

Coventry City	League	F.A.Cup
1955–56	13	–
1956–57	13	–
Total	26	–

Debut: 3/3/56 v Crystal Palace (h) 1–3 (CH)

Jim Regan was signed as a solid, dependable squad player. He had performed this role perfectly for Bristol City in 1954–55 as they comfortably won the Division 3 (South) championship. However, the following season, his opportunities were limited and he jumped at the chance of joining City. He made 13 consecutive appearances at the end of 1955–56 and kept his place at the start of 1956–57. However, injury, loss of form and the return of Iain Jamieson meant that first team football was limited.

REGIS, Cyrille
Centre Forward

Born: Mariapousoula, French Guiana 9th Feb. 1958
Career: Molesey 1974, Hayes 1975, West Bromwich Albion May 1977 (£5,000), Coventry City October 1984 (£300,000), Aston V. June 1991(F/T), Wolverhampton W. Aug.1993 (F/T).

Coventry City	League	F.A.Cup	Lge.Cup
1984–85	30+1s–5	1	–
1985–86	34 – 5	1	2 – 5
1986–87	40 – 12	6 – 2	5 – 2
1987–88	30+1s–10	2 – 1	2 – 1
1988–89	34 – 6	1	3
1989–90	32 – 4	0+1s	7 – 1
1990–91	31+3s–4	4	5 – 3
Total	231+5s–46	15+1s–3	24 – 12

Debut: 13/10/84 v Newcastle United (h) 1–1 (CF)
Honours: 5 England Full Caps (1 with City)
        3 England B Caps
        6 England U–21 Caps
        1 England XI appearance
        FA Cup Winners Medal 1987 (with City)

Regis' spell at City was full of highs and lows. The highs include playing a vital role in winning the FA Cup in 1987, scoring 5 goals versus Chester City in the League Cup in 1985 (equalling the record for any City player in 1 game), scoring 2 goals against Everton to prevent relegation at the end of 1984–85, becoming only the third City player to play for England and many fine performances as the leader of the line. The lows included far too many missed chances and an overall disappointment at the number of goals scored by Regis. He was signed by Bobby Gould in October 1984 as a proven goalscorer from WBA, in the face of competition from Manchester United. Prior to signing for City, Regis had become a feared forward and narrowly missed going to the 1982 World Cup Finals in Spain. He struggled early on at City, and it wasn't until the Curtis/Sillett partnership took over that he was restored to prime form, which enabled him to return to the England team. Regis was a fine servant in his 7 years at Highfield Road and despite his low scoring rate, is the tenth highest scorer in City's history. In the summer of 1991, Terry Butcher gave him a free transfer, much to the displeasure of the fans. This was proven to be a premature decision, for with Aston Villa he continued to display fine form until losing out to younger Dalian Atkinson.

RENNIE, David
Midfield

Born: Edinburgh 29th August 1964
Career: Apprentice Leicester City, pro 1982, Leeds United January 1986, Bristol City July 1989, Birmingham City (loan February 1992) March 1992, Coventry City March 1993 (player–exchange).

Coventry City	League	F.A.Cup	Lge.Cup
1992–93	9	–	–

Debut: 13/3/93 v Arsenal (h) 0–2 (Mid)

Scotsman Rennie started as a centre half at Leicester City, but couldn't command a regular place in the Foxes' Division 1 side. He established a regular place in midfield at Leeds, and it was at Hillsborough (in April 1987) that Rennie scored the first goal in the FA Cup semi–final against City that rocked them back on their heels. As part of Howard Wilkinson's rebuilding job at Elland Road, Rennie was sold to Bristol City, whom he helped to promotion to Division 2. Bobby Gould tried to obtain him for City in the summer of 1992 but failed. He suffered a knee injury that Autumn, and City eventually signed him once he had proved his fitness. With Stewart Robson out of action he slipped straight into the first team.

RICHARDS, C. Samuel (Sam)
Outside Left

Born: Birmingham
Career: Ruskin Social F.C., Coventry City November 1925.

Coventry City	League	F.A.Cup
1925–26	9	–

Debut: 5/12/25 v Bradford (PA) (h) 2–2 (OL)

Sam Richards was a young player who received his chance after the demise of James Walker. He had just joined City and had an extended run, but was out of his depth. He was one of 4 players dropped after the 1–8 thrashing at Doncaster in January 1926. At the end of the season he was not retained.

RICHARDS, Percy
Outside Left

Born: Merthyr Tydfil 1908
Career: Merthyr Town, Leicester City January 1931, Coventry City May 1932, Bath City April 1934, Brierley Hill Alliance c/s 1936, Hereford United c/s 1937.

Coventry City	League	F.A.Cup
1932–33	23 – 3	–
1933–34	23 – 4	–
Total	46 – 7	–

Debut: 27/8/32 v Torquay U. (a) 3–3 (OL)

Percy Richards was bought from local rivals Leicester City and played consistently for 2 seasons, but manager Harry Storer was never happy with the left wing position, and he allowed Richards to move on in 1934 when City bought Jim Liddle.

RICHARDS, William E. (Bill)

Born: Merthyr Tydfil 1905
Died: Wolverhampton 30th September 1956
Career: Troedyrhiw Carlton F.C., Merthyr Town 1925/6, Wolverhampton Wanderers c.1927, Coventry City March 1929, Fulham c/s 1931 (£100), Brighton & Hove Albion c/s 1935, Bristol Rovers 1937.

Coventry City	League	F.A.Cup
1928–29	9 – 2	–
1929–30	37 – 4	4 – 1
1930–31	31 – 6	–
Total	77 – 12	4 – 1

Debut: 23/3/29 v Swindon T. (a) 2–1 (OR)
Honours: 1 Wales Full cap

Welshman Bill Richards began with his local side Merthyr, and was signed by Wolves after only one League appearance. He played well at Molineux, but it wasn't until he arrived at Highfield Road that he produced his exciting football. Under James McIntyre, City were starting to move out of their "Stormy Period" and Richards' skills on the right wing played a big part. The sacking of McIntyre in February 1931, heralded considerable changes on the pitch. Richards was not part of Harry Storer's plans and McIntyre swooped for his former player and took him back to Fulham. He helped Fulham to promotion to Division 2 and earned his only full cap in Wales' 4–1 victory over Ireland in December 1932.

RICHMOND, Hugh
Wing Half/Forward
Born: Kilmarnock

Career: Kilmarnock Juniors 1910, Kilburnie Ladeside 1911, Kilmarnock 1912, Arthurlie 1916, Leicester City March 1919, Nuneaton Town (loan) January 1920, Coventry City May 1922, Queen's Park Rangers May 1925, Blyth Spartans July 1926.

Coventry City	League	F.A.Cup
1922–23	25 – 4	–
1923–24	28 – 11	2 – 3
1924–25	12 – 1	–
Total	65 – 16	2 – 3

Debut: 7/10/22 v Bury (h) 3–0 (RH)

Richmond had played for home town club Kilmarnock before the Great War but never made the first team. During his early days with Leicester, he was loaned out to Nuneaton Town. In his 3 seasons at Filbert Street he played only 24 times for The Foxes, and was happy to sign for City in May 1922. He was a right half but was able to play at centre forward if necessary. Whilst standing–in up front, 'Rubberneck' Richmond bagged a hat–trick against Nelson in November 1923. After a brief spell at QPR, he ended his days with Blyth Spartans as player coach.

ROBBINS, Albert
Inside Forward
Born: Penrhiwceiber

Career: Abertysswg, Coventry City, Hereford United 1930, Barry Town c/s 1931.

Coventry City	League	F.A.Cup
1928–29	2	–
1929–30	–	–
Total	2	–

Debut: 6/4/29 v Gillingham (a) 1–1 (IL)

Welshman Robbins was a reserve forward who made 2 appearances in April 1929, in place of Tommy Bowen. After these undistinguished performances he was replaced by Billy Lake. He spent a further season in the reserves before teaming up with non–league Hereford United.

ROBERTS, Brian Leslie Ford
Full Back
Born: Manchester 6th November 1955

Career: Apprentice Coventry City, pro May 1974, Hereford United (loan) February 1975, Birmingham City March 1984 (£10,000), Wolverhampton Wanderers June 1990 (F/T), Retired May 1992.

Coventry City	League	F.A.Cup	Lge.Cup
1974–75	–	–	–
1975–76	2	–	–
1976–77	12	1	–
1977–78	26	1	1+1s
1978–79	17	–	–
1979–80	10+4s	–	2+1s
1980–81	41+1s	4	9
1981–82	33+1s	1	2
1982–83	38 – 1	2 – 1	2
1983–84	30	4	3
Total	209+6s–1	13 – 1	19+2s

Debut: 19/4/76 v Tottenham Hotspur (a) 1–4 (Mid)

"Harry" was a quick and dependable full back who rose from a reserve player to become club captain. Roberts has the distinction of playing his first ten games for City away from home. He made his debut on 19th April 1976, but it wasn't until 2nd April 1977 that he played at Highfield Road. Early in his career, he played throughout the back four, but was essentially a right back. However, it was as Bobby McDonald's replacement at left back that Harry proved his worth. Roberts was not renowned as a goalscorer, so it was a great surprise that he had a purple patch, scoring 2 goals in 2 months during 1982–83. As players deserted City in the summer of 1983, Roberts was appointed as team captain by Bobby Gould. His was a shock departure, for on Saturday 10th March 1984, Harry played one of his best games ever for City, at QPR.

On Monday 12th, he signed for Birmingham, after Gould made it clear that Harry was no longer part of his plans. After 200 games for Birmingham, he moved to Wolves, returning later to Highfield Road as reserve team manager. One of the great characters to have appeared for City, he has published a book of his own entitled, "Harry's Game".

ROBERTS, Cyril
Right Back

Career: Coventry City c/s 1924.

Coventry City	League	F.A.Cup
1924–25	–	–
1925–26	1	–
Total	1	–

Debut: 5/4/26 v Ashington (h) 2–0 (RB)

Cyril Roberts is the least known of all of City's players. He was a third team player and played for the first team against Ashington, after a late injury scare forced the withdrawal of Charles Houldey. With the reserves playing away from home, Roberts stepped in for his only appearance. He was released at the end of the season.

ROBERTS, Dudley E.
Forward

Born: Derby 16th October 1945
Career: Coventry City November 1963, Mansfield Town March 1968, Doncaster Rovers (loan) February 1973, Scunthorpe United February 1974, Retired 1975.

Coventry City	League	F.A.Cup	Lge.Cup
1963–64	–	–	–
1964–65	–	–	–
1965–66	10+1s–6	–	3
1966–67	–	–	1
1967–68	1	–	–
Total	11+1s–6	–	4

Debut: 9/10/65 v Preston North End (a) 0–0 (IR)

The son of Ted Roberts, Dudley never established himself with City, for despite being with the club as a professional for 5 years he was never first choice. His only chances came when injury prevented Machin, Tudor or Gould from playing. With City buying Ernie Hunt, Roberts was surplus to Noel Cantwell's plans and he was allowed to move to

Mansfield. He became a great favourite with The Stags and was instrumental in the club's FA Cup exploits of 1968–69 and 1969–70. He scored 73 goals in 231 appearances for the Field Mill side. He moved on to Scunthorpe, where a knee injury forced him to retire.

ROBERTS, Edward (Ted)
Centre Forward

Born: Chesterfield 2nd November 1916
Career: Chapwell Colliery, Derby County 1934, Coventry City March 1937, King's Lynn c/s 1952, Banbury Spencer 1953.

Coventry City	League	F.A.Cup
1936–37	5 – 3	–
1937–38	23 – 6	1
1938–39	14 – 2	1
1945–46	WWII	–
1946–47	29 – 9	2 – 1
1947–48	26 – 10	1
1948–49	34 – 20	1
1949–50	25 – 8	1
1950–51	31 – 15	1
1951–52	25 – 12	3
Total	212 – 85	11 – 1

Debut: 26/3/37 v Burnley (a) 3–3 (IL) 1 goal

If ever a player's career was ruined by the War, then it was Roberts'. Before that period, Ted was a reserve forward who scored whenever required in the first team. In 1939, he was 22, but by the restart of the Football League, he was 29. He played for 6 seasons after the hostilities, being a prolific scorer in each season. His total of 86 goals, is the third highest in City's history – behind Clarrie Bourton and Billy Lake. City were relegated in his last season with the club. Roberts moved into non–

League football and was still playing at the age of 38. Later, he rejoined City as a coach, and the lasting thought is that but for the war, Roberts would have been an even bigger scoring success for City.

ROBERTS, Richard E. (Dick)
Full Back
Born: Rhyl
Career: Rhyl United, (Leeds City), Coventry City c/s 1914, Rhyl United 1920/1, Nuneaton Town 1921/2, Atherstone Town c/s 1922, Barwell United c/s 1923.

Coventry City	League	F.A.Cup
1914–15	20	1
1919–20	18	2
Total	38	3

Debut: 19/9/14 v Pontypridd (a) 3–2 (RB)

Roberts started with his home town club Rhyl United. Some references state that he was transferred to Leeds City before arriving at City in 1914, but there is no definite evidence to prove that he was with the Elland Road club. He played for City in the 2nd Division of the Southern League and Division 2 of the Football League. It was expected that Roberts wouldn't feature in City's post War side, but his experience and quick pace resulted in him playing another 20 games.

ROBINSON, Benjamin (Benny)
Half Back
Born: Broughton
Career: Swinburn, Coventry City 1919, Nuneaton Town.

Coventry City	League	F.A.Cup
1919–20	20	2
1920–21	5	–
1921–22	2	1
Total	27	3

Debut: 20/12/19 v Clapton Orient (h) 0–0 (RH)

Benny Robinson was pushed straight into the first team by manager Harry Pollitt when they were bottom of Division 2 in December 1919. He formed a sound half back line with Hanney and Fenwick, but was still learning the game. Therefore, new boss Albert Evans preferred to see Robinson develop in the reserves once safety was achieved. He showed himself to be a fearless player who was converted from a right half to centre forward in the Autumn of 1921.

ROBINSON, Foster
Outside Left
Born: South Shields 1903
Career: Simonside F.C., Coventry City 1920, Nuneaton Town (loan) December 1921, Bournemouth & Boscombe Athletic June 1923, Luton Town 1925/6.

Coventry City	League	F.A.Cup
1920–21	–	–
1921–22	–	–
1922–23	5	–
Total	5	–

Debut: 9/12/22 v Fulham (a) 0–4 (OL)

Youngster Foster Robinson signed for City as a 17 year old and was loaned to Nuneaton Town to gain further experience. He made his debut at Craven Cottage, after Arthur Wood pulled out at the last minute, and played 4 more games towards the end of the season before attracting the attention of Bournemouth. He played 32 League matches for The Cherries before disappearing from the professional game for 12 months, later playing one game for Luton.

ROBSON, George
Inside Forward
Born: New Delaval 1901
Career: New Delaval Villa, Walsall December 1926, Coventry City October 1929, Ashington December 1930, Retired 1935.

Coventry City	League	F.A.Cup
1929–30	4	–
1930–31	–	–
Total	4	–

Debut: 19/10/29 v Walsall (a) 2–3 (IL)

Spotted by Walsall as a free scoring forward in the North–east, Robson settled into League football immediately. He scored 9 goals in his first 22 games in his first 6 months at Fellows Park. He followed this up with 11 goals the season after (1927–28), when he formed an excellent partnership with Moses Lane. But this run ended with injury to Robson before the next season started. He didn't play until Boxing Day 1928, but still scored 7 goals in 21 games. After 3 appearances out of position on the right wing in September 1929, he was sold to City; ironically, he made his debut at Fellows Park. He failed to dislodge either Billy Lake or Alf Widdowson, and moved to his native North East to play for Ashington.

ROBSON, Stewart Ian
Midfield

Born: Billericay 6th November 1964
Career: Apprentice Arsenal, pro November 1981, West Ham United January 1987, Coventry City (loan March 1991) May 1991 (F/T).

Coventry City	League	F.A.Cup	Lge.Cup
1990–91	3+1s	–	–
1991–92	37 – 3	1	2
1992–93	14+1s	–	–
Total	54+2s–3	1	2

Debut: 9/3/91 v Leeds Utd (a) 0–2 (sub)
Full Debut: 16/3/91 v QPR (a) 0–1 (Mid)
Honours: 2 England U–21 Caps

Robson was a revelation when he burst into the Arsenal first team at only 17. His tireless running and well–timed tackling brought him lots of attention and he was talked of as a future England star. Despite being a regular under Terry Neill and Don Howe, Robson didn't figure in George Graham's plans and he was sold to West Ham United, where he continued his fine form and was rewarded with two England U–21 caps. He developed a pelvic injury in 1988 and was badly missed, before West Ham granted him a free transfer. Terry Butcher gambled with Robson and signed him after a short loan spell. In City's poor side of 1991–92, Robson was one of the few successes and missed only a handful of games. He was linked with a number of clubs in 1992 but stayed with City only to be troubled with a number of niggling injuries through the 1992–93 season.

RODGER, Graham
Centre Half

Born: Glasgow 1st April 1967
Career: Apprentice Wolverhampton Wanderers, pro August 1983, Coventry City February 1984 (F/T), Luton Town July 1989 (£190,000), Grimsby Town January 1992 (£130,000).

Coventry City	League	F.A.Cup	Lge.Cup
1984–85	–	–	–
1985–86	10	1	0+1s
1986–87	4+2s	0+1s	–
1987–88	9+3s–1	–	2
1988–89	8 – 1	–	1
Total	31+5s–2	1+1s	3+1s

Debut: 6/11/85 v WBA (a) 3–4 (Sub) League Cup
Full Debut: 9/11/85 v Liverpool (h) 0–3 (CH)
Honours: 4 England U–21 Caps (all at City)
FA Cup Winners Medal 1987

City snapped up Rodger when he was released in February 1984 by trouble hit Wolves, after only 1 appearance for them. He played only as a replacement for Trevor Peake or Brian Kilcline in his time at City and was shown to be lacking in the necessary composure for a Division 1 centre half. His most famous moment came in the FA Cup final when he laid on the pass for Lloyd McGrath's galloping right wing run for the winning goal. He struggled with injury at Luton and is currently the captain of Grimsby Town.

ROE, Thomas William
Forward

Born: Evenswood 8th December 1900
Died: December 1972
Career: Esperley Rovers, Willington Athletic, Durham City 1922, Northfleet 1923, Tottenham Hotspur c/s 1925, Nottingham Forest c/s 1927, Luton Town c/s 1928, Walsall c/s 1929, Coventry City c/s 1930.

Coventry City	League	F.A.Cup
1930–31	4	–

Debut: 20/9/30 v Norwich City (a) 2–2 (IR)

Thomas was signed as useful back up after showing his talent at Walsall, where he had scored 9 goals in 44 matches. Prior to that, he had scored 3 goals from 7 games, at Forest and Spurs, but had originally come to prominence scoring 8 goals in 17 matches for the struggling Durham City side. In his time at City he only played 4 matches, and then left the professional game.

ROGERS, James E. (Jimmy)
Forward
Born: Wednesbury 31st December 1929
Career: Rubery OFC, Wolverhampton Wanderers May 1948, Bristol City May 1950, Coventry City December 1956, Bristol City December 1958, Cinderford Town c/s 1962, Retired 1966.

Coventry City	League	F.A.Cup
1956–57	22 – 5	–
1957–58	38 – 9	2
1958–59	17 – 13	1
Total	77 – 27	3

Debut: 29/12/56 v Southend Utd (a) 2–1 (OR)

Rogers had been a prolific scorer as Bristol City moved from Division 3 (S) to Division 2. This attracted City manager Harry Warren to sign Rogers, at a time when the atmosphere at City was dire. His time at City was personally fruitful, but the club slid into Division 4. He has the distinction of scoring 3 hat–tricks for City, all in a 6 month period from March 1958, and all 3 against Aldershot. Rogers returned to Bristol City, and later became player/manager at Cinderford.

ROSARIO, Robert Michael
Centre Forward
Born: Hammersmith 4th March 1966
Career: Hillingdon Borough, Norwich City December 1983, Wolverhampton Wanderers (loan) December 1985, Coventry City March 1991 (£500,000), Nottingham Forest March 1993 (£400,000).

Coventry City	League	F.A.Cup	Lge.Cup
1990–91	0+2s	–	–
1991–92	26+3s–4	2	2+1s–2
1992–93	28 – 4	1	1
Total	54+5s–8	3	3+1s–2

Debut: 6/4/91 v Norwich City (a) 2–2 (sub)
Full Debut: 17/8/91 v Manchester City (h) 0–1 (CF)

Big centre forward Rosario was not a high scorer, but an unselfish player who contributed to the whole team effort. After signing for City as the replacement for Cyrille Regis, Rosario struggled to come to terms with the demands made upon him, but battled through to be a well respected member of the side. In the short time he and Mick Quinn were in tandem, he laid on many of Quinn's goals. He was sold to Nottingham Forest in March 1993 to ease City's financial problems, but the fee was disappointing considering the improvement Rosario made in his 2 years at Highfield Road.

ROSS, Robert
Centre Half
Born: Stenhousemuir 27th December
Career: Camelon Juniors F.C., Falkirk c/s 1919, Stenhousemuir c/s 1920, Plymouth Argyle 1923, Coventry City May 1924, Workington c/s 1925, Carlisle United c/s 1927, Wrexham June 1929, Scunthorpe & Lindsey United November 1930, Boston United September 1931.

Coventry City	League	F.A.Cup
1924–25	20	1

Debut: 6/9/24 v Stockport Co. (h) 4–2 (CH)

Ross came to England from Stenhousemuir and appeared twice for Plymouth before signing for City. He started impressively and ensured that the centre half position was his own. Despite being a big man – standing six feet tall – he had neat footwork to compliment his decisive tackling. City had a bad run and Ross was made the scapegoat. When results didn't improve, he returned to the team, but Ross's final game for City was the disastrous 0–5 defeat at Oldham. He was not retained as City cut costs and he moved to Workington and then Carlisle, helping the latter to League status.

ROWLAND, Keith
Midfield
Born: Portadown 1st September 1971
Career: YTS Bournemouth, pro October 1989, Coventry City (loan) January 1993, West Ham U. August 1993 (£110,000).

Coventry City	League	F.A.Cup	Lge.Cup
1992–93	0+2s	–	–

Debut: 16/1/93 v Norwich C. (a) 1–1 (sub)

Northern Ireland youth international Rowland came to City as part of a loan deal that took David Smith to Dean Court. Such was the speed at which the deal was struck, Rowland arrived at Highfield Road without any boots and no change of clothes. He had started well at Bournemouth, but was in the reserves when Bobby Gould offered him the opportunity to move to City. Despite laying a goal on in his first appearance, he looked out of his depth and returned to The Cherries, but moved to West Ham in 1993.

ROWLEY, Joseph (Joe)
Wing Half

Born: Wellington 13th October 1899
Died: Early 1982
Career: Oakengates Town, Coventry City October 1922, Bristol Rovers c/s 1926, Oswestry T. c/s 1928.

Coventry City	League	F.A.Cup
1922–23	29	–
1923–24	40	2
1924–25	39	3
1925–26	40 – 2	1
Total	148 – 2	6

Debut: 11/11/22 v Rotherham County (h) 2–1 (LH)

In City's struggling side of the early 1920's, there were very few players of quality playing for City, but one of the few was Joe Rowley. He moved straight into the first team in November 1922 and kept his place throughout his time at City. He was an excellent tackler and had a footballing brain. City were in dire financial straits in the summer of 1926 and the club offered reduced terms to all the players. Rowley rejected his contract and was snapped up by Bristol Rovers, for whom he continued to play well and amassed 68 appearances.

ROWLEY, Kenneth F. (Ken)
Inside Forward

Born: Pelsall 29th August 1926
Career: Elkingtons, Wolverhampton Wanderers October 1947, Birmingham C. February 1951, Coventry City November 1954.

Coventry City	League	F.A.Cup
1954–55	3	–

Debut: 18/12/54 v Bournemouth (a) 1–2 (IL)

The experienced Rowley had made one appearance for Wolves before signing for Birmingham in February 1951. He never let the side down and scored 20 goals in 42 matches at St Andrew's. He arrived at City at a time of great upheaval at the club. He only appeared as a replacement for Tommy Capel, and his spell at City lasted only 6 months.

RYAN, Reginald Alphonsus (Reg)
Inside Forward

Born: Dublin 30th October 1925
Career: SS Cars, Jaguar Cars, Nuneaton Borough (WWII), Coventry City (WWII), West Bromwich Albion September 1945, Derby County July 1955 (£3,000), Coventry City September 1958, Retired c/s 1961.

Coventry City	League	F.A.Cup	Lge.Cup
1958–59	36 – 5	2	
1959–60	19 – 3	1	
1960–61	10 – 1	–	1
Total	65 – 9	3	1

Debut: 13/9/58 v Exeter City (h) 2–0 (IL)
Honours: 16 Republic of Ireland Caps
1 Northern Ireland Cap
FA Cup Winners Medal 1954

Paddy Ryan was one of the game's great characters during the 1950's. He had been successful at WBA, gaining an FA Cup winners medal in 1954. After ten years service he moved onto Derby County, then a Division 3 team, and was a regular first team choice for 3 years. When Paddy joined City, the club was in despair. Recently relegated to the new Division 4, City were in the bottom half and Billy Frith immediately appointed him as captain. His experience, ability and attitude to the game rubbed off on City. The club raced to promotion and Ryan helped maintain City in Division 3. He finally retired at the age of 35 to help in City's commercial work. Later, he moved back to WBA in a coaching capacity. Ryan holds the distinction of being a double nation international.

ST JOHN, Ian
Midfield

Born: Motherwell, 7th June 1938
Career: Douglas Walter Thistle, North Motherwell, Motherwell August 1956, Liverpool c/s 1961 (£35,000), Hellenic February 1971, Coventry City August 1971, Tranmere Rovers 1972, Retired.

Coventry City	League	F.A.Cup	Lge.Cup
1971–72	18 – 3	2	–

Debut: 25/9/71 v Tottenham Hotspur (h) 1–0 (Mid)
Honours: 21 Full Scotland Caps
2 Scotland U–23 Caps
Lge. Champ. Medals: 1963–64 & 1965–66
FA Cup Winners Medal 1965
European Cup Wins R/up Medal 1965–66
Scottish League appearance

St John played briefly for City at the end of an illustrious career spent with Liverpool. At Anfield, St John was a prolific goal scorer, netting 118 goals in 420 League and cup games. By the time he had joined Liverpool, he was already an established Scottish international, gaining 7 of his 21 caps whilst at Motherwell. After 10 years at Anfield, St John moved to City, but his spell was not particularly successful. He opposed the sacking of Noel Cantwell and quickly moved on to Tranmere. After an unsuccessful period in management, St John is now a successful pundit on independent television.

SAMBROOK, Raymond (Ray)
Winger

Born: Wolverhampton 31st May 1933
Career: Wednesfield, Coventry City September 1953, Manchester City January 1958, Doncaster Rovers June 1962, Crewe Alexandra January 1963.

Coventry City	League	F.A.Cup
1953–54	–	–
1954–55	11 – 1	–
1955–56	35 – 9	1
1956–57	41 – 14	–
1957–58	9 – 1	2
Total	96 – 25	3

Debut: 9/10/54 v Newport Co. (a) 1–1 (OL)

The tale of Ray Sambrook summed up City's position in the mid–1950's. The club produced very talented youngsters and had great ambitions, but a side could not be put together to achieve big–time success. City were desperate for short term success and consequently experienced players arrived, which heralded the departure of younger players. Such was the case with Sambrook. He was an exciting winger who could create havoc in any defence, but he was too good for a struggling Division 3(S) side. He moved to Manchester City where he made an early impression, but soon faded away.

SAMBROOKE, Christopher L.
Centre Forward

Born: Oldbury 5th January 1895
Career: Kidderminster Harriers, Oldbury Town, Coventry City 1917, Nuneaton Town December 1919, Wellington Town, Stalybridge Celtic 1922, Redditch.

Coventry City	League	F.A.Cup
1919–20	6	–

Debut: 30/8/19 v Tottenham H. (h) 0–5 (CF)
Honours: 3 England Junior International appearances

Before playing for City, Sambrooke played 3 times for England Juniors against Scotland Juniors. He impresssed in City's Midland League side of 1918–19, and was seen as the ideal centre forward to lead City in the Football League. He had been the second highest scorer in the Midland League (which included First and Second Division reserve teams), but he lasted only 6 games in City's first team, before being sold to Nuneaton Town. He was a victim of new manager Harry Pollitt's wheeling and dealing to secure a place in the League. He later returned to League action at Stalybridge Celtic, scoring 9 goals in 20 games.

SANDERS, James Albert (Jim)
Goalkeeper

Born: Hackney 5th July 1920
Career: Longlands FC, Charlton Athletic 1939, West Bromwich Albion November 1945 (£2,250), Coventry City August 1958, Hinckley Athletic c/s 1959, Retired 1960.

Coventry City	League	F.A.Cup
1958–59	10	–

Debut: 2/8/58 v Darlington (h) 0–0 (Goal)
Honours: FA Cup Winners Medal 1954

Before arriving at City, Sanders had played 361 games for WBA, yet he did not make his League debut until the age of 26, a victim of the war years. During the war, he played for Charlton Athletic and guested briefly for Southampton, West Ham United and Exeter City. After 13 years gallant service with Albion, Jim Sanders arrived at City in August 1958 at the age of 38. He played 10 consecutive games, but broke his leg in the 7–0 defeat of Aldershot. This created a goalkeeping crisis, which forced trainer Alf Wood to go in goal, at the age of 43. This injury ended Sanders' League career.

SANSOM, Kenneth Graham (Kenny)

Left Back

Born: Camberwell 26th September 1958
Career: Apprentice Crystal Palace, pro December 1975, Arsenal August 1980 (£800,000), Newcastle United December 1988 (£300,000), Queen's Park Rangers June 1989, Coventry City March 1990 (£100,000), Everton February 1993 (F/T), Brentford March 1993 (F/T).

Coventry City	League	F.A.Cup	Lge.Cup
1990–91	9	–	–
1991–92	21	2	–
1992–93	21	–	2
Total	51	2	2

Debut: 23/3/91 v Manchester C. (h) 3–1 (LB)
Honours: 86 England Full Caps
        8 England U–21 Caps
        League Cup Winners Medal 1986–87
        League Cup Runners–up Medal 1987–88

Left back Sansom made his debut in 1975 as a 16 year old apprentice and by the time he was 18, he was a regular in the young Crystal Palace side that moved from the 3rd to the 1st Division in the late 1970's. He was first picked for England in 1979 whilst with Palace and earned 9 caps before signing for Arsenal. He made 448 appearances for Arsenal and was almost ever–present in his first eight seasons at Highbury. He progressed to win 86 caps, thereby becoming England's sixth highest capped player. 1988 was a disappointing year for Sansom, for he lost his England place to Stuart Pearce, and to Nigel Winterburn in the Arsenal team. A move to Newcastle followed, but he couldn't help The Magpies escape from relegation to Division 2. He moved back to London with QPR and played over 80 times before signing for City in March 1991. He added some much needed experience to City's defence and was given a free transfer to Everton once Phil Babb started to shine. He spent only a

month at Goodison Park before returning to the capital with Brentford in March 1993. By the summer of 1993, Sansom was close to making a total of 800 first team appearances.

SATCHWELL, Kenneth R. (Ken)

Forward

Born: Birmingham 17th January 1940
Career: U.S. Carburettors, Coventry City September 1958, Nuneaton Borough January 1963 (£2,000), Walsall October 1964.

Coventry City	League	F.A.Cup	Lge.Cup
1958–59	15 – 1	1	
1959–60	28 – 15	2	
1960–61	13 – 2	–	2 – 2
1961–62	12 – 3	1 – 1	–
1962–63	–	–	1
Total	68 – 21	4 – 1	3 – 2

Debut: 26/8/58 v Oldham Athletic (a) 0–2 (OL)

Under Billy Frith's management, Ken Satchwell burst on to the scene as City were promoted from Division 4 and became established back in Division 3. In a spell over the 1960 New Year, he scored 9 goals, starting with a 4 goal strike against Wrexham on the 25 of December (City's last game played on a Christmas Day). Injury and inconsistency meant that Satchwell played infrequently, and the purchase of Terry Bly resulted in a future in the reserves. He later impressed with Nuneaton sufficiently to earn a recall to League football, with Walsall.

SEALEY, Leslie Jesse (Les)

Goalkeeper

Born: Bethnal Green 29th September 1957
Career: Apprentice Coventry City, pro March 1976, Luton Town August 1983 (£100,000), Plymouth Argyle (loan) October 1984, Manchester United (loan December 1989), May 1990 (F/T), Aston Villa July 1991 (F/T), Coventry City (loan) March 1992, Birmingham City (loan) October 1992, Manchester United January 1993 (F/T).

Coventry City	League	F.A.Cup	Lge.Cup
1975–76	–	–	–
1976–77	11	–	–
1977–78	2	1	–
1978–79	36	–	1
1979–80	20	1	2
1980–81	35	4	6
1981–82	15	–	–
1982–83	39	3	2
1991–92	2		
Total	160	9	11

Debut: 11/4/77 v QPR (a) 1–1 (Goal)
Honours: FA Cup Winners Medal 1990
UEFA Cup Winners Medal 1991
Lge. Cup Runners–up Medal 1989 & 1991
Full Members Cup Runners–up Medal 1988

Les Sealey established himself in City's goal when injury struck Jim Blyth. The two of them vied for the number 1 shirt until the summer of 1982, when Blyth was given a free transfer because of his back problems. Despite being a tremendously confident keeper Sealey was prone to errors. It was he who helped West Ham to a 2–0 head start in the 1981 League Cup semi–final at Highfield Road, embarrassed himself in the 1988 Full Members Cup Final and gave away a needless penalty in the 1989 League Cup final. When he left City, he moved because of the club's lack of ambition. He struggled to retain his place at Luton and was loaned out to Plymouth in October 1984. Whilst in Luton's reserves, he was loaned out to Manchester United and was fortunate to gain an FA Cup winners medal when he replaced Jim Leighton in the replay of the 1990 final against Crystal Palace. When Peter Schmeichel was signed by The Red Devils, he was given a free transfer and later returned to City whilst Steve Ogrizovic was injured. He played twice and received a mixed reaction from fans who remembered his acrimonious departure from Highfield Road. He returned to Old Trafford on a free transfer.

SEDGLEY, Stephen Philip (Steve)
Centre Half/Midfield
Born: Enfield 26th May 1968
Career: YTS Coventry City, pro May 1986, Tottenham Hotspur July 1989 (£750,000).

Coventry City	League	F.A.Cup	Lge.Cup
1986–87	25+1s	0+2s	4 – 1
1987–88	25+2s–2	1	2
1988–89	31 – 1	1	3 – 1
Total	81+3s–3	2+2s	9 – 2

Debut: 26/8/86 v Arsenal (h) 2–1 (Mid)
Honours: 11 England U–21 Caps (10 at City)
FA Cup Winners Medals 1987 & 1991

Sedgley burst on to the scene in August 1986 and immediately established himself as a hard working and hard tackling midfielder. He was a substitute at Wembley in the 1987 FA Cup Final, but was not called upon. In his 3 years at City, he made over 100 appearances and matured into a Division 1 player, before signing for Tottenham. The transfer fee included additional payments if Sedgley played for England. His time at Spurs has had it's ups and downs, but he appeared in the 1991 FA Cup winning side. His progress has not continued in the way that was expected while he was at City.

SETTERS, Maurice Edgar
Defender
Born: Honiton 16th December 1936
Career: Honiton, Exeter City January 1954, West Bromwich Albion January 1955 (£4,000), Manchester United January 1960 (£35,000), Stoke City November 1964, Coventry City November 1967 (£25,000), Charlton Athletic February 1970, Retired.

Coventry City	League	F.A.Cup	Lge.Cup
1967–68	25 – 1	2	–
1968–69	17 – 2	–	4
1969–70	8+1s	1+1s	–
Total	50+1s–3	3+1s	4

Debut: 18/11/67 v Leeds United (a) 1–1 (CH)
Honours: 16 England U–23 Caps
FA Cup Winners Medal 1963

Spotted as a teenager playing for local club Exeter, Setters was bought by WBA for £4000. He played for 5 seasons, gaining the reputation for being a fierce tackler, before being sold to Manchester United. In Matt Busby's team of superb individuals, Setters provided the necessary steel for the side to be successful. He joined City from Stoke in November 1967. City were in trouble at the foot of Division 1 and were without captain George Curtis. Setters' battling performances, helped City to stay up for 2 seasons. The emergence of the Roy Barry/Jeff

Blockley partnership allowed Setters to be transferred. He later moved into management with Doncaster Rovers, before teaming up with Jack Charlton at Sheffield Wednesday, Newcastle United and now, very successfully, with the Republic of Ireland.

SHANKLY, James (Jimmy)
Centre Forward

Born: Glenbuck
Career: Glenbuck Cherrypickers, Nithsdale Wanderers c/s 1921, Portsmouth 1922, Guildford United 1923/4, Halifax Town c/s 1924, Nuneaton Town August 1925, Coventry City February 1926, Carlisle United c/s 1926, Sheffield United October 1926, Southend United c/s 1928, Barrow May 1933, Carlisle United c/s 1935.

Coventry City	League	F.A.Cup
1925–26	8 – 2	–

Debut: 27/2/26 v Accrington Stanley (h) 2–1 (CF)

A member of the famous Shankly footballing family, Jimmy will always be overshadowed by his brother Bill, who brought so much success to Liverpool as a manager. It should be remembered however, that Jimmy Shankly was an outstanding centre forward in the lower divisions for a decade. He scored 155 Football League goals and his career totalled over 200 goals. His most successful spell came at Southend United when he scored 96 goals in 147 League games. His spell at City was short, having been picked up by James Kerr, but he only stayed until the 1925–26 season's end.

SHANKS, Albert V.
Outside Right

Born: Leamington
Career: Leamington Town, Coventry City October 1926, Leamington Town, Banbury Spencer.

Coventry City	League	F.A.Cup
1926–27	1	–

Debut: 30/10/26 v Brighton & H.A. (h) 1–2 (OR)

Local boy Shanks was signed from his home team, and was pushed straight into the first team following an emergency, with Matt Hopper being indisposed on the day of the match against Brighton. He failed to impress and returned to Leamington Town. He was still playing at the Windmill Ground in 1936 and at Banbury between 1938 and 1940.

SHEA, Daniel H. (Danny)
Forward

Born: Wapping 6th November 1887
Died: 25th December 1960
Career: Manor Park Albion, West Ham United 1908, Blackburn Rovers December 1912 (£2,000), Glasgow Celtic (loan) January 1919, West Ham United c/s 1920, Fulham November 1920, Coventry City c/s 1923, Clapton Orient February 1925, Sheppey United c/s 1926.

Coventry City	League	F.A.Cup
1923–24	39 – 6	2 – 1
1924–25	21 – 5	2
Total	60 – 11	4 – 1

Debut: 25/8/23 v Barnsley (h) 2–3 (IR)
Honours: 2 England Full Caps
    2 England Victory International appearances
    League Championship Winners Medal 1914
    2 Football League appearances
    3 Southern League appearances

England international Danny Shea, was a well respected inside forward who was noted for his dribbling and close ball work, combined with a canny knack to be in the right place to score goals. He scored 122 goals in 222 games for Southern League West Ham and his £2000 transfer to Blackburn was a record for December 1912. He helped Rovers to the League Championship in 1914, scoring 29 goals. He appeared once for Celtic before re-signing for West Ham, but for only a short stay. He was 35 when City signed him from Fulham and what little pace he originally had, was gone. He made up for this however, with his knowledge of the game. With City staring relegation in the face, Shea moved to Clapton Orient. After his football retirement, he worked in the London docks.

SHELDON, Alfred (Alf)
Outside Left

Born: Worcester

Career: Worcester City, Birmingham, Oldbury, Coventry City c/s 1919, Wellington Town, Wrexham c/s 1922, Shrewsbury Town c/s 1923, Barrow 1925/6.

Coventry City	League	F.A.Cup
1919–20	12 – 1	2

Debut: 6/9/19 v Tottenham H. (a) 1–4 (IL)

Sheldon played as cover for Fred Gibson after serving Birmingham during the Great War. He played only 14 times for City, but he did score his only goal for the club in the famous 3–2 victory over Stoke at Highfield Road on Christmas Day 1919 – City's first victory in the Football League. He later returned to the League with Wrexham, playing 38 League and cup games in 1922–23. He then played for non–League Shrewsbury, before making 3 appearances for Barrow.

SHELDON, Lancelot (Lance)
Outside Right

Born: Nottingham c. 1898

Career: Selston Town, Notts County c/s 1917, Coventry City December 1918, Heanor Town c/s 1920, Mansfield Town c/s 1921.

Coventry City	League	F.A.Cup
1919–20	6	–

Debut: 30/8/19 v Tottenham H. (h) 0–5 (OR)

Sheldon was a fast, tricky outside right, who had impressed during the War. In Division 2, in a struggling side, he was out of his depth and was transferred to Heanor Town. He later played for Mansfield Town before the club achieved League status.

SHEPHERD, Brian A.
Full Back

Born: Leicester 29th January 1935

Career: Hinckley Athletic, Coventry City October 1956, Hinckley Athletic c/s 1960, Burton Albion May 1965.

Coventry City	League	F.A.Cup
1956–57	–	–
1957–58	23	–
1958–59	5	–
1959–60	1	–
Total	29	–

Debut: 25/12/57 v Port Vale (h) 1–0 (RB)

Shepherd made his debut following injury scares to Frank Austin and Charlie Timmins, and he played 23 consecutive games as City struggled but failed to escape the drop to Division 4. He was replaced by Lol Harvey and couldn't regain his place.

SHEPHERD, Trevor
Forward

Born: Sutton–In–Ashfield 25th December 1946

Career: East Kirby Miners' Welfare, Nottingham Forest December 1963, Coventry City October 1966, Torquay United (loan) March 1968, Plymouth Argyle June 1969, Nuneaton Borough 1970/71.

Coventry City	League	F.A.Cup	Lge.Cup
1966–67	–	–	–
1967–68	1	–	–
1968–69	11+2s–1	1+1s–1	–
Total	12+2s–1	1+1s–1	–

Debut: 28/10/67 v Sunderland (h) 2–2 (IR)

Shepherd was bought by Jimmy Hill as City pressed for Division 1 football in October 1966. At Forest, Shepherd had not made the first team, and it was only as cover for players such as Ernie Hannigan and Ernie Hunt that Shepherd played in the City first team. In the summer of 1969, Shepherd was allowed to move to Plymouth.

SHEPPARD, William (Bill)
Inside Left

Born: Ferryhill 1907

Career: Ferryhill Athletic, Chilton Colliery, Crook Town, Liverpool December 1925, Watford July 1927, Queen's Park Rangers June 1930, Coventry City July 1931, Walsall December 1932, Chester (loan) 1934/5, Tunbridge Wells Rangers.

Coventry City	League	F.A.Cup
1931–32	19 – 6	–
1932–33	3 – 1	–
Total	22 – 7	–

Debut: 3/10/31 v Gillingham (a) 3–1 (IL)

North–easterner Sheppard impressed sufficiently as a goalscorer in junior football for Liverpool to sign him as a professional at the age of 18. He failed to make the first team at Anfield and was sold to Watford where he made an immediate impression, scoring 25 goals in 41 appearances in his first full season. During the next season he scored 14 goals.

In 1929–30, he failed to score in 13 games and was sold to QPR, where he played only 14 games and netted 5 goals. City signed Sheppard in July 1931 and he played well whenever in the side, but he could never replace the prolific scoring Billy Lake as first choice inside left. He was sold to Walsall, and less than a month later he was one of 4 ex-City players to appear in the 2–0 FA Cup victory over Arsenal. His penalty gave The Saddlers their second goal of the game.

SHERIDAN, Anthony Joseph (Tony)
Midfield
Born: Dublin 21st October 1974
Career: YTS Coventry City, pro October 1991.

Coventry City	League	F.A.Cup	Lge.Cup
1991–92	–	–	–
1992–93	1	–	–
Total	1	–	–

Debut: 31/10/92 v Leeds Utd (a) 2–2 (Mid)
Honours: 4 Rep. of Ireland U–21 caps (all at City)

Young Dubliner Sheridan was almost lost to the professional game, as he was badly homesick whilst a trainee with City. He finally returned to Highfield Road and made his debut, replacing the injured Lloyd McGrath. He appeared for the Republic's U–21 team soon after, and is considered to be a bright prospect by both his club and country.

SHONE, Daniel (Danny)
Inside Left
Born: Wirral 27th April 1892
Died: 1974
Career: Earle F.C., Liverpool c.1915, Graysons (Garston) 1920, Liverpool May 1921, West Ham United June 1928, Coventry City January 1929 – c/s 1930.

Coventry City	League	F.A.Cup
1928–29	8 – 1	–
1929–30	–	–
Total	8 – 1	–

Debut: 5/1/29 v Brighton & H.A. (h) 3–0 (IL) 1 goal
Honours: League Championship Winners medal 1921–22.

Shone made an immediate impression as a professional, scoring 6 goals in 15 games, as Liverpool won the League Championship in 1921–22. He was in and out of the side but was an ever-present in 1924–25, making his final appearance for The Reds

in December 1925. Shone's career was resurrected by West Ham, before moving to City in The New Year of 1929. He didn't particularly impress in a poor side and soon faded out of the professional game.

SHORE, Edward
Outside Left
Born: Arley 18th October 1927
Career: Port Vale 1945, Coventry City July 1948, Hinckley Athletic c/s 1951.

Coventry City	League	F.A.Cup
1948–49	1	–
1949–50	1	–
1950–51	–	–
Total	2	–

Debut: 30/8/48 v Tottenham Hotspur (a) 0–4 (OL)

Bought as a reserve from Port Vale's 2nd team, Shore only played twice, both times as cover for Irish international, Norman Lockhart. After 3 years at City, Shore dropped into non–league football with Hinckley Athletic.

SILLETT, John Charles
Right Back
Born: Southampton 20th July 1936
Career: Nomansland, Southampton 1953, Chelsea April 1954, Coventry City April 1962 (£3,000), Plymouth Argyle July 1966, Retired 1968.

Coventry City	League	F.A.Cup	Lge.Cup
1961–62	2	–	–
1962–63	38 – 1	9	2
1963–64	41	2	2 – 1
1964–65	17	1	3
1965–66	10+1s	–	–
Total	108+1s–1	12	7 – 1

Debut: 28/4/62 v Hull City (h) 0–2 (RB)
Honours: 1 Football League appearance

John Sillett comes from a footballing family. His father Charles, played for Southampton before the war, and brother Peter appeared for Chelsea. Peter was the elder of the two brothers who played for the London team together. John came to City to gain regular first team football under Jimmy Hill. His performances at right back were instrumental in City's promotion to Division 2 and the exciting cup run in 1962–63. He was sold prematurely to Plymouth

where he spent 2 years before entering coaching. 'Snoz's' career has been more successful as a manager/coach, taking Hereford to Division 2 for the only time in the club's history, and in partnership with George Curtis he won the FA Cup whilst with City in 1987. In recent times, he has become a pundit for Central TV.

SIMCOE, Kenneth E. (Ken)
Outside Right
Born: Nottingham 14th February 1937
Career: Nottingham Forest December 1956, Coventry City June 1959, Notts County July 1960, Heanor Town, Loughborough United c/s 1963, Ilkeston Town December 1963, Heanor Town July 1964.

Coventry City	League	F.A.Cup
1959–60	8 – 1	–

Debut: 22/8/59 v Mansfield Town (h) 2–0 (OR)

Signed by Billy Frith, Simcoe started in the first team, but after 2 appearances, lost his place to Alan Daley. His other appearances were sporadic. At the end of the season, he moved back to his native city, to Notts County, and spent the rest of his career in the East Midlands, moving between clubs frequently. In this period, Simcoe had at least 3 spells with Heanor Town.

SIMMS, Gordon H.
Outside Right
Born: Leamington 26 December 1936
St. John's Leamington, South Leamington, Flavels 1953, Coventry City 1955/56, Notts County 1959, Nuneaton Borough 1960, Warwick Town 1962, Retired 1970.

Coventry City	League	F.A.Cup
1955–56	–	–
1956–57	–	–
1957–58	1	–
1958–59	–	–
Total	1	–

Debut: 5/10/57 v Colchester United (h) 1–0 (OR)

A regular reserve player, Simms' only appearance came as City struggled to gain a regular right winger. After leaving City, he finally settled down with his local club, Warwick Town, for whom he played in an 8 year spell from 1962 to 1970, when he retired. He is one of an exclusive group to have made only 1 League appearance for City.

SIMPSON, Dennis E.
Outside Right
Born: Coventry 1st November 1919
Career: Salem Baptist, Coventry City 1942, Reading May 1950, Exeter City May 1955, Exmouth Town.

Coventry City	League	F.A.Cup
1945–46	WWII	2 – 1
1946–47	12	–
1947–48	29 – 1	–
1948–49	18 – 3	–
1949–50	8 – 1	–
Total	67 – 5	2 – 1

Debut: 21/9/46 v Southampton (h) 2–0 (OR)

Local boy Simpson, was a hard working outside right, but his first team opportunities were limited by the consistent play of first team regular Les Warner. In his stay at City, he played only 1 season as a regular. He moved onto Reading, where he enjoyed 5 years as the club's right winger, followed by time at Exeter before moving out of the League at the age of 38.

SIMPSON, Frederick H. (Fred)
Wing Half
Born: Whitburn
Career: Marsden Colliery Welfare, Coventry City November 1930.

Coventry City	League	F.A.Cup
1930–31	3	–
1931–32	6	–
1932–33	5	3
Total	14	3

Debut: 24/1/31 v Norwich C. (h) 3-0 (CH)

Big Geordie centre half Fred Simpson was signed in November 1930, and made his debut 2 months later in a reshuffled side that pushed centre half Jim Baker up front. Harry Storer gave him another chance in August 1932, but he was dropped after the side lost the first 2 games conceding 7 goals. City's strength in depth led to his his future appearances out of position – at right half – and he was released in 1933.

SIMPSON, Noel H.
Left Half
Born: Mansfield 23rd December 1922
Died: 21st November 1987
Career: Nottingham Forest 1943, Coventry City August 1948 (£5,000), Exeter City February 1957, Retired c/s 1958.

Coventry City	League	F.A.Cup
1948–49	33 – 1	–
1949–50	38 – 1	1
1950–51	16 – 2	–
1951–52	35 – 1	3
1952–53	33 – 1	3
1953–54	18	–
1954–55	25	4
1955–56	37 – 1	1
1956–57	23 – 1	–
Total	258 – 8	12

Debut: 21/8/48 v Brentford (a) 2-2 (LH)

The late 1940's and 1950's saw a period of great turmoil for City. From being a successful Division 2 side, City were on the slide to Division 4. During this period, one of the few consistent performers

was Noel Simpson. Signed in August 1948 for £5000, Simpson had been a regular for Nottingham Forest and appeared for both Nottingham clubs during the War. He quickly established himself and gave nine years service before leaving for Exeter at the age of 34. Whilst at Exeter, he met up with his former City colleague, namesake Dennis Simpson. Noel later moved back to his native Nottinghamshire, where he died in 1987.

SINGLETON, Martin David
Midfield
Born: Banbury 2nd August 1963
Career: Apprentice Coventry City, pro January 1981, Bradford City December 1984 (£20,000), West Bromwich Albion December 1986 (£30,000), Northampton Town November 1987 (£57,000), Walsall October 1990 (F/T), Aylesbury United c/s 1991, Worcester City August 1991, Stafford Rangers September 1991, Banbury United 1991.

Coventry City	League	F.A.Cup	Lge.Cup
1980–81	–	–	–
1981–82	3 – 1	–	–
1982–83	3+2s	–	1
1983–84	12+1s	–	2+1s
1984–85	2	–	1 – 1
Total	20+3s–1	–	4+1s–1

Debut: 13/4/82 v Everton (h) 1–0 (Mid) 1 goal

Singleton made the dream debut, scoring the only goal of the game, versus Everton at Highfield Road. Despite this impressive start, he was never able to gain a regular first team place, even when City had the smallest squad in Division 1. Under Bobby Gould, Singleton started in favour, but lost out to David Bennett and Steve Hunt. In December 1984, he moved to Bradford, where he helped the Bantams to promotion from Division 3. He suffered severe injuries to his knees which eventually forced him out of the League.

SMAILES, Matthew (Matt)
Half Back
Born: Durham 25th March c.1905
Career: Annfield Plain, Blackburn Rovers 1925/6, West Ham United 1927, Coventry City May 1930, Ashington c/s 1931.

Coventry City	League	F.A.Cup
1930–31	11	–

Debut: 1/9/30 v Fulham (a) 0–0 (CH)

Matt Smailes had played 4 matches for Blackburn and 10 for West Ham in the First Division, before signing for City. It was anticipated that his experience would stand him and the team in good stead. After some early season indifferent performances, he lost his place to Alfred Stokes and was released by new manager Harry Storer.

SMITH, Archibald (Archie)
Outside Right

Born: Birmingham
Career: Birmingham, Coventry City October 1919

Coventry City	League	F.A.Cup
1919–20	1	–

Debut: 4/10/19 v Leicester C. (h) 1–2 (OR)

After making 1 appearance for his local club, Birmingham, Smith was signed by William Clayton with Frank Crowe and Joby Godfrey. At a time of great panic in the club, Smith was plunged into the game against Leicester, but failed to impress. He was replaced by Horace Wright for the following game and was not seen again.

SMITH, Bernard
Full back

Born: Sileby 1908
Career: Loughborough Corinthians, Birmingham 1932, Coventry City August 1935, Retired 1940.

Coventry City	League	F.A.Cup
1935–36	18	–
1936–37	34	3
1937–38	–	–
1938–39	2	–
Total	54	3

Debut: 16/1/36 v Clapton Orient (a) 1–0 (LB)

Smith came into the professional game late, signing for Birmingham at the age of 24. He played 12 games for The Blues before signing for City, and later took over from Charlie Bisby, equipping himself well, and earning a Division 3(South) Champions medal. He continued in Division 2, but manager Harry Storer was always looking to improve the team and Smith had to make way for Walter Metcalf. He retired shortly after the outbreak of war.

SMITH, Charles H. (Charlie)
Inside Forward

Born: Small Heath, Birmingham
Career: Delta Works F.C., Nuneaton Town March 1911, Northampton Town May 1912, Coventry City c/s 1919, Stourbridge c/s 1923.

Coventry City	League	F.A.Cup
1919–20	1	–
1920–21	7 – 2	1
1921–22	–	–
1922–23	–	–
Total	8 – 2	1

Debut: 3/9/19 v Leeds City (a) 0–3 (IR)

Charlie made his name before the Great War with Southern League Northampton Town, scoring 10 goals in 56 matches. During the unofficial 1918–19 season, Smith appeared 11 times for City and his signature was obtained for the following inaugural League season. He appeared in City's second League match as replacement for Chris Sambrooke, but didn't play again until the following season. He was a loyal and popular member of City's squad, albeit only as a regular reserve in his 4 years at the club.

SMITH, David
Outside Left

Born: Gloucester 29th March 1968
Career: YTS Coventry City, pro July 1986, Bournemouth (loan) January 1993, Dundee United (trial) February 1993, Birmingham City March 1993 (player–exchange).

Coventry City	League	F.A.Cup	Lge.Cup
1986–87	–	–	–
1987–88	14+2s–4	–	–
1988–89	34+1s–3	1	3
1989–90	37 – 6	1	8
1990–91	30+6s–1	3	4
1991–92	23+1s–4	1	1
1992–93	6 – 1	–	1
Total	144+10s–19	6	17

Debut: 6/2/88 v Manchester Utd. (a) 0–1 (sub)
Full Debut: 13/8/88 v Sheffield Wed. (h) 3–0 (OL)
Honours: 10 England U–21 Caps (all at City)

Smith burst onto the Division 1 scene in February 1988 when he replaced Nick Pickering on the left wing. He won admirers with his close skill and scoring ability, but he was about to be released on a free transfer when George Curtis and John Sillett took over. Smith was kept and played 10 times for

England U-21, but he stopped progressing and disappointed those who were expecting him to excel. He lost his place to Peter Ndlovu, and was injured in the warm-up in his first match on loan with Bournemouth. He had a trial in February 1993 with Dundee United but was not permitted to play a competitive match. He returned to Highfield Road and was sold to Birmingham, in a deal that brought David Rennie to City.

SMITH, F. David
Outside Right
Born: Holymoorside 27th July 1936
Career: Boston United, Chesterfield September 1953, Mansfield Town August 1955, Derby County July 1957, Coventry City November 1957, Kidderminster Harriers August 1959.

Coventry City	League	F.A.Cup
1957-58	22 - 2	-
1958-59	6	-
Total	28 - 2	-

Debut: 14/12/57 v Plymouth Argyle (a) 0-4 (OR)

Smith was signed from Derby in an attempt to keep City in Division 3 (S), but the 1957-58 season was disastrous, for they failed. In 1958-59, Peter Hill came back from injury to replace Smith, who moved on to Kidderminster Harriers for 1 season.

SMITH, George
Right Half
Born: Liverpool
Career: Runcorn, Liverpool, Gillingham 1923/4, Tranmere Rovers 1924/5, Coventry City c/s 1926, Runcorn.

Coventry City	League	F.A.Cup
1926-27	5	-

Debut: 4/9/26 v QPR (a) 1-1 (RH)

George Smith was an England Schoolboy International who only played 15 times for Gillingham before returning to Merseyside, with Tranmere Rovers. After 35 appearances, he was signed by James Kerr in the summer of 1926 as cover for William Dailey who was disappointing, and so Smith got his chance earlier than expected. After 5 poor games he was replaced by William Brown who subsequently made the right half position his own. Smith moved on, ending up at his original club, Runcorn.

SMITH, Horace
Wing Half
Born: Stourbridge
Career: Brierley Hill Alliance, Stourbridge, Coventry City c/s 1930, Merthyr Town November 1931, Stoke City January 1934, Nottingham Forest 1936, Shrewsbury Town c/s 1937, Revo Electric c/s 1939.

Coventry City	League	F.A.Cup
1930-31	5	-

Debut: 8/11/30 v Luton T. (h) 1-2 (RH)

Smith was a reserve wing half who got a look in only when Smailes and Stokes were injured. He was an energetic player who was noted for his stamina. New manager Harry Storer wanted to re-sign him but he refused terms. It took him 6 months to find a team, before playing for 2 years at Southern League Merthyr. He was signed by Stoke in January 1934, but could not break into the first team, then played 5 matches for Forest before leaving the League.

SMITH, John
Midfield
Born: Shoreditch 4th January 1939
Died: 1989
Career: West Ham United January 1956, Tottenham Hotspur March 1960, Coventry City March 1964 (£9,000), Leyton Orient October 1965, Torquay United October 1966, Swindon Town June 1968, Walsall June 1971, Dundalk June 1973.

Coventry City	League	F.A.Cup	Lge.Cup
1963-64	9	-	-
1964-65	24 - 1	-	3
1965-66	1+1s	-	1
Total	34+1s-1	-	4

Debut: 21/3/64 v Bournemouth (a) 1-2 (IL)
Honours: 1 England U-23 Cap

Early on in his career, John Smith was a revelation with the Hammers and his performances encouraged Bill Nicholson to sign him for Spurs. However, he was limited to 21 outings in 4 years. He was signed by Jimmy Hill to add some class to City's midfield. In 1964-65, he produced great form until injury struck. After regaining fitness, Smith played only a handful of games before returning to his native London with Leyton Orient. He eventually became the player-manager at Walsall and later of Dundalk. Tragically, he died at the age of 49.

SMITH, Kevan
Centre Half
Born: Yarm 13th December 1959
Career: Stockton, Darlington September 1979, Rotherham United July 1985 (£12,000), Coventry City December 1986 (£60,000), York City May 1988 (£40,000), Darlington c/s 1989, Hereford United (loan) October 1992.

Coventry City	League	F.A.Cup	Lge.Cup
1986–87	–	–	–
1987–88	5+1s	1	–
Total	5+1s	1	–

Debut: 7/11/87 v Oxford United (a) 0–1 (CH)

Smith was signed after 2 fine performances for Rotherham against City in the League Cup in 1986. However, in his first Central League game, he broke his leg, which sidelined him for the rest of the season. Season 1987–88 saw Smith play only as a replacement for Brian Kilcline when he was injured. Whilst at City, injury and reserve team football meant that his game declined. Consequently, he was delighted to move to York City, before returning to his first League club Darlington, as captain of the side in its season in the GM Vauxhall Conference. He successfully steered them back to Division 4 football and was with The Quakers as they gained promotion to and then relegation from Division 3.

SMITH, Norman L.
Centre Forward
Born: Boldon 23rd November 1919
Career: Standard Apprentices, Coventry City c/s 1938, Millwall December 1947, Bedworth Town c/s 1949.

Coventry City	League	F.A.Cup
1936–39	3	–
1945–46	WWII	–
1946–47	7	2
1947–48	3	–
Total	13	2

Debut: 24/9/38 v Nottingham Forest (a) 0–3 (CF)

It was unfortunate that War broke out when Smith was only 19 and he had just signed for City. His post–War first team outings were dependant upon injuries to players such as George Lowrie and Les Warner. In December 1947, he was transferred to Millwall.

SMITH, Stanley W. (Stan)
Wing Half
Born: Coventry 24th February 1925
Career: Nuffield Mechanisation, Coventry City 1942, Swansea Town August 1950, Stafford Rangers.

Coventry City	League	F.A.Cup
1945–46	WWII	–
1946–47	–	–
1947–48	25	2
1948–49	4	–
Total	29	2

Debut: 17/5/47 v Plymouth Argyle (h) 1–0 (CF)

Signed during the war, Stan Smith had one Football League season as a first team regular. 1947–48 was marked by injuries, particularly to full back Dennis Tooze, and the team was reshuffled with Smith coming in as wing half. His performances were solid, but once injury problems were cleared, he returned to the reserves. Swansea Town signed Smith, but he failed to make the first team.

SMITH, Wilf S.
Full Back
Born: Neumunster, West Germany 3rd September 1946
Career: Apprentice Sheffield Wednesday, pro August 1963, Coventry City August 1970 (£100,000), Brighton & Hove Albion (loan) October 1974, Millwall (loan) January 1975, Bristol Rovers March 1975 (£25,000), Chesterfield December 1976, Retired c/s 1978.

Coventry City	League	F.A.Cup	Lge.Cup
1970–71	28	1	2
1971–72	42 – 1	2	1
1972–73	32+2s	4	2
1973–74	23+1s	2	2 – 1
1974–75	7	–	–
Total	132+3s–1	9	7 – 1

Debut: 2/9/70 v Derby County (a) 4–2 (RH)
Honours: 6 England U–23 Caps
3 Football League appearances
FA Cup Runners–up Medal 1966

Born Wilfred Schmidt, the family took the Smith name when they came to Britain in Wilf's early life. He was a tremendous performer for Wednesday, earning 6 England U–23 caps, along with representing the Football League and playing in the 1966 FA Cup final. When Noel Cantwell signed him, he was the first full back to be transferred for £100,000. He quickly settled in and produced some fine form, but later lost his place to Graham Oakey and was loaned out twice before moving to Bristol Rovers. He then finished his career at Chesterfield at the relatively early age of 31.

SNAPE, John (Jack)
Wing Half

Born: Birmingham 2nd July 1917
Career: Solihull Town, Coventry City May 1936, Bedworth Town c/s 1951.

Coventry City	League	F.A.Cup
1937–38	8	–
1938–39	1	–
1945–46	WWII	1
1946–47	38 – 2	1
1947–48	17	2
1948–49	30	1
1949–50	12	–
1950–51	–	–
Total	106 – 2	5

Debut: 2/10/37 v Newcastle United (a) 2–1 (RH)

Snape started as cover for Billy Frith, and after the War, he made the right half position his own. He finally became a first team regular at the age of 29, after guesting for Leicester during hostilities. Midway through 1947–48, he suffered an injury that kept him out of action for almost 12 months. He regained his first team place, but then lost out to Harry Barratt. After a season in the reserves, he moved to local neighbours Bedworth. Snape was another player whose career was devastated by the war.

SODEN, Walter J.
Centre Forward

Born: Birmingham 22nd January 1921
Career: Boldmere St. Michael, Coventry City March 1948, Hednesford Town c/s 1949, Lockheed Leamington, Redditch Town c/s 1952.

Coventry City	League	F.A.Cup
1947–48	1	–
1948–49	1	–
Total	2	–

Debut: 24/4/48 v Millwall (a) 2–6 (CF)

Signed from a Birmingham junior team, Soden played 2 end of season games but never looked to be good enough for the first team. After 2 seasons, Soden moved back to non–league football with Hednesford Town.

SPEEDIE, David Robert
Forward

Born: Glenrothes 20th February 1960
Career: Apprentice Barnsley, pro October 1978, Darlington June 1980 (£5,000), Chelsea June 1982 (£70,000), Coventry City July 1987 (£780,000), Liverpool January 1991 (£675,000), Blackburn Rovers August 1991 (£500,000), Southampton July 1992 (£400,000), Birmingham City (loan) October 1992, West Bromwich Albion (loan) January 1993, West Ham United (loan) March 1993, Leicester City July 1993 (F/T).

Coventry City	League	F.A.Cup	Lge.Cup
1987–88	35+1s–6	1+1s	2
1988–89	36 – 14	1	3 – 1
1989–90	32 – 8	1	7 – 1
1990–91	18 – 3	–	3 – 1
Total	121+1s–31	3+1s	15 – 3

Debut: 15/8/87 v Tottenham H. (h) 2–1 (CF) 1 goal
Honours: 10 Full Scottish Caps (5 with City)
1 Scottish U–21 cap

After failing to keep a place in Barnsley's first team, Speedie was signed by Darlington and proved his goalscoring ability by scoring 17 goals in 1981–82. This attracted the attentions of Chelsea and he teamed up with Kerry Dixon as the side returned to the top Division. His later days at Chelsea were unsettled and he gratefully signed for City. To gain Speedie's signature, John Sillett broke the club's transfer record. His first League game was against Tottenham, only 3 months after the famous Cup final. He scored the opening goal and immediately became a crowd favourite. Whilst managed by John Sillett, Speedie's temper was usually under control, but he was suspended in September 1990 after an off the field incident with a member of the Vice

Presidents Club. He was sent off at Crystal Palace in Terry Butcher's 4th game in charge, and the clash of personalities resulted in Speedie being sold to Liverpool. Later, at Blackburn, he scored 26 goals for Rovers, helping them into the Premier League. He was most disgruntled when he formed part of the deal that took Alan Shearer to Ewood Park from Southampton and was not prepared to move to the South Coast. He spent 1992–93 on loan to clubs within commuting distance of his Atherstone home.

SPENCER, Derek
Goalkeeper
Born: Coventry 10th January 1931
Died: February 1989
Career: Lockheed Leamington, Coventry City December 1951, Lockheed Leamington c/s 1954, Banbury Spencer August 1956.

Coventry City	League	F.A.Cup
1951–52	1	–
1952–53	19	3
1953–54	–	–
Total	20	3

Debut: 19/4/52 v Sheffield Wednesday (h) 0–2 (Goal)

Spencer's first team debut in April 1952 against Sheffield Wednesday was a great test for the 21 year old 'keeper. City had to stay up to avoid relegation to Division 3 and Wednesday were already champions. It was not a fairy tale beginning as injury struck City lost 0–2. Spencer's first team opportunities were limited as City had 5 goal-keepers, including Peter Taylor and Reg Matthews. He played when injury forced Taylor out, but could not find a place for himself once Matthews established himself. When he died at the age of 58, the local non–league scene lost a popular figure.

SPRATT, Graham W.
Goalkeeper
Born: Leicester 17th July 1939
Career: Oadby Town, Coventry City December 1956, Rugby Town July 1959.

Coventry City	League	F.A.Cup
1956–57	–	–
1957–58	27	2
1958–59	1	–
Total	28	2

Debut: 7/9/57 v Watford (h) 2–2 (Goal)

Injury to Charlie Ashcroft allowed Spratt into the first team. He received rave reviews in his early games, but his form dwindled and his confidence was lost. He was dropped after conceding 4 goals at Colchester and 7 at Southampton. In his final 4 games for City, Spratt conceded 17 goals. Ashcroft retired but City bought in Jim Sanders to replace him. When injured, Sanders was followed by coach Alf Wood and then Arthur Lightening. Spratt's future was obviously not at City, so he moved on to a career in non–League football.

SPRING, Andrew J. (Andy)
Right Back
Born: Newcastle 17th November 1965
Career: Apprentice, Coventry City, pro November 1983, Bristol Rovers July 1985 (F/T), Cardiff City (loan) October 1985, Sligo Rovers, Drogheda United, Longford Town.

Coventry City	League	F.A.Cup	Lge.Cup
1983–84	0+1s	–	–
1984–85	3+1s	–	2
Total	3+2s	–	2

Debut: 7/4/84 v Liverpool (a) 0–5 (Sub)
Full debut: 22/9/84 v. Sunderland (a) 0–0 (RB)

Spring came through from the youth team and made 5 full appearances for the first team as a replacement for Kirk Stephens. His future at City was over once Brian Borrows arrived from Bolton. Bobby Gould (also his manager at City) signed him for Bristol Rovers. But Rovers eventually released Spring because of his off–field activities. He moved on to Ireland where he is now settled. He recently hit the headlines by winning a quarter of a million pounds in the Irish National Lottery!

SPRINGTHORPE, Terence A. (Terry)
Full Back
Born: Draycott 4th December 1923
Career: Wolverhampton Wanderers 1939, Coventry City December 1950, USA c/s 1951.

Coventry City	League	F.A.Cup
1950–51	12	1

Debut: 23/12/50 v Preston North End (a) 1–1 (RB)
Honours: FA Cup Winners Medal 1949
USA International

Signed by Wolves in 1939, Springthorpe made his debut during the war at the age of 16. During the war, Springthorpe guested for Cardiff City, Leicester

City and Wrexham. He never achieved a regular first team place at Molineux, but appeared at Wembley in the successful cup winning side of 1949. His stay at City was short as he emigrated to the USA at the end of the season. Two seasons later, he played against England for the USA, a game which England won 6–3.

STANFORD, Harry
Goalkeeper

Born: Birmingham
Career: Earle Bourne F.C., Walsall c/s 1922, Southend United 1924, Brentford 1925/6, Bristol Rovers, Brierley Hill Alliance 1926/7, Coventry City c/s 1927, Retired 1928.

Coventry City	League	F.A.Cup
1927–28	11	–

Debut: 5/9/27 v Swindon T. (h) 4–0 (Goal)

He had only played 2 League games – for Brentford in 1925–26 – before signing for City as a replacement for the injured Jack Thomson, who was to replace Stanford at City. He was signed as cover for regular goalkeeper Jimmy Newton, and injury to the latter allowed Stanford an extended run of games. He was then dropped in November 1927 after being in City's goal during the 1–9 crushing defeat at Millwall (which was City's worst defeat in the League at the time). He suffered a serious knee injury playing for the reserves in January 1928, which forced him out of the professional game.

STARSMORE, John G.
Forward

Born: Kettering
Career: Desborough Town, Kettering Town c/s 1925, Coventry City September 1928, Kettering Town c/s 1930, Swindon Town c/s 1931, Barrow 1933/4, Dartford 1934, Kettering Town c/s 1935.

Coventry City	League	F.A.Cup
1928–29	31 – 10	1 – 1
1929–30	20 – 7	–
Total	51 – 17	1 – 1

Debut: 6/10/28 v Brentford (h) 1–0 (CF) 1 goal

John Starsmore had been a successful forward with his home town club Kettering before signing for City. He started well, scoring on his debut, but James McIntyre was looking for a higher scoring centre forward. He found Jimmy Loughlin and Starsmore moved to inside right to replace the injured Alf Widdowson. With both Loughlin and Widdowson fit, Starsmore was dropped and moved back to Kettering. His career was revived at Swindon, scoring 16 goals in 71 games.

STEIN, Colin
Centre Forward

Born: Philipstoun 10th May 1947
Career: Broxburn Strollers, Armadale Thistle, Hibernian July 1965 (£200), Rangers October 1968 (£100,000) Coventry City October 1972 (£140,000), Rangers March 1975 (£80,000), Kilmarnock (loan) October 1977, Retired c/s 1978.

Coventry City	League	F.A.Cup	Lge.Cup
1972–73	31 – 10	4 – 2	–
1973–74	28 – 5	2	6 – 4
1974–75	24 – 6	2	1 – 1
Total	83 – 21	8 – 2	7 – 5

Debut: 7/10/72 v Crystal Palace (a) 1–0 (CF)
Honours: 21 Full Scotland Caps (4 with City)
      1 Scotland U–23 Cap
      Cup–Winners Cup Winners Medal 1971–72
      Scottish Lge.Cup Wins.Medal 70–71, 75–76
      Scottish FA Cup Runners–up Medal 1971
      Scottish League Representative

The signing of Colin Stein by Gordon Milne was a real coup, for he was an established international and was a consistent goalscorer. He came south from Rangers with the reputation of having one of the hardest shots in football. City were 21st in Division 1 in October 1972 when Quintin Young moved to Rangers and Stein joined City, but the latter's impact was immediate. He linked up impressively with Milne's other exciting capture, Tommy Hutchison. This partnership sparked the start of an 8 game unbeaten run to put City in mid-table. In his spell at City, Stein scored 28 goals, and gained 4 more Scotland caps to take his total to 21. His goalscoring prowess was evident in November 1968 when he scored a hat–trick in 3 minutes for Rangers against Arbroath in a Scottish Division 1 match.

STEPHENS, Kirk W.
Right Back
Born: Coventry 27th February 1955
Career: Nuneaton Borough 1972, Luton Town June 1978, Coventry City August 1984 (£50,000), Retired May 1986, Stockingford February 1987, Nuneaton Borough March 1987, Barnet c/s 1987, Nuneaton Borough c/s 1988, Retired 1989.

Coventry City	League	F.A.Cup	Lge.Cup
1984–85	32 – 2	2	–
1985–86	1+1s	–	0+1
Total	33+1s–2	2	0+1

Debut: 25/8/84 v Aston Villa (a) 0–1 (RB)

Local boy Stephens had been at Nuneaton for 6 years before getting the opportunity to play in the Football League with Luton Town. He impressed greatly as an attacking right–back in the Hatters team that returned to Division 1. In his time at Luton, Stephens barely missed a match, but his time at City was plagued with injury. He signed for City, in August 1984, with Ashley Grimes moving to Luton. In his 3rd game for City, he received a knee injury which was eventually to force him to retire in May 1986. After a break of 9 months, Stephens returned to non–league football, later becoming player–manager of Nuneaton Borough.

STEPHENS, William (Johnny)
Winger
Born: Cardiff 26th June 1935
Career: Hull City August 1952, Swindon Town June 1958, Coventry City January 1960.

Coventry City	League	F.A.Cup
1959–60	14	–

Debut: 13/2/60 v Accrington Stanley (h) 2–1 (OR)
Honours: 1 Wales U–23 cap

Johnny Stephens was a gifted, but erratic winger. His career with Hull City was a mixture of genius and dissatisfaction with professional football. He played only 18 times in 18 months at Swindon, before joining City in January 1960. In the close

season of 1960, Stephens finally moved out of the professional game which he had become disgruntled with.

STEPHENSON, William
Right Half
Born: Ryton–on–Tyne 1899
Career: Mickley Colliery Walfare, Coventry City 1920, Nuneaton Town December 1920, Scotswood 1922.

Coventry City	League	F.A.Cup
1920–21	1	–

Debut: 25/9/20 v Sheffield Wednesday (a) 0–3 (RH)

Stephenson's only appearance came at Hillsborough in September 1920. He was reserve for the first team (which was often a task for third team players) stepping in when regular left back Jim Lawrence was taken ill during the journey North. A quick reshuffle brought Alfred Fenwick to full back and Stephenson to right half. Shortly afterwards, Stephenson moved to Nuneaton.

STEVENS, Samuel (Sam)
Centre Forward
Born: Netherton 18th November 1890
Career: Cradley Heath St. Luke's, Hull City January 1912, Notts County July 1920 (£1,750), Coventry City March 1921 (£1,300), ?, Dudley Bean F.C. c/s 1925.

Coventry City	League	F.A.Cup
1920–21	11 – 3	–
1921–22	42– 21	3
1922–23	6 – 1	–
Total	59 – 25	3

Debut: 19/3/21 v Clapton Orient (h) 1–1 (CF)

Despite being considered slight for a centre forward, standing only 5 feet 8 inches tall, Sam Stevens was a potent striker both sides of The Great War. He started his professional career with Hull City after being spotted playing for Cradley Heath St Luke's. Whilst playing for The Tigers, Stevens notched up 87 goals in only 150 appearances. He was on the verge of an England cap, being a reserve for the Scotland international in 1914–15. Stevens was involved in 2 big money transfers in a 9 month period (a Notts County record fee of £1,750, and £1,300 when he joined City). Whilst at Coventry, Stevens supplied a regular helping of goals and became City's first player to score 20 goals in a League season. Injury curtailed his career and he later played in works' football.

STEWART, George T.S.
Centre Forward

Born: Buckie 17th February 1927
Career: Buckie Thistle, Dundee 1946, St. Mirren c/s 1950, Worcester City June 1954 (£3,000), Accrington Stanley September 1954, Coventry City November 1958, Carlisle United June 1960.

Coventry City	League	F.A.Cup
1958–59	25 – 15	–
1959–60	15 – 8	–
Total	40 – 23	–

Debut: 29/11/58 v Chester (h) 5–1 (CF) 1 goal

Stewart was a gifted goalscorer in the lower divisions and in Scotland, scoring a total of 203 goals in only 316 league games. He was attracted South by leading non–League club Worcester City for £3000, a significant fee for a non–League club. After a short spell at St George's Lane, Stewart left for Accrington Stanley. This was the peak of his career as he rattled in 136 goals in 182 League games. He was signed by Billy Firth in November 1958 to help City out of Division 4. In his time at City, he impressed, but injury forced him out of the first team.

STIFFLE, Nelson E.
Outside Right

Born: India 30th July 1928
Career: Ashton United, Chester December 1951, Altrincham 1952, Chesterfield May 1954, Bournemouth May 1955, Exeter City March 1958, Coventry City July 1960, Bankstown c/s 1961.

Coventry City	League	F.A.Cup	Lge.Cup
1960–61	15 – 2	2	1

Debut: 20/8/60 v Barnsley (a) 1–4 (OR)

Stiffle was a dependable outside right who moved around the lower divisions and non–league football. He was signed by Billy Frith from Exeter after some impressive performances. He started as a first team regular, but City struggled to stay in Division 3 and Stiffle failed to impress. In a bid to rise away from the relegation zone, Frith signed Stewart Imlach, who had played for Forest in the 1959 Cup final. Stiffle's appearances were limited to 4 after Imlach's arrival and in the summer of 1961, he moved to Australia to play for Bankstown in New South Wales.

STIRLING, John
Outside Right

Born: Clydebank
Died: March 1924
Career: Clydebank, Clyde September 1908, Middlesbrough September 1911, Bradford (PA) August 1914, Stoke 1919, Coventry City March 1920, Alloa Athletic c/s 1920 – March 1924.

Coventry City	League	F.A.Cup
1919–20	5	–

Debut: 6/3/20 v Stockport Co. (a) 1–1 (OR)

Scotsman Stirling arrived in England in September 1911 after spending three years with high–riding Clyde. He became a top class outside right at both Middlesbrough and Bradford before the Great War. Once League football recommenced he signed for Stoke from whom Harry Pollitt enticed him in March 1920. He played five games at outside right and returned to Scotland in the summer of 1920. He stayed with Alloa Athletic until he died suddenly in March 1924.

STODDART, William Michael C.
Centre Half

Born: Lanchester 1907
Career: Medarnsley Edge, West Stanley 1923, Manchester City March 1926, Coventry City May 1927, Southampton June 1928 (player–exchange), Bristol Rovers July 1931 (£200), Accrington Stanley July 1933, Annfield Plain May 1934.

Coventry City	League	F.A.Cup
1927–28	6 – 1	–

Debut: 27/8/27 v Watford (a) 1–3 (CF) 1 goal

Given a free transfer by Manchester City, Stoddart was bought by James Kerr and started well, scoring on his debut, but was replaced by Walter Johnstone. He came back for the last 3 games of the season as a centre half. He was sold by new boss James McIntyre to Southampton in a deal which brought Tommy Allen and Bill Henderson to City. He did not impress at Southampton and moved on to Bristol Rovers to gain first team action.

STOKES, Alfred
Wing Half

Born: West Bromwich
Career: Allen Everitt F.C., Notts County, Coventry City May 1929, Watford c/s 1931.

Coventry City	League	F.A.Cup
1929–30	24	4
1930–31	21	3
Total	45	7

Debut: 7/9/29 v Torquay Utd. (a) 3–1 (LH)

Stokes was signed by James McIntyre as a promising half back, having appeared 13 times for Notts County, and clocked up most of his appearances as replacement for the injured Jimmy Baker. He had an extended run when Baker was pushed into the centre half position in December 1930. Stokes was released by new manager Harry Storer as one of a wholesale set of changes and signed for Watford, where he played 42 times.

STONE, Joseph (Joe)
Outside Right
Born: Willenhall
Career: Willenhall Swifts, Wolverhampton Wanderers, Dudley Town, Coventry City c/s 1919.

Coventry City	League	F.A.Cup
1919/20	2	–

Debut: 6/9/19 v Tottenham H. (a) 1–4 (OR)

Prior to the War, he had been on the books of Wolves, but never played for the first team. Signed in the summer of 1919, Stone had impressed in local works' football in Worcester during the war. His stocky frame of 5 feet 7 inches, eleven and a half stone, and a turn of speed, was seen by City as an asset for their first season in Division 2. He played in 1–4 and 0–4 defeats against Tottenham and Leeds City respectively and was not seen again.

STOREY, Thomas
Outside Right
Born: Crook 23rd November
Career: Crook F.C., Middlesbrough January 1914, Crystal Palace July 1920, Coventry City July 1922.

Coventry City	League	F.A.Cup
1922–23	33 – 1	1
1923–24	21 – 2	2
1924–25	5	1
Total	59 – 3	4

Debut: 26/8/22 v Notts Co. (h) 1–2 (OR)

Storey had established himself in Middlebrough's 1st

Division side just before the Great War and returned to the Boro after hostilities. He was signed for Crystal Palace for their first season in the Football League and helped them to the Division 3 championship. Albert Evans signed him for City as an experienced outside right, but he regularly played out of position at inside right because of the form of winger Jimmy Dougall. He didn't have a goalscorer's touch and left the club when City suffered relegation in 1925.

STRAW, Raymond (Ray)
Centre Forward
Born: Ilkeston 22nd May 1933
Career: Ilkeston Town, Derby County October 1951, Coventry City November 1957, Mansfield Town August 1961, Lockheed Leamington July 1963.

Coventry City	League	F.A.Cup	Lge.Cup
1957–58	23 – 14	1	
1958–59	44 – 27	2 – 3	
1959–60	43 – 20	2 – 1	
1960–61	33 – 18	3 – 2	1
Total	143 – 79	8 – 6	1

Debut: 23/11/57 v Millwall (h) 1–4 (CF)

Derby signed Straw from local side Ilkeston but gave him limited opportunities in Division 1. Derby slipped from grace and it was not until they were in Division 3 (N) that he became a first team regular. In 1956–57, Straw scored 32 goals in 44 league games as Derby went for promotion back to Division 2. In November 1957, Billy Frith made a scoop when he brought Straw to Highfield Road. He continued his prolific goalscoring record with

City, bagging 85 goals in only 151 matches. However, his goals could not prevent City slumping to the newly formed Division 4. It was his goals that saw City bounce straight back. In his 4 year spell at City, Straw proved to be one of the most prolific goalscorers in the club's history. His 85 goals is the 4th highest in the Football League for City. Straw scored 4 hat–tricks for City and holds the post war record for goals in consecutive games. Between 1952 and 1960, Straw played in all 6 divisions of the Football League.

STRONG, Geoffrey H. (Geoff)
Wing Half

Born: Kirkheaton 19th September 1937
Career: Stanley United, Arsenal November 1957, Liverpool November 1964 (£40,000), Coventry City August 1970 (£30,000), Retired c/s 1972.

Coventry City	League	F.A.Cup	Lge.Cup
1970–71	32	1	4
1971–72	1	–	–
Total	33	1	4

Debut: 15/8/70 v Nottingham Forest (a) 0–2 (LH)
Honours: League Championship Medal 1965–66
FA Cup Winners Medal 1965

Geoff Strong did not make his League debut with Arsenal until he was 23, but he quickly established himself in the Gunners' first team. He spent four and a half seasons in the first team at Highbury, scoring a phenomenal 74 goals in 132 League and cup games, a tremendous strike record for a wing half. In November 1964, he was tempted to Liverpool, where he immediately won an FA Cup winners medal and in the following season helped the Reds to the Championship. Strong was the model professional around whom the big names could play. Strong signed for City close to his 33rd birthday, stepping straight into the first team and bringing his considerable experience to bear in City's first European tournament games. In his second season, he only played once and retired at the end of the season.

SUCKLING, Perry J.
Goalkeeper

Born: Hackney 12th October 1965
Career: Apprentice Coventry City, pro October 1983, Manchester City June 1986 (player–exchange), Chelsea (loan) December 1988, Crystal Palace January 1988, West Ham United (loan) December 1989, Brentford (loan) November 1991, Ernest Borel (Hong Kong)(loan) 1992, Watford c/s 1992.

Coventry City	League	F.A.Cup	Lge.Cup
1982–83	3	–	1
1983–84	24	–	1
1984–85	–	–	–
1985–86	–	–	–
Total	27	–	2

Debut: 28/8/82 v Southampton (h) 1–0 (Goal)
Honours: 9 England U–21 Caps (1 at City)

In the summer of 1982 manager Dave Sexton had to balance the books. He decided to release goalkeeper Jim Blyth, because first choice Les Sealey was rarely injured. However, 24 hours before the start of that season Sealey was forced out through injury. The only other goalkeeper at the club was youth team apprentice Perry Suckling who was pushed into the first team at the tender age of 16 years and 320 days. He thus became the youngest player for City in Division One and the second all time youngest, behind Brian Hill, in City's history. In his debut Suckling faced England keeper Peter Shilton and came out on the winning side. Suckling only played four times that season and when Les Sealey left the club, new manager Bobby Gould brought in the experienced Raddy Avramovic. However, Avramovic was dropped for poor performances and Suckling played every game from February to the end of the season. When Steve Ogrizovic arrived, Suckling was kept in the reserves for two years and became restless for regular football. Consequently, he moved to Manchester City at the age of 20 with David Phillips coming to Highfield Road. He lost his place and signed for Crystal Palace, playing in the crushing 9–0 defeat by Liverpool in 1989. The arrival of Nigel Martyn left Suckling in Palace's reserves and he moved to Watford after several loan spells.

SUTTON, Stephen J. (Steve)
Goalkeeper

Born: Hartington 16th April 1961
Career: Apprentice Nottingham Forest, pro April 1979, Mansfield Town (loan) March 1981, Derby County (loan) March 1985, Coventry City (loan) February 1991, Luton Town (loan) November 1991, Derby County March 1992.

Coventry City	League	F.A.Cup	Lge.Cup
1990–91	1	–	–

Debut: 2/2/91 v Wimbledon (a) 0–1 (Goal)
Honours: League Cup Winners Medal 1989 & 1990
Full Members Cup Winners Medal 1989

Sutton's only City appearance came whilst on loan from Nottingham Forest, when Steve Ogrizovic was injured. City's only other keeper was the inexperienced Tim Clarke, and manager Terry Butcher decided to go for experience. At the City Ground, Sutton had to be content with being understudy to Peter Shilton, Hans van Brenkelen and Hans Segers before making the first team place his own. Despite being a good shot stopper and at taking crosses, he lost out to Mark Crossley. He signed for Derby after an unsuccessful bid by Luton.

SWINDALE, Lancelot
Outside Right
Born: Preston, Co. Durham
Career: Preston Colliery, Blyth Spartans, Coventry City 1921, Shildon Athletic, Blyth Spartans April 1923.

Coventry City	League	F.A.Cup
1921–22	4	–

Debut: 17/11/21 v Derby Co. (h) 1–2 (OR)

With an injury to first choice outside right Jimmy Dougall, the young reserve winger Swindale was pushed into the side against Derby County. He played well and managed a run of 4 games, but relinquished his place once Dougall regained full fitness. After the end of his first season, he was released.

TAYLOR, George Thomas
Outside Right
Born: Walsall
Career: Talbot Stead, Walsall Wood, Bloxwich Strollers, Stourbridge, Notts County 1925, Bolton Wanderers December 1933, Coventry City October 1937, Retired 1943.

Coventry City	League	F.A.Cup
1937–38	30 – 5	1
1938–39	35 – 6	1
Total	65 – 11	2

Debut: 9/10/37 v Luton T. (h) 2–1 (OR) 1 goal

Harry Storer was never satisfied with the wingers that he bought for City and he chopped and changed to get a combination he could be happy with. He paid over £2,000 for the highly experienced Taylor, who had made 265 League appearances for Notts County and 170 League and Cup appearances for Bolton. He was an almost ever–present for three seasons in Division 1 before signing for City. He played on both flanks, but preferred to play on the right side. He continued to play until 1943.

TAYLOR, Peter T.
Goalkeeper
Born: Nottingham 2nd July 1928
Died: Majorca 4th October 1990
Career: Christchurch, Nottingham Forest WWII, Coventry City May 1946, Middlesbrough August 1955 (£3,500), Port Vale June 1961, Burton Albion c/s 1962.

Coventry City	League	F.A.Cup
1946–47	–	–
1947–48	–	–
1948–49	–	–
1949–50	–	–
1950–51	1	–
1951–52	26	3
1952–53	8	–
1953–54	41	1
1954–55	10	–
Total	86	4

Debut: 28/4/51 v Luton Town (a) 1–1 (Goal)

Peter Taylor played for 9 seasons at City, but he only ever played one season as a regular in the first team. He made his debut on the final day of the 1950–51 season, ending Alf Wood's run of 215 consecutive League and cup games. In the early fifties, City had a surplus of goalkeeping talent, consequently, after shaking off the challenge of Wood, Billy Gilbert and Derek Spencer, Taylor lost his place to the fast emerging Reg Matthews. Later spells at Port Vale and Burton Albion included some coaching, which set him in good stead for his management partnership with Brian Clough whom Taylor met whilst at Middlesbrough. Together, they brought the League championship to Derby and Nottingham Forest and the European Cup twice to Forest. In later life, illness struck Taylor and it was tragic that he should die whilst on holiday in Majorca in October 1990.

TEDDS, William H. (Billy)
Right Back
Born: Bedworth 27th July 1943
Career: Coventry City September 1960, Cambridge United c/s 1965, Lockheed Leamington July 1967.

Coventry City	League	F.A.Cup	Lge.Cup
1960–61	–	–	–
1961–62	4	–	–
1962–63	1	–	–
1963–64	–	–	–
1964–65	3	–	1
Total	8	–	1

Debut: 16/9/61 v Shrewsbury Town (a) 1–1 (RB)

Local boy Bill Tedds, spent 5 years at City as a professional, but never gained a regular first team place. He only ever played when injury struck Frank Kletzenbauer, John Sillet or John Burckitt. His games included the 1–8 thrashing by Leicester City in the League Cup in December 1964. With Mick Kearns taking over the right back spot and John Sillett in the reserves, there was no place for Tedds.

THOMAS, Brinley (Bryn)
Centre Forward
Born: Coventry 13th December 1932
Career: Longford Rovers, Coventry City September 1950, Banbury Spencer c/s 1954, Rugby Town, Bedworth Town, Banbury Spencer c/s 1957.

Coventry City	League	F.A.Cup
1950–51	–	–
1951–52	–	–
1952–53	8 – 1	–
1953–54	4	–
Total	12 – 1	–

Debut: 3/4/53 v Colchester United (a) 1–0 (CF)

Early in his career Thomas was kept out of the first team by the experience of Eddy Brown, George Lowrie and Ted Roberts, but his chance came in April 1953. Les Warner was injured, Brown moved to the wing and Thomas came in as centre forward. He played until the end of the season and made an occasional appearance in 1953–54 before being released.

THOMAS, Daniel J. (Danny)
Right Back
Born: Worksop 12th November 1961
Career: Apprentice Coventry City, pro December 1978, Tottenham Hotspur June 1983 (£300,000), Retired December 1987.

Coventry City	League	F.A.Cup	Lge.Cup
1978–79	–	–	–
1979–80	0+3s	–	1
1980–81	23+2s–1	2+1s–1	5+1s
1981–82	39 – 1	4	2
1982–83	41 – 3	3	3
Total	103+5s–5	9+1s–1	11+1s

Debut: 26/9/79 v W.B.A. (a) 1–2 (Mid) League Cup
Honours: 2 England full Caps (both at City)
7 England U–21 Caps (5 with City)

When Danny Thomas arrived at Highfield Road, his elder brother Valmore was already a professional with the club. However, as Danny's career took off, his brother moved on to Hereford United. When Danny played for England, Valmore was in non-league football. Originally, Danny Thomas gained a chance in midfield, although at the time, Mick Coop was the regular right back and Brian Roberts also staked a claim to the position. However, the tremendous ability shown by Thomas encouraged Gordon Milne to push him into his natural position and he immediately shone through. Such was his ability, that Coop was allowed to move to Derby and Roberts became left back. After less than 20 full games, Thomas was an England U–21 international and by the summer of 1983, he became only City's second full England international (after Reg Matthews). However, this was somewhat tarnished by his determination to leave the club following the dismissal of Dave Sexton. Several clubs wanted him but he finally chose Tottenham Hotspur. He never recaptured his City sparkle with 'Spurs, and tragically, as he seemed to be running into form, he suffered a sickening injury to his knee against QPR which ended his career. After attempting a comeback, he retired in December 1987, at the age of 26. Since then, he has turned his attention to gaining a degree in physiotherapy and is now the club physio at WBA.

THOMAS, Peter J.
Goalkeeper
Born: Coventry 20th November 1944
Career: St. Mary's Youth Club, GEC (Coventry), Coventry City c/s 1965, Waterford (loan) c/s 1966 to November 1966, Waterford c/s 1967 (F/T), Retired early 1980's.

Coventry City	League	F.A.Cup	Lge.Cup
1965–66	–	–	–
1966–67	1	–	–
Total	1	–	–

Debut: 26/11/66 v Cardiff City (h) 3–2 (Goal)
Honours: 2 Republic of Ireland full Caps
         4 League of Ireland appearances
         Republic of Ireland XI appearance
         FAI Cup Winners Medal 1980
         FAI Cup Runners–up Medal 1968, 72, 79

Signed from local football, Thomas was loaned out to Waterford, who played in the League of Ireland, in the summer of 1966. Meanwhile, Jimmy Hill sold reserve keeper Bob Wesson to Walsall, and regular keeper Bill Glazier picked up an injury. Thomas was hastily recalled from Ireland to play his only League game, against Cardiff. Glazier returned, but Thomas remained as cover. At the end of the season, he was allowed a permanent move back to Waterford where he had considerable success, including two international apperances plus 13 European club matches – quite an achievement for a former City reserve!

THOMPSON, Garry Lindsey
Centre Forward
Born: Birmingham 7th October 1959
Career: Apprentice Coventry City, pro June 1977, West Bromwich Albion February 1983 (£225,000), Sheffield Wednesday August 1985 (£450,000), Aston Villa May 1986 (£450,000), Watford December 1988 (£325,000), Crystal Palace March 1990, Queen's Park Rangers August 1991, Cardiff City August 1993.

Coventry City	League	F.A.Cup	Lge.Cup
1977–78	5+1s–2	–	–
1978–79	19+1s–8	2	0+1s–1
1979–80	16+1s–6	–	–
1980–81	34+1s–8	4 – 1	7 – 6
1981–82	36 – 10	3 – 2	2
1982–83	18+2s–4	2 – 1	3
Total	128+6s–38	11 – 4	12+1s–7

Debut: 21/3/78 v Aston Villa (h) 2–3 (CF)
Honours: 6 England U–21 Caps (all at City)

Garry Thompson was a great find for City. Early in his career, he filled in for the injured Mick Ferguson, but soon emerged as a goalscorer in his own right. Gordon Milne put faith in his young striker, who repaid Milne's confidence. Thompson's tally of 49 goals for City has only been bettered in Division 1 by Ian Wallace, Mick Ferguson and Cyrille Regis. He built up an excellent partnership, for City and with the England U–21 team, with Mark Hateley. Thompson was always the more consistent goal-scorer, but whilst Hateley went on to play for England and on the Continent, Thompson has become a striking journeyman. He was sold to West Bromwich Albion, on the insistence of chairman Jimmy Hill and over the head of manager Dave Sexton. The money was never used to strengthen the depleted squad, and this sparked off a players' revolt which resulted in most of the first team leaving in the summer of 1983. Thompson's most memorable game for City must be the League Cup semi-final against West Ham in 1981. On a bitterly cold night, Tommo put through his own goal and scored twice, the second in injury time to bring City a 3–2 victory after trailing 0–2.

THOMPSON, George Wilfred
Centre Half
Born: Witton–le–Wear 1896
Career: Southwick F.C, Norwich City November 1913, Aberdare 1920, Dundee 1921, Torquay United 1922, Reading c/s 1923, Coventry City c/s 1924, Nuneaton Town January 1925, Walsall 1925/6, Caernarvon Town July 1926 (player-manager).

Coventry City	League	F.A.Cup
1924–25	2	–

Debut: 30/8/24 v Chelsea (a) 0–1 (CH)
Honours: England Schoolboy International

Big centre half Thompson had been a schoolboy international before signing for Norwich City. He played 5 games for The Canaries, either side of The Great War. Afterwards, he moved around the country and made a brief stop at City. He was dropped after 2 consecutive defeats. His final League appearance was at Walsall and he became player-manager of Caernarvon, taking them to the Welsh National League title in his first season.

THOMPSON, James William J. (Jimmy)
Centre Forward
Born: Plaistow 19th April 1898
Died: Epsom August 1984
Career: Custom House, Charlton Athletic August 1921, Wimbledon September 1921, Millwall Athletic December 1921, Coventry City June 1923, Clapton Orient August 1924, Luton Town July 1925, Chelsea c/s 1927, Norwich City May 1929, Sunderland May 1930, Fulham October 1930 £300, Hull City October 1931, Tunbridge Wells Rangers January 1932, Peterborough & Fletton United 1934/5, Linfield 1935, Aldershot 1935, Lucerne October 1935.

Coventry City	League	F.A.Cup
1923–24	2	–

Debut: 22/12/23 v Stoke (a) 1–2 (CF)

Jimmy Thompson spent a season at City, making only 2 appearances at centre forward. It was later in his career that he established himself as a first team centre forward, at Luton and Chelsea, where he had the happy knack of scoring. At Stamford Bridge, he scored 34 goals in only 42 games, yet was dropped. There followed an impressive spell at Norwich, which encouraged First Division Sunderland to sign him. He spent only 3 months at Roker without making an appearance, before moving back South to Fulham. His great achievement in football came after his retirement, when he became a scout for Chelsea and holds the distinction of recommending Jimmy Greaves to The Blues.

THOMPSON, Keith A.
Left Midfield
Born: Birmingham 24th April 1965
Career: Apprentice Coventry City, pro January 1983, Wimbledon (loan) October 1983, Northampton Town (loan) March 1985, Real Oviedo September 1985 (£10,000), Coventry City September 1988 Sing Toa (Hong Kong).

Coventry City	League	F.A.Cup	Lge.Cup
1982–83	2+3s	–	–
1983–84	6	1	–
1984–85	1	–	0+1s
1985–86	–	–	–
1988–89	2+7s–1	–	0+1s
1989–90	0+1s	–	0+1s
1990–91	0+1s	1	0–1s
Total	11+12s–1	2	0+4s

Debut: 18/9/82 v Birmingham C. (a) 0–1 (OL)

The younger brother of Garry Thompson, Keith was a talented left–sided midfield player who was expected to go far. He failed to deliver and has since tried his luck abroad. He made his debut whilst still an apprentice and was loaned out to gain experience. He failed to break into the side and Don Mackay sold him to Real Oviedo. He enjoyed himself in Spain, learned the language and married, but the offer from John Sillett to return was too good to be true and he bought himself out of his contract. He struggled again at City and moved to Sing Toa in Hong Kong.

THOMSON, Arthur
Inside Forward
Born: Whitby
Career: West Stanley, Morecambe, Manchester United c/s 1928, Southend United 1931, Coventry City c/s 1932, Tranmere Rovers, Morecambe 1934/5.

Coventry City	League	F.A.Cup
1932–33	1	–

Debut: 10/9/32 v Luton T. (a) 1–4 (IR)

Thomson was a fringe player at Old Trafford when Manchester United struggled in the late 1920's and early 30's. He was then released when the Red Devils were relegated to Division 2 in 1931 and impressed at Southend, scoring 6 goals in 14 games. Signed for City by Harry Storer in the summer of 1932, Thomson's only appearance came as a replacement for Jock Lauderdale.

THOMSON, John Y. (Jack)
Goalkeeper
Born: Glasgow
Career: Benburb, Bristol Rovers 1921/2, Alloa Athletic c/s 1922, Partick Thistle 1923, Aberaman, Aberdare December 1924, Brentford c/s 1925, Plymouth Argyle c/s 1926, Coventry City January 1928, New York Nationals (USA) 1928/9, Nuneaton Town August 1929.

Coventry City	League	F.A.Cup
1927–28	3	–

Debut: 11/2/28 v Walsall (a) 0–7 (Goal)

Thomson had been a successful keeper in Scotland before moving South. Impressive performances encouraged Aberdare and then Brentford to sign him, being a regular at both clubs (during his season at Griffin Park, he only missed 2 games). In his 18 months at Plymouth, he played 7 times before signing for City. City's reserve keeper Stanford was injured and Thomson was signed as cover for Jimmy Newton, who himself received an injury. Thomson played 3 consecutive games, conceding 11 goals, including 7 on his debut in the humiliating drubbing by Walsall. Newton regained his place and Thomson moved to the USA to experience football in their new league.

TILFORD, Arthur
Left Back

Born: Ilkeston 19th May 1903
Career: Trowell St. Helens, Nottingham Forest May 1924, Blackpool May 1926, Coventry City May 1929, Fulham February 1932 (£750), Southampton (loan) February 1933, Walsall May 1934.

Coventry City	League	F.A.Cup
1929–30	1	–
1930–31	29	3
1931–32	27	2
Total	57	5

Debut: 26/10/29 v QPR (h) 2–3 (LB)

Tilford was signed from 2nd Division Blackpool and expected to slot straight into the City side at left back. He played only once in his first season however, due to the good form of Ted Watson. Injury to Watson in November 1930 gave Tilford his chance. He never looked back and played 61 consecutive League and cup games before ex–City manager James McIntyre of Fulham swooped for his signature to assist in their promotion to Division 2. Whilst at Fulham, Tilford suffered personal tragedy. His son died and the club felt that a loan spell at Southampton would help. After 5 months, he moved back to Craven Cottage, but was unable to regain his place in the side.

TIMMINS, Charles (Charlie)
Right Back

Born: Birmingham 29th May 1922
Career: Jack Moulds Athletic, Coventry City September 1946, Lockhead Leamington c/s 1958.

Coventry City	League	F.A.Cup
1946–47	–	–
1947–48	–	–
1948–49	–	–
1949–50	23	–
1950–51	33	1
1951–52	7	–
1952–53	11	–
1953–54	16	–
1954–55	9 – 1	
1955–56	19 – 2	1
1956–57	23 – 1	1
1957–58	20 – 1	1
Total	161 – 5	4

Debut: 24/8/49 v Luton Town (a) 0–2 (RB)

Charlie Timmins came into professional football at the age of 24, from Birmingham junior football and it took him 3 years to break into the first team. He established a regular place, but injury cost him his position, and thereafter he vied with Martin McDonnell, Ken Jones and Frank Austin for the right back spot. His loyalty was second–to–none and he was rewarded with the club captaincy in 1957.

TINNING, George E.
Right Back

Born: Kirkintilloch
Career: Clydebank, Coventry City 1925/6.

Coventry City	League	F.A.Cup
1925–26	5	–
1926–27	9	–
1927–28	11	1
1928–29	1	
Total	26	1

Debut: 2/4/26 v New Brighton (a) 1–5 (RB)

Scotsman Tinning was signed in season 1925–26 by James Kerr but didn't break through to gain a regular place in the team. He was not the quickest or strongest full back and often got the run around. He was released in 1929 and had the distinction of playing in a large number of games in which City got a pasting!

TITTERTON, David S.J.
Left Back
Born: Hatton 25th September 1971
Career: YTS Coventry City, pro June 1990, Hereford United 1991 (£10,000), Wycombe Wanderers August 1993 (F/T).

Coventry City	League	F.A.Cup	Lge.Cup
1989–90	0+1s	–	–
1990–91	0+1s	–	1
1991–92	–	–	–
Total	0+2s	–	1

Debut: 5/5/90 v Liverpool (h) 1–6 (Sub)
Full debut: 26/9/90 v Bolton W. (h) 4–2 (LB) League Cup

Combative defender Titterton holds the distinction of being booked for a challenge before he kicked a ball in first team football, having illegally tackled Ray Houghton when he came on a substitute on the last day of the 1989–90 season. When his chance came in September 1990, he was injured early in the League Cup match against Bolton and didn't figure in new manager Terry Butcher's plans. He was sold to Hereford and met up with former City manager Sillett, where he continued his uncompromising style, before his free transfer in the summer of 1993.

TOMS, William
Inside Left
Born: Manchester 19th May
Career: Eccles Borough 1914, Southport Central, Manchester United October 1919, Plymouth Argyle September 1920 (£500), Oldham Athletic July 1921 (£250), Coventry City July 1922 (£150), Stockport County June 1923, Wrexham October 1923, Crewe Alexandra December 1924, Winsford United 1925.

Coventry City	League	F.A.Cup
1922–23	30 – 19	1

Debut: 26/8/22 v Notts Co. (h) 1–2 (IL)
Honours: Welsh Cup Winners Medal 1923–24

Toms became a professional after the Great War, in which he was awarded the Military Cross. City was the only club where he was successful, which was surprising considering the shambolic state of the club at the time! He holds the distinction of scoring City's first hat–trick in The Football League, in the 7–1 victory over Wolves on Christmas Day 1922. His departure was certain after he was suspended by the club for an undisclosed act of "misconduct", along with Arthur Ormston. Toms was a stocky inside forward who was considered an asset to each side he played for, but he moved out of League football only 2 years after leaving City.

TOOZE, Dennis G.
Full Back
Born: Swansea 12th October 1917
Career: Redditch Town Coventry City c/s 1937, Retired c/s 1949.

Coventry City	League	F.A.Cup
1937–38	–	–
1938–39	–	–
1945–46	WWII	–
1946–47	17	–
1947–48	15	–
1948–49	4	–
Total	36	–

Debut: 2/9/46 v West Bromwich Albion (h) 3–2 (RB)

Tooze signed for City in 1937, but it was not until September 1946, at the age of 28, that he made his debut. His versatility meant that he could play at either left or right back, although his appearances were limited by the consistency of regular full backs Dick Mason and Harry Barratt. The majority of Tooze's outings came at right back as the versatile Barratt moved into the forward line. In 1949, Tooze received a bad injury which forced him out of the professional game. During the war, he guested for Darlington.

TOSELAND, Ernest (Ernie)
Outside Right
Born: Northampton 17th March 1905
Died: Northampton 19th October 1987
Career: Higham Ferriers Town, Coventry City c/s 1925, Manchester City March 1929, Sheffield Wednesday March 1939.

Coventry City	League	F.A.Cup
1925–26	–	–
1926–27	–	–
1927–28	–	–
1928–29	22 – 11	1
Total	22 – 11	1

Debut: 5/9/28 v Watford (a) 2–4 (OR)
Honours: League Champs. Winners Medal 1936–37
FA Cup Winners Medal 1934
FA Cup Runners–up Medal 1933
1 Football League appearance

Toseland burst into City's team in September 1928 at the age of 23. He was a fast and tricky winger, but his debut had been delayed by injuries, including a broken collarbone. He upstaged the experienced Bill Henderson and was the talk of the City.

The problem for the club, was that the players around him were not of sufficient quality to form the nucleus of a good side. Consequently, he was sold for a club record fee of £3000 to 1st Division Manchester City, despite not having played a full season of League football. Whilst at Maine Road, Toseland won FA Cup and championship winners medals and played for the Football League. The only honour that he didn't win was an England cap, which surprised many people. In his 10 years, he appeared 409 times for Manchester City, scoring 75 goals. He moved to Sheffield Wednesday, but the War interrupted his career after 12 appearances. He finally hung up his boots in 1946.

TOWNSEND, Jack S.
Outside Left

Born: Nuneaton 1906
Career: Griff Colliery 1922, Nuneaton Town c/s 1923, Coventry City May 1927, Nuneaton Town, Hinckley United, Burton Town March 1930, Nuneaton Town c/s 1930.

Coventry City	League	F.A.Cup
1927–28	15 – 1	–
1928–29	16 – 3	1
Total	31 – 4	1

Debut: 3/9/27 v Charlton Athletic (h) 3–3 (OL)

Local lad Jack Townsend was signed by James Kerr after a remarkable improvement in his form at Nuneaton Town. He was a quick left winger who could cross well and in his first few games showed

he was as hard as nails and as keen as mustard. He was in and out of the side, but lost out to the pacey and experienced Billy Pick. He then played for a number of local sides.

TUDOR, John A.
Forward

Born: Ilkeston 25th June 1946
Career: Ilkeston Town, Coventry City January 1965, Sheffield United December 1968, Newcastle United January 1971, Stoke City October 1976, A.C. Ghent c/s 1977, Gateshead 1980, Bedlington Terriers 1982, Retired 1983.

Coventry City	League	F.A.Cup	Lge.Cup
1964–65	–	–	–
1965–66	–	–	–
1966–67	16 – 8	–	1
1967–68	34+2s–4	3	–
1968–69	13+1s–1	–	3+1s–2
Total	63+6s–13	3	4+1s–2

Debut: 5/5/66 v Brighton & HA (a) 1–1 (IR)
Honours: FA Cup Runners–up Medal 1974
        Texaco Cup Winners Medal 1974 and 1975
        Anglo/Italian Tournament Winners Medal 1974

John Tudor emerged in season 1966–67, just when City needed him. This was the season in which City were determined to reach Division 1, after just failing the season before. Jimmy Hill needed cover for scoring sensation Bobby Gould and the scheming partnership of Ian Gibson and Ernie Machin. Tudor provided this, notching 9 goals in 16 games. He scored some important goals, including City's goal at Ipswich in the penultimate game of the season which ended 1–1, plus 1 against Millwall in the 3–1 victory which clinched the Division 2 championship. In Division 1, Tudor struggled, as did the whole team. His scoring declined, and, in a crisis was asked to play in defence. He regained his scoring touch at Sheffield United and then played with Malcolm MacDonald at Newcastle in one of the most potent in Division 1 partnerships. He eventually settled in his native Derbyshire to run a pub.

TURNER, Alan
Inside Right

Born: Hull 5th July 1943
Career: Scunthorpe Utd 1960, Coventry City March 1962, Shrewsbury Town July 1966, Bradford (P.A.) May 1967, Wigan Athletic c/s 1968.

Coventry City	League	F.A.Cup	Lge.Cup
1961–62	1	–	–
1962–63	–	–	–
1963–64	–	–	–
1964–65	2	–	–
1965–66	1	–	–
Total	4		–

Debut: 24/4/62 v Bristol City (a) 2–3 (IR)

Signed by Jimmy Hill early in his career at City, Turner played only 4 games in 5 seasons. He was essentially a reserve team player, who moved on to Shrewsbury Town in July 1966, and after retirement to non–league management.

TURNER, Herbert L.
Inside Right
Born: Birmingham
Career: Darlaston, Birmingham, Merthyr Town c/s 1919, Coventry City March 1925, Brierley Hill Alliance c/s 1926, Torquay United c/s 1927, Bristol Rovers 1928, Brierley Hill Alliance 1929, Market Harborough Town, Bournemouth & Boscombe Athletic 1930/1.

Coventry City	League	F.A.Cup
1924–25	9 – 1	–
1925–26	21 – 6	1
Total	30 – 7	1

Debut: 21/3/25 v Wolverhampton W. (a) 1–3 (IR)

Turner was signed in March 1925 with City in dire straits trying to avoid relegation from Division 2. He had scored 45 goals in 6 seasons at Merthyr Town, but could not help City to survive. He put in some good performances in Division 3(N) being predominately an inside right who would link between the half backs, outside right and centre forward. City were in financial trouble and were insistent that players take a pay cut for the 1926–27 season. Turner refused to re–sign, and linked up with Brierley Hill before being signed by ex–City player Percy Mackrill as an experienced forward for Torquay, scoring The Gulls' opening goal in The Football League in August 1927.

TURNER, Wayne L.
Midfield
Born: Luton 9th March 1961
Career: Apprentice Luton Town, pro April 1977, Lincoln City (loan) October 1981, Coventry City July 1985 (£75,000), Brentford September 1986 (£30,000), Barnet c/s 1988 (F/T).

Coventry City	League	F.A.Cup	Lge.Cup
1985–86	14+1s–1	1	1
1986–87	–	–	–
Total	14+1s–1	1	1

Debut: 3/9/85 v Oxford Utd (h) 5–2 (Mid)

Bought by Don Mackay in the summer of 1985, Turner was appointed club captain. However, his 14 month stay at City was filled with disappointment. He suffered injury, never played really well, and was eventually dropped. He did not feature in the plans of the Sillett/Curtis partnership and was sold to Brentford for half the fee paid to Luton. After a spell at non–league Barnet he is now coaching back at Luton.

UNDERWOOD, Benjamin Riley (Ben)
Half Back
Born: Newton 30th September 1901
Died: 9th March 1958
Career: New Hucknall Colliery 1920, Sutton Town 1924, Derby County December 1924, Doncaster Rovers c/s 1926, Leeds United May 1929, Coventry City c/s 1931, Retired 1934.

Coventry City	League	F.A.Cup
1931–32	11	1
1932–33	9	–
1933–34	–	–
Total	20	1

Debut: 19/8/31 v Fulham (a) 3–5 (RH)

Ben Underwood was a more than useful wing half who had been a reserve at Derby whilst Harry Storer was there. He impressed at Doncaster and was sold to First Division Leeds United. He only played 6 times for the Elland Road club before signing for City. He suffered serious injury in only his second match and struggled thereafter. He was forced to retire through injury in 1934.

UPHILL, Denis Edward
Inside Right
Born: Bath 11th August 1931
Career: Finchley, Tottenham Hotspur September 1949, Reading February 1953, Coventry City October 1955, Mansfield Town March 1957, Watford June 1959, Crystal Palace October 1960, Rugby Town 1963, Romford, Dartford February 1964.

Coventry City	League	F.A.Cup
1955–56	31 – 13	1
1956–57	18 – 4	–
Total	49 – 17	1

Denis Uphill was a football journeyman, playing for 6 Football League and several non-league clubs. He started as a promising youngster at Tottenham, but after 6 games and a successful time at Reading, he moved to City. His 18 months stay was a turbulent period in City's history. Uphill nevertheless, impressed and it was unfortunate that he moved to Mansfield Town. The 1950's was an unusual time for City in that 4 players named Hill (all unrelated) and Uphill played during that time. In 1955–56, Uphill, Peter Hill and Jimmy Hill (not the future manager) all played in City's forward line.

VAN GOOL, Roger
Outside Right

Born: Belgium 1st June 1950
Career: F.C. Bruges, F.C. Cologne, Coventry City February 1980 (£250,000), Antwerp 1981 (player exchange).

Coventry City	League	F.A.Cup	Lge.Cup
1979–80	8	–	–
1980–81	9	–	2
Total	17	–	2

Debut: 8/3/80 v West Bromwich Albion (h) 0–2 (OR)

After the 1978 World Cup, English football became enriched with foreign players. Ardiles and Villa came to Spurs, Tarantini to Birmingham, Muhren and Thijssen to Ipswich and Roger Van Gool to City; in February 1980, Gordon Milne announced the exciting signing. However, Van Gool was almost 30, could not speak English, and could never fit in at City. He played 19 games at the end of 1979–80 and early 1980–81, but he could not capture any form and was a big disappointment. He faded into City's reserves and became somewhat of a forgotten man as Peter Bodak took over at outside right. Van Gool left in August 1981 in a straight swap that saw young Dutchman Rudi Kaiser come to City.

WALDOCK, Ronald (Ron)
Inside Left

Born: Heanor 6th December 1932
Career: Loscoe Youth Club, Coventry City February 1950, Sheffield United May 1954, Scunthorpe United February 1957, Plymouth Argyle September 1959, Middlesbrough January 1960, Gillingham October 1961, Margate c/s 1964.

Coventry City	League	F.A.Cup
1949–50	–	–
1950–51	–	–
1951–52	–	–
1952–53	9 – 2	1 – 1
1953–54	18 – 7	1
Total	27 – 9	2 – 1

Debut: 27/9/52 v Millwall (a) 0–2 (OL)

Waldock made his debut at the age of 19 as a replacement for the injured Peter Hill. He impressed greatly, but could not keep a regular first team place. Rather than keeping Waldock as a valuable squad player, City allowed him to move to Sheffield United. This upward step was a difficult move to tackle, but he was a great success at Scunthorpe, scoring 45 goals in 92 League games. Waldock was one of many City players who the club let move in the 1950's, preferring to aim for immediate success rather than groom players for the future.

WALKER, James
Outside Left

Born: Glasgow c.1902
Career: Arniston Rovers, Dundee 1923, Dundee United, Broxburn United 1924/5, Coventry City c/s 1925, Bathgate November 1926, Bo'ness December 1926.

Coventry City	League	F.A.Cup
1925–26	16 – 1	1
1926–27	–	–
Total	16 – 1	1

Debut: 29/8/25 v Lincoln C. (h) 3–2 (OL)

Yet another of James Kerr's Scottish signings, Walker was bought from Scottish 2nd Division side Broxburn United. He was played out of position as he was a right winger, but showed his potential by scoring on his debut at Lincoln. He was a quick wide man who had played with Michael McIlvanney at Broxburn and they later linked up with City. After 16 games, he received an injury which lost him his place.

WALKER, William Baird (Billy)
Inside Forward

Born: New Cumnock 1892
Career: Lugar Boswell, Bradford City August 1911, Lanemark c/s 1913, Birmingham November 1913, Coventry City November 1919, Merthyr Town c/s 1920, Bristol City late 1922, Sheffield Wednesday October 1923, Weymouth 1924 (player-manager), Leamington Town.

Coventry City	League	F.A.Cup
1919-20	20 - 7	2 - 1

Debut: 22/11/19 v Blackpool (h) 0-0 (IL)

Scotsman Billy Walker was signed from Birmingham by Harry Pollitt as he tried to get City out of relegation trouble. Walker achieved what he was signed for – to score some much needed goals – the first coming in the 3–2 victory against Stoke on Christmas Day 1919 (This was City's first goal since October the 4th, and the longest League run without a goal until Hartlepool beat this unenviable record in 1992–93). After a good period at Bristol City, he played 19 games for Sheffield Wednesday before becoming player manager of Weymouth.

WALLACE, Ian Andrew
Forward

Born: Glasgow 23rd May 1956
Career: Yoker Athletic, Dumbarton c/s 1974, Coventry City August 1976 (£40,000), Nottingham Forest July 1980 (£1.25 million), Brest (France) c/s 1984 (£40,000), Sunderland January 1985 (£50,000), Maritimo (Portugal) c/s 1986, Croatia (Australia) March 1987.

Coventry City	League	F.A.Cup	Lge.Cup
1976-77	24+2s-9	-	-
1977-78	41 - 20	1	4 - 2
1978-79	38 - 15	2	1
1979-80	25 - 13	1	1
Total	128+2s-57	4	6 - 2

Debut: 30/10/76 v Sunderland (h) 1-2 (Sub)
Honours: 3 full Scotland Caps (all with City)
　　　　　1 Scotland U-21 Cap (with Cap)
　　　　　League Cup Runners-up Medal 1984-85

Gordon Milne spotted the flame–haired Wallace playing for Scottish 2nd Division club Dumbarton in August 1976. It was a big gamble to sign him and at first, things did not look promising. Early during his time at City, he suffered an horrific car accident, which threatened his sight. In his first full comeback game, versus Norwich, Wallace was hit directly in the eye by the ball and it was hit and miss as to the effect that this may have had on his sight. Happily, there were no side effects and he started to show City fans what he was capable of. City struggled in this first season but Milne started to form a partnership with Mick Ferguson. In 1977–78, Wallace became the only City player in Division 1 to score 20 goals in a season. His prolific goalscoring, pushed City to the brink of a European place. His record goalscoring has been overtaken by Cyrille Regis, but Wallace's 57 goals is the highest number scored by a single player in Division 1 for City. When signed by Brian Clough for Forest, Wallace was in City's reserves. His fee of £1.25million, is the second highest fee ever received by City. He scored regularly, but not prolifically, for Forest and his continental experience was not a success, so Wallace returned to Sunderland. He ended his career in Australia, where he now coaching after breaking his leg. Wallace enjoyed a brief international career whilst at City, typically scoring in his only U–21 international and in his full Scottish debut. Wally will always be remembered as being one of the great strikers for Coventry City.

WALTERS, Michael (Mick)
Full Back

Born: Banbury 17th November 1939
Career: Coventry City December 1956, Rugby Town July 1959, Bradford City January 1962, Burton Albion June 1963.

Coventry City	League	F.A.Cup
1956-57	-	-
1957-58	3	1
1958-59	-	-
Total	3	1

Debut: 23/11/57 v Millwall (h) 1-4 (LB)

Walters was a reserve player , drafted into the Division 3(S) team in late 1957 as a result of an injury to Charlie Timmins. He struggled to succeed and was quickly replaced by Brian Shepherd. Walters never regained a place. His league opportunity arose again in 1962 with Bradford City, but after 20 appearances, Walters returned to non-league football.

WALTON, John A. (Johnny)
Forward
Born: Horwich 21st March 1928
Died: 1979
Career: Bury (amateur) May 1949, Manchester United July 1951, Bury July 1952, Burnley February 1954, Coventry City October 1956, Kettering Town 1958, Chester July 1959.

Coventry City	League	F.A.Cup
1956–57	8	1
1957–58	5	–
Total	13	1

Debut: 20/10/56 v Brighton & HA (a) 1–2 (IL)
Honours: 19 England Amateur Caps

Walton was one of the few players to play First Division football as an amateur after the War. He began with Bury, impressing sufficiently for Manchester United (Champions elect) to sign him, but appeared only twice for the latter. He was later signed by City in an attempt to generate some goals, but this did not happen. He returned to League action briefly with Chester before retiring. Walton was never a regular first team choice at any of his clubs and played only 89 League games in 11 seasons, but appeared frequently for England at amateur level. He died in 1979 at the relatively early age of 51.

WARD, David
Centre Forward
Born: Barry 19th July 1901
Died: Barry 1959
Career: Pentrebach Harriers, Merthyr Town 1924/5, Aberaman 1925/6, Barry A.F.C. 1926/7, Coventry City 1927/8, Newport County November 1928, Barry Town c/s 1929.

Coventry City	League	F.A.Cup
1927–28	10 – 2	–
1928–29	1	–
Total	11 – 2	–

Debut: 18/2/28 v Gillingham (h) 1–2 (CF)

Ward's League career was revived by City. After scoring 6 goals in 21 games for Merthyr Town, he drifted out of League action. He was not a big centre forward, standing at only 5 feet 8 inches. He was sold to Newport County as part of the deal that brought Billy Pick to Highfield Road. He appeared only 6 times for The Ironsides before signing for Barry Town. He was the father of Welsh International Dai Ward, who played for Bristol Rovers and Cardiff City.

WARD, Robert A. (Bob)
Right Back
Born: c.1916
Died: Autumn 1990
Career: Bedworth Town, AWA Baginton, Coventry City 1944, Bedworth Town, Rugby Town.

Coventry City	League	F.A.Cup
1945–46	WWII	1

Debut: 8/1/46 v Aston Villa (a) 0–2 (RH) FA Cup

Bob Ward joined City during the War whilst in his late 20's, and played several games at right back during this period. His only official appearance came when he played out of position at right half. With the return of City's experienced squad for the recommencement of League football, Ward was released. It was while at Rugby that he started his coaching and he formed a partnership with Jimmy Knox at AP Leamington and VS Rugby.

WARNER, Leslie H. (Les)
Outside Right
Born: Birmingham 19th December 1918
Died: Coventry 1982
Career: Shirley Juniors, Jack Moulds Athletic, Coventry City September 1937, Retired c/s 1954.

Coventry City	League	F.A.Cup
1937–38	2	–
1938–39	6	–
1945–46	WWII	2
1946–47	16	–
1947–48	7 – 3	2 – 2
1948–49	29 – 3	1
1949–50	30 – 3	1
1950–51	41 – 4	1
1951–52	31 – 1	–
1952–53	34 – 5	3 – 1
1953–54	3	–
Total	199 – 19	10 – 3

Debut: 26/2/38 v Swansea Town (h) 5–0 (OR)

Les "Plum" Warner was a great favourite of the City fans during the War and the eight years following it. His pace and skill along the right wing provided a tremendous supply of crosses for forwards such as Welsh international George Lowrie and Ted Roberts. Warner was however, another player whose career was severely hampered by the War. At the cessation of football by the FA in September 1939, Warner had played 8 League games after signing from Birmingham junior side Jack Moulds Athletic. His all-round ability was being recognised, but he

Clem Warren was a local lad, and moved into the inside right position in City's struggling Division 2 side. He didn't fit in well, was sold to Yeovil, and later failed to make the first team at Walsall.

WASSALL, John Charles

Defender

Born: Birmingham 9th June 1933
Career: Modern Machines 1948, Coventry City May 1951, Southport August 1957, Bromsgrove Rovers November 1957, Retired 1961.

Coventry City	League	F.A.Cup
1951–52	–	–
1952–53	–	–
1953–54	–	–
1954–55	–	–
1955–56	11	–
1956–57	6	–
Total	17	–

Debut: 21/9/55 v Reading (a) 0–1 (LB)

Wassall was one of the many players groomed by City's excellent youth policy in the period after the war. His first team opportunity arose when an injury to Noel Simpson allowed him in at left back in a reshuffled defence. He kept his place as a result of an injury to right back Ken Jones. His versatility meant that in 11 appearances in 1955–56, he played in 4 positions, both backs, centre half and outside left. The following season, his 6 appearances came as cover for the injured Roy Kirk. Wassall was however surplus to requirements and he was released to Southport, where he played 4 matches, but was released after clashing with the board. He had been asked to move from the Midlands to Southport, but did not want to do so. He retired in 1961 at the age of 28, to concentrate on his business activities.

was still in reserve to first team regulars George Ashall and George Taylor – who was coming to the end of his career. During the War, he guested briefly for Watford, and by the end of wartime football, in 1946, Warner was 27. He played in 8 seasons afterwards, always bringing a sparkle to any game. His style of play always left him open to harsh tackling. Consequently, Warner only played 209 first team games. In the Division 3 relegation season of 1951–52, Warner was sidelined for 3 months, making only 3 appearances between late December and late March; he was sorely missed. The following season, Warner was in magnificent form as he took apart 3rd Division full backs and the team were on the edge of the promotion race. Injury cruelly struck, and "Plum" did not play in the last 9 games in which City won only once to finish in a disappointing 6th place. By the time Warner was fit again, the promising Gordon Nutt had established himself as the first team's outside right. Warner duly retired at the age of 35. He was a great servant for City, his only League club, whose skill was appreciated by all those who saw it.

WARREN, Clement E. (Clem)

Inside Right

Born: Nuneaton
Career: Edgewick F.C., Herberts Athletic, Coventry City January 1922, Yeovil Town June 1923, Walsall August 1924, Worcester City April 1925.

Coventry City	League	F.A.Cup
1921–22	16 – 3	–
1922–23	2	–
Total	18 – 3	–

Debut: 11/2/22 v Bradford (PA) (h) 2–2 (IR)

WATSON, Edward George (Ted)

Full Back

Born: Felling–on–Tyne 28th April 1895
Career: Sunderland WWI, Felling Colliery, Portsmouth 1919/20, Pontypridd, Wolverhampton Wanderers May 1921, Coventry City March 1929, Oakengates Town October 1932.

Coventry City	League	F.A.Cup
1928–29	10	–
1929–30	42	4
1930–31	14	3
1931–32	19	1
1932–33	–	–
Total	85	8

Debut: 16/3/29 v Crystal Palace (h) 1–3 (LB)
Honours: Welsh Cup Runners–up Medal 1920–21

After playing for Sunderland during The Great War, Watson made his senior debut for Southern League Portsmouth. His stay at Fratton Park was short and he moved to Pontypridd, in the 2nd Division of The Southern League. He was spotted by Wolves as he helped his side to the final of The Welsh Cup in 1921. In his 8 years at Molineux, Watson made 206 appearances, being a first choice right back for 5 years. He missed only 1 match in Wolves Division 3(N) championship side of 1923–24. Having lost his place in 1928, Watson was signed by James McIntyre in March 1929 as a left back to form a partnership with Laurie Crown. He made some sterling performances but injury saw him replaced by Arthur Tilford. His final appearances came as right back after Crown had retired. Once Harry Storer bought Jesse Bennett, Watson was allowed to move to Oakengates.

WATSON, John Gordon
Outside Left
Born: Wolsingham, Co. Durham
Career: Cambois Welfare, Blyth Spartans August 1932, Everton January 1933, Coventry City October 1934, Crystal Palace May 1936, Ashington c/s 1937.

Coventry City	League	F.A.Cup
1934–35	10 – 1	–
1935–36	7	–
Total	17 – 1	–

Debut: 13/10/34 v Crystal Palace (a) 1–3 (OL)

Signed after making 2 appearances for the Everton, Watson was another of the many wingers manager Harry Storer used. He could play on either flank, but was only used as a replacement for players like Arthur Fitton and George McNestry. He moved to Crystal Palace and played in 12 matches.

WATSON, William
Centre Half
Born: Scotland
Career: Vale of Clyde, Ayr United c/s 1923, Vale of Leven, Coventry City 1925.

Coventry City	League	F.A.Cup
1925–26	32 – 1	1

Debut: 5/9/25 v Southport (a) 2–1 (CH)

Watson was signed by James Kerr and replaced fellow Scot Bobby Jones at centre half. He was slow and cumbersome, but was surprisingly chosen ahead of Fred MacLachlan. He was a regular choice in City's only season in Division 3(North) and was offered lower terms due to City's financial troubles. He refused and returned to Scotland.

WAUGH, Keith
Goalkeeper
Born: Sunderland 27th October 1956
Career: Apprentice Sunderland pro July 1974, Peterborough Utd July 1976, Sheffield Utd August 1981, Bristol City (loan) November 1984, Cambridge Utd (loan) December 1984, Bristol City July 1985, Coventry City August 1989 (£40,000), Watford (loan December 1990) February 1991 (F/T), Retired c/s 1993.

Coventry City	League	F.A.Cup	Lge.Cup
1989–90	1	–	1
1990–91	–	–	–
Total	1	–	1

Debut: 16/9/89 v Luton Town (h) 1–0 (Goal)
Honours: Associate Membs. Cup Winners Medal 1986
Associate Membs. Cup Runs.–up Medal 1987

Keith Waugh had been well established and respected in the lower divisions for 15 years. It was not however, until approaching his 33rd birthday, that he made his First Division debut. Waugh lost his first team place at Sheffield United and attracted the attentions of Bristol City, where he had his most successful period to date, appearing in 2 Wembley finals and helping The Robins to a League Cup semi–final clash with Nottingham Forest in 1989. He was always understudy to Steve Ogrizovic at City and his 2 appearances came when Oggy was injured. He saved a penalty on his debut against Luton. His appearances for Watford were limited, firstly by David James and latterly by ex–City keeper, Perry Suckling. Keith joined the Watford coaching staff in August.

WEBB, Harold
Full Back
Born: Fulham
Career: Walthamstow Avenue, Park Royal, Fulham March 1931, Exeter City March 1933, Coventry City c/s 1935, Newport County c/s 1936, Bristol Rovers c/s 1938.

Coventry City	League	F.A.Cup
1935–36	3	–

Debut: 18/1/36 v Exeter C. (h) 3–0 (RB)

Webb was attracted to Harry Storer because of his versatility. He made 7 appearances for Fulham and 70 for Exeter City, in the right wing, wing half and right back positions. In his season at Highfield Road, Webb played at both right and left back and was always on the winning side. With the arrival of Jack Astley, Webb was sold to Newport County, for whom he played 54 League games. In the season before the outbreak of war, he made a single appearances for Bristol Rovers.

WEGERLE, Roy Connon
Forward
Born: Johannesburg 19th March 1964
Career: Tampa Bay Rowdies 1981, Chelsea June 1986, Swindon Town (loan) March 1988, Luton Town July 1988, Queen's Park Rangers December 1989 (£1 million), Blackburn Rovers March 1992 (£1.2 million) Coventry City March 1993 (£1 million).

Coventry City	League	F.A.Cup	Lge.Cup
1992–93	5+1s	–	–

Debut: 3/4/93 v. Southampton (h) 2–0 (F)
Honours: USA International
      League Cup Runners–up Medal 1989

Wegerle is a highly skilful forward who learnt his trade under Rodney Marsh at Tampa Bay Rowdies. He moved to Chelsea, where he showed some of his sparkle. But his two years were frustrating and Wegerle was happy to move to Luton, where he displayed his skill and scoring ability which encouraged QPR to spend £1 million. He was leading scorer at Loftus Road, netting 19 goals in season 1990–91. In March 1992 his former Luton boss Ray Harford, the number two to Kenny Dalglish, recommended Wegerle as the man to help Blackburn to the Premier League. He never hit it off at Ewood Park and was happy to move to City. The deal saw the £2.5 million Kevin Gallacher move North with Wegerle valued at £1 million. This was Wegerle's third £1 million move and he became City's record signing. He appeared for the USA in his country's 2–0 defeat of England in June 1993, and became City's second USA international, after Gerry Baker in the 1960's.

WESSON, Robert W. (Bob)
Goalkeeper
Born: Thornaby–on–Tees 15th October 1940
Career: Thornaby Boys Brigade, Coventry City November 1958, Walsall September 1966 (£15,000), Doncaster Rovers (loan) February 1970, Retired 1973.

Coventry City	League	F.A.Cup	Lge.Cup
1958–59	–	–	
1959–60	–	–	
1960–61	12	–	–
1961–62	4	–	–
1962–63	27	9	–
1963–64	41	2	2
1964–65	14	–	2
1965–66	35	4	4
1966–67	–	–	–
Total	133	15	8

Debut: 20/3/61 v Newport County (a) 3–3 (Goal)

Wesson started as understudy to South African goalkeeper Arthur Lightening. His opportunity arose in March 1961 as injury hit Lightening. He played 12 consecutive games at the end of the season, but Lightening regained his place at the start of the following season. Jimmy Hill sold Lightening to Middlesbrough, but Wesson could not command a first team place. Dave Meeson was bought from Reading, but his form was indifferent, which let Wesson in. He became the regular keeper as City pushed for promotion and reached the sixth round of the FA Cup. He lost out to Bill Glazier but regained his place when Glazier broke his leg. With a fit Glazier, Jimmy Hill allowed Wesson to move to Walsall. He spent 7 seasons at Fellows Park before retiring. During that time, he was loaned out to Doncaster Rovers, because he was unable to keep Phil Parkes, the future QPR and West Ham United favourite, out of the side. He was constantly overlooked, due to his unassuming manner, in favour of more stylish keepers. He is currently landlord of the Royal Oak in Kenilworth.

WHITE, Francis (Frank)
Outside Right
Born: Warwick 30th June 1910
Died: 1981
Career: St. Paul's, Warwick Town August 1926, West Bromwich Albion 1930, Coventry City May 1931, Newport County c/s 1935, Dudley Town c/s 1936, Racing Club de Paris 1937/8, Grantham October 1938, Peterborough United November 1938.

Coventry City	League	F.A.Cup
1931–32	40 – 6	2
1932–33	40 – 11	4
1933–34	31 – 7	2
1934–35	7 – 2	–
Total	118 – 26	8

Debut: 31/8/31 v Southend U. (h) 0-2 (OR)

Signed on a free transfer from WBA, White was a speedy winger who could play on either flank, but much preferred the right. He was quick and elusive and provided many superb crosses for the striking partnership of Bourton, Lauderdale and Lake. White chipped in with a useful supply of goals, including 2 in the Club's record victory, 9–0 against Bristol City in April 1934. He lost his place and moved onto Newport. He played only 17 times for the Somerton Park club, before bowing out of League football aged 25.

WHITEHOUSE, James A. (Jimmy)
Inside Left
Born: West Bromwich 19th September 1934
Career: Greets Green, West Bromwich Albion 1950, Reading June 1956, Coventry City May 1962 (F/T), Millwall March 1964, Hillingdon Borough c/s 1965.

Coventry City	League	F.A.Cup	Lge.Cup
1962–63	37 – 9	9 – 6	2 – 1
1963–64	9 – 3	–	1
Total	46 – 12	9 – 6	3 – 1

Debut: 18/8/62 v Notts County (h) 2-0 (IL)

Jimmy Hill pulled off a coup when signing Jimmy Whitehouse from Reading on a free transfer. At the age of 27, Whitehouse was still at his best, which he proved during his time at City. He started as a junior at WBA, but after no first team appearances he moved on to Reading. The tall, blond haired forward became a crowd favourite, scoring 61 goals in 221 League and Cup games. His departure from Reading was clouded in controversy as fans protested. In Jimmy Hill's rebuilding work at City,

Whitehouse was an important factor, for he made an immediate impact at City and scored regularly. He was particularly prolific in the great cup run of 1962–63, scoring 6 goals in 9 games. Injury forced Whitehouse out and he could not regain his place. His brother Brian, was also a professional footballer, playing for WBA, Norwich City, Wrexham, Charlton, Crystal Palace and Leyton Orient.

WHITTON, Stephen Philip (Steve)
Forward
Born: East Ham 4th December 1960
Career: Apprentice Coventry City, pro September 1978, Seiko (loan) 1980, West Ham United July 1983, Birmingham City (loan January 1986) August 1986 (£70,000), Sheffield Wednesday March 1989 (£300,000), Halmstad (Finland)(loan) c/s 1990, Ipswich Town January 1991 (£150,000).

Coventry City	League	F.A.Cup	Lge.Cup
1978–79	–	–	–
1979–80	1+6s	–	–
1980–81	0+1s	–	–
1981–82	26+2s–9	–	2
1982–83	37+1s12	3 – 2	1+2s
Total	64+10s–21	3 – 2	3+2s

Debut: 29/9/79 v Tottenham Hotspur (h) 1-1 (Mid)

Whitton struggled to establish himself at City during Gordon Milne's reign, but drastic cuts during Dave Sexton's period as manager resulted in City having the smallest squad in Division 1. In that time, Whitton established himself as a regular. He scored some spectacular goals, but his cumbersome style left him open to criticism. He was not a sharp forward for City, but relied on his shooting ability. In the mass exodus of 1983, Whitton was tempted away by his local side West Ham United. He proved to be a regular scorer in Division 2 with Birmingham City, which attracted Ron Atkinson to spend £300,000 to take him to Sheffield Wednesday. Opportunities were limited and the emergence of the David Hirst–Paul Williams partnership left Whitton in the cold. He moved in January 1991, to Ipswich, where he teamed up with John Lyall, his boss at West Ham.

WIDDOWSON, Alfred (Alf)
Inside Forward
Born: Nottingham 16th September 1900
Died: 1970
Career: Boots Athletic, Notts County 1919/20, Coventry City March 1928, Newark Town c/s 1932, Heanor Town c/s 1933.

Coventry City	League	F.A.Cup
1927–28	12 – 1	–
1928–29	17 – 3	–
1929–30	28 – 11	4 – 1
1930–31	12 – 1	–
1931–32	–	–
Total	69 – 16	4 – 1

Debut: 10/3/28 v Bournemouth & B. Ath. (a) 3–2 (IR)

Alf Widdowson was a highly experienced, strong, and determined inside forward, who was noted for scoring important goals in his time at Notts County. He had made about 150 appearances for The Magpies in Divisions 1 and 2, before being bought, along with Norman Dinsdale, by City director Mr. Saunders. The combined fee was £500, but the club's bank refused to sanction the payment. The situation was saved by former chairman David Cooke and County were paid. His time at City was disrupted by injury, which restricted him to only 73 appearances. Towards the end of his playing days, he became a fringe player and was released by Harry Storer in the summer of 1932 after 18 months spent mainly in the reserves. He returned to his native Nottinghamshire.

WILLIAMS, Andrew (Andy)
Midfield
Born: Dudley 29th July 1962
Career: Dudley Town, Solihull Borough, Coventry City July 1985, Rotherham United October 1986 (player–exchange), Leeds United November 1988, Port Vale (loan) December 1991, Notts County (loan February 1993) March 1993 (£115,000).

Coventry City	League	F.A.Cup	Lge.Cup
1985–86	3+5s	–	–
1986–87	0+1s	–	–
Total	3+6s	–	–

Debut: 7/11/85 v Liverpool (h) 0–3 (Sub)
Full Debut: 11/1/86 v Aston Villa (h) 3–3 (Mid)

Signed by Don Mackay in July 1985, Williams came into League football at the age of 23, leaving his job as a trained accountant. He struggled to find a position at City and when it looked as if he might be given a run in the first team, Mackay bought Nick Pickering to play on the left side of midfield. Williams was languishing in the reserves when he and Gareth Evans moved to Rotherham in exchange for Dean Emerson. He earned regular plaudits at Rotherham, which enticed Howard Wilkinson to buy

him for Leeds United. He was never a regular at Elland Road and despite later adding some composure to Notts County's midfield, he couldn't prevent them from being relegated from Division 1.

WILLIAMS, John N.
Forward
Born: Birmingham 11th May 1968
Career: Cradley Town, Swansea City c/s 1991, Coventry City July 1992 (£250,000).

Coventry City	League	F.A.Cup	Lge.Cup
1992–93	38+3s–8	1	2

Debut: 15/8/92 v Middlesbrough (h) 2–1 (CF) 1 goal

Ex–postman Williams signed for Swansea City and his electrifying pace helped him to win the 'Rumbelows Spring Challenge', which was a competition to find the quickest sprinter in the Football League. Bobby Gould signed him for City and he had a dream start, scoring three goals in his first two games. Given that he was still a novice, his form through the 1992/93 season was sporadic, but on his day he could frighten any full back and, with Kevin Gallacher and Peter Ndlovu, formed part of probably City's fastest ever forward line.

WILLIAMS, Paul A.
Centre Forward
Born: Sheffield 8th September 1963
Career: Distillery, Leeds United, Arcadia (Pretoria) 1986, Grinaker Rovers (Johannesburg) 1986, Nuneaton Borough 1986, Preston North End December 1986, Newport County August 1987, Sheffield United (loan March 1988) June 1988 (£17,000), Hartlepool United c/s 1989 (F/T), Stockport County c/s 1990 (F/T), West Bromwich Albion March 1991 (£250,000), Coventry City (loan) October 1992, Stockport County January 1993 (£25,000).

Coventry City	League	F.A.Cup	Lge.Cup
1992–93	1+1s	–	–

Debut: 24/10/92 v Chelsea (h) 1–2 (Sub)
Full Debut: 31/10/92 v Leeds Utd (a) 2–2 (CF)
Honours: 1 Northern Ireland Full Cap

Despite being born in Sheffield, Williams was brought up in Northern Ireland and worked in his father's coal business. After playing over 200 games for Distillery, Williams tried his luck on the mainland. After failing at Elland Road, he tried his luck in South Africa. He established himself at Newport, at centre half, but in the club's final season in the Football League, he was sold to Sheffield

United. It was at Bramall Lane that he was converted to a centre forward. Signed by Bobby Gould at WBA, he performed ably, but was overlooked by new boss Ossie Ardilles. Gould brought him to City during an injury crisis, but didn't take up the option to sign him. He is the son of Betty Williams, who was awarded the Nobel Peace Prize for her peace campaigning in Northern Ireland.

WILMOT, Kenneth (Ken)
Left Back
Born: Nuneaton 3rd April 1911
Career: Nuneaton Town, Hinckley United, Coventry City November 1932, Nuneaton Town, Walsall 1935/6, Dudley Town c/s 1936.

Coventry City	League	F.A.Cup
1932–33	12	–
1933–34	–	–
Total	12	–

Debut: 4/3/33 QPR (h) 7–0 (LB)

Signed in November 1932, Wilmot got his chance in March 1933. He played at left back until the end of the season and appeared to have a bright future. Full back Charlie Bisby regained his place for the start of the 1933–34 season and was a revelation. Wilmot's only other appearance came in the Division 3(S) Cup in February 1934. He later appeared 3 times for Walsall before moving to Dudley Town. Wilmot played first class cricket for Warwickshire through most of the 1930's as a medium pace bowler.

WILSON, Charles (Charlie)
Inside Forward/Wing Half
Born: Heeley, Sheffield 20th July 1905
Died: Kidderminster April 1985
Career: Stonehouse, Hallam F.C., West Bromwich Albion December 1920, Sheffield Wednesday February 1928, Grimsby Town, March 1932, Aston Villa August 1933, Coventry City June 1934, Kidderminster Harriers c/s 1935, Peterborough United October 1935, Worcester City 1936, Kidderminster Harriers 1937, Kidderminster Police 1946, Retired 1947.

Coventry City	League	F.A.Cup
1934–35	10 – 4	2

Debut: 13/10/34 v Crystal Palace (a) 1–3 (IL) 1 goal

At the age of 16, Wilson made his League debut in what was one of the most difficult sides to break into, WBA. It took some time for him to settle, but he soon started scoring regularly. His ability was to score the unexpected goal. He was signed by Sheffield Wednesday and was converted to a left half. He was a fringe player in Wednesday's consecutive championship winning sides of 1928–29 and 29–30. He was signed by Harry Storer for City from Villa's reserves and was cover for City's exciting forwards. He lasted 12 months before entering non–League football. He played throughout the War and retired at the age of 42.

WINSNIP, Edward (Eddie)
Right Back
Born: Prudhoe
Died: 1929
Career: Prudhoe Castle, Crystal Palace 1920/1, Prudhoe Castle 1921/2, Coventry City c/s 1922, Kidderminster Harriers c/s 1925, Brentford 1926/7 – 1929.

Coventry City	League	F.A.Cup
1922–23	35	1
1923–24	29	1
1924–25	15	3
Total	79	5

Debut: 16/9/22 v Port Vale (a) 1–0 (RB)

Winship had been rejected by Crystal Palace after an unsuccessful season at The Nest. His career was revived by Albert Evans, who bought him for City from Prudhoe Castle. He established himself as a strong full back, standing 5 feet 8 inches and weighing 11½ stone. He lost his place to the up and coming Jackie Randle and the wily Jack Bellas. As City were relegated from Division 2 in 1925, the club cut costs and released Winship. He later played 85 League games for Brentford, but died in 1929, whilst still registered as a player.

WITHEY, Graham A.
Centre Forward
Born: Bristol 11th June 1960
Career: Pucklechurch Sports 1976, Welton Rovers 1977, Bath City 1978, Bristol Rovers August 1982, Coventry City August 1983 (£5,000), Seiko (loan) 1984, Cardiff City December 1984, Bath City (loan) 1985, Bristol City September 1986, Bath City December 1986, Cheltenham Town 1988, Exeter City c/s 1988, Brisbane City 1989, Gloucester City late 1989, Bath City 1990.

Coventry City	League	F.A.Cup	Lge.Cup
1983–84	10+10s4	4 – 3	1
1984–85	1+1s	–	–
Total	11+11s4	4 – 3	1

Debut: 29/8/83 v Tottenham H. (a) 1–1 (sub) 1 Goal
Full Debut: 10/9/83 v West Ham Utd (a) 2–5 (CF)

Bobby Gould's biggest gamble when becoming manager in 1983, was to buy 2 players from his previous club Bristol Rovers – Nicky Platnauer and Graham Withey. Withey cost £5,000, and had played only 19 full League games for Rovers. He was signed as a squad player and made his debut against Tottenham at White Hart Lane as a second half substitute. He proceeded to score in the last 10 minutes. He could not command a regular place, and moved to Cardiff which started a football trek across the South West. In his career, Withey has had 4 spells at Bath City and played for both Bristol clubs, drifting in and out of League football. His last spell with a League club was at Exeter when he teamed up with ex–City player Tommy Langley.

WOLFE, Thomas Henry
Inside Left

Born: Barry Dock 7th March 1900
Died: Edgware 23rd March 1954
Career: Atlantic Mills F.C., Swansea Town, Sheffield Wednesday c/s 1922, Coventry City c/s 1923, Southend United June 1924, Fulham March 1925, Charlton Athletic June 1927, Bristol Rovers May 1929 – January 1930.

Coventry City	League	F.A.Cup
1923–24	10 – 1	–

Debut: 25/8/23 v Barnsley (h) 2–3 (IL) 1 goal
Honours: 1 Wales Amateur Cap

Signed by Albert Evans as a promising youngster from Sheffield Wednesday. He had failed to make the grade at Hillsborough, after making his international debut for Wales Amateurs v England Amateurs in January 1922 whilst at Swansea. He lost out to "Cute" Herbert at City and was sold to Southend United. After 11 appearances for The Shrimpers, he played 27 times for Fulham. He had the ability to play at inside left and outside left and later played 12 times for Charlton and twice for Bristol Rovers before leaving League football.

WOOD, Alfred Robert (Alf)
Goalkeeper

Born: Aldridge 14th May 1915
Career: Sutton Town, Nuneaton Town, Coventry City December 1935, Northampton Town December 1951, Coventry City July 1955 (player–coach), Retired 1959.

Coventry City	League	F.A.Cup
1935–36	–	–
1936–37	–	–
1937–38	1	–
1938–39	1	–
1945–46	WWII	2
1946–47	42	2
1947–48	42	2
1948–49	42	1
1949–50	42	1
1950–51	41	1
1951–52	10	–
1955–56	1	–
1956–57	2	1
1957–58	–	–
1958–59	10	2
Total	234	12

Debut: 26/2/38 v Swansea Town (h) 5–0 (G)

Alf Wood was a tremendous servant for Coventry City. His period of service for the club coincided with a period of great change and uncertainty, but throughout his playing days, his commitment to the club and his performances never wavered, making him a much respected professional throughout the game. City manager Harry Storer signed the 20 year old and he made steady progress making 2 appearances before the war. He made an impressive debut against Swansea Town in February 1938 when he kept a clean sheet in a 5–0 victory. The all round ability of regular keeper Bill Morgan kept Wood out, but his chance came when he was discharged from the army, suffering from spinal meningitis. After a great fight back, Wood claimed the City's goalkeeper's jersey as his own in 1944 when injury forced the premature retirement of Morgan. In 1945–46, Wood played in every match, although these matches were not recognised as first class games, since guest players still appeared for many sides. Including these games, Wood would have played 260 consecutive official matches. It was on the final day of the 1950–51 season that this fabulous run ended, when Peter Taylor took over in goal. In 1951, City had strength in depth and Wood was considered past his best at the age of 36. He served the Northampton ably for 4 years, before returning to City in a coaching capacity. Injury scares to regular goalkeepers Reg Matthews and Alf Bentley, forced the 41 year old Wood to play against Reading. Further mishaps were to follow, for in September 1958, City's new experienced goalkeeper Jim Sanders broke his ankle against Aldershot and young reserve goalkeeper Graham Spratt was considered ill–equipped. Consequently, the 43 year old Wood, stepped in to play 12 consecutive games, of which City lost only 2. He was replaced by the young and exciting Arthur Lightening and moved back into coaching, where he stayed until 1961. His departure coincided with those of Billy Frith and Arthur Jepson who made way for Jimmy Hill. It was a splendid career that Alf Wood had, for the sight of 43 year old goalkeepers in the 1950's was even rarer than the modern day. He has the pride of place as City's oldest first team player, but it is as Northampton's keeper against City that many will remember him, when in November 1954, City's Roy Kirk scored the only goal of the First round FA Cup tie. It was a freak 80 yard effort that Wood failed to stop!

WOOD, Arthur H.
Outside Left

Born: Walsall
Career: Talbot Stead, Crystal Palace 1919, Coventry City c/s 1922, Willenhall 1925/6.

Coventry City	League	F.A.Cup
1922–23	41 – 10	1
1923–24	30 – 7	2
1924–25	11	–
1925–26	1	–
Total	83 – 17	3

Debut: 26/8/22 v Notts Co. (h) 1–2 (OL)

Wood had been in and out of the Crystal Palace side and had scored 11 goals in 51 games before being picked up by Albert Evans for City in the summer of 1922 at the same time that "Mollie" Morgan left for Selhurst Park. He was a quick outside left who could cross a ball well, and had the knack of scoring his fair share of goals. He scored a hat–trick in April 1923 against Barnsley, when pushed up to centre forward. He was adept up front, even though he was a little lightweight, 5 feet 8 inches tall and 11½ stone. He lost his place to the up and coming "Cute" Herbert.

WOODS, Raymond Guy (Ray)
Outside Right

Born: Birkenhead 7th June 1965
Career: Apprentice Tranmere Rovers, pro 1983, Bangor City November 1984, Northwich Victoria, Runcorn, Caernarfon Town 1986, Colne Dynamoes 1988, Wigan Athletic March 1989, Coventry City January 1991 (£200,000), Wigan Athletic (loan) January 1993.

Coventry City	League	F.A.Cup	Lge.Cup
1990–91	12 – 1	–	–
1991–92	9	0+1s	1
1992–93	–	–	–
Total	21 – 1	0+1s	1

Debut: 2/3/91 v Crystal Palace (h) 3–1 (OR)

Woods started at Tranmere Rovers in 1983 and made only 15 appearances before moving on and spending five years moving around the North–West non–League scene, eventually signing for Wigan Athletic. He had been in the reserve side of Colne Dynamoes, when his former Tranmere boss Bryan Hamilton signed him, and put him straight in his Division 3 side! He suffered a bad groin injury which kept him out of the game for 12 months, but he was spotted when he played two outstanding games against City in the FA Cup in January 1991. He was signed up and played well until a recurrence of his groin injury, which kept him out of action for almost 18 months. He was trying to revive his career with a loan spell back at Wigan in 1993.

WOOLHOUSE, Reuben
Outside Left

Born: Sheffield, November 1906
Career: Ecclesfield United, Birmingham May 1925, Southend United c/s 1928, Loughborough Corinthians c/s 1929, Bradford City May 1930, Coventry City July 1932, Walsall June 1933, Swindon Town August 1938.

Coventry City	League	F.A.Cup
1932–33	7 – 1	4 – 1

Debut: 5/11/32 v Crystal Palace (a) 3–1 (OL) 1 goal

The son of a Barnsley St Peters player of the early 1890's, Woolhouse was recruited by Birmingham from the same Sheffield junior side that his father played for. He didn't make the first team in his 3 seasons at St. Andrew's. He seemed unlikely to make the grade after being released by Southend having played only 2 games. His career was revitalised at Valley Parade and he was signed by Harry Storer for City. He played only 11 games for City, as a replacement for Percy Richards. He was allowed to move to Walsall and this slender winger was a fine servant for The Saddlers in his 5 years, scoring 47 goals in 204 appearances, which was an excellent return for a winger.

WRIGHT, Horace D.
Outside Right
Born: Derbyshire
Career: Ilkeston United, Bulwell White Star, Derby County September 1910, Portsmouth September 1912, Darlington c/s 1913, Mansfield Mechanics 1914, Coventry City September 1919, Exeter City 1919/20, Aberaman c/s 1920, Abertillery May 1921, Chesterfield 1921/2, Coalville Town, Kettering c/s 1923.

Coventry City	League	F.A.Cup
1919–20	10	–

Debut: 27/9/19 v Leicester C. (a) 0–1 (OR)

Wright started before the Great War with Derby County, and played 15 times in 2 seasons, including 3 in their promotion season of 1911–12. He joined Portsmouth in August 1912 and played 27 times for the Southern League side. He was signed by William Clayton in September 1919, to add experience to City's struggling side, and had the dubious distinction of playing 10 games for City during which the club didn't score a single goal. He made 1 appearance for Chesterfield in 1921–22.

WYER, Peter William
Forward
Born: Coventry 10th February 1937
Career: Coventry City October 1955, Derby County June 1956, Coventry City August 1958, Nuneaton Borough, Rugby Town July 1959.

Coventry City	League	F.A.Cup
1955–56	1	–
1958–59	4	–
Total	5	–

Debut: 22/10/56 v Crystal Palace (a) 0–3 (IL)

A reserve player, Peter Wyer played one game before moving to Derby County. He played 2 matches for the Rams in his 2 season spell, before returning to his home city in 1958. He was once again in reserve, playing only when there were injuries to Ray Straw and Peter Hill. He never looked liked a long term prospect and moved into non–league football with local side, Nuneaton Borough.

WYNN, George Arthur
Inside Right
Born: Treflach, Llansilin, nr. Oswestry 14th Oct. 1886
Died: Abergele, Denbighshire 28th October 1966
Career: Pant Glas, Oswestry United April 1906, Wrexham May 1908, Manchester City April 1909 (£250), Coventry City November 1919 (£300), Llandudno Town, Halifax January 1922, Mansfield Town February 1922, Mossley September 1922, Oswestry Town.

Coventry City	League	F.A.Cup
1919–20	17 – 2	2
1920–21	7 – 1	–
Total	24 – 3	2

Debut: 22/11/19 v Blackpool (h) 0–0 (IR)
Honours: 11 Wales Full Caps
2 Wales Victory internationals
Welsh Cup Winners Medal 1908–09

Wynn came to prominence in Wrexham's Welsh Cup winning side of 1909 and earned the first of his 11 Welsh caps. He was enticed to step up from the Birmingham League to Manchester City, where he settled in at inside right. Despite his short stature and slight frame, (he was only 5 feet 6 inches and weighed 10 stone), his tremendous skill earned him many plaudits. In total, he scored 58 goals for the Maine Road club. He was signed for City in the club's attempt to escape from their desperate position in their first season in the Football League. His career came close to being ended when, during the Great War, his leg was nearly amputated following a bad injury.

YORATH, Terence C. (Terry)
Midfield

Born: Cardiff 27th March 1950
Career: Apprentice Leeds United, pro April 1967, Coventry City August 1976 (£125,000), Tottenham Hotspur August 1979 (£275,000), Vancouver Whitecaps 1981, Bradford City December 1982, Swansea City July 1986 (player–manager), Retired 1987.

Coventry City	League	F.A.Cup	Lge.Cup
1976–77	38 – 1	1	3
1977–78	40 – 2	1	3
1978–79	21	–	–
Total	99 – 3	2	6

Debut: 4/9/76 v Liverpool (a) 1–3 (Mid)
Honours: 59 full Wales Caps (20 with City)
7 Wales U–23 Caps
European Cup Runners–up Medal 1975
Cup Winners Cup Runners–up Medal 1973
League Championship Medal 1973–74
FA Cup Runners–up Medal 1973

Terry Yorath was a great signing by Gordon Milne. At £125,000, it was an astute piece of work to bring the Welsh national captain to City from a formidable Leeds United side. It took some t.me for Yorath to establish himself at Leeds because of the consistency of players such as Johnny Giles, Billy Bremner and Eddie Gray. He finally became an important and regular part in the club's championship season of 1973–74. Yorath came to City at the peak of his career, and played a significant part in City's transformation from a relegation threatened side, to a team that played attractive football. Yorath's no–nonsense midfield battling won great admiration, and was the pivot around which City operated. Injury towards the end of his spell with City allowed younger players like Andy Blair into the first team. Yorath wanted to play for a team more likely to win honours, so he moved to Spurs, before playing in Canada and then for Bradford City. He moved to Swansea as manager, where he played his final League match. Yorath is currently manager of the Wales National side and is at the forefront of the campaign for sportsmen and women to be more aware of heart problems, following the tragic death of his son Daniel, 15 from a sudden heart failure.

YORKE, Andrew
Left Back

Born: Blyth 1899
Career: Blyth Spartans 1919, Sleekburn Albion 1920/1, Sunderland 1921/2, Coventry City c/s 1923, Northampton Town c/s 1923, Lincoln City c/s 1927, Newark Town c/s 1930.

Coventry City	League	F.A.Cup
1923–24	2	–
1924–25	14	1
Total	16	1

Debut: 29/8/23 v Barnsley (h) 2–3 (LB)

Signed by Albert Evans from First Division Sunderland, Yorke had made one appearance for the Roker club and was to take over from James Lawrence as left back. He turned out to be a liability with little idea of positional play. The result was that he was overkeen and tended to chase all over the field, leaving his colleagues vulnerable. He was duly dropped and only played when there was an injury to Lawrence or Jackie Randle. He moved to Northampton and after 21 games was transferred to Lincoln, where he played 105 matches before leaving the League.

YOUNG, Clarence W. (Clarrie)
Outside Left
Born: Bow 23rd February 1920
Career: Margate, Coventry City August 1938, Retired 1948.

Coventry City	League	F.A.Cup
1938–39	–	–
1945–46	WWII	–
1946–47	1	–
1947–48	–	–
Total	1	–

Debut: 15/3/47 v Manchester City (h) 1–1 (OL)

Clarrie Young came to City as an exciting prospect in 1938, but in his time at City he played only 1 League game. He failed to achieve the standards expected of him and lost out first to George Ashall and then to Irish international, Norman Lockhart. He was forced to retire through injury in 1948.

YOUNG, Quintin
Outside Right
Born: Irburne 19th September 1947
Career: Ayr Utd 1969, Coventry City July 1971, Rangers October 1972, East Fife c/s 1976, Retired c/s 1980.

Coventry City	League	F.A.Cup	Lge.Cup
1971–72	21 – 2	1	0+1s
1972–73	4+1s	–	1
Total	25+1s–2	1	1+1s

Debut: 24/8/71 v Derby County (h) 2–2 (OR)

Young started his career at Ayr at the relatively late age of 22, but impressed greatly. This encouraged Noel Cantwell to buy him, but he never really settled in England and lost his place to Mick McGuire. He was grateful for a move back to Scotland with Rangers, being part of the deal that brought Colin Stein to City. Young was never a regular at Ibrox and moved to East Fife where he played until retiring in 1980, at the age of 33.

Addendum – Players signed during Summer 1993 and made early season appearances.

HARFORD, Michael G.

Born: Sunderland 12th February 1959
Career: Lambton Street Old Boys, Lincoln City July 1977, Newcastle United December 1980 (£180,000), Bristol City August 1981 (£160,000), Birmingham City March 1982 (£100,000), Luton Town December 1984, Derby County January 1990, Luton Town September 1991, Chelsea c/s 1992, Sunderland March 1993, Coventry City July 1993 (£200,000)

Mick came on as a substitute for Coventry against Newcastle United and scored within 10 minutes – already a favourite with the crowd.

MORGAN, Stephen A.

Born: Oldham 19th September 1968
Career: Apprentice Blackpool pro c/s 1986, Plymouth Argyle July 1990 (£150,000), Coventry City July 1993 (£110,000)

> **Steve became the 600th Football League player to appear for Coventry City.**

WILLIAMS, Paul R.C.

Born: Leicester 11th September 1969
Career: YTS Leicester City pro June 1988, Stockport County July 1989, Coventry City August 1993 (£150,000)

'YORE PUBLICATIONS'
12 The Furrows, Harefield,
Middx. UB9 6AT

A SELECTION OF TITLES (For latest list please send a S.A.E.)

REJECTED F.C. VOLUME 1 (Reprint) *(By Dave Twydell)* The 2nd Edition of this popular book – now in hardback – has minor additions, updates, corrections and has been re-typeset. This volume provides the comprehensive histories of: Aberdare Athletic, Ashington, Bootle, Bradford (Park Avenue), Burton (Swifts, Wanderers and United), Gateshead/South Shields, Glossop, Loughborough, Nelson, Stalybridge Celtic and Workington. The 288 well illustrated pages also contain the basic statistical details of each club. Price £12–95 plus £1–30 postage.

REJECTED F.C. OF SCOTLAND – *Vol. 1: Edinburgh and The South.* *(By Dave Twydell)* The first of three volumes on the written and basic statistical details of the Scottish ex-League Clubs (Edinburgh City, Leith Athletic, St.Bernards, Armadale, Broxburn United, Bathgate, Peebles Rovers, Mid-Annandale, Nithsdale Wanderers and Solway Star). Price £12–95 Plus £1–30 Postage. **(Volume 2 – Glasgow and District.** Same price with another 11 Clubs' histories, including Third Lanark).

'GONE BUT NOT FORGOTTEN – PART 2' *(By Dave Twydell)* The abbreviated histories of a variety of defunct non-League Clubs and Grounds; the old Hillingdon Borough, Wycombe's Loakes Park, Oswestry Town and Shirley Town are included in this edition (Part 1 is now sold out). A particular merit of these books is the high illustrative content, and with details for readers to track down the sites of the Grounds – 64 pages. Price £4–95 plus 45p postage

PETERBOROUGH UNITED – *The Official History of The Posh.* *(By Andy Groom and Mick Robinson)* 273 x 202 m.m. hardback (with full colour dust jacket) containing 240 (high quality paper) pages. An extensive and well illustrated text section details the club's history from the earliest days. The statistical section contains the complete match and team details from the Club's formation in 1934. (Reprint – The first print run sold out within five days). Price £14–95 plus £3–40 postage.

CARDIFF CITY F.C. – *The Official History of The Bluebirds:* *(By John Crooks).* Large format (273 x 202 m.m.), cased (hardback) with a full colour dust jacket and containing 320 pages, printed on high quality paper. Separate sections deal with the history of the Club in words and pictures, an abbreviated 'Who's Who' section (every League player recorded), a section on Ninian Park, and the full statistics (including line-ups) of every major competitive match from 1910–1991. *("In the Super League of Club Histories" – South Wales Echo)* Price £16–95 Plus £3–50 Postage.

AMBER IN THE BLOOD – A History of Newport County: *(Tony Ambrosen).* The book tells the full written story of football in Newport from the pre-County days right up to the newly formed Newport AFC club. The text is well illustrtated, and a comprehensive statistical section provides all the results, attendances, goalscorers, etc. from 1912 to 1993 – the various Leagues and principal Cup competitions; additionally seasonal total players' appearances are included. This hardback book, printed on high quality paper, and containing 176 large pages is exceptional value at only £13–95 plus £2–60 postage.

FOOTBALL LEAGUE – GROUNDS FOR A CHANGE (By Dave Twydell). A 424 page, A5 sized, Hardback book. A comprehensive study of all the Grounds on which the current Football League Clubs previously played. Every Club that has moved Grounds is treated separately, with a 'Potted' history of each, plus 250 illustrations. As well as plenty of 'reading' material, this is likely to become a standard reference book. Price £13–95 Plus £1–70 Postage.

THROUGH THE TURNSTILES (by Brian Tabner) This incredible book which provides the average attendance of every Football League Club, for every season from 1888/89 to 1991/92. *('The best Football Book I have ever read'* – was one reader's comment. " *'Yore Publications' best book to date – at the bottom end of the price range for a quality book.* " – The Footballer Magazine) Well illustrated, and also relates the development of the game (angled towards attendances). Other sections give details of the best supported 'away' teams, season ticket sales over the years, etc. Large format (251x174 m.m.) hardback and 208 packed pages on high quality paper. An excellent read at £13–95 plus £1–70 Postage

HISTORY OF THE LANCASHIRE FOOTBALL ASSOCIATION 1878–1928. A rare historical and fascinating hardback reprint (first published in 1928). Contains the history of the formative days of Lancashire football. Sections within the 288 pages include the early histories of about 20 Clubs (Manchester Utd., Wigan Borough, Rochdale, etc.), Lancashire Cup competitions, Biographies, etc. For those interested in the development of the game, this is a 'must', and you will definitely not be disappointed. Price £12–95 Plus £1–30 Postage.

THE IRONSIDES. A Lifetime in the League – Who's Who of Newport County (By Tony Ambrosen) ("Providing a hugely enjoyable read and a valuable reference book" – South Wales Argus). Every player who appeared for the Club in the Football League is given a potted football and personal history, plus lengthy sections on the players during the Club's three periods in non–League football and details of all the Managers and Trainers. There are over 100 players' photographs within this A5 size 224 page book. A 'must' for statisticians and others interested in this former League club. Limited number of copies left. Price £8–95 Plus £1–00 Postage

MORE DEFUNCT F.C. (By Dave Twydell). A follow up to the successful 'Defunct F.C.' book (Now out of print). Detailed and well illustrated histories of defunct Clubs – *Bedford Avenue, Lovell's Athletic, Romford, Rugby Town, Slough Centre and West Stanley* – including basic statistics, 230 pages. Price £6–75 Plus £1 postage.

Football Videos – available from major Video Outlets or send a S.A.E. to:

> **Trans Video Productions,**
> **Regent House, 16 Old Road,**
> **Linslade, Leighton Buzzard, LU7 7RD.**

(For full lists of these, plus other football and general interest videos)

REJECTED F.C. – The Video The video of the books (Rejected F.C. Volumes 1 and 2). Several hours of repeated entertainment. Includes extensive modern film shots, interviews with many personalities related to these teams, still shots to aid the telling of these Clubs' Histories... and an amazing collection of archive film (e.g. Ashington in 1924, pre–war New Brighton, Workington's last home League match, etc.). Every 'Rejected' club (from Accrington in 1888) is featured. Price £12–99 (incl. VAT) plus postage.

FOOTBALL PHOENIX – The sequel to 'Rejected F.C. – The Video'. The stories on film of the five post–war League Clubs who became defunct and have successfully reformed (Gateshead, Accrington Stanley, Bradford P.A., Newport County and Aldershot). Film clips include all the goals from County's last game, Aldershot's last League game, footage from 1970 of the new Stanley, etc. 80 minutes of excellent entertainment at only £10–99 (incl. VAT) plus postage.